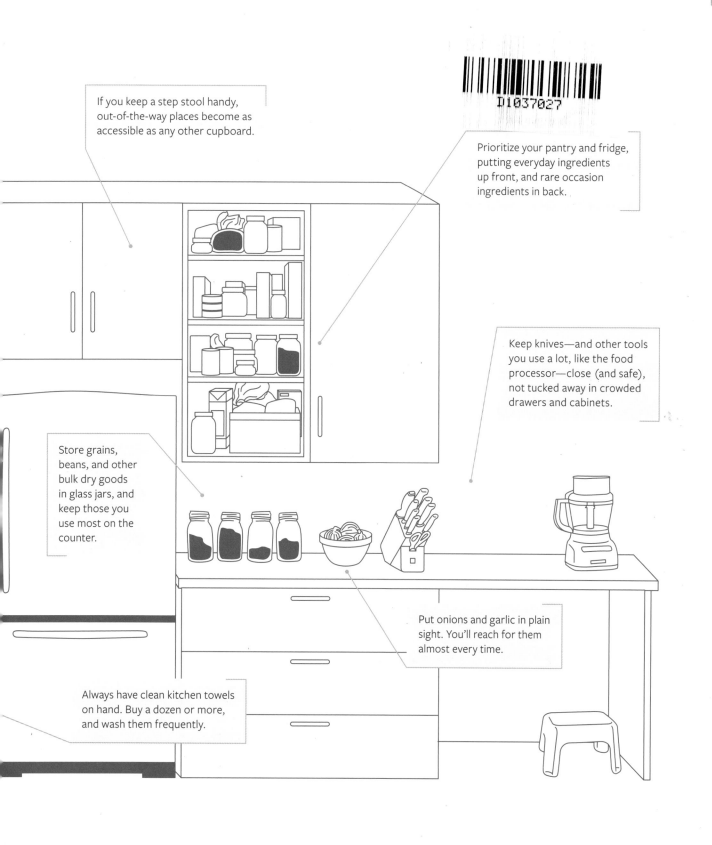

If you keep a step stool handy, out-of-the-way places become as accessible as any other cupboard.

Prioritize your pantry and fridge, putting everyday ingredients up front, and rare occasion ingredients in back.

Keep knives—and other tools you use a lot, like the food processor—close (and safe), not tucked away in crowded drawers and cabinets.

Store grains, beans, and other bulk dry goods in glass jars, and keep those you use most on the counter.

Put onions and garlic in plain sight. You'll reach for them almost every time.

Always have clean kitchen towels on hand. Buy a dozen or more, and wash them frequently.

How to Cook
Everything
fast

Provençal Chicken,
page 387

COMPLETELY REVISED AND UPDATED

How to Cook
Everything
fast

GREAT FOOD
IN 30 MINUTES
OR LESS

Mark Bittman

PHOTOGRAPHY BY JIM HENKENS

HARVEST
An Imprint of WILLIAM MORROW

Other Books by Mark Bittman

How to Cook Everything

How to Cook Everything Vegetarian

How to Cook Everything The Basics

How to Grill Everything

How to Bake Everything

Bittman Bread

Animal, Vegetable, Junk

How to Eat

Dinner for Everyone

A Bone to Pick

Mark Bittman's Kitchen Matrix

VB6: Eat Vegan Before 6:00

The VB6 Cookbook

Food Matters

The Food Matters Cookbook

The Best Recipes in the World

Fish: The Complete Guide to Buying and Cooking

Leafy Greens

Mark Bittman's Kitchen Express

Mark Bittman's Quick and Easy Recipes from the
  New York Times

The Mini Minimalist

Jean-Georges: Cooking at Home with a Four-Star Chef

Simple to Spectacular

HarperCollins books may be purchased for
educational, business, or sales promotional use.
For information, please email the Special Markets
Department at SPsales@harpercollins.com.

FIRST EDITION

Book design by Toni Tajima
Food styling by Callie Meyer
Photography © 2022 by Jim Henkens
Front endpaper illustration © Olivia de Salve Villedieu

Library of Congress Cataloging-in-Publication Data
has been applied for.

ISBN 978-0-544-79031-5

22 23 24 25 26 TC 10 9 8 7 6 5 4 3 2 1

Contents

Acknowledgments

Putting together a cookbook about fast cooking is slow. Like any other big book project, it's a deliberate process that spans several years and relies upon the creativity, hard work, and good nature of many people.

First of all there is my team: Kerri Conan, Kate Bittman, Melissa McCart, Danielle Svetcov, and our former colleagues who worked especially hard on this book, Daniel Meyer and Kelly Doe.

Endless gratitude goes to all the editorial, copy, design, and production pros at HarperCollins/Harvest Books (and the people they bring to the party), most of whom have been working on How to Cook Everything for years: Deb Brody, Stephanie Fletcher, Melissa Lotfy, Toni Tajima, Jacqueline Quirk, Karen Murgolo, Rebecca Springer, Rachel Meyers, Kimberly Kiefer, and Suzanne Fass. I want to also recognize Adam Kowit, who had a profound impact on the first edition of this book.

And from the HarperCollins marketing, sales, and publicity teams, thank you for your support for updating this title: Anwesha Basu, Katie Tull, and Andrea Dewerd.

This edition of the book is lush with images of food, all belying the fact that they're fast recipes. They are, though, and they're beautiful, which was no small feat, especially during a pandemic. Kerri ran this shoot in Seattle with photographer Jim Henkens and food stylist Callie Meyer. Together with the generosity of designer Kelie Grosso, they did all the props and sets, with help in the kitchen from Milana Zettel, Laura McQueen, and Dawnelle DeMarco.

We've lost count of how many times we've been through this process, and it never fails to excite, delight, and reward. Kerri and I have been huge advocates and fans of *How to Cook Everything Fast*, which we believe is a unique book with a fantastic approach to cooking and, of course, great recipes. Enjoy it, and thank you for joining us.

Time to Cook

The way we feed ourselves is always changing, evolving with the stages in our lives, the expanding availability of ingredients, and our knowledge of different preparation and cooking techniques.

As eaters we've become more sophisticated. We're learning to understand and appreciate global flavors and cooking traditions, while paying closer attention to where our food comes from and where it's going in the future. We know what eating well is but don't always have the time to prepare meals at home, so we settle for some spin on eating fast.

Yet as I asserted in 2014 with the first edition of this book, cooking remains an essential human activity. It can relax us after long, stressful days, bring us closer to our families, and put a lifetime of nourishment and endless eating possibilities right at our fingertips. The trick is to get food on the table faster—and better—than the abundance of restaurants and food companies jockeying to feed us.

Life may have become more complicated, but cooking can become simpler.

The fact is that you do have time to cook: You just need better recipes. Imagine a road map that captures the rhythm of the kitchen, where preparation and cooking happen seamlessly. Soup begins to simmer while you prepare more vegetables for the pot; oil shimmers in a skillet as you chop an onion; broiled meat rests while rice steams. This is naturally fast cooking, the kind experienced cooks do intuitively.

Fast cooking involves strategy not compromise. Here I take seemingly complicated dishes like wonton soup and chicken Parmesan and reduce them to their essentials, taking them apart and reconstructing them with all the flavors and textures you love about the originals. Smart, easy techniques, like cutting meat into smaller pieces for lightning-quick braises and harnessing the power of the broiler, give you all the pleasure of eating homemade meals with minimal work and—perhaps more important—time.

The result is delicious food prepared from real ingredients—quickly. There are plenty of shortcuts here, and for the most part they don't compromise flavor or texture. (When they do, they're worth it.) As a practical purist, I open cans and boxes like everyone else, provided what's inside is nutritious and minimally processed. (There's a checklist of what qualifies as convenience food in this book on page 11; if you're already a *How to Cook Everything* fan, there won't be any surprises.)

This completely revised and updated *How to Cook Everything Fast* is both a series of strategies and a collection of innovative recipes that do the planning and organizing for you. And this time, photographs both inspire and provide additional details.

Whether you're a beginner hoping to learn how to weave homemade meals into your regular routine or an experienced cook looking to become more efficient, I can help you get where you want to be—all in 30 minutes or less.

The Fast Kitchen

Fast doesn't have to mean frantic. If you use your head, cooking quickly can be pleasurable and rewarding. As with many skills, learning to be fluid, comfortable, and confident in the kitchen comes with practice. Here the lessons are built into the recipes, so you can just dive in and, without realizing it, hone your skills and become naturally more efficient whenever you cook.

REAL-TIME COOKING

The process of getting a home-cooked meal on the table involves four tasks: shopping, preparing, cooking, and cleaning up. Common "wisdom" would have you complete these steps linearly, finishing one before beginning the next. Shop. Unpack the groceries. Wash, trim, chop, slice, dice. Stand at the stove. Serve. Eat. Tackle the dishes.

But that approach ignores the natural rhythm of experienced cooks. For them, the action ebbs and flows within a span of time rather than to the beat of a ticking clock. While something simmers, roasts, or sautés, you have the flexibility to make a loop between counter, fridge, and stove, pause at the sink to wash some dishes, or work on making a salad. Efficiency comes when you put time on your side and maximize every minute.

This is real-time cooking, where gathering, preparing, and combining ingredients become one seamless endeavor. It's both faster and easier than the more common step-by-step process and embodies concepts that are not only fundamental to these recipes but applicable to all others. Embrace real-time cooking, and you'll be looking at the components of cooking—food, tools, and techniques—from a completely different perspective.

Helping Hands

Too many cooks don't spoil the broth; some of the best moments in the kitchen involve sharing a countertop with family and friends. Even one extra set of hands can be a huge help. (If there's a youngster around who's willing and able, you'll be spreading the joy into the next generation.) In fact these recipes are perfect for divvying up tasks among all your helpers; see "Do the Blue" on page 18.

Rethinking the Meal

It's not a new concept, but you can cook one dish—like pasta, salad, soup, or even eggs—and call it dinner; or build a more substantial meal by adding simply executed snacks, sides, or desserts. So the bulk of the recipes in this book are for main courses that eat like meals, dishes that bring several components (such as meat, vegetables, and starches) together on one plate in ways that both retain their distinction and integrity and create a whole that's more than the sum of its parts.

To reflect the way I—and many others—are eating now, one big difference since the first edition of this book is the balance of meat to vegetables in these recipes. There are also a lot more vegetarian and vegan main dishes and variations.

If you have the inclination, you can make a snack to begin the meal or try a salad, vegetable, noodle, rice, or grain dish from Components and Sides (page 479), which are easy to prepare while you're cooking the mains (you'll find specific suggestions in many of the recipe headnotes). These strategies provide plenty of options for assembling all kinds of fast meals, from everyday kitchen-table lunches and dinners to breakfasts, parties, and celebrations. (For a tutorial on other recipe features, see A New Kind of Recipe on the back inside cover of the book.)

FAST INGREDIENTS

A well-stocked kitchen is the backbone of fast cooking; this section lists the staples to keep in your pantry, fridge, and freezer and provides a quick rundown of which time-saving ingredients are worth buying. I've also included a substitution chart to inspire improvisation when you don't have (or don't fancy) a particular ingredient. And so you can vary both flavor profiles and key ingredients easily, many recipes include additional spins—variations—on the main recipe. But before you can cook, you've got to shop.

Shopping for Speed

The faster you shop, the sooner you get into the kitchen. Making a shopping list is an obvious advantage and worth reminding you about here; it's easier to keep one perpetually going on your phone or an old-fashioned notepad than to create one from scratch every time you shop. Then try to strike a balance between spontaneous, impromptu shopping—like stopping after work for fresh vegetables and meat—and weekly or even biweekly stocking up. Since the most efficient scenario is to cook from what you already have at home as often as possible, the goal is to get in the habit of using short-storing foods first. The lists here will help you do that.

Every kitchen should have the foods in the charts that follow. Some, like salt and pepper, are common sense, while others are the kinds of instant flavor boosters that are essential for fast cooking, like soy sauce and real Parmesan cheese. Other flavor-packed ingredients (not absolute essentials but nice to have around) include olives, capers, anchovies, dried tomatoes, tahini, miso, and (of course) bacon.

THE MYTH OF MISE EN PLACE

Although many terrific ideas have moved from restaurants to home kitchens, mise en place—prepping all the ingredients ahead of time—isn't one of them. The term, which means "put in place," is perfect if you have an assistant who gets all the food chopped, measured, neatly arranged in cups on a tray, and put within arm's reach of the stove before you turn it on. But for people in home kitchens, doing all the prep ahead of time often leaves you twiddling your thumbs, waiting for food to cook. Yet this is how most cookbooks and videos direct you to work through recipes. Consider this book a call to break the habit of getting everything "put in place" before you start cooking.

Pantry Staples

Consider these the long-storing essentials you keep in either the fridge or a cupboard. As you explore the recipes, you'll customize this list (and those that follow) to prioritize, add, and subtract depending on what you cook most.

INGREDIENT	DETAILS	STORAGE
Extra virgin olive oil	What I mean when I write *olive oil*. It doesn't have to be expensive—and don't let anyone tell you it doesn't work for frying. But if you like the flavor of olive oil, you should consider buying the freshest good-quality oil you can afford and use it for drizzling, and either a milder olive oil or good-quality vegetable oil for cooking. If that's you, look for single-source, cold-pressed oil in bottles or cans stamped with the date of harvest.	To maintain freshness, keep a small bottle on the counter, to be refilled from a big bottle or you can keep it in the fridge. Store small, more expensive bottles in a dark cabinet.
Good-quality vegetable oils	Here I keep the qualifier in the recipe ingredient lists to emphasize my suggestion to use relatively neutral-tasting oils pressed from a particular seed *not* the generic stuff labeled "vegetable oil," which is made from highly processed soybeans. The best for general cooking are grapeseed, safflower, and sunflower oils. Canola is a good one if you like and already use it (I find it a bit thick and sometimes sticky). Peanut and corn oils can also be of good quality though they have more pronounced flavors. Use vegetable oils when you want a more neutral flavor than olive oil.	Best refrigerated; keep a small jar or bottle on the counter or in a cabinet for immediate use.
Specialty oils	The most common in these recipes is sesame oil—use the dark, toasted kind; it's a special case and used judiciously as a flavorful condiment and rarely for cooking. Though people seem to be cooking more with coconut, avocado, and nut oils, they're usually too heavy and strong-tasting—with a wide range of heat tolerances—for all-purpose use, but I won't stop you if you like them and want to explore different options.	Some of these oils are highly saturated fats (like the coconut), meaning, among other things, that they're solid at room temperature. Many will go rancid quickly. Buy only what you'll use quickly, and keep all in a cool, dark place or the refrigerator.

INGREDIENT	DETAILS	STORAGE
Vinegars	Sherry vinegar (a tad higher in acidity than other vinegars) is my favorite; wine vinegars are also quite good for all-purpose cooking. Balsamic and rice vinegars are the lowest in acidity and useful for their mild sweetness. I suggest stocking one wine, rice, and balsamic vinegar, as well as apple cider vinegar if you like it; the unfiltered kind has a slight apple flavor with pleasant acidity.	Vinegar keeps for at least a year at room temperature. A cloudy sediment might settle at the bottom of the bottle—the "mother" from the fermentation process—it's edible. If you're worried about the appearance or texture, try to pour so that it stays at the bottom of the bottle.
Salt and black pepper	I use the coarse and all-purpose kosher salt for almost everything and sea salt for times the slightly briny flavor will be appreciated. Iodized salt is intense and tastes a little like iodine. Good-quality preground pepper is fine, but grinding your own is preferable and easy.	Keep a small bowl or jar of kosher salt and a sturdy hand-held pepper mill (or preground pepper in a small jar) on the counter. A little sea salt on the table is a nice touch for final seasoning.
Spices and dried herbs	The essentials: chili and curry powders, cayenne, smoked paprika, ground cumin, ground ginger, ground coriander, and five-spice. Dried oregano, sage, rosemary, tarragon, dill, bay leaves, and thyme are acceptable substitutes for fresh, so consider them options even when not specifically mentioned in recipes. Start with one-third the quantity of fresh and taste as you go. There are so many good spice blends available now I encourage you to try substituting any you like in the recipes here, especially the stir-fries and soups, which easily take to flavor changes.	Keep spices and dried herbs in a cool, dark (and handy) place. Replace what you don't use within a year. (Note the date on the label when it goes in, and you'll know when the time's up.)
Garlic, onions, and ginger	Known collectively as "aromatics." Loads of recipes in this book (and elsewhere) start with garlic, onions, or both. Ginger is an essential flavor in a wide range of Asian cuisines. Other aromatics like shallots, scallions (immature or green onions), and leeks can all be good substitutes, though their flavors are different. Ground ginger is quite different from fresh, so in a pinch you can substitute just a pinch for every inch of fresh. I've been seeing more fresh turmeric available lately, which I also like to use in combination with ginger, but go easy since it's a tad bitter (and turns everything it touches yellow).	Keep garlic, onions, and ginger in a basket or bowl on the counter; they'll last for weeks. (Refrigerate for longer storage.) Once you slice into a knob of ginger, store it loosely wrapped in the fridge until it starts to look funky—usually a couple of weeks.

INGREDIENT	DETAILS	STORAGE
Rice and other grains	The quickest-cooking, and therefore most used here, are white rice (short- or long-grain), couscous, bulgur, and quinoa. There are other options if you can work ahead or have a little more time. See page 208 for how to substitute brown rice in any recipe.	A cabinet or closet is fine, but if you don't use them often and have the room, they'll keep better and longer in the freezer. (Cooked grains freeze well for several months too. See the recipe on page 497.)
Dried pasta and noodles	There are plenty of different shapes to choose from in both white and whole wheat varieties; the shapes are mostly interchangeable, though the rule of thumb is smooth sauces with long strands and chunky sauces with cut pastas. Italian pastas are usually better than those made in the United States, though specialty and local producers are changing that. The recipes that include Asian-style noodles are scattered throughout the book and give you directions for how to prepare them.	These are usually dated for expiration but will keep longer than you'll use them.
Dried and canned beans	Dried beans are inexpensive, versatile, and easy to cook from scratch (see page 505 for a basic recipe). But you've got to plan ahead. With the exception of lentils, the recipes in this book call for canned, frozen, or your own home-cooked beans—and I can't encourage you strongly enough to make a big batch whenever possible. All the recipes here give canned quantities as an option. Each type of canned bean measures slightly differently, but the ingredient list assumes that 1 (15-ounce) can equals 1¾ cups.	Canned store for years; frozen cooked beans keep for months. The older dried beans are, the longer they'll take to cook, though they also keep for at least a year.
Canned tomatoes and tomato paste	Depending on the desired texture, I use whole peeled, diced, and crushed tomatoes. All come in "small" 15-ounce (approximately) and "large" 28-ounce cans. Tomato paste in a tube (like toothpaste) or in jars is more convenient than canned, but all are fine to use in these recipes.	Canned, jarred, and boxed tomatoes are marked with a best-by date, as is tomato paste. If you don't use all of the package, put the leftovers in a resealable bag (or container), squeeze the air out as best you can, and freeze. Next time, just thaw or cut off a chunk. Tubed paste stores for weeks in the fridge; freezing paste in an ice cube tray before storing is super-handy.

INGREDIENT	DETAILS	STORAGE
Peanut butter	Should contain peanuts and maybe salt and nothing else. Some stores let you grind it yourself. Whether you like smooth or chunky is always your call; they cook the same.	Keep in the fridge after opening. Before using, stir with a butter knife to reincorporate any separated oil.
Coconut milk	You'll use it more than you think. In cans and in refrigerated and shelf-stable cartons; full- and reduced-fat coconut milk will both work fine in the recipes here. Just be sure to buy real unsweetened coconut milk not water, cream, or some other coconut beverage.	Leftover coconut milk keeps in an airtight container in the fridge for several days after opening and freezes well for months.
Soy sauce and fish sauce	Two slightly different hits of intense flavors straight from the bottle. Soy sauce is essential; fish sauce (also called "nam pla" or "nuoc mam") is great to have around too.	Both last a long time, but fish sauce stays fresher longer when stored in the fridge.
Sugar, honey, and maple syrup	I used to say sugar is sugar, though of course it's not really since there are a few different kinds like granulated, golden and dark brown, or turbinado; each has a slightly different flavor. Use whichever you like and have handy in these recipes. Honey and maple syrup should be real, meaning free of additives or additional sweeteners.	Sugar and honey never go bad, but if honey crystalizes, warm gently in the microwave until it becomes liquid again. Maple syrup is best refrigerated after opening.
Flour, cornmeal, baking powder, and baking soda	Unbleached flour, please (I like having both white and whole wheat), and stone-ground cornmeal.	Baking powder and soda are marked with expiration dates. Flour and cornmeal keep for a year or so, longer if you freeze them.
Condiments	Ketchup, mayonnaise, Dijon mustard, hot sauce, and whatever else you crave. To make your own salsa, see pages 350, 364, and 480.	Mayonnaise, mustard, hot sauce, and ketchup all keep longer when stored in the fridge after opening.
Nuts and seeds	As big a variety as you think you'll use. Walnuts, almonds, and peanuts are most essential, though for crunch they're virtually interchangeable.	Use within a few months or store in the freezer.

Fridge Staples

For the most part, these are the least perishable of the perishables.

INGREDIENT	DETAILS	STORAGE
Butter, milk, and yogurt	I prefer the fresh taste of unsalted butter and used it in all the recipes here, but you can taste and adjust seasoning whenever you use salted. Milk and yogurt, preferably full fat, are also essential. Buttermilk, cream, sour cream, cream cheese, or crème fraîche appear occasionally.	Keep a little butter in the fridge or covered on the counter and the rest in the freezer. The rest are all dated.
Eggs	From true free-ranging birds if possible. Locally or regionally raised are usually good choices, too. You will notice the difference in flavor.	Supermarket eggs are dated but generally keep much longer than the carton indicates. Recently laid eggs (like those you find at a farmers' market or get from a neighbor) are best when still fresh but will keep for weeks.
Parmesan cheese	Get a chunk of real Parmigiano-Reggiano from Italy (what is listed as "Parmesan cheese" in the recipes). It's worth the price and extra time to grate fresh. Grana Padano and the saltier pecorino Romano are nearly as versatile though stronger tasting. Everything else is an imitation.	Wrap a chunk in wax paper, and it will keep for months in the refrigerator. (It is virtually indestructible; if it gets a spot of mold, just cut it off.)
Fresh herbs	Unless you have an herb garden, there's no need to keep more than one handy in the fridge at a time. Consider these the most versatile to keep in rotation: parsley, cilantro, basil, rosemary, thyme, and dill. Sage, tarragon, chives, and oregano as extras. I'm not saying they're utterly interchangeable, but the flavor boost that fresh herbs give is unmatched.	Thyme, rosemary, oregano, and sage can simply be wrapped in plastic. Others will live longer if you trim the bottoms and set the bunch in a jar of water like flowers. Best to use fresh herbs within a few days.
Lemons, limes, and oranges	You'll want both juice and zest, so get real fruit not bottled juice.	These will keep for a few weeks in the fridge; use before they get rotten or shrivel and dry.
Fresh chiles	Jalapeños strike a good balance of availability and moderate but real heat; all are useful.	Most will last for several weeks in the fridge and the heat level can vary fruit to fruit within the same variety. So if you like the heat, explore a couple different kinds. The easiest way to use them is to hold by the stem and snip from the bottom up with scissors. I like to keep them in a small bowl so they're handy.

INGREDIENT	DETAILS	STORAGE
Apples, pears, cabbage, broccoli and cauliflower, winter and summer squashes, potatoes, sweet potatoes, and other root vegetables	Long-keeping fruits and vegetables are always useful.	Ripe apples and pears, cabbage, summer squash, and cauliflower and broccoli keep best in the fridge—often up to several weeks. Store potatoes and sweet potatoes in the dark if possible. Store everything else on the counter.

Freezer Staples

I treat the freezer like the pantry on ice. Lucky you if you've got space for a big one.

INGREDIENT	DETAILS	STORAGE
Homemade stock	When I don't have homemade stock, I use water; the canned and boxed stuff just doesn't taste all that good to me (and it's rather expensive), though you can certainly use it. All the stock recipes you'll need are on page 489.	Refrigerate in airtight containers for several days or freeze in ice cube trays or resealable bags.
Frozen vegetables	Convenient and often better tasting and more nutritious than out-of-season "fresh" produce. Corn, peas, spinach and other greens, and edamame and shell beans like limas or black-eyed peas are best; other vegetables can also be valuable if you like them.	Don't overbuy. These will last for months, but using them sooner is better.
Frozen fruit	Essential for making fast smoothies and frozen desserts (see pages 24 and 466). I always try to keep at least one or two from this list in the freezer: strawberries, raspberries, peaches, and mangoes.	Best within weeks; will last for months.
Cooked beans	The perfect setup for fast—and excellent—cooking. See page 505 for a big-batch beans recipe.	Freeze beans in containers, covered with their cooking liquid, for up to a few months. Thaw in the fridge or microwave or during cooking.
Cooked grains	Like beans, indispensable for fast, spontaneous meals. See the master recipe and variations on page 496.	Store grains in resealable bags with all air squeezed out. Thaw in the fridge or microwave or during cooking.

INGREDIENT	DETAILS	STORAGE
Summertime tomatoes	It's almost unbelievable, but these freeze beautifully. And then you've got "fresh" tomatoes for cooking sauces, soups, chilis, and stews all winter.	Rinse perfectly ripe whole tomatoes and pop them in airtight containers. Pull them out as you need them. After they thaw a bit, cut out the core and slip the skins right off if you don't want to use them.
Homemade tomato sauce	Infinitely better than store-bought. And easier and more customizable than you think. See the recipe on page 492.	Refrigerate for days or cook a big batch, divide it among freezer containers, and freeze for months—or longer. Thaw in the refrigerator or the microwave.

Interchangeable Ingredients

Whenever a recipe calls for something you don't have, use this chart for Plan B. (Cooking times may vary.)

INGREDIENT	SUBSTITUTION	INGREDIENT	SUBSTITUTION
Stock	Water, wine, beer, apple cider	**Cauliflower**	Broccoli
Fresh tomatoes	Canned tomatoes (drained canned diced tomatoes can even work in some salads)	**Fennel**	Celery
Nuts and dried fruit	Any nut or dried fruit can be substituted for another.	**Asparagus**	Green beans or sugar snap peas
Vinegar	Any type will work; lemon and lime juice too.	**Fresh peas, sugar snap peas, or snow peas**	Frozen shelled peas
Fish sauce	Soy sauce	**Jícama**	Radishes, daikon, kohlrabi
Dried or fresh red chiles	Red chile flakes or cayenne	**Parsnips**	Carrots
Cooked/canned beans	All types are totally interchangeable.	**Pears**	Apples
Cilantro	Parsley, basil	**Sweet potatoes**	Carrots, parsnips, or winter squash
Tarragon	Dill, mint, chives, chervil	**Sour cream**	Yogurt
Rosemary	Thyme, sage, oregano	**Heavy cream (called "cream" in recipes)**	Half-and-half (unless you're whipping it)

INGREDIENT	SUBSTITUTION	INGREDIENT	SUBSTITUTION
Shallots	Onions, leeks	**Scallops**	Shrimp, squid
Lemongrass	Lemon zest (alone or mixed with a little lime zest)	**Mussels**	Clams (they're heavier, so I usually figure 2 pounds clams to every pound of mussels)
Salad greens	Lettuces and arugula and other greens are totally interchangeable.	**Fish fillets**	More interchangeable than you think; thin delicate fillets cook more quickly and are more fragile than thicker fish.
Kale	Collards, chard, spinach, escarole, bok choy	**Boneless, skinless chicken breasts**	Boneless, skinless chicken thighs (which will take a few minutes longer to cook); or chicken tenders (which will cook more quickly than breasts)

SHORTCUT CHEAT SHEET

Many will tell you that the key to fast cooking is to stock your kitchen with prepared "convenience" foods so that you're left with very little work to do once you get home. While some might occasionally be useful, others sacrifice too much in the way of quality, flavor, and nutritional value. It's best to make them yourself; see the page references for recipes and information. Here's my breakdown:

Worth It

Canned tomatoes

Canned beans

Canned tuna (preferably packed in olive oil but water packed is fine too)

Frozen fruits and vegetables

Panko (sort of; see page 488 for even better bread crumbs)

Deli meat (as long as it's of superior quality and you can get it sliced to order; otherwise roast your own proteins from the recipes on page 507)

Preground spices and spice blends

Some dried herbs (see the discussion on page 5)

Not Worth It

Canned or packaged stock (see the recipes on page 489) or use water

Jarred salsa and tomato sauce (see pages 480 and 492 to make your own)

Packaged hummus (see the recipe on page 96)

Rotisserie chicken (to roast whole chicken, see page 507)

Prechopped vegetables

Pregrated Parmesan

Prewashed salad greens (just invest in a spinner)

Bottled salad dressing (see Vinaigrette on page 485)

Just about any other shortcut ingredient or component

FAST EQUIPMENT

A cluttered kitchen is a slow kitchen. I've grouped all the equipment you'll need to cook from this book according to how it will be used, loosely in order of importance and frequency.

TYPE OF EQUIPMENT	WHAT YOU NEED	KITCHEN NOTES
Stoveware	Large (12-inch) skillets; large pot (at least 1 gallon, but bigger is more useful); medium skillet (8 to 10 inches); 1- to 2-quart small and medium saucepans. All of these should have tight-fitting lids and ideally be ovenproof or broiler-proof.	You'll use large skillets (often several at the same time) for everything. So get two: maybe one cast iron and one nonstick or stainless steel. 12 inches is fine; 13 or 14 inches is even better. (The more food you can comfortably fit in a skillet without crowding, the better it will brown—and in fewer batches.)
Ovenware	Large (18 × 13-inch) and small (9 x 13-inch) rimmed baking sheets; metal roasting pan (ideally also 18 x 13-inch); 9 × 13-inch baking pan or dish; 9-inch square baking pan; wire racks; muffin tin with standard-size cups; 9-inch pie plate; 9-inch round cake pan (springform is ideal).	You can never have enough rimmed baking sheets; some recipes here use two at the same time, so stock up (they're cheap, and you can stack them). Baking dishes should be metal, glass, ceramic, or enameled cast iron. Muffin tins, pie plates, and cake pans don't get much action in this book but have some uses beyond baking.
Small appliances	Food processor; blender; microwave oven; electric mixer; maybe an immersion blender	If you don't have a food processor, buy one; even a small size will change your life. (Used ones are really inexpensive.) An electric mixer is less critical but will make desserts easier; a powerful hand-held one is fine. You can live without a microwave, but there are recipes in this book that use one. And a blender makes smoother purées than anything else—not critical but nice; consider at least an immersion blender.
Knives	Chef's knife; long serrated knife; paring knife	You'll rely on a chef's knife (8 to 10 inches is best for most people) to make quick work of prep; it should feel as comfortable in your hand as possible. You'll use the serrated knife for bread and fine slicing. I keep a half dozen cheap paring knives on hand all the time. And then add knives as you develop a need for, say, a boning blade or wider cleaver-like options.

TYPE OF EQUIPMENT	WHAT YOU NEED	KITCHEN NOTES
Utensils	Large spoons; spatulas; tongs; peeler; box grater and/or fine grater (Microplane); kitchen scissors; can opener; liquid and dry measuring cups and spoons; quick-read thermometer; whisk; ladle; brushes; potato masher; rolling pin; mandoline (nice, and there are cheap but good ones out there)	You should have a few wooden spoons and two metal: one slotted, one not. You'll need one flexible metal spatula for turning and a rubber or silicone version for scraping. A rolling pin is handy but used sparingly in this book; a wine bottle does the trick in a pinch (especially if you've already consumed its contents). And truth be told, I probably use a fork for whisking much more often than I use an actual whisk; it's just as fast, although you've got to work a little harder.
Accessories	Cutting boards (wood, bamboo, and plastic if you like); kitchen towels; pot holders; kitchen timer; pepper mill; parchment paper	I like a big, sturdy wooden cutting board that lives on the counter and a smaller plastic one that I stash somewhere else. A clean kitchen is a fast kitchen, so keep lots of kitchen towels on hand. A kitchen timer is a bit of a relic in a smart phone world, but if you're worried about keeping your phone dry, digital timers are even handier.
Bowls and storage	Mixing bowls; large colander; strainers; salad spinner; glass jars; plastic storage containers (silicone are the ideal choice); resealable bags; foil; wax or parchment paper; plastic wrap	A salad spinner is by far the most efficient way to clean, dry, and store greens. I store vinaigrettes and homemade condiments in glass jars in the fridge and always keep plenty of containers and freezer bags for storing big batches of cooked beans, grains, and leftovers.

FAST STRATEGIES

The practice of prepping and cooking simultaneously is by far the biggest key to fast cooking that I have to offer here; it can be applied to boiling, steaming, pan-cooking, roasting, baking, broiling, grilling, and even braising and frying. But I'm always thinking about ways to be more efficient in the kitchen, so here is a preview of the other time-saving tips that are incorporated into recipes throughout the book.

The Rinse Cycle

Rinsing fruits and vegetables isn't always included in recipe Prep directions because I assume you will do it how and when you see fit (or not). But here are a few efficient ways to work it into the flow: If you have a bunch of different produce, consider putting them all in a colander together and rinsing under cold water all at once. If you run out of room in the colander, do them in batches and put what's done on towels.

If vegetables are going to be used toward the end of a recipe, wash while you have downtime as other things cook. Sometimes it's easiest to run water over foods like carrots, cabbage, or leeks after they've been trimmed or peeled or even sliced, since you're going to get rid of the peels anyway. (For more about food safety, see page 19.)

Consolidate Chopping

If a recipe uses chopped garlic, ginger, and/or chiles at the same time, don't chop those things one at a time. Instead, peel the garlic and ginger, trim the chiles, put them all in a pile, then start chopping them all together using a rocking motion until they're chopped fairly evenly. I rarely call for mincing, but when I do, just keep going until the bits are smaller.

Thinner (and Smaller) = Faster

This is obvious but worth remembering: Big, thick pieces take longer to cook through than foods cut small or sliced thin. That's as true of vegetables as it is of meat, and with a knife in your hand, you have quite a bit of control over the size and shape of the ingredients before they hit the pan. And grated vegetables cook the fastest of all; see the next point.

Grate for Puréeing

If you're making a puréed vegetable soup, grate the vegetables so that they become tender as quickly as possible. After all, it makes no difference what they look like at the beginning.

Start with Heat

Appliances, pots, pans, water, and fat take time to get hot. So before doing anything else, turn on the oven, heat the broiler, and/or set water to boil. And since many of the recipes start with sautéing or pan-cooking, you can preheat skillets too. (In cases where the Prep will take more than a couple minutes, I direct you to heat pans on one of the lowest settings until you're ready to cook.)

Adjust the Heat

While I've tried my best to balance the simultaneous flows of cooking and prepping, there may be times when you get slightly out of sync. Don't worry! You can always raise, lower, or turn off the heat on the stove to accommodate the speed of your prep work. So if the oil in a skillet is hot, but you haven't finished chopping the onion that's supposed to go in it, lower or turn off the heat until you're ready.

Don't Wait for the Oven

Unless you're baking bread, cookies, pie, or cake—or roasting something that requires an initial blast of very high heat—you don't have to wait for the oven to reach its final temperature before putting the food in. Vegetables are the best examples, but slow-roasted or braised meat and chicken can be started in an oven that hasn't yet come up to temperature. In some cases the recipe prompts you. In other cases, just judge doneness by visual cues since cooking times will differ from those in the recipes.

Heat Oil in the Oven

Put a rimmed baking sheet or roasting pan with a little oil in the oven as it heats. When you add whatever you're roasting to the pan, you'll immediately get the sizzle and sear that you're looking for on the bottom.

Embrace the Broiler

Broiling is a useful way to provide quick blasts of heat to a lot of food at once while freeing up space on the stove and sparing you the work of cooking in batches. With the rack farther away from the heat, the broiler can also be used for thicker cuts of meat or firmer vegetables that need a little more time to cook through. (I call this "long-distance broiling"; see page 420 for the details.)

Take Advantage of Steam

More efficient than using a real steamer is employing the steam that occurs naturally when you sauté or simmer something with moisture in it—usually vegetables or starches—to cook something else, especially proteins like fish, chicken, or eggs. A skillet of beans simmering with a splash of stock gives off steam, as does bubbling tomato sauce or zucchini cooking with olive oil. Put a lid on any of those pans and you've got yourself a steamer for whatever you might lay on top of the cooking food. (For recipes that effectively use steam, including in the microwave, see pages 324, 359, and 373. Or see page 498 for how to rig a steamer and cook simple vegetables.)

Use Less Liquid for Braising

The amount of liquid that we normally use for braising can take a while to come to an initial boil and a long time at the end to reduce into a sauce. Cut down time on both ends by adding less liquid. Submerge your ingredients in about 1 inch of liquid, cover the pot, and cook, turning occasionally and adding a little more liquid as necessary.

Clean as You Go

A delicious meal is less enjoyable when there's a messy kitchen waiting for you. Just like you use some natural breaks in the cooking process to prep, use other bits of downtime to clean dishes you're done using, wipe down counters and cutting boards—that sort of thing.

HOW TO USE THIS BOOK

The diagram on the back inside cover is a handy reference for using the recipes. Some of the book's unique features are worth further explanation.

Gathering Ingredients

To save valuable prep time, I always focus on streamlining ingredients to what's absolutely necessary. And since the lists for the recipes are essentially shopping lists, all you need to do before you start cooking is to put the required items on the kitchen counter, or at least make sure that you have everything you need handy. Ideally there isn't much advance planning required—defrosting meat or poultry a day ahead in the fridge perhaps, developing a menu that includes a side or two, that sort of thing.

You should use the ingredients list to give you an accurate idea of how much you need of each item; the recipe directions tell you how to prepare and cook them. To keep shopping simple, I've listed produce by simple count unless the amount sort of matters; then the size will be included as a description. If the exact quantity is important, the weight appears.

Fresh herbs are a special case. Unless you have an herb garden, you buy them by the bunch—the size of which will vary—or pick up a small container when you just need a few sprigs. Though how much you need is revealed in the directions, it's tough for even experienced cooks to estimate the yield. Here's my solution: When you need a little, the recipe calls for a few sprigs. Otherwise, a whole bunch is directed. Check the quantity in the recipe; if you've already got some in the fridge (or again, have a garden), you might not need to buy more. When you do need to buy fresh herbs, figure there will almost certainly be extra. And that's good news. The section in the table on page 8 gives you permission to make substitutions, and describes how to store them.

"Do the Blue"

All recipe directions are listed in blue (Prep) or in black numbered steps (Cook) and reflect the most efficient order and timing of tasks. They might look longer than traditional recipes, but all activity—preparation and cooking—is included in the detail. Believe me, they're faster.

The sequence and timing of the Prep and Cook steps are written for a single cook, working at a steady pace. There is some overlap and repetition of detail so you don't have to keep looking back at the ingredient list or the previous instruction. And sometimes cooking continues through multiple steps while you work on the Prep.

The recipes can also accommodate those who feel more comfortable prepping ingredients ahead of time, as well as those who are lucky enough to have a helper in the kitchen. Since Prep steps are highlighted in blue, you can easily identify them when you first look at a recipe and do all the necessary chopping and slicing before you start cooking. Or you can simply say to your helper, "You do the blue steps while I do the black" (or vice versa). This is really cool.

Component Recipes

How much faster could you cook if some of the work was already done when you started? A lot. So in addition to the hundreds of recipes and variations in this book, I've included a handful of Component Recipes (you can think of them as "master recipes") that are the basic homemade staples I like to keep stocked in my fridge or freezer at all times—things like vinaigrette, cooked beans, stock, roasted proteins, and tomato sauce. You can buy these, of course, but they're significantly better if you make them yourself.

Spotlights on Ingredients and Techniques

All How to Cook Everything books include detailed information about buying and storing key ingredients—in lists and tables I call "Lexicons." This latest addition to the family works similarly. The difference is that the ingredient features here are streamlined to target their focus on precisely what you need to know in order to cook fast from scratch. These tidbits appear in the recipe introductions, or sometimes in separate notes or sections where they are most useful.

The same goes for techniques. From general topics like maximizing your grill and broiler, to ingredient-specific topics like pressing tofu or shaving hard cheese, these tips will help you cook both better and faster—and learn by doing.

A Word About Food Safety

Fussing over kitchen hygiene while you're trying to cook isn't particularly fast. But neither is getting sidelined with a food-borne illness. And though I'm not obsessed with cleanliness, I always say it's well worth your time to practice the most basic food safety habits.

This means washing your hands before, during, and after handling food, especially when going from raw meats to anything else. Keep all of your work surfaces, sinks, and utensils clean the same way. (Soap and hot water will do the trick; antimicrobial concoctions can promote germ resistance. Use a weak bleach solution once in a while for deep cleaning.) Your refrigerator should always be between 35 and 40°F and your freezer around 0°F (this temperature also helps minimize freezer burn).

Washing fruits and vegetables is really a matter of personal choice. At one end of the spectrum are people who use soapy water, especially on produce that's visibly dirty or has been known to have problems—like melons, greens, and squash; other folks wash virtually nothing. I usually come down somewhere in the middle and decide case by case based on what it looks like and whether I'm going to eat it raw or cooked; I tend to be quite blasé about food that I'm cooking, for better or worse.

All of those rules are easy enough to follow. But things do get a little more complicated when we talk about bacteria and cooking temperatures. Sometimes meat, poultry, fish, or eggs contain disease-causing bacteria. There are two ways to minimize the risk: The first is to cook thoroughly, which can result in dry food that isn't ideal from your palate's perspective. (I don't do that myself, and my recipes don't recommend doing it either, but it's a judgment call.) The second way to minimize the risk of harmful bacteria is to buy the best-quality products you can from sources you trust the most. This I do recommend. It's not a failsafe, but it's much less of a sacrifice than a life of eating well-done steak.

Browsing the Recipe Titles

Deciding what sounds good to eat on any given day is a crucial part of efficient cooking. The recipe titles should be clear, descriptive, or instantly familiar. For at-a-glance navigation, I've listed all the recipe titles and page numbers in the contents, beginning on page v. The first you'll notice: Most of the recipe names include the main ingredients and seasonings, so they're rather long. With iconic dishes—whether identified with American or global cooking traditions—the name is usually its own best description, a beacon that signals something you've made before, enjoyed at a friend's house, or had in a restaurant.

Since everything in this book can be made in 30 minutes or less, from accessible supermarket ingredients and often nontraditional techniques, these recipes cannot be considered authentic. I usually try to amplify that in their titles, with qualifiers or by identifying the flavors of a specific cuisine. In other cases—like tacos, burritos, and frittatas—ingredients provide additional description. When more detail is helpful, the recipe introductions describe a little bit about the recipe's origins and how my version is different.

My intention is to balance respect for culinary cultures and traditions with accessibility. I want home cooks—with all kinds of experiences, budgets, and individual preferences—to prepare and enjoy meals with their families and friends. Along the way, I hope these recipes inspire you to continue learning and exploring, as only the journey of cooking can.

Breakfast

Weekday mornings are notorious for mealtime madness—the kind of crunch that tempts us to grab junk on the run or skip breakfast entirely. My goal is to change all that by providing a bundle of flexible recipes you can pull together in advance or on the fly. It's a simple strategy: Use the hectic pace and your proximity to the fridge and coffee pot to make something really good really fast. I mean, as long as you're in the kitchen anyway, why not pull together real, satisfying, nourishing food?

That might mean a bowl of homemade cold cereal (page 21), toast that eats like a meal (page 25), a spiced apple couscous or savory oatmeal to make in advance (pages 28 and 34), ways to prep and store fruit (page 26), and of course extraordinary smoothies (page 24).

On more leisurely days, you can hang around the stove and flip pancakes or tend to eggs. Or maybe you fancy breakfast for dinner. Either way, this chapter has you covered. From Tortilla Scramble (page 31) to ham-and-biscuit sandwiches (page 36) and citrusy ricotta pancakes (page 38), between the main recipes and variations, you've got options.

Loaded Muesli

Untoasted granola—muesli—is always better than boxed cereal and comes together in a flash from oats and whatever else you like. Purists insist on an overnight soaking in milk or yogurt for maximal nutritional benefit and a pleasant creaminess, which is lovely if you remember before going to bed. I usually just mix it up at the last minute. (And it should be noted that nondairy milks are lovely with muesli.) Granola takes longer than 30 minutes but not by much, so I'm including it as a variation below. Either way, multiply the ingredients as you like for a big batch. **Serves 2**

Ingredients

½ cup raisins or chopped dried fruit

3 cups rolled oats

1 cup any roasted or raw nuts and/or seeds

½ cup unsweetened shredded coconut

½ teaspoon ground cinnamon

Salt

Yogurt or milk for serving

▫ Prep · Cook

▫ Measure ½ cup raisins or other dried fruit; if the pieces are big, take a few minutes to chop them into bits.

1. Combine the fruit, 3 cups rolled oats, 1 cup nuts and/or seeds, ½ cup coconut, ½ teaspoon ground cinnamon, and a sprinkle of salt.

2. Taste and adjust the seasoning. Serve with yogurt or milk, or store in sealed containers. (The main recipe and the variations will last in the pantry for weeks and the freezer for months.)

Variations

Candied Ginger–Clove Muesli. The spice is nice. Substitute ½ cup chopped candied ginger for the raisins and ground cloves for the ground cinnamon.

Apricot-Cardamom Muesli. Use chopped dried apricots for the fruit and ground cardamom instead of ground cinnamon.

Loaded Granola. Use raw nuts so they don't overtoast, or add roasted nuts with the coconut. Put the oats and nuts in a large bowl and sprinkle with salt. Drizzle with ¼ to ½ cup honey or maple syrup (to taste) and toss to combine. Spread the oat mixture on a rimmed baking sheet and bake at 350°F, stirring occasionally until lightly browned, about 30 minutes. Toss in the spice, then sprinkle the coconut on top and return to the oven until the granola is fragrant and the coconut is golden. Remove from the oven, stir in the fruit, and cool completely before storing.

6 Dried Fruit, Spice, and Nut or Seed Combinations to Try

The variations offer a couple of my favorite ingredient mixtures for muesli and granola. Here are a handful more:

1. Cranberries, ground allspice, pepitas (hulled green pumpkin seeds)
2. Cherries, vanilla bean seeds, pistachios
3. Golden raisins, sunflower seeds
4. Pineapple, ground coriander, cashews
5. Mangoes, chili powder, peanuts
6. Apples, ground ginger, almonds

Sunshine Smoothie

You can have a different smoothie every day without repeating flavors for weeks. Here are four very different ideas to get your gears moving. Yogurt used to be the go-to ingredient for creaminess, but vegan options like oat or nut milks and silken tofu deliver a similar richness. For frostier—and faster—smoothies, start with frozen fruit; see Faster Fruit on page 26 for directions on how to prepare your own fruit. **Serves 2 to 4**

Ingredients

1 medium pineapple

2 bananas

1 (14-ounce) can coconut milk (reduced-fat is okay)

Ice cubes

Water or orange juice, if needed

Prep · Cook

☐ Cut the top and bottom off the pineapple; stand it upright and slice around the outside to remove the skin. Still cutting from top to bottom, slice around the core; you'll have at least 4 pieces. Discard the core (I gnaw on it first); chop the flesh. Refrigerate half for another use.

☐ Peel and chop the bananas.

1. Put the pineapple, bananas, coconut milk, and a few ice cubes in a blender.

2. Blend until completely smooth, adding some water or orange juice to thin the drink if necessary, and serve. Leftovers will keep for a day or two in the fridge.

Variations

Crimson Smoothie. Instead of the coconut milk, use 1½ cups yogurt. Replace the pineapple and banana with 2 cups each fresh strawberries and cubed watermelon.

Green Smoothie. Substitute 1½ cups oat milk for the coconut milk. Instead of the pineapple and banana, use the flesh from 1 ripe avocado and 3 cups green grapes.

Blue Smoothie. Replace the coconut milk with 12 ounces soft silken tofu (about 1½ cups; reserve any left over for another use or toss it in the smoothie if you like). Instead of the pineapple and banana, use a total of 4 cups mixed blackberries and blueberries.

Toast with Toasted Almond Butter and Strawberries

Nuts, fruit, and whole grains are always a good way to start the day. And you'll be amazed how simple it is to make chunky, fresh-tasting nut butter at home. All you do is give some nuts (or seeds, for that matter; I toast them, but you don't have to) a whirl in the food processor with water. To make a big batch so you always have some handy, figure 2 cups nuts or seeds will yield more than 1 cup butter, so you'll have some extra for another time.
Serves 4

Ingredients

2 cups raw almonds

2 cups strawberries

4 thick slices whole grain bread

Salt

Honey for drizzling

▫ Prep · Cook

1. If you don't have a toaster, heat the oven to 400°F.

2. Put 2 cups almonds in a large dry skillet over medium heat. Cook, shaking the skillet frequently, until lightly browned and fragrant, 3 to 5 minutes.

   ▫ Hull and slice 2 cups strawberries.

3. Toast 4 slices bread in a toaster or on a rimmed baking sheet in the oven, turning once, until it's as dark as you like.

4. Transfer the toasted almonds to a food processor; add a sprinkle of salt. Grind to the consistency of coarse meal.

5. Add ½ cup water. Process until creamy, 1 to 2 minutes. Add more water, 1 tablespoon at a time, and process until spreadable. Taste and add salt if you like.

6. Spread the toast generously with almond butter. Top with sliced strawberries, drizzle with honey, and serve. (Refrigerate leftover almond butter in a sealed container for up to a month.)

● recipe continues →

● Toast with Toasted Almond Butter and Strawberries, continued

Variations

Toast with Toasted Pecan Butter and Peaches. Replace the almonds with pecans. Instead of the strawberries, halve and pit 2 large or 3 medium peaches; slice thin.

Toast with Toasted Walnut Butter and Apples. Substitute walnuts for the almonds. Instead of the strawberries, core 1 large or 2 medium crisp apples, peel if you like, and thinly slice or chop into bite-sized pieces.

Toast with Toasted Cashew Butter and Tomatoes. Use only the ripest, juiciest fruit. Substitute cashews for the almonds. Instead of the strawberries, top with chopped or sliced tomatoes; you'll want 1 large or 2 medium.

FASTER FRUIT

The trick to eating more fruit—especially during the mad rush of a hectic morning—is to do the rinsing, trimming, peeling, pitting, slicing, and chopping in advance and capture the perfect moment of ripeness by either freezing, macerating, or cooking.

To freeze your own fruit for smoothies, sauces, desserts, or compotes, simply chop or slice it as needed, spread the pieces out on a rimmed baking sheet or two, and pop in the freezer until the pieces are frozen solid, just a couple hours or overnight. Then pack the fruit into airtight containers to use as you need it. The best fruits for freezing are berries, melons, pineapple, bananas (in or out of the peel), and mangoes; peaches, nectarines, and apricots can work well if you douse them generously in lemon juice first.

Macerating marinates cut fruit in its own juices and leaves you with a thin sauce. Most macerated fruits last in the fridge for a day or two before the pieces brown or break down. Juicy fresh fruits like berries, citrus, and peaches only need a sprinkle of sugar or salt to help them release water; sprinkle, stir, then let sit for 15 to 20 minutes. Firmer fruits, like apples, pineapple, and mangoes, benefit from added liquid—simple syrup, fruit juice, vinegar, wine, or brandy. Drizzle a bowl of cut fruit with 1 or 2 tablespoons, toss, and let sit for about 30 minutes. You can season the fruit with spices or herbs too. Macerate when you want to improve imperfect fruit or make a quick topping for yogurt, pancakes, French toast, baked goods—even toast.

Fruit compote takes things a step further by applying heat. Start by macerating as described above, then cook the fruit at a gentle bubble in a covered pot on the stove or a glass dish in the microwave. How long you go depends on whether you want a chunky or smooth texture; stop a stage before you ultimately want it, remove from heat, then let sit for a few minutes to cool and thicken. Compote keeps for up to a week in the refrigerator.

Candy-Apple Couscous

Steeping couscous and a couple key ingredients in something besides water makes for a hot cereal that eats like dessert. Don't worry: Nothing is too sweet; the hearty taste of whole wheat couscous provides a nutty backdrop. **Serves 2 to 4**

Ingredients

2 tablespoons butter

1 tablespoon packed brown sugar

½ teaspoon ground cinnamon

Salt

1½ cups apple cider

1 large or 2 medium apples

1 cup couscous (preferably whole wheat)

⬜ Prep · Cook

1. Put 2 tablespoons butter in a medium saucepan over medium-high heat. When it starts to melt, add 1 tablespoon brown sugar, ½ teaspoon ground cinnamon, and a sprinkle of salt, and cook, stirring frequently until the sugar melts.

2. Carefully stir in 1½ cups apple cider; remove from the heat.

   ⬜ Core, peel, and chop the apple(s).

3. Add the apples and couscous to the pot. Bring the mixture to a boil. Cover the pot and turn off the heat.

4. Let the couscous steep until the liquid is absorbed, about 10 minutes. Fluff the couscous with a fork, taste, adjust the seasoning, and serve.

Variations

Chocolate Bar Couscous.
Omit the apple. Instead of the sugar, use 2 ounces chopped dark chocolate. Substitute milk for the apple cider (cow's or a nondairy alternative). Keep the ground cinnamon if you like or try a pinch of ground ancho chile or cayenne. Stir in ½ cup unsweetened shredded coconut along with the couscous.

Orange-sicle Couscous.
Instead of the cider, use ¾ cup each orange juice and milk (cow's or a nondairy alternative); add 1 teaspoon vanilla extract. Substitute 2 oranges for the apples. Grate about 1 tablespoon zest, then peel the oranges. Separate them into sections and remove the seeds if necessary. Add the orange sections and zest as described in Step 3.

Sugar-Plum Couscous.
Substitute turbinado sugar for the brown sugar. Instead of the apple cider, squeeze the juice of 1 lemon into 1¼ cups water through a strainer to catch the seeds. Substitute ¼ teaspoon ground cardamom for the ground cinnamon. Thinly slice a dozen (or more) pitted prunes to replace the apples.

Roasting-Pan French Toast

What slows French toast down is cooking it in batches in a skillet. A griddle solves that problem, but if you don't have one, I bet you do have a roasting pan, which works the same way. If you decide to go the skillet route or are making several batches, keep finished slices warm in a 200°F oven on a wire rack over a rimmed baking sheet to keep them crisp. For bread, consider cinnamon raisin or an eggy brioche- or challah-style loaf; slices an inch thick or less are ideal. **Serves 4**

Ingredients

4 eggs

½ cup milk

1 tablespoon sugar

1 teaspoon vanilla extract

Salt

4 tablespoons (½ stick) butter, plus more as needed and for serving

8 slices any bread

Maple syrup for serving

☐ Prep · **Cook**

1. Set a roasting pan on 2 burners over medium-low heat.

2. Crack the eggs into a large shallow bowl or dish. Add ½ cup milk, 1 tablespoon sugar, 1 teaspoon vanilla, and a sprinkle of salt; whisk to combine.

3. Add 4 tablespoons butter to the roasting pan and swirl it around. Raise the heat to medium.

4. One slice at a time, dip the bread in the egg mixture, soaking it well and coating both sides. As you finish, lay each slice in the roasting pan.

5. Cook, turning once and adding more butter if the toast starts to stick, until browned on both sides, 3 to 5 minutes per side. You might need to rotate them on the second side to promote even browning. Serve with maple syrup and more butter.

Variations

Roasting-Pan Coconut Toast. Delightfully vegan. Pick an eggless bread. Instead of the eggs and milk, whisk 1 (14-ounce) can coconut milk and ½ cup unsweetened shredded coconut for dipping the bread. Use coconut oil or other vegetable oil for greasing the pan. For a real treat, serve these with lime wedges and sorghum syrup for drizzling.

Roasting-Pan Parmesan Toast. A savory spin. Omit the sugar, vanilla, and maple syrup. Add 2 teaspoons chopped fresh rosemary and ½ cup grated Parmesan cheese to the egg mixture in Step 2. Serve drizzled with olive oil or sprinkled with more cheese.

Tortilla Scramble

Okay, frying your own tortillas isn't faster than buying chips—but it is better. So with an investment of just a couple extra minutes, you'll get phenomenal texture. Depending on where you've lived or traveled, this recipe might sound a lot like migas, which can also be made from leftover bread. **Serves 2**

Ingredients

4 corn tortillas

1 medium onion

⅓ cup vegetable oil

2 poblano chiles

Salt and pepper

1 large ripe tomato

1 avocado

2 scallions

4 eggs

4 ounces queso fresco or Cotija cheese (1 cup crumbled)

Prep · Cook

- Line a plate with towels.

- Stack 4 tortillas, cut them in half, then cut into ½-inch-wide strips.

- Trim, peel, and slice the onion.

1. Put ⅓ cup vegetable oil in a medium skillet over medium heat.

   - Core, seed, and slice the chiles.

2. When the oil is hot (toss in a bit of tortilla; it will sizzle), add the tortilla strips. Cook, stirring constantly until they are golden brown and crisp, 1 or 2 minutes. Transfer the strips to the towels with a slotted spoon and sprinkle with salt.

3. Raise the heat to medium-high. Add the onion and poblanos to the skillet, sprinkle with salt and pepper, and cook, stirring occasionally, until they soften and begin to brown, 5 to 10 minutes.

   - Core and chop the tomato.

   - Halve and pit the avocado, scoop out the flesh, and chop.

   - Trim and chop the scallions.

   - Crack the eggs into a medium bowl, sprinkle with salt and pepper, and whisk or beat with a fork until smooth.

   - Crumble 1 cup queso fresco.

4. Add the eggs to the skillet and cook, stirring frequently and scraping the sides until they begin to curdle, 3 to 5 minutes.

5. Add the tomato and tortilla strips and stir gently. If some parts of the eggs are drying out, remove the skillet from the heat and continue stirring until the cooking slows down a bit. Then return to the heat.

6. The eggs are done when they're creamy, soft, and still a bit runny, just another minute or two. Scatter the avocado, scallions, and crumbled cheese over the top and serve.

Broiled Eggs,
right, and Broiled
Prosciutto and
Eggs, left

Broiled Eggs

If you're cooking for a crowd but want something other than a scramble, this muffin-tin method gets you pretty close to the elegance of poached eggs, with the added benefit of all the eggs cooking—and finishing—at the same time. The keys to making the recipe work: Use a pan with standard-size cups; position it as far away from the heat as you can so the eggs cook all the way through before the top gets too firm. If you can't get the rack 6 inches from the heat source, then heat the oven to 425°F with a rack fitted toward the top; put the eggs in and figure they'll take about twice as long. Toast is the natural accompaniment, cut into sticks or "soldiers" for easy dipping. **Serves 3 to 6**

Ingredients

2 to 4 tablespoons (¼ to ½ stick) butter

6 to 12 eggs (depending on your muffin tin)

Salt and pepper

1 small bunch chives for garnish (optional)

▢ Prep · Cook

1. Turn the broiler to high; put the rack 6 inches from the heat.

   ▢ Grease 1 or 2 muffin tins (for a total of 6 or 12 cups) with 2 to 4 tablespoons butter.

2. Carefully crack 1 egg into each of the cups.

3. Put the muffin tin in the oven and broil until the eggs are just set (the yolks should still be slightly runny and the whites opaque), 6 to 8 minutes.

   ▢ Chop 2 or 3 tablespoons chives for garnish if you're using them.

4. Gently remove each egg from the muffin tin with a spoon. Sprinkle with salt and pepper and serve, garnished with the chives if you like.

Variations

Broiled Cheesy Eggs. Divide ½ to 1 cup grated sharp cheddar or Gruyère cheese among the cups before cracking in the eggs in Step 2. It will take an extra couple minutes for the cheese to melt and the eggs to cook.

Broiled Prosciutto and Eggs. Cut 3 to 6 thin slices of prosciutto in half crosswise; drape a slice into each buttered cup before cracking in the egg in Step 2. It will take an extra couple minutes for the prosciutto to crisp and the eggs to cook.

Creamed Broiled Eggs. Decadent. After buttering the cups, divide ⅓ to ¾ cup cream among them (that's 1 tablespoon in each cup). Then crack in the eggs. This will only take an extra minute or two to cook the eggs. After scooping them out, drizzle any cream remaining in the cups over the top.

Salt-and-Pepper Oats

Breakfast porridge—made from rice, corn, rolled oats, or ground wheat—is a staple that falls in and out of favor and is usually served sweet. This savory option is more like pilaf, only without the fuss of stirring. You just bring the grains to a boil, cover the pot, then walk away. (You can also substitute quinoa in this recipe.) To save even more time, start with already cooked grains out of the fridge and just pop them in the microwave. All the more reason to double the quantities here or make a big batch from the master recipe and variations on page 496. **Serves 4**

Ingredients

1½ cups steel-cut oats

Salt

2 tablespoons butter or olive oil, or more to taste

Pepper

▢ Prep · Cook

1. Combine 1½ cups oats with a large pinch of salt and water to cover by about an inch in a medium saucepan. Bring to a boil, then adjust the heat so the liquid bubbles gently. Cover the pot.

2. Cook undisturbed until the water is absorbed and holes appear in the top of the grains, 15 to 20 minutes; the oats should be tender.

   ▢ If you're using butter, cut it into small bits.

3. Add a generous sprinkle of black pepper and 2 tablespoons butter or olive oil; stir them into the oats with a fork. Taste and adjust the seasoning, adding more butter or oil if you like, and serve.

Variations

Salsa Oats. When you put the oats in the pot, add 1 cup cooked or raw salsa then add water to cover the oats by 1 inch. Cook as directed, only seasoning less. To finish, use olive oil.

Soy Sauce Oats. Go easy on the salt in Step 1; add 2 tablespoons soy sauce. Try a pinch of red chile flakes with the black pepper. Use 1 tablespoon sesame oil and 1 tablespoon butter when you fluff the grains in Step 3.

10 Toppers for Salt-and-Pepper Oats

Any of these—alone or in combination—are terrific additions to the main recipe or the variations. How much depends on you.

1. Chopped ripe tomatoes
2. Chopped fresh herbs like parsley, cilantro, basil, dill, or mint
3. Sliced hard-boiled eggs
4. Chopped nuts like peanuts, cashews, almonds, or pistachios
5. Chopped scallions
6. Chopped pickles or pickled vegetables
7. Anchovies, sardines, tuna, or other canned or jarred fish
8. Leftover simply cooked vegetables
9. Chopped tender greens like spinach or arugula
10. A sprinkle of ground spices like curry powder, ground chiles, or smoked paprika

Pork 'n' Greens Breakfast

The best thing about making your own breakfast sausages is customizing them. Serve any of these with toast, and/or cook eggs as you like in a separate skillet or pot at the same time (page 483). **Serves 4**

Ingredients

2 tablespoons olive oil

2 or 3 sprigs fresh sage or ½ teaspoon dried

1 pound ground pork

Pinch of ground nutmeg

Salt and pepper

1 bunch kale (1 pound)

▫ Prep · Cook

1. Put 2 tablespoons olive oil in a large skillet over low heat.

   ▫ If you're using fresh sage, strip the leaves from 2 or 3 sprigs and chop.

2. Put the ground pork in a bowl along with the chopped fresh sage or ½ teaspoon dried, a pinch of ground nutmeg, and a sprinkle of salt and pepper. Gently mix the seasonings into the pork with a fork.

3. Raise the heat to medium-high. Break off a small piece of the sausage mixture, flatten it, and fry it in the skillet until cooked through. Taste and adjust the seasoning of the sausage mixture.

4. Shape the sausage mixture into 4 large or 8 small patties (the thinner they are, the faster they'll crisp). Cook undisturbed until the patties release easily from the skillet, 3 to 5 minutes. Turn and cook on the other side.

   ▫ Trim and chop the kale.

5. Transfer the cooked sausages to a plate. Spoon out all but 2 tablespoons of the fat in the pan. Add the kale to the skillet, sprinkle with salt and pepper, and cook, stirring occasionally until it's just tender, 4 to 5 minutes. Serve with the sausage patties.

Variations

Spicy Pork and Apples Breakfast. Replace the sage with ½ teaspoon cayenne and the ground nutmeg with 2 teaspoons minced garlic. Instead of the kale, core and slice 1 pound apples (I don't bother to peel them but you can). Cook the apples until slightly softened and lightly browned; you still want them to be a little crisp.

Chorizo Breakfast with Peppers. Instead of the sage and ground nutmeg, use 1 tablespoon chili powder, 2 teaspoons minced garlic, 1 teaspoon ground cumin, and ½ teaspoon cayenne. Substitute 3 thinly sliced bell peppers (any color) for the kale.

Drop Biscuit Ham Sandwiches

Yes, you can have biscuits on the table in 30 minutes—when you make them like this. The simple fillings come together while the biscuits bake. The main recipe features a quick fruity-mustardy "mostarda" you'll want to use on all sorts of sandwiches. **Serves 4 (makes 12 baby biscuits)**

Ingredients

4 tablespoons (½ stick) cold butter, plus a little more for greasing the pan

2 cups flour, plus more if needed

1 teaspoon salt

¼ teaspoon pepper

1 tablespoon baking powder

1 teaspoon baking soda

1 cup buttermilk, plus more if needed

⅓ cup fruit preserves (like cherry or apricot)

⅓ cup Dijon mustard

8 ounces thinly sliced ham

▢ Prep · Cook

1. Heat the oven to 450°F.

   ▢ Cut 4 tablespoons butter into cubes.

2. Put 2 cups flour, 1 teaspoon salt, ¼ teaspoon pepper, 1 tablespoon baking powder, and 1 teaspoon baking soda in a food processor. Pulse to combine.

3. Add the butter to the food processor, and pulse until the bits of butter are the size of peas.

4. Add 1 cup buttermilk and pulse just until the mixture forms a ball. (If it seems very sticky and wet, pulse in more flour, a tablespoon at a time, until the dough comes together. If it's too dry, do the same with buttermilk.)

5. Grease a rimmed baking sheet with butter. Drop heaping tablespoons of the dough onto the baking sheet; press down slightly with the back of a spoon. (You should have 12 biscuits.) Bake the biscuits until golden brown, 7 to 9 minutes.

6. Put the ⅓ cup preserves and ⅓ cup Dijon mustard in a small bowl and stir to combine.

   ▢ Cut 8 ounces ham into pieces about the same size as the biscuits.

7. When the biscuits are done and just cool enough to handle, cut them in half along the equator, spread some of the mustard mixture inside, and fill with ham. Serve hot or warm.

Variations

Drop Biscuit Smoked Salmon Sandwiches. Instead of the ham, use thinly sliced cold-smoked salmon (lox style). Replace the preserves and mustard with ½ cup crème fraîche, 2 tablespoons chopped fresh dill, and 1 tablespoon lemon juice.

Drop Biscuit Egg Sandwiches. Omit the ham. While the biscuits bake, scramble or fry 8 eggs (page 483). For the spread, mash 2 tablespoons honey into 3 tablespoons butter.

Drop Biscuit Pimento Cheese Sandwiches. Instead of the ham and spread, put ¼ cup cream cheese in a medium bowl with 4 ounces grated sharp cheddar (1 cup), 1 tablespoon Dijon mustard, and ½ cup chopped jarred pimiento or roasted red bell peppers; sprinkle with lots of black pepper and stir with a fork to combine. Use this cheese mixture to fill the warm biscuits.

Orange-Ricotta Pancakes

Ricotta works magic on pancake batter, so you end up with incredibly light and fluffy cakes with a little more substance than diner flapjacks. Orange zest adds brightness. Promise me one thing: You won't fret over the lumps. Doing so will only take more time to mix and make for less fluffiness. **Serves 4**

Ingredients

2 cups flour

½ teaspoon baking soda

½ teaspoon salt

2 eggs

About 2 cups ricotta cheese (one 15-ounce container)

1 tablespoon sugar

1 orange

Butter for cooking

Maple syrup or powdered sugar for serving

▫ Prep · Cook

1. Heat the oven to 200°F and put a large rimmed baking sheet on the center rack.

2. In a large bowl, combine 2 cups flour, ½ teaspoon baking soda, and ½ teaspoon salt.

3. Crack the eggs into a medium bowl and beat. Stir in 2 cups ricotta and 1 tablespoon sugar.

4. Put a large skillet over medium-low heat.

   ▫ Grate 1 tablespoon zest from the orange; then halve the orange.

5. Add the orange zest to the wet ingredients and squeeze in the orange juice through a strainer or your fingers to catch the seeds. Gently stir the wet ingredients into the dry. Mix only enough to moisten the flour; don't worry about lumps.

6. Put a tablespoon or so butter in the skillet and swirl it around. When the butter foam subsides, work in batches with a serving spoon to make any size pancakes you like, careful to avoid crowding the pan. Cook until the bottoms are golden brown and bubbles appear in the centers of the pancakes, 2 to 4 minutes.

7. Turn the pancakes and cook, adjusting the heat so they don't burn, until the second sides are lightly browned, another few minutes.

8. As they finish, transfer the cooked pancakes to the pan in the oven to keep warm. Continue cooking, adding a little more butter for each batch, until you've used up all the batter. Serve warm with maple syrup or a dusting of powdered sugar.

Snacks

et's agree right up front that whether you call these little dishes snacks, hors d'oeuvre, or appetizers doesn't matter. Nor will it make any difference if you eat them before dinner, between meals, or make an assortment for a cocktail party or lazy grazing supper in front of the television. These recipes always deliver a lot of bang for your bite.

Some ideas: Combine a couple—like my easy deconstructed deviled eggs (page 52) and Skewerless Chicken Satay (page 49)—with a salad or soup. Start a celebration with something elegant and make-ahead like Goat Cheese Truffles (page 45), which are nothing more than fresh cheese balls rolled in seasonings. Or make a double batch of Gingery Cashews with Honey-Soy Glaze (page 40) to nosh on your next road trip.

For vegetable lovers, there are two spins on crudités (page 42) and Edamame with Chili Salt (page 41). And no snack chapter would be complete without shrimp and something to dip them in (page 48).

Spiced Cashews with Bacon

Sautéing nuts in rendered bacon fat is luxurious—and much faster than roasting. **Serves 4**

Ingredients

4 slices bacon

2 cups unsalted raw cashews

Salt

2 teaspoons curry powder

☐ Prep · **Cook**

1. Put a large skillet over medium heat.

    ☐ Chop 4 slices bacon into ½-inch pieces.

2. Add the chopped bacon to the skillet. Cook, stirring occasionally until crisp, 5 to 10 minutes.

3. Transfer the bacon to a paper towel with a slotted spoon; keep about 2 tablespoons of the rendered fat in the skillet and pour off the rest.

4. Add 2 cups cashews and a sprinkle of salt to the skillet. Cook, stirring frequently and adjusting the heat to prevent burning if necessary until the nuts are lightly browned, 3 to 5 minutes.

5. Sprinkle the nuts with 2 teaspoons curry powder; stir constantly until fragrant, about a minute.

6. Stir the bacon into the nuts. Let the mixture cool for a few minutes before serving. If there are any leftovers after a couple hours at room temperature, refrigerate them.

Variations

Pecans with Bacon and Brown Sugar. Substitute pecan halves for the cashews and ⅓ cup packed dark brown sugar for the curry powder.

Briny Spiced Peanuts. Use raw unsalted peanuts instead of the cashews. Substitute 4 sheets nori for the bacon. Stack them and use kitchen scissors to cut them into 1-inch strips; then stack those and snip crosswise as thinly as you can. Substitute five-spice powder for the curry. Instead of cooking the bacon in Step 2, heat 1 tablespoon each vegetable and sesame oils in the skillet and use that to toast the nuts. When you add the spice in Step 5, toss in the nori.

Gingery Cashews with Honey-Soy Glaze. Omit the bacon and curry powder. Peel and chop about 1 inch fresh ginger. Instead of cooking the bacon in Step 2, heat 2 tablespoons vegetable oil in the skillet and use that to toast the nuts and soften the ginger at the same time. While the nuts are cooking, combine ¼ cup honey with 2 tablespoons soy sauce in a small bowl. When the nuts are toasted, turn off the heat and drizzle with the honey mixture. Toss to coat the nuts with the glaze.

Edamame with Chili Salt

Boiled or steamed in-shell edamame with salt is a classic Japanese snack that's become super-popular here too. Few finger foods are simpler to make or eat. After they're cool enough to handle, you eat them by squeezing the beans from the shells as you would a tube of toothpaste—only they go directly into your mouth. **Serves 4**

Ingredients

Salt

2 teaspoons chili powder

1½ pounds edamame in their pods (fresh or frozen)

1 tablespoon sesame oil

Prep · Cook

1. Bring a medium pot of water to a boil and salt it.

   ☐ Combine 2 teaspoons chili powder and 1 teaspoon salt in a bowl.

2. When the water boils, add 1½ pounds edamame and cook until they're hot all the way through and you can pierce a bean with a fork, 3 to 5 minutes, depending on the beans.

3. Drain well, toss with 1 tablespoon sesame oil and the chili salt, and serve hot or warm.

Variations

Microwaved Seasoned Edamame. Works for the main recipe and either of the following variations. Put the beans in a covered microwave-safe dish with ¼ cup water. Cook on high, checking and stirring every minute or so until they're hot and plump, usually just 2 or 3 minutes.

Sesame Edamame. Omit the chili powder. While the edamame cook, toast 3 tablespoons sesame seeds in a small dry skillet over medium heat, shaking almost constantly until golden, just a couple minutes. When the beans are tender, toss them with the sesame oil, seeds, and salt.

Garlicky Edamame. Omit the chili powder. While the water comes to a boil, peel and chop 4 large cloves garlic; add them to the pot with the beans. Use a strainer to drain the edamame so you capture the bits of softened garlic too. Toss with the sesame oil and salt before serving.

Snacking Vegetables with Quick Romesco

Crudités seem sort of fussy for this book, especially since the dips are why people eat this appetizer anyway. The main recipe takes a shortcut to the traditional Spanish almond sauce; the variation demonstrates the power of warm olive oil. Here's the secret to pulling vegetables together in a snap: Choose no more than three and be okay with one or two if that's all you have handy. **Serves 4**

Ingredients

3 cloves garlic

1 cup ripe cherry tomatoes

2 tablespoons roasted almonds

1½ pounds assorted vegetables for eating raw (like carrots, bell peppers, fennel, celery, radishes, and/or cucumbers)

2 tablespoons sherry vinegar

⅓ cup olive oil

½ teaspoon smoked paprika or chili powder

Salt and pepper

☐ Prep · Cook

1. Put a large dry skillet over medium heat.

   ☐ Peel 3 cloves garlic and chop them.

2. When the skillet is hot, add the garlic, 1 cup cherry tomatoes, and 2 tablespoons almonds. Cook, shaking the skillet occasionally so the almonds don't burn, until the tomatoes are a bit charred and begin to burst and the almonds and garlic are lightly browned, 4 to 6 minutes.

   ☐ Trim, peel, core, and seed any vegetables that need it. Cut the vegetables into pieces you can use for dipping. Put them on a platter.

3. Transfer the charred tomatoes, almonds, and garlic to a food processor. Add 2 tablespoons sherry vinegar, ⅓ cup olive oil, ½ teaspoon smoked paprika, and a sprinkle of salt and pepper.

4. Process until the mixture is thick and relatively smooth but still has some crunch from the almonds. Taste and adjust the seasoning.

5. Transfer the romesco sauce to a serving bowl and serve with the vegetables alongside for dipping.

Variation

Snacking Vegetables with Warm Garlicky Olive Oil. Omit the tomatoes, almonds, and vinegar. In Step 1, instead of heating the skillet dry, add the olive oil. Increase the garlic to 4 or 5 cloves and add them to the pan; they should sizzle a little and soften while you prepare the vegetables. Season the oil with some salt and pepper and serve it warm with the vegetables for dipping.

Warm-Pickled Cucumber Spears

Steeping vegetables in hot brine infuses them with lots of flavor quickly. If you're in a hurry, serve them at room temperature. Or pop them in the freezer for 20 minutes to blast chill. Either way, their tang is a welcome snack. **Serves 4**

Ingredients

½ cup red wine vinegar

1 bay leaf

1 teaspoon salt

½ teaspoon sugar

3 medium cucumbers
(1 to 1½ pounds)

1 bunch fresh dill

☐ Prep · Cook

1. Put ½ cup red wine vinegar, 1 bay leaf, 1 teaspoon salt, ½ teaspoon sugar, and 2 cups water in a large pot (use stainless steel or enameled so it doesn't react with the brine) and bring to a boil.

   ☐ Trim the cucumbers and peel them if they're thick or waxed; cut them into thick spears and remove the seeds with a spoon if you like.

   ☐ Chop ¼ cup fresh dill leaves and tender stems.

2. When the brine comes to a boil, add the cucumbers and dill; cover and turn off the heat.

3. Let the cucumbers sit for 10 to 15 minutes. Serve warm or at room temperature. To store, let the cucumbers cool a bit, then submerge them in the brine in a jar or other airtight container and refrigerate. They'll keep for about a week and pickle further in the fridge.

Variations

Warm-Pickled Bell Peppers. Substitute 1 pound red or yellow bell peppers for the cucumbers and 2 tablespoons chopped fresh oregano or 2 teaspoons dried for the dill. Core the peppers, then cut into slices about ½ inch wide.

Warm-Pickled Zucchini. Replace the cucumbers with 1 pound zucchini. Add 2 teaspoons grated lemon zest to the pot along with the dill.

Warm-Pickled Carrots. Use 1 pound carrots instead of cucumbers and 1 tablespoon cumin seeds instead of dill. Peel the carrots if you like, then cut them crosswise diagonally into coins or lengthwise into sticks.

Goat Cheese Truffles

We think of truffles as dessert—little balls of chocolate rolled around in cocoa powder, or something along those lines. These take the shape and preparation in an utterly savory direction. **Serves 4**

Ingredients

2 tablespoons olive oil

2 thick slices any rustic bread (a little stale is fine)

1 bunch fresh parsley

Salt and pepper

8 ounces fresh goat cheese

☐ Prep · **Cook**

1. Put 2 tablespoons olive oil in a large skillet over low heat.

   ☐ Tear 2 slices bread into pieces and put them in a food processor. Pulse into coarse crumbs; you need 1 cup.

   ☐ Chop ¼ cup fresh parsley leaves.

2. Raise the heat to medium. Add the bread crumbs to the skillet, sprinkle with a little salt and some pepper, and stir gently to coat in the oil. Cook, stirring frequently, until the crumbs are golden and crisp, 6 or 7 minutes. Shake the pan every minute or so to keep the crumbs from burning.

   ☐ Break the goat cheese with your fingers into 16 pieces and roll them into 1-inch balls.

3. When the crumbs are crisp, pour them into a rimmed baking sheet with the parsley and toss with a fork until cool.

4. Roll the goat cheese balls in the bread crumbs to coat lightly, pressing the crumbs into the cheese a bit if needed to make them stick. Put them on a plate and serve.

---

10 RECIPES FROM ELSEWHERE IN THE BOOK THAT MAKE GREAT SNACKS

1. Broiled Eggs (page 33)
2. Warm-Pickled Cauliflower Salad with Roasted Red Peppers (page 71)
3. Drop Meatballs (without the spaghetti; page 187)
4. Masa and Rajas (page 229)
5. Potato Rösti with Warmed Apples (page 261)
6. Bok Choy Pancake with Soy Dipping Sauce (page 277)
7. Tofu and Cauliflower, à la Suvir (page 322)
8. Buffalo Shrimp (page 343)
9. Chile Chicken and Bubbling Cheese (page 398)
10. BBQ Baby Back Ribs (page 441)

Crab Toast

Cooked crabmeat is an incredibly useful fast ingredient with a wonderful sweet, briny flavor. This is a good way to stretch it, since it's expensive. Or try the economical canned alternatives in the last two variations. **Serves 4 to 8**

Ingredients

Several sprigs fresh dill

1 lemon

1 cup lump crabmeat (about 8 ounces)

2 tablespoons mayonnaise

2 teaspoons Dijon mustard

Salt and pepper

4 thick slices any rustic bread

Olive oil

▢ Prep · **Cook**

1. Turn the broiler to high; put the rack 4 inches from the heat.

   ▢ Chop 3 tablespoons dill leaves and tender stems. Put 2 tablespoons in a medium bowl. Save what's left for garnish.

   ▢ Grate 2 teaspoons lemon zest and add to the bowl; refrigerate the fruit for another use.

   ▢ Pick through 1 cup crabmeat, discarding any pieces of shell or cartilage you find. Add the crabmeat to the bowl.

2. Add 2 tablespoons mayonnaise, 2 teaspoons Dijon mustard, and a sprinkle of salt and pepper to the bowl. Stir to combine.

3. Drizzle 4 slices of bread with olive oil. Broil the bread until lightly browned on top, 1 to 3 minutes.

4. Turn the toast and spread the crab mixture on the uncooked side, pressing it down lightly with a fork. Return the bread to the broiler until the crab mixture is bubbling, about 3 minutes. Cut each slice of bread into 2 or 3 pieces, garnish with the remaining dill, and serve.

Variations

Curried Crab Toast. Substitute cilantro for the dill and add ½ teaspoon curry powder to the crab mixture.

Sardine Toast. Instead of the mayonnaise and Dijon mustard, use ¼ cup tomato paste seasoned with 1 teaspoon minced garlic and a pinch of red chile flakes. Drain 3 cans olive oil–packed sardines (about 5 ounces each) and fold the fish into the tomato mixture. Use this to spread on the toast. Garnish with chopped fresh chives instead of the dill.

Anchovy Toast. Follow the directions for the sardine variation, only use 4 to 8 olive oil–packed anchovy fillets (to taste). Or if you have access to pickled white anchovies, use 8 to 12 for a real treat. Garnish with chopped fresh parsley.

Peel-and-Dip Shrimp

Broiling shrimp with their shells on saves you time on peeling and imparts flavor while protecting them from overcooking. Consider the seasoned mayonnaise dip—or the spins that follow—as a reward for the effort at the table. Grilling the shrimp on a baking sheet is another speedy option and saves you fussing with skewers or trying to keep up with a lot of turning: Prepare a charcoal or gas grill for hot indirect cooking; when the fire is ready, put the pan on the cool side, close the lid, and let them cook until pink, just a couple minutes. **Serves 4**

Ingredients

1½ pounds any size shell-on shrimp

1 cup mayonnaise

2 teaspoons seasoning (your choice: curry powder, chili powder, ground cumin, ground coriander, paprika, smoked paprika, or Old Bay)

Salt and pepper

1 lemon

1 tablespoon olive oil

□ Prep · Cook

1. Turn the broiler to high; put the rack 4 inches from the heat.

   □ If the shrimp is frozen, put it in a colander and run it under cold water for a minute or two to thaw. Let it sit to drain.

2. Put 1 cup mayonnaise, 2 teaspoons seasoning, and a sprinkle of salt and pepper in a serving bowl; stir to combine.

   □ Halve the lemon and squeeze the juice into the dip through a strainer or your fingers to catch the seeds. Stir again.

3. Put the shrimp on a rimmed baking sheet and toss with 1 tablespoon olive oil and a sprinkle of salt and pepper.

4. When the broiler is hot, cook the shrimp, turning once, until they're lightly charred on the outside and just cooked through, 3 to 4 minutes per side.

5. Serve with the dip, letting people peel the shrimp at the table.

Variations

Peel-and-Dip Shrimp with Warm Butter. Instead of the mayonnaise, use 2 sticks butter. Melt them in a small pot over medium heat without disturbing, so that the milk solids sink to the bottom. Sprinkle the seasoning into a small heatproof bowl and carefully pour the clear melted butter on top. Stir, then taste and adjust the seasoning; keep warm for serving as the dip.

Peel-and-Dip Shrimp Cocktail. Instead of the mayonnaise, use 1 cup ketchup; season it as described.

Boiled Peel-and-Dip Shrimp. Instead of heating the broiler, bring a large pot of water to a boil and salt it. Cook the shrimp until just pink, 2 to 5 minutes depending on the size. Use any of the dips above.

Skewerless Chicken Satay

Follow the thinking here: You can either spend time threading chicken on skewers before cooking, then unthreading it before eating, or you can simply skip the long sticks and small swords and get to the best part even faster. And for an easy switch-up, instead of the chicken, use about 1½ pounds boneless pork or beef sirloin steaks. **Serves 4**

Ingredients

6 to 8 boneless, skinless chicken thighs (1½ pounds)

1 lime

2 cloves garlic

1 inch fresh ginger

1 tablespoon soy sauce

1 tablespoon rice vinegar

1 tablespoon sugar

1 teaspoon ground cumin

1 teaspoon chili powder

⅓ cup peanut butter

▫ Prep · **Cook**

1. Turn the broiler to high; put the rack 4 inches from the heat. Put the chicken in the freezer.

   ▫ Halve the lime; squeeze the juice into a large bowl.

   ▫ Peel 1 clove garlic and 1 inch ginger. Mince them together and add them to the bowl.

2. Add 1 tablespoon soy sauce, 1 tablespoon rice vinegar, 1 tablespoon sugar, 1 teaspoon ground cumin, and 1 teaspoon chili powder to the bowl. Whisk to combine. Divide the marinade in half, reserving half for making the dipping sauce.

3. Remove the chicken thighs from the freezer, cut them into thin slices, and add to 1 portion of the marinade; toss to coat.

4. Line a rimmed baking sheet with foil; using tongs, transfer the chicken to the foil, discarding the marinade left behind. Spread out the chicken so it overlaps as little as possible.

5. When the broiler is hot, cook the chicken, turning as necessary until lightly charred all over, 6 to 8 minutes.

6. While the chicken cooks, whisk ⅓ cup hot water and ⅓ cup peanut butter into the reserved portion of the marinade until smooth.

7. Pour the sauce into a serving bowl. When the chicken is done, let it cool for a minute or two before chopping into bite-sized pieces. Serve with toothpicks or cocktail forks and the peanut sauce for dipping.

Tortillas Rojas

Take a quick blended salsa, toss it with warm chips, and sprinkle everything with fresh cheese, and you've got a keeper you'll make again and again. In fact, you'll probably like them better than nachos. **Serves 4**

Ingredients

1 (9-ounce) bag tortilla chips

1 tablespoon vegetable oil

1 fresh hot green chile (like serrano)

2 cloves garlic

1 (14-ounce) can diced tomatoes

Salt

Several sprigs fresh cilantro

1 lime

4 ounces queso fresco (1 cup crumbled)

Dash of hot sauce (optional)

☐ Prep · Cook

1. Heat the oven to 300°F. Spread the tortilla chips on a rimmed baking sheet; put them in the oven to warm as it heats.

2. Put 1 tablespoon vegetable oil in a small saucepan over medium heat.

   ☐ Trim the chile; seed it if you like. Peel 2 cloves garlic. Chop 1 chile and the garlic together; it's okay if the pieces are sort of big.

3. Add the chile and garlic to the saucepan and cook, stirring frequently until fragrant, 15 to 30 seconds.

4. Add the tomatoes and their juice to the pan, sprinkle with salt, and raise the heat to medium-high. Cook, stirring once or twice until the tomatoes start to break apart, 5 to 8 minutes.

   ☐ Chop several cilantro sprigs.   ☐ Crumble the 4 ounces queso fresco.

   ☐ Cut the lime into wedges.

5. Carefully transfer the salsa to an upright blender. Start the machine on low to avoid splashing, then increase the speed gradually until the salsa is smooth. Taste and adjust the seasoning, adding a dash of hot sauce if you like.

6. Put the warmed chips in a large bowl. Add the salsa a few spoonfuls at a time, tossing constantly so the chips are evenly coated.

7. Put the chips on a platter or in a shallow bowl; sprinkle the queso fresco on top. Garnish with cilantro and lime wedges and serve right away.

Variations

Tortillas Verdes. Instead of diced tomatoes, use canned tomatillos.

Tortillas Queso. After cooking the chiles and garlic in Step 3, reduce the heat to medium-low. Instead of the tomatoes, add 1½ cups Mexican crema or sour cream to the pan and cook, stirring constantly, until steaming; be careful not to let the mixture boil and curdle. Increase the queso fresco to 8 ounces (2 cups crumbled) and add half to the warm cream. Use this sauce to coat the chips, garnishing as described in Step 7.

Tortillas Frijoles. Cook the chiles and garlic as described in Step 3. Instead of the tomatoes, drain and add 1 (15-ounce) can black beans and stir until heated through. Purée as described in Step 5, adding enough water to make a thick sauce. Use this bean sauce to coat the chips, garnishing as described in Step 7.

Hard-Boiled Eggs with Dijon Mayo

Everything you love about deviled eggs with none of the hassle. You can even prepare the recipe through Step 2 up to a day or two ahead of serving. For more ways to flavor the sauce, see the list that follows. **Serves 4 or more**

Ingredients

8 eggs

Ice cubes

½ cup mayonnaise

1 tablespoon Dijon mustard

½ teaspoon paprika

Salt and pepper

1 bunch chives

▢ Prep · Cook

1. Fill a large pot halfway with water and bring to a boil. One at a time, gently lower the eggs straight from the fridge (or not) into the boiling water with a spoon so they don't crack. Cover, turn off the heat, and set the timer for 10 minutes (if you want the yolks set but not chalky; adjust less or more as you like).

    ▢ Fill a large bowl with ice water.

2. Put ½ cup mayonnaise, 1 tablespoon Dijon mustard, ½ teaspoon paprika, and a sprinkle of salt and pepper in a small bowl. Stir to combine.

    ▢ Chop ¼ cup chives.

3. When the time is up, the eggs are done. Transfer them to the ice water with a slotted spoon. Leave them submerged for at least 1 minute.

4. Crack and peel the eggs. Transfer them to a cutting board and halve them lengthwise.

5. Sprinkle the eggs with a little salt and dollop the mayonnaise mixture on top of each half. Garnish with a little more salt and pepper and the chives and serve.

• recipe continues →

• Hard-Boiled Eggs with Dijon Mayo, continued

Variations

Hard-Boiled Eggs with Curry Mayo. Omit the Dijon mustard and chives. Substitute 1½ teaspoons curry powder for the paprika.

Hard-Boiled Eggs with Saffron Mayo. Omit the Dijon mustard. Substitute ¼ teaspoon crumbled saffron threads for the paprika.

Jammy Eggs with Any Mayo. Terrific with any flavored mayonnaise (below). Instead of letting the eggs sit for 10 minutes in Step 1, reduce the steeping time to 8 minutes. Be careful peeling and cutting into these eggs since the yolks are still a little runny.

7 WAYS TO FLAVOR MAYONNAISE

Use the ideas in this list any time you want to spike mayonnaise for salads, sandwiches, or dips. To ½ cup, add any of the following, alone or in combination:

1. 1 tablespoon minced garlic, fresh ginger, or chile
2. ¼ cup chopped fresh basil, cilantro, parsley, or chives
3. 1 tablespoon chopped fresh rosemary, oregano, or thyme
4. 2 tablespoons soy sauce
5. 1 to 2 teaspoons grated citrus zest
6. 1 teaspoon prepared horseradish, hot sauce, or Worcestershire sauce
7. 1 or 2 mashed anchovies

Salads

My **idea** of salad might be a little different from yours. There are definitely lots of vegetables involved, raw and/or cooked. Lettuce is optional; flip through a few pages for a rundown of possible greens and how to prepare and store them.

As long as there's a tangy dressing, I like most salads at room temperature, especially those that have starchy ingredients like potatoes or grains, since the texture is more appealing. For quick-chilled ice-cold salads, pop the bowl in the freezer for 5 to 10 minutes before tossing.

It is totally acceptable to eat a salad and piece of bread and call it a meal, even if it doesn't have much meat; vegetables are satisfying too. In fact, I often prefer plant proteins like legumes; they're lighter and easier to digest.

Speaking of the lighter, vegetarian side, this chapter starts with arugula and eggs in a lemony dressing (page 57). I also am amazed how satisfying a simple bean, cucumber, and yogurt salad can be (page 84). For heartier recipes, try Corn Salad with Garlic Chicken (page 85) or Kimchi and Snow Pea Salad with Grilled or Broiled Beef (page 90).

Each salad has the dressing incorporated; the variations might swap out ingredients or flavors. And for basic vinaigrette with a couple new spins and homemade croutons, see pages 485 and 488.

Arugula with Fried Eggs and Shaved Parmesan

Sharp-tasting, bright green arugula, dressed simply with lemon juice and olive oil, is an ideal bed for an oozing fried egg. As you eat, the yolk mixes with the olive oil, lemon, and Parmesan to form an irresistibly rich dressing. Make this heartier by cooking twice as many eggs and serving with Croutons (page 488) or a dense whole grain bread. **Serves 4**

Ingredients

1 lemon

3 tablespoons olive oil

Salt and pepper

4 ounces Parmesan cheese
(1 cup shaved; see Shaving Parmesan)

1 large bunch arugula
(12 ounces)

2 tablespoons butter

4 eggs

□ Prep · Cook

1. Halve the lemon and squeeze the juice into a large bowl through a strainer or your fingers to catch the seeds. Add 3 tablespoons olive oil and a sprinkle of salt and pepper.

   □ Shave about 1 cup Parmesan with a vegetable peeler, add to the bowl, and stir.

   □ Trim the arugula and add it to the bowl, but wait to toss the salad.

2. Put a large skillet over medium-high heat. After about a minute, add 2 tablespoons butter and swirl the pan.

3. When the butter has melted, swirl it around to coat the bottom of the skillet. Crack the eggs into the skillet and cook, spooning some of the pooling butter or oil on top if you like, until the whites are no longer translucent, 2 to 3 minutes. Turn the heat to low and sprinkle the eggs with salt and pepper. Cook undisturbed until the whites are firm and the yolks are as runny as you like, just a couple minutes more.

4. Toss the salad; taste and adjust the seasoning. Divide among serving plates. Top each with a fried egg.

SHAVING PARMESAN

For cooking and garnishing, I almost always grate Parmesan cheese, since I want it to melt easily. In salads, however, a little more heft delivers an appealing texture. To make thin shavings or shards, take a chunk of cheese, find a side that's fairly smooth, and use a vegetable peeler to slice, pulling toward you. To best control the blade, work in short strokes, anchoring the cheese with your thumb. For smaller shreds, grate the cheese over the biggest holes of a box grater.

Endive and Radicchio with Warm Bacon Vinaigrette

With a warm dressing that features bacon and its cooking fat, you get two types of smoky saltiness—perfect to balance the assertiveness of endive and radicchio. The crunch factor is a knockout too. To turn the salad into a more substantial meal, toss in a handful of cannellini beans (see page 505 for home-cooked) and serve with a fresh baguette. **Serves 4**

Ingredients

8 slices bacon

4 to 6 heads endive (1½ pounds)

1 small head radicchio (4 to 6 ounces)

1 large shallot

1 teaspoon Dijon mustard

¼ cup olive oil

3 tablespoons balsamic vinegar

Salt and pepper

☐ Prep · Cook

1. Put a large skillet over medium-high heat.

   ☐ Chop 8 slices bacon. Line a plate with towels.

2. Add the bacon to the skillet and cook, stirring occasionally until crisp, 5 to 10 minutes.

   ☐ Trim and chop the endive and radicchio and put them in a large bowl.

   ☐ Trim, peel, and mince the shallot.

3. When the bacon is crisp, transfer it to the towels with a slotted spoon. Add the shallot to the skillet and stir until it sizzles. Turn off the heat and pour off all but 2 tablespoons of the fat, leaving the shallot in the pan.

4. To make the dressing in the skillet, whisk in 1 teaspoon Dijon mustard, ¼ cup olive oil, 3 tablespoons balsamic vinegar, and a sprinkle of salt and pepper.

5. Pour the dressing over the endive and radicchio, add the cooked bacon, and toss. Taste and adjust the seasoning, and serve.

Antipasto Wedge

The wedge salad is a steakhouse classic made with iceberg lettuce, tomatoes, crisp bacon, and blue cheese dressing. This Italian-style version features Gorgonzola dressing, pepperoncini, and crisp salami instead. It's more flavorful than the original and can be prepared in little more time than it takes to crisp the meat. Croutons (page 488) are the best embellishment, though the salad is satisfying without them. **Serves 4**

Ingredients

1 tablespoon olive oil

4 ounces salami

1 large head iceberg lettuce

1 lemon

½ cup sour cream

½ cup plain yogurt

Salt and pepper

4 ounces Gorgonzola cheese (1 cup crumbled)

1 pint ripe cherry tomatoes

2 or more pickled peppers (mild like pepperoncini or hot like jalapeños)

Prep · Cook

1. Put 1 tablespoon olive oil in a large skillet over medium heat.

   □ Chop 4 ounces salami.

   □ Line a plate with towels.

2. When the oil is hot, add the salami and cook, stirring occasionally until crisp, 5 to 10 minutes. Transfer the salami to the towels with a slotted spoon.

   □ Trim the bottom and outer leaves from the lettuce, leaving the core and head intact. Cut the head top-to-bottom into quarters.

   □ Halve the lemon; refrigerate 1 half for another use.

3. Put ½ cup sour cream, ½ cup yogurt, the juice of ½ lemon, and a sprinkle of salt and pepper in a small bowl. Crumble 1 cup Gorgonzola, add it to the bowl, and stir to combine. Taste and adjust the seasoning.

   □ Halve the cherry tomatoes.

   □ Trim and chop 2 or more pickled peppers.

4. Put each iceberg quarter cut side up on a plate and top with the dressing, then scatter the tomatoes, peppers, and salami over all and serve.

Variations

Tapas Bar Wedge. Omit the pickled peppers. Use 4 ounces chopped Spanish chorizo instead of the salami. Substitute 3 ounces Manchego cheese for the Gorgonzola (about ¾ cup grated) and stir ½ teaspoon smoked paprika into the dressing.

Crab Wedge. With a lemony ranch dressing. Omit the pickled peppers. Substitute 12 ounces lump crabmeat (about 1½ cups) for the salami and skip Steps 1 and 2; substitute melted butter for the olive oil, drizzle it over the crab, and toss. Instead of the Gorgonzola, whisk ¼ cup powdered buttermilk and 2 tablespoons chopped fresh chives into the dressing.

Taco Wedge. Steak *and* salad in every bite. Instead of the salami, chop 8 ounces sirloin steak into bits no bigger than ½ inch. Cook as described in Steps 1 and 2, only raise the heat to medium-high and reduce the cooking time to 3 to 5 minutes; you want it crisp in places and pink in others. Sprinkle with salt and pepper and toss. Substitute queso fresco for the Gorgonzola. After assembling the salad, crumble some tortilla chips over the top if you like.

Chickpea and Carrot Salad with Warm Cumin Oil

An uncommon warm salad you can easily customize: Grating the vegetables in a food processor, rather than chopping them as in the recipe, makes the salad more like a slaw. I like the teeny surprise of cumin seeds, but if you prefer a smooth dressing, pour the oil through a strainer into the bowl before serving. Home-cooked chickpeas (page 505) are always excellent here, as are cannellini beans. And toasted pita wedges are the perfect accompaniment no matter what tweaks you make to the recipe. **Serves 4**

Ingredients

½ cup olive oil

1 clove garlic

1 lemon

2 tablespoons cumin seeds

5 to 7 medium carrots (1 pound)

3½ cups cooked or canned chickpeas (two 15-ounce cans)

1 bunch fresh mint

Salt and pepper

□ Prep · Cook

1. Put ½ cup olive oil in a small saucepan over low heat.

   □ Crush and peel 1 clove garlic; add it to the oil.

   □ Zest the lemon directly into the oil. Refrigerate the fruit for another use.

2. Stir 2 tablespoons cumin seeds into the oil. Let the oil warm up slowly undisturbed until it starts to bubble steadily, 5 to 10 minutes.

   □ Trim and peel the carrots; slice them into thin coins or half-moons. Put them in a large bowl.

   □ If you're using canned chickpeas, rinse and drain them. Add the chickpeas to the bowl.

   □ Chop ½ cup mint leaves; add to the bowl.

3. When the oil is warm and slightly bubbling, discard the garlic and pour the oil over the chickpeas and carrots; stir to coat well. Sprinkle the mixture with salt and pepper and toss. Taste and adjust the seasoning, and serve.

Variations

Chickpea and Red Pepper Salad with Warm Paprika Dressing. Substitute 1 tablespoon smoked paprika for the cumin seeds. Instead of carrots, thinly slice 3 red bell peppers; add them to the oil with the garlic in Step 3 and toss to coat. Use parsley instead of mint.

Edamame and Daikon Salad with Warm Ginger Dressing. Substitute 2 tablespoons sesame oil and ⅓ cup vegetable oil for the olive oil, lime zest for the lemon, 1 tablespoon minced fresh ginger for the cumin seeds, 1 pound daikon radish for the carrots, and scallions for the mint. Use shelled edamame instead of chickpeas; add them to the oil with the garlic in Step 3 and toss to coat. Garnish with sesame seeds if you like.

Beet Salad with Cashews and Warm Curry Dressing. Substitute 1 pound beets for the carrots, 1⅓ cups cashews (raw or roasted) for the chickpeas, and 1 tablespoon curry powder for the ground cumin. Everything else stays the same.

Crab and Celery Root Rémoulade

Easier and more interesting than classic celery root rémoulade, with variations that open the door to all sorts of easy substitutions—any and all of which could start with celery stalks and leaves instead of celery root. Tuck this salad into sandwiches, serve on a bed of greens, or spread on crackers for a casual lunch or supper. **Serves 4**

Ingredients

1 cup mayonnaise

1 tablespoon Dijon mustard

1 clove garlic

2 tablespoons capers

2 anchovy fillets

1 bunch fresh parsley

¼ teaspoon cayenne

Salt and pepper

1 pound cooked lump crabmeat

1 large or 2 medium celery roots (1½ pounds)

▢ Prep · Cook

1. Put 1 cup mayonnaise and 1 tablespoon Dijon mustard in a large bowl.

   ▢ Peel and mince 1 clove garlic; add to the bowl.

   ▢ Chop 2 tablespoons capers and 2 anchovy fillets; add them to the bowl.

   ▢ Chop ¼ cup parsley leaves and add them to the bowl; reserve some leaves for garnish.

2. Add ¼ teaspoon cayenne and a sprinkle of salt and pepper to the bowl and stir.

   ▢ Pick through the crabmeat, discarding pieces of shell or cartilage. Add the crabmeat to the bowl.

   ▢ Trim and peel the celery root(s). If you're using a food processor for grating, cut the celery root into chunks that will fit through the feed tube. Shred the celery root in a food processor with a grating disk or by hand with a box grater.

3. Add the celery root to the bowl and toss to combine. Taste and adjust the seasoning, garnish with the reserved parsley leaves, and serve.

Variations

Celery Root Rémoulade with Hard-Boiled Eggs. Instead of using crabmeat, start by cooking 8 hard-boiled eggs (page 52). Rinse under cold water to cool, peel them, then chop and add to the salad in Step 3.

Tuna and Celery Root Rémoulade. Substitute 12 ounces canned or jarred tuna (preferably packed in olive oil) for the crabmeat. Drain well, then add to the salad in Step 3.

Chicken and Celery Root Rémoulade. Instead of crabmeat, use about 1½ cups shredded or chopped cooked chicken.

Poached Shrimp Salad with Herby Tartar Sauce

Cooking shrimp is always effortless. And when the shrimp simply steeps in just-boiled water off the heat, you can turn your full attention to a special tartar sauce. This poaching technique also works for scallops, chunks of fish, and even chicken—and might become your go-to kitchen hack. For a bigger deal, serve with plain white rice (page 496), add another head of lettuce, and make wraps at the table. **Serves 4**

Ingredients

Salt

1 large or 2 small heads Boston lettuce

½ cup mayonnaise

2 teaspoons Dijon mustard

1½ pounds medium peeled shrimp

1 bunch fresh dill

3 sprigs fresh tarragon

2 sweet pickles or ¼ cup capers

1 lemon

Salt and pepper

□ Prep · Cook

1. Bring a medium saucepan of water to a boil and salt it.

   □ Trim the lettuce and tear off the leaves whole.

2. Put the lettuce leaves overlapping on a platter.

3. Put ½ cup mayonnaise and 2 teaspoons Dijon mustard in a medium bowl.

4. When the water comes to a boil, add the shrimp, cover, and turn off the heat. Let sit for 10 minutes.

   □ Chop ¼ cup dill leaves and tender stems; add them to the bowl.

   □ Strip the leaves from 3 tarragon sprigs, chop, and add them to the bowl.

   □ Chop 2 sweet pickles or ¼ cup capers; add to the bowl.

   □ Halve the lemon; squeeze the juice of 1 half into the bowl through a strainer or your fingers to catch the seeds. Refrigerate the remaining half for another use.

5. Add a sprinkle of salt and pepper to the bowl and stir to combine. Taste and adjust the seasoning.

6. When the shrimp are cooked through, drain them; rinse under cold water to cool. Add the shrimp to the bowl with the tartar sauce and toss to coat. Spoon the shrimp over the lettuce leaves and serve.

Canned Tuna Salad with Avocado and Green Beans

There are so many ways to buy "canned" tuna now. Packed in olive oil is almost always my preference, large chunks or small fillets if possible. Bonus points if you find some in jars. In general stay away from tuna in pouches since it tends to be mushy. Another way to serve this (and the tofu variation that follows) is over mesclun with lemon wedges and whole grain bread or crackers. **Serves 4**

Ingredients

Salt

1 pound green beans

1 lime

¼ cup olive oil, plus more as needed

1 tablespoon soy sauce

1 small red onion

Ice cubes

12 ounces oil-packed tuna (in jars or cans)

2 avocados

□ Prep · **Cook**

1. Bring about 2 inches of water to a boil in a large skillet and salt it.

   □ Trim the green beans and cut into 2-inch pieces.

   □ Halve the lime; squeeze the juice into a large bowl.

2. Add ¼ cup olive oil and 1 tablespoon soy sauce to the bowl and whisk to combine.

   □ Trim, peel, halve, and thinly slice the onion; add it to the bowl.

   □ Halve and pit the avocados, scoop out the flesh, cut into chunks; add them to the bowl.

   □ Prepare a bowl of ice water big enough to hold the green beans.

3. When the water comes to a boil, add the green beans, cover, and cook until they're just tender, about 3 minutes.

4. Drain the beans and immediately transfer them to the ice bath.

5. Break the tuna into chunks and add it to the bowl. Toss gently, adding more olive oil if the salad looks too dry. Taste and adjust the seasoning, and serve.

Variations

Tofu Salad with Avocado and Green Beans. Replace the olive oil with ¼ quarter cup good-quality vegetable oil and 2 tablespoons sesame oil. Use 1 brick firm tofu (14 to 16 ounces) instead of the tuna. Cut the tofu (no need to cook it) into cubes and gently toss it with the rest of the salad.

Seared Scallops with Grilled or Broiled Romaine

One of the best things about searing scallops is the sauce you make afterward with their pan juices. Here it's a rich, lemony dressing that's perfect over grilled or broiled romaine. Croutons (page 488) are terrific here, or serve with ciabatta or any other thick-crusted loaf.
Serves 4

Ingredients

4 hearts romaine lettuce (or 2 whole heads romaine lettuce)

6 tablespoons olive oil

Salt and pepper

1 clove garlic

1 lemon

2 tablespoons butter

1 pound sea scallops

1 small red bell pepper

½ cup white wine

▫ Prep · Cook

1. Prepare a grill for direct cooking or turn the broiler to high; put the rack 4 inches from the heat.

    ▫ Halve the hearts of romaine lengthwise, leaving them attached at the stem end. For whole heads, remove the distressed outer leaves and cut the heads into quarters the same way.

2. Put the romaine on a rimmed baking sheet, drizzle with 4 tablespoons olive oil and sprinkle with salt and pepper. Grill (directly over the fire) or broil (in the pan), cut side toward the heat, until the lettuce is lightly charred, 2 to 5 minutes. Transfer the romaine, cut side up, to 4 plates or a platter.

3. Put a large skillet over medium-high heat.

    ▫ Peel and mince 1 clove garlic.   ▫ Halve the lemon.

4. Add 2 tablespoons butter, 2 tablespoons olive oil, and the garlic to the skillet. After about 30 seconds, add the scallops and sprinkle with salt and pepper. Cook, turning once when the scallops release easily, until both flat sides are browned but the center is still slightly translucent, about 2 minutes per side. Transfer to a plate.

    ▫ Core, seed, and chop the bell pepper.

5. Squeeze the lemon juice into the skillet through a strainer or your fingers to capture the seeds. Add ½ cup white wine and the bell pepper. Cook until the liquid reduces slightly, just a minute or two. Add the scallops and any juices back to the skillet and stir to coat with the dressing. Spoon the scallops, bell pepper, and dressing over the romaine and serve.

● recipe continues →

Variations

Seared Shrimp with Grilled or Broiled Romaine. Instead of the scallops, use 1 pound thawed peeled large shrimp. Sear them in Step 4, only reduce the cooking time to about 1 minute per side; they should be pink outside but not yet opaque at the thickest part.

Seared Squid with Grilled or Broiled Escarole. Instead of the romaine, trim and halve 2 small heads escarole as described. Substitute 1 pound cleaned and cut squid for the scallops. (Frozen is fine; rinse under cold running water to thaw first, drain, and dry well.) Grill the escarole as you would the romaine; they might take a minute or so longer to char. Cook the squid as described in Steps 4 and 5, shaking the pan to sear the pieces until they're opaque, just a couple minutes total, before proceeding.

Seared Scallops, Shrimp, or Squid with Grilled or Broiled Baby Bok Choy and Ginger Dressing. You can use scallops, shrimp, or squid here. Instead of the romaine, use 4 or more heads baby bok choy (you want at least 1 pound). Substitute 1 fresh hot green chile for the bell pepper, 2 limes for the lemon, 1 tablespoon minced fresh ginger for the garlic, and sake for the white wine. Trim and halve the bok choy as you would the romaine; they'll cook a little faster.

GRILLING GREENS

A quick blast of heat transforms lettuce and other greens by crisping the outside and adding smokiness. Just make sure to choose greens that can stand up to the heat. Romaine, iceberg, cabbage, and bok choy all do wonderfully; very tender greens like arugula, Boston lettuce, and Bibb lettuces will wilt too quickly. For greens that come in bunches (like dandelion and kale), it can be nice to keep them all together, tied with wet string, so that they're easy to turn, and the outside leaves char while the inside leaves are protected.

Warm-Pickled Cauliflower Salad with Roasted Red Peppers

Simmering cauliflower in a vinegar brine is essentially a quick pickling technique. The idea is to cook the vegetable a little less than you ultimately want it, so it retains plenty of crunch. Then as a time-saving, underrated treat, serve the salad still warm. Or make it up to a day ahead and serve it ice cold. For even more substance, serve the cauliflower draped with a couple thin slices of prosciutto and pass breadsticks at the table. **Serves 4**

Ingredients

½ cup red wine vinegar

1 bay leaf

2 teaspoons salt

1 teaspoon dried oregano

1 large or 2 small heads cauliflower (about 2 pounds)

4 celery stalks

8 roasted red peppers (jarred is fine)

⅔ cup green olives

¼ cup olive oil

Pepper

◻ Prep · **Cook**

1. In a large pot (stainless steel or enameled), combine ½ cup red wine vinegar, 4 cups water, 1 bay leaf, 2 teaspoons salt, and 1 teaspoon dried oregano; turn the heat to high.

   ◻ Break or chop the cauliflower into florets.

2. When the brine comes to a boil, add the cauliflower, cover the pot, and cook until you can barely pierce the cauliflower with the tip of a sharp knife, 5 to 10 minutes.

   ◻ Trim and chop 4 celery stalks; put in a large bowl.

   ◻ Slice 8 roasted red peppers; add them to the bowl.

   ◻ Pit ⅔ cup green olives if necessary; chop them up a bit. Add to the bowl.

3. When the cauliflower is ready, drain it, reserving about ½ cup of the brine. Add the cauliflower to the bowl along with ¼ cup olive oil, a splash of the brine, and a sprinkle of pepper. Toss, taste, and adjust the seasoning, adding more brine if it needs it. Serve warm.

• recipe continues →

Variations

Warm Broccoli Salad with Balsamic Vinaigrette. Deeply colored and slightly sweeter. Substitute ¼ cup balsamic vinegar for ¼ cup of the red wine vinegar, broccoli for the cauliflower, and ¼ cup pine nuts and ¼ cup raisins for the celery. Use black olives (oil-cured are my favorite here) instead of green and add up to 1 cup grated Parmesan cheese before tossing. Broccoli cooks faster than cauliflower, so start checking on it after 2 minutes.

Warm-Pickled Kale Salad with Roasted Red Peppers. Ideal served over a thick slice of toasted Italian bread. Instead of the cauliflower, trim the bottom stems from 1 pound lacinato kale; slice the leaves crosswise into ribbons about 1 inch thick. Simmer the kale in the brine until slightly softened, just a minute or two. Use kalamata instead of green olives; the rest of the recipe stays the same. Serve the salad topped with shaved Parmesan (page 57).

Warm-Pickled Brussels Sprouts Salad with Roasted Red Peppers. You need a food processor for this one. Omit the olives. Substitute 1 pound Brussels sprouts for the cauliflower. After trimming the bottoms, push them through the feed tube of a machine fitted with a ¼-inch (6 mm) slicing disk. Simmer the Brussels sprouts in the brine until slightly softened, just a minute or two. Add 1 tablespoon whole grain mustard to the salad when you toss it in Step 4.

ROASTED PEPPERS FROM A JAR

Using jarred peppers is undeniably convenient. Most come packed in an acidic brine; you rinse, then pat them dry with a towel. If you can find peppers packed in olive oil, use them right out of the jar, holding them up with a fork to drain any excess oil back inside; save what remains after the peppers are gone for dressings and sauces. (Once the jar is opened the contents will keep in the refrigerator for several weeks.) To roast your own fresh bell peppers, see page 501.

Broiled Eggplant Salad with Tangy Tahini Dressing

Broiling vegetables is perfect for when you want some char but don't feel like firing up the grill—or if you don't have one. The only trick is to preheat the broiler and get the pan as close as you can to the heat source. I always lean toward eggplant for this salad, but other options are zucchini, tomato, or asparagus; all go well with the bright and rich dressing. For more of a main course, crumble feta cheese on top and serve with a stack of warm pita or over a bowl of couscous (page 497). **Serves 4**

Ingredients

2 large, 3 medium, or 4 to 6 small eggplants

6 tablespoons olive oil, plus more as needed

Salt and pepper

1 clove garlic

1 lemon

¼ cup tahini

¼ cup Greek yogurt

¼ teaspoon ground cumin

Hot tap water as needed

1 small red onion

Several sprigs fresh parsley

Dried Aleppo (or other) pepper flakes, to taste

Prep · Cook

1. Turn the broiler to high; put the rack 4 inches from the heat.

   ☐ Trim and cut the eggplant(s) on the diagonal into slices no more than 1 inch thick.

2. Put the eggplant slices on a rimmed baking sheet, drizzle with 4 tablespoons olive oil, and turn the slices to spread it generously on both sides; it's okay if they're touching. Sprinkle with salt and pepper.

3. Broil, turning the eggplant once until it's tender and browned in places, 8 to 12 minutes total.

   ☐ Peel and mince 1 clove garlic.

   ☐ Cut a lemon in half and squeeze the juice into a medium bowl through a strainer or your fingers to catch the seeds.

4. Put ¼ cup tahini in the bowl with ¼ cup Greek yogurt, ¼ teaspoon ground cumin, the garlic, 2 tablespoons olive oil, and a sprinkle of salt and pepper. Whisk until smooth, adding hot tap water 1 tablespoon at a time to get a pourable consistency. Taste and adjust the seasoning.

   ☐ Trim, peel, and halve the onion; thinly slice 1 half and refrigerate the other for another use.

   ☐ Chop several parsley sprigs.

5. When the eggplant is ready, transfer the slices to a platter and spoon on the dressing. Scatter the onion and parsley over the dressing, sprinkle with the Aleppo to taste, and serve.

Cabbage Slaw with Crisp Tofu and Peanut-Lime Dressing

This salad is a dream if you like a lot of crunch: There's shredded cabbage, thinly sliced red onion, peanuts, and crisp crumbled tofu. Broiling the tofu away from the flame allows it to crisp quickly without burning; tossed with some salt and red chile flakes, the crumbles make an irresistible stir-in or garnish. Try them on other salads, cooked vegetables, grains, or noodles and see the first variation for another way to season them. **Serves 4**

Ingredients

2 bricks firm tofu (14 to 16 ounces each)

¼ cup plus 2 tablespoons good-quality vegetable oil

1 teaspoon red chile flakes

Salt

1 lime

3 tablespoons peanut butter

Hot sauce (optional)

1 small head savoy or green cabbage (1 pound)

1 small red onion

½ cup peanuts

▢ Prep · Cook

1. Turn the broiler to high; put the rack 6 inches from the heat.

   ▢ Press the tofu between towels to squeeze out as much water as you can. Crumble the tofu onto a rimmed baking sheet.

2. Toss the tofu with 2 tablespoons vegetable oil, 1 teaspoon red chile flakes, and a sprinkle of salt. Broil, checking and stirring occasionally, until the tofu crumbles are brown and crisp in places, 20 to 25 minutes.

   ▢ Halve the lime.

3. In a large bowl, whisk together ¼ cup vegetable oil, the juice of the lime, 3 tablespoons peanut butter, 3 tablespoons hot water, some salt, and a dash of hot sauce if you're using it.

   ▢ Trim, core, and quarter the cabbage. Cut each quarter crosswise into thin ribbons; add to the bowl.

   ▢ Trim, peel, halve, and thinly slice the onion; add to the bowl.

   ▢ Chop ½ cup peanuts; add them to the bowl.

4. When the tofu is ready, add it to the bowl. Toss, taste, and adjust the seasoning, then serve.

Variations

Cabbage Slaw with Crisp Tofu and Coconut-Lime Dressing. Instead of the vegetable oil, peanut butter, and water in the dressing, use ½ cup full-fat coconut milk. When the tofu is ready, sprinkle ¼ cup unsweetened shredded coconut over it and return it to the broiler until the coconut is golden, about a minute.

Kohlrabi Slaw with Crisp Tofu or Pork and Peanut-Lime Dressing. Replace half the cabbage with 2 kohlrabis. Peel and grate them when you prepare the cabbage.

Curried Tofu Salad with Apples, Pecans, and Golden Raisins

Sometimes chicken is an irreplaceable ingredient in a dish; other times it's not. In curried "chicken" salad, for instance, all I want is something with a firm texture and a mild flavor to soak up the dressing—and extra-firm tofu fits the bill perfectly without any cooking. The variations give you other options. All work well in a bowl with plain white rice (page 496) or rice noodles (page 495); if you go that route, chop the lettuce. **Serves 4**

Ingredients

1 small head romaine or red-leaf lettuce

½ cup mayonnaise

½ cup Greek yogurt

1 tablespoon curry powder

Salt and pepper

1 brick extra-firm tofu (14 to 16 ounces)

2 apples

3 celery stalks

1 shallot

1 bunch fresh cilantro

½ cup pecans

½ cup golden raisins

□ Prep · Cook

□ Trim the lettuce and tear the leaves off whole. Put the lettuce leaves, overlapping, on a platter.

1. Put ½ cup mayonnaise, ½ cup Greek yogurt, 1 tablespoon curry powder, and a sprinkle of salt and pepper in a large bowl. Stir until smooth and evenly colored.

   □ Drain the tofu well and crumble it into the bowl.

   □ Core and chop the 2 apples; trim and chop 3 celery stalks, including any leaves. Add both to the bowl.

   □ Trim, peel, and chop the shallot; add to the bowl.

   □ Chop ½ cup cilantro and add to the bowl.

   □ Chop ½ cup pecans; add to the bowl.

2. Add ½ cup golden raisins to the bowl. Stir to combine. Taste and adjust the seasoning. Spoon the salad over the lettuce leaves and serve.

Variations

Chipotle Tofu Salad with Jícama, Pepitas, and Raisins. Substitute 1 to 2 tablespoons chopped chipotle chile in adobo (to taste) for the curry powder; 1 small jícama, peeled and chopped, for the apples; and pepitas (hulled green pumpkin seeds; no need to chop them) for the pecans.

Curried Chicken Salad with Almonds and Dried Apricots. A perfect use for leftover simply cooked chicken; shred or chop it before starting (you'll need about 2 cups). Or cook 1½ pounds chicken tenders as described in the variation for Poached Shrimp Salad with Herby Tartar Sauce on page 65. Substitute the chicken for the tofu. Instead of the pecans and golden raisins, use chopped almonds and dried apricots.

Bulgur, Apple, and Fennel Salad

Chewy, hearty bulgur is a terrific match for crisp slices of apple and fennel. If you have a mandoline or good knife skills, or you just don't mind eating the slightly tough center of the fennel, you can thinly slice the bulbs, cores and all. Otherwise, carefully cut out the core with a paring knife before slicing. To up-size this, top with thinly sliced grilled chicken or whole large shrimp, or toss in 2 cups cannellini beans; you'll need to add a little more olive oil and lemon juice. **Serves 4**

Ingredients

3 medium apples

2 medium fennel bulbs (1 pound)

1 lemon

½ cup shelled pistachios

¼ cup olive oil

Salt and pepper

1 cup bulgur

▢ Prep · Cook

1. Bring 2½ cups water to a boil in a medium saucepan.

   ▢ Core and slice the apples; put in a large bowl.

   ▢ Trim the fennel and thinly slice crosswise to get a pile of crescent-shaped pieces (pull apart any that are stuck together). Discard any hard center pieces. Add to the bowl.

   ▢ Halve the lemon; squeeze the juice into the bowl through a strainer or your fingers to catch the seeds.

2. Add ½ cup pistachios to the bowl with the apples and fennel. Add ¼ cup olive oil, sprinkle with salt and pepper, and toss.

3. Put 1 cup bulgur in another large bowl with a large pinch of salt. Pour the boiling water over the bulgur and cover with a plate. Finely ground bulgur will take 10 to 15 minutes to become tender, medium 15 to 20, and coarse 20 to 25.

4. When the bulgur is tender, drain off any excess water through a strainer and add the bulgur to the bowl with the apples and fennel. Toss, taste, and adjust the seasoning, then serve.

Vegetable Fajita Salad

Salad with most of the components of a traditional fajita minus the steak. (For that, see the variations.) Mushrooms and zucchini get a run under the broiler, while peppers and onions sizzle away in a skillet. All are tossed with a salsa of sorts—fresh corn, tomatoes, cilantro, lime—and sour cream. For a fancier presentation, you can plate the components separately on a large platter and let everyone serve themselves and toss their own. Serve with warmed corn or flour tortillas or chips, if you like. **Serves 4**

Ingredients

2 portobello mushrooms (8 ounces)

2 medium zucchini (1 pound)

¼ cup good-quality vegetable oil

Salt and pepper

2 bell peppers (1 pound; any color)

1 medium onion

2 ears fresh corn, or 1½ cups frozen kernels

1 large ripe tomato

1 bunch fresh cilantro

2 limes

Sour cream for serving (optional)

▢ Prep · Cook

1. Turn the broiler to high; put the rack 4 inches from the heat.

    ▢ Trim the stems from the mushrooms; trim the zucchini. Halve the zucchini lengthwise.

2. Put the mushrooms and zucchini, cut side up, on a rimmed baking sheet, rub with 2 tablespoons vegetable oil, and sprinkle with salt and pepper. Broil, turning the mushrooms once and leaving the zucchini cut side up, until they're tender and browned in places, 10 to 15 minutes.

    ▢ Core, seed, and slice the bell peppers.

    ▢ Trim, peel, halve, and slice the onion.

3. Put 2 tablespoons vegetable oil in a large skillet over medium-high heat.

4. When the oil is hot, add the peppers and onion and sprinkle with salt and pepper. Cook, stirring occasionally until they're tender, 5 to 10 minutes.

    ▢ If using fresh corn, husk the corn and cut the kernels off the ears. Put the corn kernels in a large bowl.

    ▢ Core and chop the tomato; add it to the bowl.

    ▢ Chop ½ cup cilantro and add it to the bowl.

    ▢ Halve the limes; squeeze their juice into the bowl. Sprinkle with salt and pepper.

5. When the mushrooms and zucchini are tender and browned, slice or chop them as you like and add them to the bowl. When the peppers and onions are tender and browned, add them to the bowl. Toss, taste, and adjust the seasoning. Serve with sour cream if you like.

Variations

Steak Fajita Salad. Adds some time but truly makes a meal. Broil 1 pound skirt steak before cooking the vegetables: Pat it dry, put it on the rimmed baking sheet, drizzle with an additional tablespoon oil, and sprinkle with salt and pepper. It should take 5 to 10 minutes total to get to medium-rare; turn once as soon as the top begins to brown. Transfer the steak to a cutting board to rest. Then use the same baking sheet to broil the vegetables as described above. When the salad is ready to serve, slice the steak thinly against the grain, add any juices to the salsa, and drape the steak pieces across the top.

Vegetable and Black Bean Fajita Salad. Add 2 cups cooked or drained canned black beans to the corn, tomato, and cilantro mixture before serving.

Broiled Vegetable Salad with White Bean Dressing, with or Without Pasta. The best creamy vegan dressing ever— perfect for tossing with cut pasta. If you go that route, put a pot of water to boil before doing anything else and it won't add that much extra time. Omit the cilantro, lime, and sour cream. In a food processor, combine 1 cup cooked or canned drained white beans, 1 small clove garlic, the juice of a lemon, ⅓ cup olive oil, and a sprinkle of salt and pepper. Process until the mixture is smooth and thin enough to pour; add a splash of water if necessary. Taste and adjust the seasoning. Toss half of this dressing with the corn and tomato mixture and save the other half to drizzle over the broiled vegetables. Garnish with chopped fresh parsley or basil.

Warm Three-Bean Potato Salad

Typical three-bean salads are usually swimming in a sickly sweet vinegar dressing. I use just a touch of honey for sweetness and add potatoes for extra body. Boiling the green beans and potatoes in shallow water in the same pot—in the bare minimum of water—saves time and extra dishes. Serve with endive leaves for scooping if you like; the bitterness is a lovely counterpoint. **Serves 4**

Ingredients

Salt

1 pound russet or Yukon Gold potatoes

½ cup olive oil

3 tablespoons red wine vinegar

2 teaspoons Dijon mustard

1 teaspoon honey

Pepper

1 small red onion

8 ounces green beans

1¾ cups cooked or canned kidney beans (one 15-ounce can)

1¾ cups cooked or canned chickpeas (one 15-ounce can)

1 bunch fresh parsley

☐ Prep · Cook

1. Put about 2 inches of water and a large pinch of salt in a medium pot; turn the heat to high.

   ☐ Peel the potatoes if you like. Cut them into ½-inch chunks and add them to the pot.

2. Whisk ½ cup olive oil, 3 tablespoons red wine vinegar, 2 teaspoons Dijon mustard, 1 teaspoon honey, and a sprinkle of salt and pepper together in a large bowl.

   ☐ Trim, peel, halve, and thinly slice the onion; add it to the dressing.

   ☐ Trim and chop the green beans.

3. When the water comes to a boil, cover the pot and continue to boil, stirring once or twice until the potatoes are a little short of tender, about 5 minutes.

   ☐ If you're using canned kidney beans and chickpeas, rinse and drain them. Add the kidney beans and chickpeas to the bowl.

4. When the potatoes are nearly tender, add the green beans to the pot. Cook, stirring occasionally, until the potatoes and green beans are fully tender, 2 to 5 minutes.

   ☐ Chop ½ cup parsley and add it to the bowl.

5. When the potatoes and green beans are tender, drain them and add to the bowl. Toss, taste, and adjust the seasoning, then serve.

White Bean and Cucumber Salad with Yogurt and Dill

Dressing white beans in a light yogurt sauce enhances their natural creaminess and adds a refreshing tang. While cucumbers and red onion provide the necessary crunch and sharpness, lemon and dill brighten the whole thing into oblivion. I suggest using your own cooked beans (page 505) if at all possible, and instead of serving a starchy side, try piling the salad on a bed of Boston lettuce leaves. **Serves 4**

Ingredients

¾ cup Greek yogurt

3 tablespoons olive oil

1 lemon

1 bunch fresh dill

Salt and pepper

3½ cups cooked or canned white beans (two 15-ounce cans)

4 small cucumbers (about 1 pound)

1 small red onion

▢ **Prep · Cook**

1. Put ¾ cup yogurt and 3 tablespoons olive oil in a large bowl and whisk to combine.

   ▢ Halve the lemon; squeeze the juice into the bowl through a strainer or your fingers to catch the seeds.

   ▢ Chop ¼ cup fresh dill leaves and tender stems; add them to the bowl.

2. Sprinkle salt and pepper into the yogurt sauce and whisk until smooth. Add a little water if necessary to make it the consistency of a thick dressing.

   ▢ If you're using canned beans, rinse and drain them. Add the beans to the bowl.

   ▢ Trim and peel the cucumbers. Cut them in half lengthwise and scoop out the seeds with a spoon. Chop the flesh and add it to the bowl.

   ▢ Trim, peel, halve, and slice the onion; add it to the bowl.

3. Toss the beans and vegetables with the dressing until coated. Taste and adjust the seasoning, and serve.

Variation

Chickpea and Cucumber Salad with Tahini and Parsley. Replace ¼ cup of the yogurt with ¼ cup tahini, the dill with parsley, and the white beans with chickpeas. (I like to mash them with a fork in the dressing.) Add 1 teaspoon ground cumin to the dressing.

Corn Salad with Garlic Chicken

Charred corn kernels add a smoky dimension to salads. Fresh corn in season is always best, but frozen works well here too. Broiled chicken, sprinkled with spices and rubbed with garlic (see Garlic-Rubbed Chicken), makes it a meal, though you can always toss in a cup of cooked plain rice (page 496) for a little more oomph. Just be sure to take the rice out of the fridge when you start the recipe to take the chill off. **Serves 4**

Ingredients

4 ears fresh corn or 4 cups frozen kernels

Salt

2 cloves garlic

3 or 4 boneless, skinless chicken thighs (about 12 ounces)

2 tablespoons good-quality vegetable oil

¼ teaspoon cayenne

2 teaspoons ground cumin

Pepper

8 radishes

1 bunch scallions

1 bunch fresh cilantro

2 limes

Sour cream for garnish (optional)

Prep · Cook

1. Put a large skillet over medium-high heat. Turn the broiler to high; put the rack 4 inches from the heat.

   ▫ If you're using frozen corn, proceed to Step 2. Husk the corn, trim, and cut the kernels off the cob.

2. Put the corn in the skillet and sprinkle with salt. Cook, stirring occasionally, until the corn chars lightly, 5 to 10 minutes.

   ▫ Peel and halve 2 cloves garlic.

3. Put the chicken on a rimmed baking sheet; rub with 2 tablespoons vegetable oil and sprinkle with ¼ teaspoon cayenne, 2 teaspoons ground cumin, salt, and pepper. Broil, turning once, until lightly browned on both sides and just cooked through, 5 to 10 minutes per side.

4. When the corn is lightly charred, put it in a large bowl.

   ▫ Trim and chop 8 radishes; add them to the bowl.

   ▫ Chop 1 cup cilantro and add it to the bowl.

   ▫ Trim and chop the scallions and add them to the bowl.

   ▫ Halve the limes; squeeze the juice into the bowl.

5. When the chicken is done, remove it from the broiler and rub all over with the raw garlic.

6. Toss the corn mixture together; taste and adjust the seasoning. To serve, slice the chicken as thick as you like and lay the slices over the top of the corn salad. Garnish with a dollop of sour cream if you like.

● recipe continues →

Variations

Edamame Salad with Ginger Chicken. Omit the cayenne and ground cumin. Substitute 4 cups frozen shelled edamame for the corn. Instead of rubbing the chicken thighs with garlic, rub them with a piece of peeled fresh ginger. Substitute sesame oil for 1 tablespoon of the vegetable oil, and 1 cup chopped peeled daikon radish for the red radishes.

Pozole Salad with Garlic Chicken. Instead of the corn, use 3½ cups cooked or canned hominy (two 15-ounce or one 29-ounce can). Rinse and drain it well. Everything else stays the same, except the hominy

won't char like the corn. And you might want to add 1 cup thinly sliced cabbage to the salad bowl in Step 6.

Corn Salad with Shrimp. Omit the ground cumin. Use olive oil instead of vegetable oil, red chile flakes instead of cayenne, and 1 pint ripe cherry tomatoes, halved, in place of radishes. Use 1½ pounds thawed peeled large shrimp instead of the chicken. Rather than rubbing all those shrimp with garlic, mince the garlic and toss it with the shrimp before broiling for 2 or 3 minutes per side.

GARLIC-RUBBED CHICKEN

The way you season bruschetta is by rubbing grilled or broiled toast with a cut raw garlic clove, which cooks very gently on the surface of the hot bread. The same technique works wonderfully for chicken and even steak or pork chops: Just rub the garlic directly on the meat after cooking. Plus, it eliminates the possibility of minced garlic burning during high-heat, fast cooking.

Chicken and Pita Salad

This is essentially a spin on the classic fattoush with some extra protein added in the main recipe and first variation. The last two options take the idea into totally different directions. The pita—grilled or broiled like the meat—soaks up the flavor like a sponge without getting soggy. **Serves 4**

Ingredients

2 or 3 medium ripe tomatoes

1 medium cucumber

1 small red onion

3 or 4 boneless, skinless chicken thighs (about 12 ounces)

6 tablespoons olive oil

Salt and pepper

4 pitas

1 bunch fresh parsley

1 lemon

☐ Prep · Cook

1. Prepare a grill for direct cooking or turn the broiler to high; put the rack 4 inches from the heat.

   ☐ Core the tomatoes, cut them into chunks, and put them in a large bowl.

   ☐ Trim the cucumber; peel if necessary. Cut it in half lengthwise and scoop out the seeds with a spoon. Chop the flesh and add to the bowl.

   ☐ Trim, peel, halve, and thinly slice the onion; add it to the bowl.

2. Put the chicken on a large rimmed baking sheet. Drizzle with 2 tablespoons olive oil and sprinkle with salt and pepper. When the grill or broiler is hot, cook the chicken, turning once until browned on both sides and just cooked through, 5 to 10 minutes per side.

   ☐ Brush the pitas with 2 tablespoons olive oil and sprinkle with salt and pepper.

   ☐ Chop ½ cup parsley and add it to the bowl.

   ☐ Halve the lemon; squeeze the juice into the bowl through a strainer or your fingers to catch the seeds.

3. When the chicken is just cooked through, transfer it to a cutting board. Grill the pitas directly on the grates or broil them on a rimmed baking sheet, turning once until toasted, a minute or two per side.

4. When the pitas are ready, transfer them to the cutting board. Chop the pita and the chicken; add them to the bowl. Add 2 tablespoons olive oil and a sprinkle of salt and pepper. Toss, taste, and adjust the seasoning, and serve.

Variations

Lamb and Pita Salad. A whole 'nuther level. Just be sure you add the lamb to the salad while it's still warm. Instead of the chicken, grill or broil about 1½ pounds lamb shoulder chops to your desired doneness (I like them medium-rare) as described in Step 2; they may take another couple minutes depending on the thickness. After resting, cut the lamb into bite-sized pieces, discarding the bones and any excess fat.

Chicken and Bread Salad. Think dinnertime panzanella. Substitute 4 thick slices crusty Italian or French bread for the pita and 2 tablespoons balsamic vinegar for the lemon juice. Add a handful of chopped pitted olives and some shaved Parmesan to the salad as well.

Chicken and Rice or Grain Salad. Perfect repurposing of leftover cooked grains. Instead of the pitas, spread 3 cups cooked rice or grains on a rimmed baking sheet, drizzle with the oil, and toss with a fork. Broil as described in Step 3, shaking the pan once, just long enough to warm and lightly toast it, about 3 minutes. The rest of the ingredients and seasonings remain the same.

Kimchi and Snow Pea Salad with Grilled or Broiled Beef

Crunch galore: Combine sliced raw snow peas and kimchi, then top it with tender grilled or broiled beef. For a bigger bowl, start with plain-cooked rice (page 496) or rice noodles (page 495). And for more about kimchi, see the note that follows on page 92. **Serves 4**

Ingredients

12 ounces snow peas

2 cups kimchi

1 pound boneless beef sirloin or rib-eye steak

Salt and pepper

Several sprigs fresh mint

4 scallions

1 tablespoon sesame oil

Soy sauce to pass at the table

☐ Prep · Cook

1. Prepare a grill for direct cooking or turn the broiler to high; put the rack 4 inches from the heat.

   ☐ Slice the snow peas on a diagonal into bite-sized pieces and put them in a large bowl.

2. Add 2 cups kimchi to the bowl along with some of its juice. Toss to combine.

3. When the grill or broiler is hot, put the steak on a rimmed baking sheet and sprinkle all over with salt and pepper. Grill on the grates or broil in the pan, turning once, until charred on both sides but still one shade pinker inside than you like. Figure 2 to 5 minutes per side, depending on your grill or broiler; use a knife to nick and peek. Transfer the meat to a cutting board to let it rest.

   ☐ Strip the leaves from several mint sprigs, chop, and add them to the bowl.

   ☐ Trim and chop the scallions and add them to the bowl.

4. Toss the salad, taste, and adjust the seasoning. Serve individually in shallow bowls or spread on a platter. Slice the steak thinly against the grain; drape it across the top of the salad and drizzle with any accumulated juices and 1 tablespoon sesame oil. Serve with soy sauce.

● recipe continues →

Variations

Kimchi and Celery Salad with Grilled or Broiled Beef. Instead of the snow peas, thinly slice the tender heart and leaves of 1 bunch celery.

Kimchi and Snow Pea or Celery Salad with Grilled or Broiled Pork. For the vegetables, use either the main recipe or the first variation. Instead of beef, use about 1 pound pork tenderloin. Slice it across into medallions about ½ inch thick. Grill or broil as described in Step 3 until browned on both sides and just slightly pink in the middle, about 2 minutes a side.

Sauerkraut and Apple Salad with Grilled or Broiled Pork. Seek out super-fresh sauerkraut to replace the kimchi and you'll be amazed. Instead of the snow peas, core and slice 3 green apples as thinly as you can manage. Instead of beef, use about 1 pound pork tenderloin. Slice it across into medallions about ½ inch thick. Grill or broil as described in Step 3 until browned on both sides and just slightly pink in the middle, about 2 minutes a side. Substitute 2 tablespoons chopped chives for the mint.

KIMCHI

Kimchi, the spicy fermented vegetables ubiquitous to Korean cooking, packs a huge punch of flavor and texture. It's usually made with cabbage, but sometimes you find daikon, scallions, or other vegetables. The chile version—as opposed to a "water kimchi" soaked in a much milder brine—is both tangy and hot, and even though it's fermented for a long time, it retains a vibrant crunch.

Like sauerkraut, you can approximate kimchi quickly by combining cabbage, salt, vinegar, and Korean red pepper paste. I've got this shortcut version on page 303. But the real deal is definitely not fast. And that's really what you want here. Luckily, high-quality kimchi is easy to find, certainly at Asian grocery stores and increasingly at mainstream supermarkets. Don't hesitate to buy a big jar if you find one; it will keep for a few months in your fridge, and there are a number of ways to use it, from mixing it with plain rice or Asian noodles to stirring it into soup to stir-frying it. Or eat it straight like a piquant side dish.

Sandwiches

You already know how to make a sandwich. But how often do you venture beyond grilled cheese and sliced deli meat?

Time to branch out—as in Salmon Sandwiches with Peanut Vinaigrette and its variations (page 106). Or for a vegetarian option, try the Smoky Pinto Burgers on page 101. And I love to go for open-face and deconstructed numbers, like Egg Salad Bruschetta (page 103).

Sandwiches are of course a vehicle for eating excellent bread. Though I make suggestions with each recipe, feel free to use what you like, especially if you either bake your own or have access to a good bakery. There are also a couple tacos and a burrito here, as well as guidance for making wraps, which are an excellent way to use leftovers.

There are lots of ways to round out hot or cold sandwich meals. Soup or salad are naturals, as are chips. I also like a cooked vegetable (see page 498) or some kind of crudité, like the recipe and variations on page 42. Which reminds me: Vegetables and dips and other snacks can help you build a do-it-yourself sandwich bar—one of my favorite kid-friendly ways to feed a large, festive gathering or weekend family lunch.

Broiled Cheese

When you want to make more than one crisp-outside-gooey-inside sandwich, long-distance broiling is the right technique. Even if you have a big griddle, try this way; the radiant heat delivers some nice crunch to the crust. **Serves 4**

Ingredients

4 tablespoons (½ stick) butter

8 ounces cheddar cheese (2 cups grated)

8 slices sandwich bread

☐ Prep · Cook

1. Turn the broiler to high; put the rack 6 inches from the heat.

   ☐ Melt 4 tablespoons butter in the microwave or in a small pot over medium-low heat.

   ☐ Slice 8 ounces cheddar cheese or grate 2 cups.

2. Use the cheese and bread to fill and assemble 4 sandwiches. Brush the tops with about half of the butter. Or dab with a fork if you don't have a brush.

3. Put the sandwiches on a rimmed baking sheet, butter side up, and broil until the tops are browned, 2 to 3 minutes. Carefully turn and brush or dab the other side with the remaining butter and return the pan to the broiler. Cook until the bread is toasted on this side and the cheese is melted, another couple minutes. Press down on the sandwiches with the back of a spatula if you like and serve right away.

Variations

Broiled Peanut Butter and Jelly. A template for any nut butter combination, including cashew and tomato sandwiches, or even tahini and kimchi. Instead of the cheese, use ½ cup peanut butter and ¼ cup jam (or to taste). For vegan sandwiches, substitute coconut oil, the corresponding nut or seed oil, or good-quality vegetable oil for the butter. Fill and broil the sandwiches as described.

Broiled Cheese, Don't Hold the Mayo. Terrific crunch and flavor, if slightly unorthodox. Instead of butter, use mayo to brush or dab on the outside of the sandwiches.

10 Additions to Broiled Cheese

Add any of the following when you assemble the sandwiches. Spread on the bread or scatter with the cheese as appropriate:

1. Thinly sliced tomato
2. Thinly sliced onion
3. Thinly sliced green or red bell peppers
4. Cooked and crumbled bacon or sausage
5. Bits of prosciutto, ham, or salami
6. Chopped roasted or canned green chiles
7. Mustard
8. Chopped canned chipotle chiles in adobo
9. Maple syrup or honey
10. Thinly sliced apple or pear

Hummus and Vegetable Pita Pockets

Pita is the ideal vehicle for hummus: Spread it thickly inside slightly crisp pockets, then fill with fresh vegetables and briny feta. The recipe here gives you about 2 cups hummus, enough for a generous ½ cup for each sandwich. For a lighter approach, halve the portion of hummus, refrigerate the rest for up to a few days, and finish with lettuce, olives, or more cucumbers. The variations and list that follow will inspire your own creations and include directions for handling pocketless pitas. And you can always use cannellini or fava beans to make the hummus. **Serves 4**

Ingredients

Four 8-inch pitas with pockets

¼ cup olive oil, plus more for drizzling

Salt and pepper

1 lemon

2 cloves garlic

1¾ cups cooked or canned chickpeas (one 15-ounce can)

½ cup tahini

1 teaspoon ground cumin or paprika

2 or 3 medium ripe tomatoes

1 large cucumber

4 ounces feta cheese (1 cup crumbled)

☐ Prep · Cook

1. Turn the broiler to high; put the rack 4 inches from the heat.

   - ☐ Drizzle the pitas with olive oil (about ½ teaspoon per side) and rub it over all with your fingers. Sprinkle salt and pepper on both sides and spread the pitas out on a large rimmed baking sheet.

   - ☐ Halve the lemon; squeeze the juice into a food processor or blender through a strainer or your fingers to catch the seeds.

   - ☐ Peel and chop 2 cloves garlic.

   - ☐ If you're using canned chickpeas, rinse and drain them.

2. Add the garlic and chickpeas to the machine along with ½ cup tahini, ¼ cup olive oil, 1 teaspoon ground cumin or paprika, and a sprinkle of salt and pepper. Let the machine run, adding water, chickpea-cooking liquid, or more olive oil a tablespoon at a time until the purée is smooth but not watery. Taste and adjust the seasoning.

   - ☐ Core the tomatoes and cut them into chunks; put them in a medium bowl.

   - ☐ Peel the cucumber if necessary, cut it in half lengthwise, and scoop out the seeds with a spoon if you like. Chop the flesh and add it to the bowl.

3. Put the pitas on a rimmed baking sheet and grill, turning once, until browned—even slightly charred—on both sides, 2 to 5 minutes total.

   - ☐ Crumble 1 cup feta cheese and add to the tomatoes and cucumber. Sprinkle with salt and pepper, drizzle with a little olive oil, and toss.

4. When the pitas are browned, cut each one in half, spreading them apart a bit to widen the pocket.

5. Spoon some hummus into each pocket and spread it around the inside. Spoon in the vegetable and feta mixture, top with a little more hummus if you like, and serve.

Variations

Hummus and Eggplant Pita Pockets. Instead of using the cucumber and tomatoes, before making the hummus, trim 1½ pounds eggplant and cut into slices about ¼ inch thick. Lay out the slices on a rimmed baking sheet and rub them all over with the oil; sprinkle with salt. Grill or broil the eggplant until it's pliable and browned on both sides, 5 to 10 minutes total. Meanwhile make the hummus, crumble the feta, and toast the pita. After spreading the insides of the pita with hummus, tuck in some rolled eggplant slices and sprinkle with some feta.

Tofu and Vegetable Pita Pockets. Instead of the chickpeas, purée one 14- to 16-ounce brick firm tofu in the food processor or blender with the other ingredients in Step 3.

Pocketless Pita Sandwiches. More of an eating than a cooking technique. It works with the main recipe and the first two variations, and anything in the list that follows. Use pocketless pita, which is usually a little thicker and chewier, and increasingly available made from whole wheat. Rub the olive oil on both sides and grill or broil the pita as described in the main recipe. Prepare the hummus and the vegetable mixture, then use them to top the warm bread, which you can then fold in half or tear off in pieces to eat with the filling.

5 Additions to Hummus and Vegetable Pita Pockets

Add any of the following, alone or in combination, to the tomato, cucumber, and feta mixture:

1. Sliced red onions
2. Chopped red peppers (roasted are nice if you've got 'em)
3. Chopped pitted olives
4. Chopped fresh parsley, dill, or mint
5. Cooked bulgur (page 497)

Sassy Sardine Open-Face Sandwich, page 100

Tangy Tuna Sandwich

Everybody has a favorite spin on a tuna salad sandwich, and mine usually veers toward piquant, tangy flavors to offset the richness of the fish. Get oil-packed tuna in a jar if you can find it; the quality is generally better. And don't shy away from the pickles and brine here; they're crucial. **Serves 4**

Ingredients

Two 6-ounce jars or 5-ounce cans tuna (packed in olive oil)

1 small shallot

2 large or 3 medium dill pickles

1 bunch fresh parsley

8 slices sandwich bread

1 tablespoon Dijon mustard

Salt and pepper

Olive oil

□ Prep · Cook

1. Turn the broiler to high; put the rack 6 inches from the heat.

   □ Put the tuna and its oil in a medium bowl.

   □ Peel and chop the shallot; add it to the bowl.

   □ Chop 2 or 3 pickles; add them to the bowl.

   □ Chop ¼ cup parsley and add it to the bowl.

   □ Put 8 slices bread on a rimmed baking sheet.

2. Broil the bread, turning once until lightly browned on both sides, 2 to 5 minutes total.

3. Add 1 tablespoon Dijon mustard to the tuna in the bowl and sprinkle with salt and pepper. Stir with a fork to break apart the tuna, mashing it a bit against the side of the bowl as you work. Add olive oil a teaspoon at a time until the tuna is glossy, then add 1 teaspoon brine from the pickle jar. Taste and adjust the seasoning, adding more brine if you like.

4. When the bread is lightly toasted, remove it from the broiler. Assemble the sandwiches while the toast is still warm and serve.

• recipe continues →

● Tangy Tuna Sandwich, continued

Variations

Provençal Tuna Sandwich.
I particularly like this on a
chunk of split baguette, but
hearty Italian or olive breads
are also good choices. Replace
the pickles and parsley with
1 small fennel bulb; chop it and
some of the fronds as finely
as you can manage. Instead
of the Dijon mustard, use
2 tablespoons capers. Since
you won't be using pickle
brine, add the juice of a lemon
along with the olive oil.

**Sassy Sardine (or Mackerel)
Open-Face Sandwich.**
Substitute jarred or canned
sardines or mackerel for
the tuna; you want skin-on
fillets, ideally packed in oil.
Use 8 slices thinly sliced
whole grain rye instead of the
sandwich bread. In Step 1,
keep the fish in the cans and
make the dressing alone as
described. After toasting the
bread, spread each slice with
some dressing and top with
the sardines (or mackerel).
Garnish with thinly sliced
lemon and parsley.

Tangy Tuna Melt. Forget
cheddar here—for both the
main recipe and the first
variation, provolone is the
way to go. After you flip the
bread in Step 2, divide the
tuna salad among 4 slices and
top with 1 or 2 thin slices
cheese. Continue broiling until
the cheese melts, close the
sandwiches, and serve.

10 PERFECT DISHES FOR FILLING SANDWICHES FROM ELSEWHERE IN THE BOOK

Whether you fill two slices or a split roll, eat
open face, or wrap in a big flour tortilla or other
flatbread, all of these are easy to turn into handheld
meals. And be sure to check out the burgers
(pages 405 and 427), chicken pita sandwich
(page 388), and Sloppy Joes (page 429).

1. Skewerless Chicken Satay (page 49)
2. Broiled Eggplant Salad with Tangy Tahini
   Dressing (page 74)
3. Broiled Caprese (page 251)
4. Buffalo Shrimp (page 343)
5. Broiled Chicken Breasts with Avocado Salsa
   (page 364)
6. Jerk-Inspired Chicken and Onions
   (page 393)
7. Steak, Lettuce, and Herb Wraps (page 411)
8. Skillet Meat Loaf (page 431)
9. Cumin-Rubbed Pork with Mangoes
   (page 444)
10. Eggs, Cooked Four Ways (page 483)

Smoky Pinto Burgers

Patties made out of pink pinto beans and oats are easier (and better!) than any vegetarian burger you've ever tried. **Serves 4**

Ingredients

2 canned chipotle chiles in adobo

1 medium carrot

1 large clove garlic

3½ cups cooked or canned pinto beans (two 15-ounce cans)

½ cup rolled oats, plus more if needed

¼ cup coconut oil

2 teaspoons ground cumin

Salt and pepper

Good-quality vegetable oil for frying

4 hamburger buns

1 small red onion

Several sprigs fresh cilantro

2 limes

⅓ cup mayonnaise

▫ Prep · **Cook**

- ▫ Put 2 chipotle chiles and some adobo from the can in a large flat-bottom bowl; mash with a fork until relatively smooth.

- ▫ Trim and peel the carrot; grate it on the large holes of a box grater. Add it to the bowl.

- ▫ Peel and mince 1 clove garlic; add it to the bowl.

- ▫ If you're using canned beans, rinse and drain them. Add the pinto beans to the bowl.

1. Measure ½ cup oats. Grab about half and crumble them between your hands over the bowl; repeat with the remaining oats. Add ¼ cup coconut oil, 2 teaspoons ground cumin, and a sprinkle of salt and pepper to the bowl.

2. Use a potato masher or fork to mash and stir the ingredients in the bowl until combined and the mixture holds together when you pinch some between your fingers.

3. Put a thin film of vegetable oil in a large skillet over medium heat. Turn the broiler to high; put the rack 6 inches from the heat.

4. Shape the bean mixture into 4 patties, about ½ inch thick.

5. When the oil is hot, cook the burgers, turning once, until crisp on both sides and firm at the center, 4 or 5 minutes per side, adding more vegetable oil if the pan is dry.

6. Split the buns in half, brush with a little vegetable oil, and broil until lightly toasted, 2 or 3 minutes.

- ▫ Trim, peel, halve, and thinly slice the onion.

- ▫ Trim the toughest stems from several cilantro sprigs.

- ▫ Cut the limes into wedges.

7. When the buns are toasted, remove them from the broiler. Spread ⅓ cup mayonnaise on the cut sides of the buns. Add the onion, cilantro, and burgers. Close the sandwiches and serve with lime wedges.

● recipe continues →

• Smoky Pinto Burgers, continued

Variations

White Bean and Zucchini Burgers. Substitute 1 small zucchini for the carrot, white beans for the pintos, 1 tablespoon grated lemon zest for the chipotles, 2 teaspoons chopped fresh rosemary for the ground cumin, and basil for the cilantro. After you grate the zucchini, put it in a clean kitchen towel and wring it dry before proceeding.

BBQ Black-Eyed Pea and Sweet Potato Burgers. Replace the carrot with ½ small sweet potato, the pinto beans with black-eyed peas, and the chipotles with 2 tablespoons barbecue sauce.

Curried Chickpea Burgers. Omit the ground cumin. Instead of the chipotles, mash 2 tablespoons curry powder with 1 chopped scallion in the large bowl. Substitute chickpeas for the pinto beans. Everything else stays the same.

Egg Salad Bruschetta

Loaded with fresh cucumbers and tomatoes and tossed with a quick Italian-style dressing, this open-face sandwich puts the "salad" back in egg salad. **Serves 4**

Ingredients

6 eggs

Ice cubes

1 medium cucumber

2 medium ripe tomatoes

1 small red onion

2 sprigs fresh oregano
or 1 teaspoon dried

8 slices Italian bread

1 lemon

¼ cup olive oil

Salt and pepper

□ Prep · **Cook**

1. Turn the broiler to high; put the rack 6 inches from the heat.

2. Fill a medium saucepan about two-thirds with water and gently submerge the eggs. Bring to a boil, turn off the heat, and cover. Set a timer for 9 minutes.

   □ Fill a large bowl with ice water.

   □ Peel the cucumber if necessary, cut it in half lengthwise, scoop out the seeds with a spoon, and chop the flesh. Put it in a large bowl.

   □ Core and chop the tomatoes; add to the bowl.

   □ Trim, peel, and chop the onion; add to the bowl.

   □ If you're using fresh oregano, strip the leaves from 2 sprigs and chop. Add the oregano to the bowl.

   □ Put 8 slices of bread on a rimmed baking sheet.

3. Broil the bread, turning once until lightly browned on both sides, 2 to 5 minutes total.

   □ Grate the lemon zest into the bowl; refrigerate the remaining fruit for another use.

4. When the eggs are done, transfer them to the ice water with a slotted spoon. Leave them submerged for at least 1 minute to cool.

5. Crack and peel the eggs. Transfer them to a cutting board and chop. Add them to the bowl.

6. Add ¼ cup olive oil and a sprinkle of salt and pepper; toss, taste, and adjust the seasoning. Spoon the egg salad on top of the bread and serve.

• recipe continues →

Variations

Egg Salad Bruschetta with Aïoli. Substitute 1 or 2 celery hearts (several tender stalks with leaves) for the cucumber and tomatoes, 1 clove garlic for the oregano, and mayonnaise for the olive oil. Start by mincing the garlic and combining it in the large bowl with the mayonnaise and lemon zest; squeeze the juice from the lemon into the bowl through a strainer or your fingers; add salt and pepper, and stir to make the dressing. Then build in the onions and eggs.

Egg and Arugula Bruschetta. Instead of the cucumber, use 2 cups arugula; substitute 1 pint ripe cherry tomatoes for the medium tomatoes, and halve them instead of chopping.

Egg and Radicchio Bruschetta. Especially delicious on a hearty multigrain or olive loaf. Substitute a small head radicchio for the cucumber and tomatoes; after coring and trimming, slice the leaves crosswise as thinly as you can. Instead of the lemon, use 2 tablespoons balsamic vinegar in the dressing.

Non-Egg Salad Bruschetta. A vegan twist that tastes and looks like the main recipe. Instead of the eggs, use 1 small celery root (about 12 ounces). After trimming and peeling, chop the flesh or cut it into matchsticks. Everything else stays the same.

Eggplant Parmesan Sub

The components are all here: eggplant, Italian cheeses, and tomato sauce; the bread crumbs come in the form of toasted sub rolls. Crunch, check. Silky tomatoey cheesiness, check. The only thing missing is you standing at the stove breading and frying. **Serves 4**

Ingredients

3 tablespoons olive oil

2 large eggplants (1½ pounds)

Salt and pepper

4 sub rolls

4 ounces low-moisture mozzarella cheese (1 cup grated)

4 ounces Parmesan cheese (1 cup grated)

1 (15-ounce) can crushed tomatoes

Several sprigs fresh basil

▫ Prep · **Cook**

1. Turn the broiler to high; put the rack 6 inches from the heat. Put 3 tablespoons olive oil in a large skillet over medium heat.

   ▫ Trim the eggplants and cut them into ½-inch cubes.

2. Add the eggplant to the oil, sprinkle with salt and pepper, and raise the heat to medium-high. Cook, stirring occasionally until lightly browned all over, 6 to 8 minutes.

3. Split the sub rolls lengthwise and open them on a rimmed baking sheet and broil until lightly toasted on the inside, 1 to 3 minutes.

   ▫ Grate 1 cup each mozzarella and Parmesan.

4. Remove the rolls from the broiler; leave the broiler on.

5. When the eggplant is lightly browned, add the tomatoes. Stir to combine and cook until the eggplant is tender, another 2 or 3 minutes.

   ▫ Strip the leaves from several basil sprigs.

6. When the eggplant is tender, spoon the eggplant and tomato mixture onto the bottom half of each roll; top with the basil leaves and then the cheeses.

7. Return the sandwiches to the broiler and broil until the cheeses are bubbling and browned. Top the sandwiches with the other half of the roll and serve right away.

Variations

Chicken Parm Sub. Instead of the eggplant, use 1½ pounds boneless, skinless chicken thighs, cut into 1-inch chunks. Cook them as you would the eggplant in Step 2; they'll brown in 5 to 6 minutes. Add the tomatoes and cook until the chicken is just cooked through, 2 to 3 minutes more.

Portobello Parm Sub. Instead of the eggplant, remove the stems from 1½ pounds portobello mushrooms and cut the caps into 1-inch chunks. Cook them as you would the eggplant in Step 2, then add the tomatoes and proceed.

Salmon Sandwiches with Peanut Vinaigrette

The sandwich for salmon lovers, not burger lovers. Please use a wild-caught variety. Or you can use another type of fish (see the last variation) with the peanut vinaigrette or any of the sauces in the variations. **Serves 4**

Ingredients

1½ pounds salmon fillets

1 tablespoon vegetable oil

Salt and pepper

¼ cup peanuts

2 limes

1 tablespoon soy sauce

1 tablespoon sesame oil

3 scallions

Several sprigs fresh cilantro

4 hamburger buns

▫ Prep · Cook

1. Prepare a grill for direct cooking or turn on the broiler; put the rack 4 inches from the heat.

   ▫ Put the salmon on a rimmed baking sheet skin side up, rub with 1 tablespoon vegetable oil, and sprinkle with salt and pepper.

   ▫ Chop ¼ cup peanuts; put them in a small bowl.

   ▫ Halve 1 lime and squeeze the juice into the bowl; cut the other into wedges and reserve.

2. Add 1 tablespoon soy sauce and 1 tablespoon sesame oil to the bowl. Stir to combine.

3. Grill the salmon directly on the grates or broil in the pan, turning once, until browned on both sides and cooked as you like, 3 to 4 minutes per side if you like it a little soft in the middle, another minute or two if you like it firmer.

   ▫ Trim and slice the scallions.

   ▫ Strip the leaves from several cilantro sprigs.

4. When the salmon is done, remove it from the grill or broiler.

5. Split the buns and grill or broil (on a fresh baking sheet) until the inside is lightly toasted, a minute or two.

6. Using a knife or metal spatula, break the salmon (including the skin if you like) into chunks and put them on the bun bottoms. Drizzle the peanut vinaigrette on the salmon and top with the scallions and cilantro. Close the sandwiches and serve with lime wedges.

Variations

Salmon Sandwiches with Tarragon Dijonnaise. Rub the salmon with olive oil instead of vegetable. Instead of the peanuts, lime, soy sauce, and sesame oil for the vinaigrette, combine 3 tablespoons mayonnaise with 2 tablespoons Dijon mustard, 1 tablespoon chopped fresh tarragon (or a little more if you like), and some salt and pepper. Spread the mixture on the toasted buns before adding the salmon. Top with sliced tomatoes instead of the scallions and cilantro.

Salmon Sandwiches with Candied Ginger Butter. Instead of the vinaigrette, heat 4 tablespoons (½ stick) butter and ⅓ cup chopped candied ginger in the microwave or a small pot. Use this sauce to dab on the toasted rolls and drizzle over the salmon when assembling the sandwiches. Keep the scallions and cilantro, or garnish with watercress.

Fish Sandwiches with Tartar Sauce. Use whatever thick, white fish fillets work best for you, like rockfish or cod. Omit the scallions and cilantro. Instead of the vinaigrette, combine ¼ cup each mayonnaise and chopped dill pickles with 1 tablespoon Dijon mustard; taste and add a little salt and pepper if you like. In Step 3, grill the fish as you would the salmon. Spread the tartar sauce on the toasted buns before adding the fish. Top with shredded iceberg lettuce if you like.

Warm Chicken Salad Sandwich with Grapes and Rosemary

To me, chicken salad is actually better when it's slightly warm. But it only takes 10 minutes in the freezer to chill, so you can always go that route. Be sure to check out the turkey variation: It's perfect—and even faster—with holiday leftovers but also easy enough to make anytime with quick-cooking turkey cutlets. Or try swapping other ingredients for your own flavor combinations. **Serves 4**

Ingredients

1½ pounds chicken tenders

1 cup white wine or water

1 bay leaf

Salt

3 sprigs fresh rosemary

⅓ cup mayonnaise

2 teaspoons Dijon mustard

Pepper

1 bunch red or green grapes

1 baguette

⬚ Prep · Cook

1. Put the chicken, 1 cup wine or water, 1 bay leaf, and a pinch of salt in a medium skillet over high heat.

2. As soon as the liquid comes to a boil, lower the heat so it barely bubbles. Cover and cook for 3 minutes. Remove from the heat but don't open the lid. Let it sit for 10 minutes.

   ⬚ Strip the leaves from 3 rosemary sprigs, chop, and put them in a large bowl.

   ⬚ Add ⅓ cup mayonnaise, 2 teaspoons Dijon mustard, and a sprinkle of salt and pepper to the bowl; stir to combine.

   ⬚ Pick off 1 cup grapes from the bunch, slice each grape in half, and add them to the bowl.

   ⬚ Halve the baguette lengthwise.

3. Nick the thickest pieces of chicken with a small knife to make sure the interior is no longer pink; if it is, bring the water to a boil again, cover, shut it off, and let sit for another 3 minutes or so. When the chicken is cooked, transfer it to a cutting board. (Save the broth for another use.) Chop or shred the chicken and add it to the bowl. Stir to coat the chicken and grapes in the dressing. Taste and adjust the seasoning.

4. Spoon the chicken salad onto the bottom half of the baguette, then top with the other half. Cut the sandwich into 4 sections and serve.

Roll-Your-Own Chicken Burritos with Canned Tomato Salsa

The unorthodox salsa makes all the difference in these big, meal-sized burritos you serve open face to let everyone fold their own. Since it's made with canned diced tomatoes, you don't have to worry about finding—and chopping—ripe fresh tomatoes outside of tomato season. The results are a cross between fresh and cooked salsa. When excellent fresh tomatoes are in season, try the recipe on page 480. **Serves 4**

Ingredients

1 large (28-ounce) can diced tomatoes

2 scallions

1 fresh hot green chile (like jalapeño)

1 bunch fresh cilantro

2 limes

Salt and pepper

2 tablespoons vegetable oil

4 to 6 boneless, skinless chicken thighs (about 1 pound)

1¾ cups cooked or canned black beans (one 15-ounce can)

2 cloves garlic

1 tablespoon chili powder

1 teaspoon ground cumin

4 large flour tortillas

Sour cream (optional)

Prep · Cook

- Drain the tomatoes, reserving the juice for another use; put the tomatoes in a medium bowl.

- Trim and chop the scallions; add them to the bowl.

- Trim and mince the chile; add it to the bowl.

- Chop ½ cup cilantro leaves and add it to the bowl.

- Halve 1 lime and squeeze the juice into the bowl; quarter the other lime and reserve for serving. Sprinkle the salsa with a little salt and pepper, stir, and let sit.

1. Put 2 tablespoons vegetable oil in a large skillet over medium-high heat.

   - Chop the chicken into ½-inch chunks.

2. When the oil is hot, add the chicken to the skillet, sprinkle with salt and pepper, and cook, stirring occasionally until it loses its pink color, 3 or 4 minutes.

   - If you're using canned beans, rinse and drain them.

   - Peel and mince 2 cloves garlic.

3. When the chicken is no longer pink, add the beans and garlic along with 1 tablespoon chili powder, 1 teaspoon ground cumin, and a sprinkle of salt and pepper. Cook, stirring occasionally, until the beans are hot and the chicken is cooked through, 3 to 5 minutes.

• recipe continues →

4. Put the tortillas in the microwave for 15 seconds or so to warm them up (or see page 113 for other ways).

5. When the chicken and beans are done, spoon the mixture onto the center of the tortillas. Top with the salsa and a few dollops of sour cream if you like and serve, passing the salsa at the table. (If anyone needs help wrapping, here are some directions to share: Fold the bottom of the tortilla up and over the filling, then fold in the sides to hold it in place; roll the burrito over so the seam side ends up underneath.)

Variations

Roll-Your-Own Steak and Black Bean Burritos with Canned Tomatillo Salsa. Substitute 1 large (28-ounce) can tomatillos for the tomatoes; drain and chop them as directed before Step 1. Use 1 pound sliced skirt steak instead of the chicken; for medium rare, cook it only 2 to 3 minutes in Step 2.

Roll-Your-Own Pork and Black Bean Burritos with Orange Salsa. Any orange is good here, especially the small varieties like satsuma or the larger pink cara cara that are now common in winter. Substitute 1 pound fresh oranges for the canned tomatoes. Peel, seed them if necessary, and chop them. Use 1 pound boneless pork chops instead of the chicken; prepare and cook them as described in Step 2.

Roll-Your-Own Shrimp and White Bean Burritos with Frozen Corn Salsa. Substitute 2 cups frozen corn kernels for the tomatoes; they'll thaw as they sit with the other salsa ingredients. Use 1 pound peeled shrimp instead of the chicken; put them in a colander under cold running water for about a minute to thaw them. Replace the black beans with navy or cannellini beans and add them at the same time as the shrimp; by the time the beans are hot, the shrimp will be cooked but not overcooked.

Steak Tacos (and Beyond)

Consider this recipe and the variations a template: I'm giving you specifics for how to cook and garnish simple proteins for quick fillings. With leftovers—cooked meat and fish, cooked vegetables and greens, raw salads, or not-too-soupy bean dishes—and a stack of tortillas in the fridge, your taco making is limited only by your imagination. See the list that follows and the instructions for warming tortillas on the opposite page. **Serves 4**

Ingredients

Several cabbage or lettuce leaves

4 large radishes

2 limes

Several sprigs fresh cilantro

1 pound skirt or sirloin steak

Salt and pepper

12 corn tortillas

Salsas and hot sauces for serving

Sour cream or Mexican crema for serving (optional)

☐ Prep · Cook

1. Prepare a grill for direct cooking or turn the broiler to high; put the rack 4 inches from the heat.

   ☐ Rinse and dry the cabbage or lettuce leaves and slice them crosswise into thin ribbons; you should have about 2 cups.

   ☐ Trim and chop 4 large radishes.

   ☐ Halve the limes.

   ☐ Strip the leaves from several cilantro sprigs.

2. When the grill or broiler is hot, put the steak on a rimmed baking sheet and sprinkle all over with salt and pepper. Grill directly on the grates or broil in the pan, turning once, until browned on both sides but still one shade pinker inside than you like it. Figure 2 to 5 minutes per side, depending on the thickness of the steak and your grill or broiler; use a knife to nick and peek.

3. Transfer the meat to a cutting board and let it rest.

4. Put the tortillas in the microwave for 15 seconds or so to warm them up (or see opposite for other ways). (Or if grilling, heat them directly over the fire, careful not to burn them.)

5. Slice the steak thinly against the grain. Assemble the tacos: on each tortilla, steak first, then cabbage or lettuce, radishes, and cilantro, then a squeeze of lime. Serve right away, passing salsa or hot sauce at the table along with sour cream or crema if you'd like.

Variations

Chicken Tacos. Instead of the steak, grill or broil about 1 pound boneless, skinless chicken thighs. You want them cooked through, so figure 3 to 5 minutes a side.

Fish Tacos. Substitute a firm, sturdy white fish for the steak. Catfish, rockfish, cod, halibut, or whatever looks freshest. Grilling fish can be tricky, so just broil it. Rub the baking sheet and the fish generously with some good-quality vegetable oil before seasoning in Step 2. Broil the fish until it's just opaque at the center but isn't dry, 2 to 4 minutes a side depending on the thickness.

Tofu Tacos. Instead of the steak, use 2 bricks firm tofu (14 or 16 ounces each). Cut each brick in half through its equator so you have 4 "steaks" about 1 inch thick. Cut each steak crosswise into 6 sticks. Put the tofu sticks on the baking sheet and rub them generously all over with vegetable oil before sprinkling with salt and pepper. Grill directly on the grates or broil in the pan until a crust forms, about 5 minutes. Then turn the sticks and cook on the other side until crisp, 3 to 5 minutes.

WARMING TORTILLAS

Microwaving isn't the only way to make flour and corn tortillas hot and pliable for filling. To heat bigger batches, wrap 6 to 8 tortillas in foil or put them in a small oven-safe skillet with a tight-fitting lid and warm them in a 375°F oven until steaming, 5 to 10 minutes. To get some charring and blistering, warm them over direct heat, like a grill or the flame of a gas stove, turning them with tongs every few seconds, or warm them on a dry skillet or griddle, turning once. Whatever method you choose, as they're ready, keep them hot in a tortilla holder (a shallow round container with a lid) or wrapped in a clean kitchen towel.

18 OTHER TACO OR BURRITO FILLINGS FROM ELSEWHERE IN THE BOOK

Use any of the plant- or meat-based fillings listed below to fill warmed corn or flour tortillas (see page 113). Then add shredded lettuce or cabbage if you like and serve with salsa or hot sauce.

1. Skewerless Chicken Satay (page 49)
2. Chickpea and Carrot Salad with Warm Cumin Oil (page 62)
3. Salmon Sandwiches with Peanut Vinaigrette (minus the buns, page 106)
4. Eggplant Steaks with Fresh Tomato Sauce (page 253)
5. Celery Root Tempura With or Without Shrimp (page 279)
6. Pan-Seared Corn With or Without Pork (page 285)
7. Beans and Greens (page 291)
8. Pan-Fried Tofu with Peanut Sauce and Scallions (page 320)
9. Broiled Fish with Fresh Salsa (page 334)
10. Smoky Shrimp Scampi (page 339)
11. Broiled Chicken Breasts with Avocado Salsa (page 364)
12. Jerk-Inspired Chicken and Onions (page 393)
13. Steak and Vegetables with Chimichurri (page 417)
14. Beef and Mushroom Kebabs with Spicy Pepita Sauce (page 424)
15. Cumin-Rubbed Pork with Mangoes (page 444)
16. Homemade Chorizo with Pinto Beans (page 452)
17. Stir-Fried Lamb with Green Peppers and Cumin (page 460)
18. Cook-Ahead Roasts, Starting with Chicken (page 507)

Crisp Pork and Watermelon Tacos

This bundle of taco ideas is a lesson in counterpoints: pairing something crisp and sort of fatty with something cool and juicy. Since the fruit is unadorned, I try to choose whatever is in season: In winter, citrus, mango, or pineapple are good; strawberries in spring; apricots and plums in late summer—you get the idea. **Serves 4**

Ingredients

2 tablespoons vegetable oil

1 pound boneless pork sirloin or loin chops

Salt and pepper

1 small seedless watermelon (you'll need only 2 cups chopped)

2 cloves garlic

1 teaspoon ground cumin

1 teaspoon chili powder

2 limes

Several sprigs fresh cilantro

12 corn tortillas

4 ounces queso fresco (1 cup crumbled; optional)

☐ Prep · Cook

1. Put 2 tablespoons vegetable oil in a large skillet over medium-high heat.

   ☐ Cut the pork into thin strips about 2 inches long and ¼ inch wide.

2. Add the pork to the skillet in a single layer, sprinkle with salt and pepper, and cook undisturbed until it begins to crisp on the bottom and release from the pan, about 3 minutes.

   ☐ Halve and peel the watermelon. Chop the flesh into ½-inch chunks; you'll need 2 cups for the tacos. Refrigerate the rest for another use.

   ☐ Peel and mince 2 cloves garlic.

3. When the pork begins to crisp, stir in the garlic, 1 teaspoon ground cumin, and 1 teaspoon chili powder. Continue cooking, stirring occasionally, until the spices are fragrant and the pork is crisp and no longer bright pink at the center, 3 to 5 minutes more.

   ☐ Halve the limes.

   ☐ Strip the leaves from several cilantro sprigs.

   ☐ Put the tortillas in the microwave for 15 seconds or so to warm them up (or see page 113 for other ways).

   ☐ Crumble 1 cup queso fresco if you're using it.

4. When the pork is crisp all over, assemble the tacos: Put the pork on a tortilla, top with watermelon and cilantro, and squeeze lime juice over the top. Sprinkle with queso fresco if you're using it and serve.

• recipe continues →

Variations

Crisp Pork and Pear Tacos.
Omit the cilantro and queso fresco. Substitute 2 cups chopped pears (about 2 pears) for the watermelon; peel, seed, and chop them after Step 2. Use 1 tablespoon chopped fresh sage instead of the ground cumin and 1 teaspoon dry mustard instead of the chili powder. Use 1 lemon in place of the limes.

Crisp Chicken and Mango Tacos.
Use 2 cups chopped mangoes instead of the watermelon. Instead of the pork, cut and cook 1 pound boneless, skinless chicken thighs as described in Steps 1 through 3. Everything else stays the same.

Crisp Bacon and Peach Tacos.
Only when peaches are at peak season. Figure you'll need 4; cut them into chunks (peeling is optional). Substitute 12 slices thick-cut bacon for the pork; chop it into 1-inch pieces. It will crisp a little faster than the sliced pork. Drain the bacon on towels before assembling the tacos.

Big T's (and MB's) Meat Sauce Sub

Back in the 1990s, the now-long-gone and much-missed Big T's sub shop in Cambridge, Massachusetts, sold this sandwich—which contained only the sauce used to bathe its meatballs—for a dollar. My version and the variations take a stab at re-creating the experience in a modern way. **Serves 4**

Ingredients

2 tablespoons olive oil

8 ounces ground beef

8 ounces ground pork

Salt and pepper

2 cloves garlic

1 bunch fresh parsley

1 tablespoon dried oregano

1 ounce Parmesan cheese (¼ cup grated)

8 ounces provolone cheese (2 cups grated or chopped)

4 sub rolls

1 (15-ounce) can crushed tomatoes

Pickled vegetables for serving

☐ Prep · **Cook**

1. Put 2 tablespoons olive oil in a medium skillet over medium heat. Turn the broiler to high; put the rack 6 inches from the heat.

2. Put the ground beef and pork in the skillet and sprinkle with salt and pepper.

   ☐ Chop 2 cloves garlic and add them to the skillet.

   ☐ Chop ¼ cup parsley leaves and add it and the oregano to the skillet.

   ☐ Grate ¼ cup Parmesan and add to the skillet.

3. Stir the meat to break it up a bit and combine all the ingredients. Cook, stirring once or twice, until the meat loses its pink color, 3 to 4 minutes.

   ☐ Grate or chop 2 cups provolone.

   ☐ Split the sub rolls in half lengthwise with a serrated knife or your fingers, and open them on a rimmed baking sheet, cut sides up.

4. When the meat loses its pink color, add the tomatoes and stir to combine. Adjust the heat so the mixture bubbles gently but steadily and simmer until it thickens like pasta sauce, about 5 minutes.

5. Put the rolls under the broiler, turning once until lightly toasted on both sides, 1 to 3 minutes total. Turn the rolls cut sides up; leave the broiler on.

6. Once the sauce is ready, spoon it onto the bottom halves of the rolls. Scatter the top halves of the rolls with the provolone, return the sandwiches to the broiler, and broil until the cheese is bubbling and browned. Serve right away, with pickled vegetables on the side.

• recipe continues

Variations

MB's Chili Sub. Use 8 ounces ground beef instead of the beef-pork combination. Substitute 2 tablespoons chili powder for the oregano and cilantro for the parsley. When you add the tomatoes in Step 4, stir in about 1¾ cups cooked or canned kidney beans, drained (one 15-ounce can). For the cheeses, use a Mexican melting cheese like asadero and/or a crumbling cheese like queso fresco or Cotija.

MB's Curried Tomato Sauce Sub. Use 12 ounces ground lamb instead of the beef-pork combination. Substitute 2 tablespoons curry powder for the oregano and fresh mint for the parsley. For the provolone and Parmesan cheeses, use 8 ounces crumbled paneer, or if you can't find that, feta.

MB's Vegetarian or Vegan Sauce Sub. Substitute 1 medium onion, 1 medium carrot, and 1 large bell pepper, all chopped, for the beef and pork. Increase the oil to 3 tablespoons and sauté the vegetables until they begin to soften, then add the tomatoes and parsley and simmer until the vegetables are tender, 5 to 10 minutes. For a vegetarian sandwich, use the cheeses as described in the main recipe; for a vegan sandwich, spread the sauce on both sides of the bread before the final broiling, and garnish the subs with ½ cup chopped almonds, hazelnuts, or pecans.

Soups

'm about to debunk any notion that soups are time consuming. All of the recipes in this chapter are foolproof and fast: You chop up some ingredients, maybe get them cooking in oil, pour liquid over everything, crank up the heat, and suddenly you have a pot of soup going. One that you'll be eating in 30 minutes or less.

Soups give you plenty of leeway and put you in complete control of pacing. If you need more time to get other food ready, simmer slowly or even stop the cooking. If you're in a hurry, cook steadily. Whatever's in the pot will wait for you. And unlike cooking a perfect steak, the fate of the dish doesn't hinge on a few key minutes.

For that flexibility you can thank what I call "the time–texture continuum." You decide how long your soup will cook based on how much of a hurry you're in and how tender (or not) you like your vegetables. As vegetables release starch and break down during cooking, the soup thickens and develops more flavor. Sometimes it's worth an extra 10, 20, 30 minutes for a richer texture and deeper flavor; other times you may not care.

Melon Gazpacho with Crisp Prosciutto

I'm not kidding when I say gazpacho works well with almost every juicy fruit. You can replace the melon in the main recipe with tomato or tomatillo for something more familiar. But also consider substitutions like citrus, berries, or plums. A little heft on top makes this more of a meal; fried bread crumbs, crumbled chickpeas, and chopped nuts are vegan options. My trick to quick chilling: ice cubes. If you want the soup colder and have a little time, pop it in the freezer for 10 or 15 minutes before serving. **Serves 4**

Ingredients

5 tablespoons olive oil, plus more for drizzling

4 ounces sliced prosciutto

1 clove garlic

Any large melon (like honeydew) or small seedless watermelon (2 pounds)

3 large or 4 medium ripe tomatoes (about 1 pound)

1 bunch fresh basil

2 tablespoons sherry vinegar, or to taste

Salt and pepper

Ice cubes

Prep · Cook

1. Put 1 tablespoon olive oil in a medium skillet over medium-low heat.

   ☐ Chop the prosciutto into smaller-than-bite-sized pieces.

2. When the oil is warm, add the prosciutto to the skillet and cook, stirring occasionally, until crisp, 5 to 10 minutes.

   ☐ Line a plate with towels.

   ☐ Peel 1 clove garlic and put it in a food processor or blender. Pulse once or twice to chop.

   ☐ Halve the melon, remove any seeds, and scoop the flesh into the food processor or blender.

   ☐ Core and quarter the tomatoes.

   ☐ Chop ½ cup basil leaves.

3. When the prosciutto is crisp, transfer it to the towels.

4. Add the tomatoes to the food processor along with 2 tablespoons sherry vinegar, 4 tablespoons olive oil, and a sprinkle of salt and pepper.

5. Let the machine run if you want a smooth gazpacho, or pulse if you want it chunky, scraping down the sides if necessary and adding ice cubes one at a time until you get the consistency you like. Taste and adjust the seasoning. Serve garnished with the prosciutto, basil, and a drizzle of olive oil.

Spicy Black Bean Soup

With canned or home-cooked beans from the fridge or freezer (page 505), you can make a bold-flavored black bean soup in 15 minutes. and. No need to drain home-cooked beans; include some of their cooking liquid and adjust the amount of stock or water to compensate. Ditto for soup based on other kinds of beans, of course. **Serves 4**

Ingredients

3 tablespoons olive oil

1 large onion

2 cloves garlic

1 or more chipotle chiles in adobo (to taste)

3½ cups cooked or canned black beans (two 15-ounce cans)

1 tablespoon ground cumin

4 cups chicken or vegetable stock or water

Salt and pepper

1 lime

Several sprigs fresh cilantro for garnish

Sour cream for garnish

□ Prep · Cook

1. Put 3 tablespoons olive oil in a large pot over medium heat.

   □ Trim, peel, and chop the onion.

2. Add the onion to the oil and cook, stirring occasionally, until softened, 3 to 5 minutes.

   □ Peel and mince 2 cloves garlic; add them to the pot and stir.

   □ Chop 1 or more chipotle chiles.

   □ If you're using canned beans, rinse and drain them.

3. Add the chipotle chiles with a little of the adobo, 1 tablespoon ground cumin, the beans, 4 cups stock or water (including bean-cooking liquid if you have some), and a sprinkle of salt and pepper to the pot and stir. Bring the soup to a boil, then turn the heat down to medium-low, cover, and simmer until the beans begin to break down, 5 to 10 minutes.

   □ Halve the lime.

   □ Chop several sprigs cilantro.

4. When the beans begin to break down, remove the pot from the heat. Run a potato masher or immersion blender through the soup, just enough to mash or purée about half of the beans.

5. Squeeze in the lime juice. Taste and adjust the seasoning. Serve garnished with the cilantro and a dollop of sour cream.

Bacon and Egg Drop Soup

Any way you make them, naturally fast-cooking eggs are always welcome in soup. With this technique—used both for the classic Chinese restaurant soup and Italian stracciatella soup—you magically get gorgeous flowerlike petals in every bite (see Cracking Eggs into Soup, page 126). Also try the nontraditional flavors in the variations. **Serves 4**

Ingredients

8 slices bacon

6 cups any stock

Salt and pepper

4 eggs

2 scallions

Sesame oil for drizzling

Soy sauce for serving

□ Prep · Cook

1. Put a large pot over medium heat.

   □ Chop the bacon into 1-inch pieces.

2. Add the bacon to the pot. Cook, stirring occasionally, until crisp, 5 to 10 minutes.

   □ Line a plate with towels.

3. Transfer the bacon to the towels with a slotted spoon and pour off all but 2 tablespoons of the fat.

4. Put 6 cups stock in the pot and bring to a boil. Add a sprinkle of salt (if you think the stock needs it) and pepper and lower the heat so the stock bubbles gently but steadily.

   □ Crack the eggs into a liquid measuring cup or medium pitcher and beat them lightly.

   □ Slice the scallions thinly on a diagonal.

5. While the stock is bubbling gently, slowly pour in the eggs, stirring constantly, so that they cook softly and appear as silky flowerlike strands; don't let them overheat and curdle. Remove from the heat; taste and adjust the seasoning.

6. To serve, top each bowl with some bacon and a few drops of sesame oil, garnish with the scallions, and pass the soy sauce at the table.

• recipe continues →

Variations

Bacon and Egg Drop Soup with Greens. Chop 1 head bok choy or 1 bunch mustard greens. Before adding the eggs in Step 5, stir in the greens and let them cook while the stock returns to a gentle bubble, then stir in the eggs and finish the soup.

Toast, Bacon, and Egg Drop Soup. The flavors of breakfast in a bowl. Instead of the sesame oil and soy sauce, have some good-quality store-bought or homemade salsa (page 480) handy. While the bacon cooks in Step 2, toast 4 thick slices bread (any kind). Put a slice of toast in each bowl before adding the soup, then garnish with the scallions and a spoonful of salsa.

Carbonara Soup. Omit the sesame oil and soy sauce. Instead of the scallions, chop several fresh parsley sprigs. Two or 3 cups leftover plain or lightly sauced pasta is perfect here and saves a little time; add it to the stock in Step 5 after the eggs cook, but before you take the soup off the heat. If you don't have any handy, boil 12 ounces any pasta in salted water until tender but not mushy, 8 to 12 minutes; start the recipe while it cooks. Use pancetta instead of bacon. Drain the pasta, reserving the cooking water for the soup if you don't have stock. When you stir in the eggs, add 1 cup grated Parmesan cheese (4 ounces). Serve garnished with the parsley.

CRACKING EGGS INTO SOUP

It's easy to get that "flower petal" wispy egg-drop texture in your soup. And even if you don't, the soup will still be delicious. For wisps, the temperature of the liquid needs to remain consistent even as you add the cool eggs. So adjust the heat to maintain a steady but gentle bubble, and add the eggs in a slow, steady stream, using a container with a pour spout. Too fast and they will drop the temperature of the liquid and simply thicken the soup without forming strands; too hot and they'll curdle like scrambled eggs. Any way, you win; it just won't be as beautiful.

Frozen Vegetable Soup

Almost all frozen vegetables are minimally processed and flash-frozen right after harvest, without any additions. Many are grown in the United States. They're a gift to hurried cooks, and this recipe coaxes out every bit of flavor from virtually any vegetable. For ideas to make this more of a meal, see the second variation. And a hearty loaf of whole grain bread on the side is always welcome. **Serves 4**

Ingredients

3 tablespoons olive oil, plus more for drizzling

1 large onion

Salt and pepper

2 cloves garlic

6 cups any chopped frozen vegetables, including beans (1½ to 2 pounds)

Several sprigs fresh thyme

2 bay leaves

1 (15-ounce) can diced tomatoes

4 cups chicken or vegetable stock or water

Prep · Cook

1. Put 3 tablespoons olive oil in a large pot over medium-high heat.

   - Trim, peel, and chop the onion; add it to the pot, sprinkle with salt and pepper, and stir.

   - Peel and chop 2 cloves garlic; add them to the pot and stir.

2. Cook, stirring occasionally, until the onion softens, 3 to 5 minutes.

   - Organize the packages of vegetables on your counter from the firmest, longest cooking—like squash or shell beans—to the most tender, quickest cooking, like spinach and other greens.

3. When the onion mixture is soft, start adding the vegetables, firmest first, stirring occasionally until they thaw and begin to get tender. (Timing will depend on the vegetable; keep an eye on the pot and test frequently.)

4. Continue adding and stirring, adjusting the heat to prevent burning, until the vegetables in the pot begin to brown in places and become almost as soft as you like.

   - Tie the thyme sprigs and bay leaves securely with a piece of kitchen twine to make a bouquet garni. (If you don't have any twine, just continue.)

5. Add the canned tomatoes and their juice with the 4 cups stock or water, bring the soup to a boil, then lower the heat so it bubbles steadily but gently. Add the bouquet garni (or loose herb sprigs and bay leaves) and

recipe continues →

cook, stirring once or twice, until the vegetables are fully tender and the broth darkens, between 10 and 20 minutes (or even more) depending on how tender you want the vegetables and how much time you have.

6. Taste and adjust the seasoning. Fish out the bouquet garni (or the thyme sprigs and bay leaves). Serve drizzled with more olive oil.

Variations

Creamy Frozen Vegetable Soup. When the soup is ready, turn off the heat and purée it, using an immersion blender or carefully working in batches in an upright blender so it's never filled more than halfway. Add 1 cup cream if you like and reheat before serving.

Hearty Frozen Vegetable Soup. More substantial and won't take more time if you have any ingredients like bits of leftover braises and stews parked in the fridge. When the soup is ready, add chopped roasted or grilled chicken or other meat or fish; canned or cooked beans (page 505); any cooked rice or grain (page 496); or buttered egg noodles (page 493). Then cook long enough to just heat through before serving.

Frozen and Fresh Vegetable Soup. If you've got time to trim and chop any fresh vegetables, go for it, substituting them for part of the 6 cups total volume (or weight) in the ingredient list. The same technique will work perfectly. Trim and chop whatever vegetables you'd like, then organize and cook them as described.

6 Ways to Flavor Frozen Vegetable Soup

1. 1 tablespoon chili powder (add with the onion and garlic)
2. The zest of 1 lemon or lime (add with the onion and garlic)
3. 1 large (28-ounce) can whole peeled or diced tomatoes (add with the first vegetables; reduce the stock to 4 cups)
4. 1 tablespoon chopped fresh rosemary, sage, thyme, or oregano (add with the last vegetables)
5. 1 cup any grated or crumbled cheese (for garnish)
6. ¼ cup chopped fresh parsley, basil, cilantro, or dill (for garnish)

Tomato Soup with Fennel

Fennel, olives, rosemary, and orange zest are four Provençal ingredients with punch. They may be used alone or combined, frequently with tomatoes. You can make the soup even more substantial by adding seafood; see the variations that follow. **Serves 4**

Ingredients

3 tablespoons olive oil, plus more for garnish

1 large onion

2 cloves garlic

Salt and pepper

2 medium fennel bulbs (1 pound)

⅔ cup any olives

2 sprigs fresh rosemary

1 orange

1 tablespoon tomato paste

1 large (28-ounce) can diced tomatoes

4 cups vegetable or chicken stock or water

▢ Prep · Cook

1. Put 3 tablespoons olive oil in a large pot over low heat.

   ▢ Trim, peel, and chop the onion; add to the pot.

   ▢ Peel and mince 2 cloves garlic; add to the pot. Sprinkle with salt and pepper.

2. When the onion and garlic start to sizzle, raise the heat to medium and cook, stirring occasionally, until they begin to soften and color, 5 to 10 minutes.

   ▢ Trim and chop the fennel bulbs, saving a few of the fronds for garnish.

3. Add the fennel to the pot and cook, stirring occasionally until the fennel begins to soften, 3 to 5 minutes.

   ▢ Pit ⅔ cup olives if necessary; chop them up a bit.

   ▢ Strip the leaves from 2 rosemary sprigs, and chop.

   ▢ Grate 1 tablespoon zest from the orange; squeeze the juice into a small bowl through a strainer or your fingers to capture the seeds; then add the zest.

4. Add 1 tablespoon tomato paste to the pot and cook, stirring constantly until it darkens slightly, a minute or two.

5. Add the olives, rosemary, and orange juice and zest and cook, stirring until fragrant, less than a minute.

6. Add the tomatoes and their juice and scrape any browned bits off the bottom of the pot. Add 4 cups stock or water and raise the heat to high.

● recipe continues →

7. When the soup comes to a boil, adjust the heat so it bubbles gently but steadily and cook, stirring once in a while until the tomatoes break down, 5 to 10 minutes.

   ☐ Chop the reserved fennel fronds.

8. Taste and adjust the seasoning. To serve, drizzle with more olive oil and garnish with the fennel fronds.

Variations

Tomato Soup with Fennel and Shrimp. In Step 7, after the tomatoes break down, add 1 pound peeled shrimp to the soup. Cook, stirring constantly, until the shrimp turn pink and are just cooked through, 2 to 5 minutes, depending on whether or not it was frozen. Garnish and serve right away.

Tomato Soup with Fennel and Fish. One pound of any 1-inch-thick, sturdy white fish fillets—like bass, catfish, or halibut—will work. In Step 7, after about 5 minutes of cooking, lay the fish on top of the soup and cover the pot. Cook undisturbed until the fillets flake easily with a fork but are still a little soft, 3 to 5 minutes. Stir the fish into the soup; garnish and serve.

Tomato Soup with Fennel and Squid. While the soup is cooking in Step 7, rinse 1 pound squid (frozen is fine); if necessary, cut the bodies crosswise into rings, and cut the tentacles free. In Step 7 after the tomatoes break down, add the squid to the pot. Cook, stirring constantly, until the rings and tentacles turn white and are just cooked through, 2 to 5 minutes, depending on if they were still frozen. Garnish and serve.

Creamy Creamless Mushroom Soup with Parsley Pesto

This vegetable soup serves as a model for many others: Sliced mushrooms soften quickly in the main recipe; ditto asparagus in the first variation. The next two options provide techniques for softening moderately firm and sturdy vegetables enough to purée in relatively short order. You can always add a splash of cream to any of these, of course, but with the pesto—a slightly chunky sauce that comes together while the soup cooks—it's not necessary. If you don't have a blender or want to save time, smush the vegetables with a potato masher a few times just before serving. **Serves 4**

Ingredients

2 tablespoons butter

1 medium onion

1½ pounds cremini mushrooms

Salt and pepper

6 cups vegetable or chicken stock or water

1 bunch fresh parsley

1 clove garlic

⅓ cup chopped walnuts

3 tablespoons olive oil

▢ Prep · Cook

1. Put 2 tablespoons butter in a large pot over medium-low heat.

   ▢ Trim, peel, and chop the onion.

2. When the butter starts to foam, add the onion and cook, stirring occasionally until it softens and becomes translucent, about 10 minutes.

   ▢ Trim, rinse, and slice the mushrooms.

3. Raise the heat to medium-high. Add the mushrooms and a sprinkle of salt and pepper, and stir constantly until they start to shrivel and release liquid, a minute or two. Add 6 cups stock or water. Bring to a boil, then reduce the heat so that it bubbles gently but steadily; cook until the mushrooms are tender, 5 to 10 minutes.

   ▢ Chop 1 cup parsley leaves.

   ▢ Peel and mince 1 clove garlic.

   ▢ Chop ⅓ cup walnuts into smaller pieces.

4. Combine the parsley, garlic, walnuts, 3 tablespoons olive oil, and a sprinkle of salt and pepper in a small mixing bowl. Mash and stir with a fork against the sides of the bowl until the pesto becomes a loose paste.

5. Turn off the heat under the soup and run an immersion blender through the soup or, carefully working in batches, transfer it to an upright blender so it's never filled more than halfway and purée. Reheat the soup for 1 to 2 minutes if necessary. Taste and adjust the seasoning. Serve with the pesto spooned on the top.

Variations

Creamy Creamless Asparagus Soup with Mint Pesto. Radiant green. Use asparagus, cut into 1-inch pieces, instead of the mushrooms, and mint instead of the parsley.

Creamy Creamless Butternut Soup with Chive Pesto. Winter squash takes a tad longer than mushrooms or asparagus, but this is still a fast soup. Substitute butternut squash—or any winter squash—for the mushrooms and chives for half the parsley. Trim and peel the squash and scoop the seeds out with a spoon. Chop the flesh into chunks no bigger than 1 inch. Double the cooking time in Step 3.

Creamy Creamless Root Soup with Parsley Pesto. Carrots, parsnips, celery root, turnips, and sweet potatoes or potatoes (tubers, but same idea). Grating is the trick. With the investment of a few minutes prep, you'll save at least 20 minutes in the pot (the time it would take for chunks to get tender). Before Step 3, trim and peel the vegetables. Shred them in a food processor with a grating disk.

PEELING BUTTERNUT SQUASH

Peeling butternut and other winter squashes can be time consuming. Two ways to do it: Cut the squash to create flat sides so you can work downward with a chef's or paring knife to slice the skin from the flesh, turning the piece as you work, then trim off the ends. Or if you've got a sharp and sturdy vegetable peeler, remove the skin from a whole butternut squash, working from top to bottom. The top half of the squash should be solid meat; cut apart the top and bulbous bottom half, split the bottom, scoop out the seeds, and you're done.

Red Lentil Soup with Apples

The fastest bean soup from scratch, with the added bonus of some sweetness and spice. The variations take the lentils in totally different directions. **Serves 4**

Ingredients

1 cup red lentils

1 small onion

6 cups vegetable stock or water

2 large apples

1 teaspoon ground allspice

½ teaspoon ground ginger

Salt and pepper

3 tablespoons butter

▢ Prep · Cook

▢ Rinse and toss the lentils in a strainer under cold water, discarding any that look discolored.

▢ Trim, peel, and chop the onion.

1. Put the lentils and onion in a large pot with 6 cups stock or water. Bring to a boil.

   ▢ Peel, quarter, and core the apples; chop them into bite-sized pieces and add them to the pot.

2. When the soup comes to a boil, adjust the heat so it bubbles steadily but gently. Add 1 teaspoon ground allspice, ½ teaspoon ground ginger, and a sprinkle of salt and pepper. Cover and cook, stirring once in a while, until the lentils and apples are quite soft, 15 to 20 minutes. Stir in the butter, taste, and adjust the seasoning, then serve.

Variations

Curried Red Lentil Soup with Cauliflower. Instead of the apples, use 1 small head cauliflower (about 1 pound). Before starting the recipe, core it then chop the whole head into pea-sized pieces; add it to the pot with the lentils in Step 1. Use 1 tablespoon curry powder instead of the ground allspice and ginger. Garnish with yogurt if you like.

Red Lentil Soup with Rhubarb. Instead of the apples, chop 3 large rhubarb ribs. Substitute 1 teaspoon cinnamon for the ground allspice and keep the ½ teaspoon ground ginger. Garnish with chopped pistachios if you like.

Red Lentil Soup with Chard. Instead of the apples, chop 1 bunch any color chard, ribs and all. Substitute ¼ teaspoon ground nutmeg for the ground allspice and ginger. Garnish with chopped hazelnuts if you like.

Tomato and Bread Soup with White Beans

Pour garlicky tomato broth over toasted bread and watch it become hearty soup. Add a few drops of olive oil, and you've got something truly delicious with a distinctive, satisfying texture. I add body with beans too. Just because. There are even more vegetable options in the variations. **Serves 4**

Ingredients

2 tablespoons olive oil, plus more for drizzling

1 large onion

4 cloves garlic

Salt and pepper

1 large carrot

4 or 5 large ripe tomatoes (1½ pounds), or 1 large (28-ounce) can whole peeled tomatoes

2 tablespoons tomato paste

4 sprigs fresh thyme or 1 teaspoon dried

4 thick slices any rustic bread

1¾ cups cooked or canned white beans (one 15-ounce can)

3 cups vegetable or beef stock or water

Several sprigs fresh basil

▢ Prep · **Cook**

1. Put 2 tablespoons olive oil in a large pot over medium heat.

   ▢ Trim, peel, and chop the onion.

   ▢ Crush 4 cloves garlic on a cutting board with the flat side of a knife; peel them.

2. When the oil is hot, add the onion and garlic and a sprinkle of salt and pepper. Cook, stirring occasionally, until the onion softens, 3 to 5 minutes.

   ▢ Trim, peel, and chop the carrot; add it to the pot and stir.

   ▢ If you're using fresh tomatoes, core and chop them. Or break up the canned tomatoes with your hands.

3. Turn the broiler to high; put the rack 4 inches from the heat.

4. When the onion and carrot are soft, add 2 tablespoons tomato paste and cook, stirring until it darkens a bit, 1 to 2 minutes. Add the tomatoes (include the juice from the can) and cook, stirring occasionally, until they thicken into a chunky sauce, 10 to 15 minutes.

   ▢ If you're using fresh thyme, strip the leaves from 4 sprigs and chop.

   ▢ Put 4 slices bread on a rimmed baking sheet and drizzle each with a little olive oil.

5. Broil the bread, turning once until toasted on both sides, 2 to 5 minutes total. Add the fresh thyme or 1 teaspoon dried to the pot and stir.

   ▢ If you're using canned beans, rinse and drain them.

   ▢ Tear the toasted bread into bite-sized pieces and put in the bottom of 4 soup bowls.

6. Add 3 cups stock or water to the pot along with the beans. Adjust the heat so the soup bubbles gently but steadily; cook, stirring occasionally and adding a little liquid if necessary, until it heats through, another 3 minutes.

   ☐ Strip the leaves from several basil sprigs and chop.

7. Taste and adjust the seasoning. Pour the soup over the bread. Garnish with the basil, drizzle with olive oil, and serve.

Variations

Tomato and Bread Soup with Eggplant. In Step 1, add 3 tablespoons olive oil to the pot. Cut 1 large or 3 small eggplants into 1-inch chunks. Add them with the onion and garlic in Step 2; cook until they begin to soften, 5 to 10 minutes, and proceed.

Tomato and Bread Soup with Zucchini. Trim, then cut 2 medium zucchini into 1-inch chunks. Add them with the tomatoes in Step 4.

Tomato and Bread Soup with Arugula. Add about 5 ounces arugula (if the leaves are large, tear them) with the stock in Step 6.

Pasta e Fagioli

This quick take on the Italian classic is stew-like, thick with vegetables, beans, and pasta in every bite. You can omit the parsley, but don't skimp on the Parmesan or olive oil. If you've got leftover pasta or noodles in the fridge, go ahead and use them, even if they're lightly sauced in a flavor-compatible way. Figure 2 to 3 cups cooked pasta and then reduce the stock or water to 4 cups. **Serves 4**

Ingredients

3 tablespoons olive oil, plus more for drizzling

1 medium onion

2 medium carrots

2 celery stalks

Salt and pepper

2 cloves garlic

1¾ cups cooked or canned cannellini or pinto beans (one 15-ounce can)

2 sprigs fresh rosemary

1 (15-ounce) can whole peeled tomatoes

6 cups chicken or vegetable stock or water

1 cup tiny cut pasta (like ditalini or orzo)

1 bunch fresh parsley

4 ounces Parmesan cheese (1 cup grated)

▢ Prep · Cook

1. Put 3 tablespoons olive oil in a large pot over low heat.

   ▢ Trim, peel, and chop the onion; add it to the pot.

   ▢ Trim and peel the carrots.

   ▢ Trim 2 celery stalks.

   ▢ Chop the carrots and celery, add them to the pot, and stir.

2. Raise the heat to medium-high. When the vegetables start sizzling after a minute or so, sprinkle with salt and pepper. Cook, stirring occasionally, until they soften and begin to brown, 3 to 5 minutes.

   ▢ Peel and chop 2 cloves garlic; add to the pot and stir.

   ▢ If you're using canned beans, rinse and drain them.

3. When the vegetables are soft, add 2 sprigs rosemary to the pot. Stir until fragrant, less than 1 minute. Add the tomatoes and their juice, breaking them up with a spoon and scraping any browned bits off the bottom of the pot. Add 6 cups stock or water and raise the heat to high.

4. When the soup comes to a boil, stir in the beans and 1 cup pasta. Return the mixture to a boil; adjust the heat so it bubbles steadily. Start tasting the pasta after 5 minutes; it should be tender but not mushy. If the pot starts to look dry, add water a little at a time.

   ▢ Chop ½ cup parsley leaves.

   ▢ Grate 1 cup Parmesan cheese.

5. When the pasta is tender, turn off the heat. Fish out the rosemary sprigs and discard. Taste and adjust the seasoning. To serve, garnish each serving with 2 tablespoons parsley, ¼ cup Parmesan, and a drizzle of olive oil.

Chickpea and Couscous Stew with Carrots and Warm Spices

When you cook pasta or grains into soup, they release starch and work as a thickener, leaving you with the satisfying texture of a stew-like porridge. A chunk of the time here is unattended cooking, so once you get things going, there's an opportunity to set the table or get a jump on the dishes. **Serves 4**

Ingredients

¼ cup olive oil

1 large onion

1 teaspoon ground cumin

1 teaspoon ground coriander

1 teaspoon ground cinnamon

2 or 3 large carrots (about 1 pound)

Salt and pepper

1¾ cups cooked or canned chickpeas (one 15-ounce can)

2 cloves garlic

1 tablespoon tomato paste

1 large (28-ounce) can whole peeled tomatoes

4 cups vegetable or chicken stock or water

1 lemon

1 bunch fresh mint

½ cup couscous

☐ Prep · Cook

1. Put ¼ cup olive oil in a large pot over medium heat.

   ☐ Trim, peel, and chop the onion.

2. Add 1 teaspoon ground cumin, 1 teaspoon ground coriander, and 1 teaspoon ground cinnamon to the pot; cook, stirring until dark and fragrant, about 1 minute.

3. Add the onion to the pot and cook, stirring occasionally, until it begins to soften, 3 to 5 minutes.

   ☐ Trim, peel, and chop the carrots; add them to the pot and stir.

4. Raise the heat to medium-high. When the vegetables start sizzling, sprinkle with salt and pepper and cook, stirring occasionally, until they soften and begin to brown, 5 to 10 minutes.

   ☐ If you're using canned chickpeas, rinse and drain them.

   ☐ Peel and chop 2 cloves garlic; add them to the pot and stir.

5. Add 1 tablespoon tomato paste and cook, stirring until it darkens slightly, a minute or two. Stir in the chickpeas. Add the tomatoes and their juice, breaking them up with a spoon and scraping any browned bits off the bottom of the pot. Add 4 cups stock or water and raise the heat to high.

   ☐ Grate the zest of the lemon; refrigerate the fruit for another use.

   ☐ Chop 1 cup mint leaves.

6. When the stew begins to boil, lower the heat so it bubbles gently. Stir in ½ cup couscous; cover and turn off the heat. After 5 minutes, stir in the lemon zest and mint. Taste and adjust the seasoning, and serve.

Variations

Chickpea and Couscous Soup with Cauliflower and Warm Spices. Instead of the carrots, add 1 small head cauliflower, trimmed and chopped, to the stew with the tomatoes and stock in Step 5. After reducing the heat in Step 6, cook, stirring occasionally, until the cauliflower is almost as tender as you like it, 5 to 10 minutes. Then add the couscous and proceed with the recipe.

Chickpea and Bulgur Soup with Cabbage and Warm Spices. Substitute 1 small head green cabbage, chopped, for the carrots and fine- or medium-grind bulgur for the couscous. Or try another sturdy green like collards, kale, or mustard.

White Bean and Couscous (or Bulgur) Soup with Broccoli and Oregano. Broccolini or broccoli rabe also work well here; whichever you choose, wait to add it until you stir in the tomatoes in Step 5. Instead of the ground cumin, coriander, and cinnamon, use 2 tablespoons chopped fresh oregano or 2 teaspoons dried in Step 2. Use either couscous or fine- or medium-grind bulgur for the grain.

Clam (or Mussel) Chowder

Since seafood brings the briny character of the ocean to the pot—and there are lots of vegetables here too—all you need is water, not stock, to make this soup. Fish or chicken stock will change the flavor to be less like the ocean; that may be what you want. For a more elegant presentation, fish the clams or mussels out of the pot before serving, discard the shells, and return the seafood to the chowder. **Serves 4**

Ingredients

2 tablespoons butter

4 sprigs fresh thyme or 2 teaspoons dried

Salt

2 large or 3 small russet or Yukon Gold potatoes

1 large leek

1 large carrot

2 celery stalks

2 cloves garlic

3 pounds littleneck or other hard-shell clams, or 2 pounds mussels

1 cup cream or milk

Pepper (optional)

Prep · Cook

1. Put 5 cups water and 2 tablespoons butter in a large pot over medium-high heat. Add 4 sprigs fresh thyme or 2 teaspoons dried, and sprinkle with salt.

   - Scrub the potatoes; peel them if you like. Cut them into small chunks and add them to the pot.

   - Trim the leek and slice the white and light green parts only. Rinse thoroughly in a colander under cold water, drain well, and add it to the pot.

   - Trim and peel the carrot; trim the celery. Cut them into small chunks and add them to the pot along with the leek.

   - Peel and slice 2 cloves garlic and add to the pot.

2. When the liquid comes to a boil, adjust the heat so it bubbles gently but steadily. Cook, stirring occasionally, until the potatoes are fork-tender but not yet breaking apart, 10 to 15 minutes.

   - Scrub the clams or scrub and debeard the mussels; discard any that don't close when you tap them.

3. When the potatoes are tender, add the clams or mussels to the chowder. Pour in 1 cup cream or milk. Adjust the heat so the liquid bubbles gently but steadily. Cover and cook just until the clams or mussels open, 3 to 5 minutes.

4. When the shellfish have opened, stir the pot gently to combine everything. (You can discard those that remain tightly closed or gently pry them open with a butter knife to see if they release easily and look and smell normal.) Taste and adjust the seasoning, adding a sprinkle of pepper if you'd like. Fish out and discard the thyme sprigs if you used them. Serve right away, with extra bowls on the table for the empty shells.

• recipe continues →

Variations

Fish Chowder. Instead of the clams or mussels, use 1 pound thick white fish fillets, like cod or halibut. Remove any bones, but leave the fillets intact when you nestle them in the chowder in Step 3. They'll take about the same amount of time to cook until they just begin to flake. Be careful not to overcook.

Shrimp Chowder. Instead of the clams, use 1 pound medium or large peeled shrimp, thawed and cut into bite-sized chunks. They'll cook in 1 to 2 minutes, so don't wander off.

Corn and Cheddar Chowder. Summer special. Instead of the clams or mussels, use 2 cups corn kernels (frozen is fine, but freshly cut from the cob is much better). When you add the cream in Step 3, also stir in 1 cup grated cheddar cheese, the sharper the better.

Miso Soup with Scallops, Soba, and Spinach

Japanese stock, dashi, is a real change from chicken or vegetable broth, and since the main ingredients are sea greens and bonito flakes—a type of dried fish that you can find now in many supermarkets—it's as simple as steeping tea. (See the recipe variation on page 490 to make just seaweed stock.) It's easy to do while you assemble the soup and worth using an extra pot. Feel free to vary the vegetables based on whatever you like and have handy. **Serves 4**

Ingredients

1 large piece dried kelp
(kombu; 4 to 6 inches long)

Salt

1 bunch spinach (1 pound)

8 ounces sea scallops

½ cup dried bonito flakes

8 ounces soba noodles

⅓ cup any miso

Pinch of five-spice or black pepper

□ Prep · Cook

1. Put the dried kelp and 8 cups water in a large pot over medium heat. Bring another large pot of water to boil; salt it.

   □ Trim off any thick stems from the spinach and chop the leaves.

   □ Cut each scallop crosswise into 2 or 3 thin rounds.

2. When the water with the kelp just starts to bubble, turn off the heat, remove the kelp (you can save it for stir-fries if you want), and stir in ½ cup bonito flakes. (The broth is the dashi.)

3. When the pot of salted water comes to a boil, add 8 ounces soba noodles. Cook, stirring occasionally, until the noodles are barely tender, 3 to 5 minutes.

4. When the noodles are ready, drain them and rinse under warm water, then return them to the pot. Add the spinach and put the raw scallop slices on top.

5. Strain all but 1 cup of the dashi into the pot with the noodles and cover. Return the pot to high heat. Cook undisturbed until it just starts to bubble, the scallops are barely opaque at the center, and the spinach is tender, 3 to 5 minutes.

   □ Strain the remaining dashi into a small bowl. Add ⅓ cup miso and whisk until smooth.

6. When the soup is ready, turn off the heat and stir the miso mixture into the pot.

7. Taste and add more salt if necessary. Serve with a sprinkle of five-spice or pepper over the top.

• recipe continues →

Variations

Miso Soup with Shrimp, Soba, and Spinach. Substitute thawed peeled shrimp for the scallops. Chop them into bite-sized pieces or—slightly fancier—slice them in half lengthwise into crescents.

Miso Soup with Tofu, Soba, and Bok Choy. Substitute one 12-ounce brick firm silken tofu for the scallops and bok choy (include the stems) for the spinach. When you stir in the miso mixture, break the tofu into big, irregular pieces with a large spoon.

Miso Soup with Chicken, Udon, and Snow Peas. Quite substantial. Use 1 medium boneless, skinless chicken breast (8 ounces), thinly sliced, instead of the scallops and snow peas instead of the spinach. Substitute udon for the soba; they will take a minute or two longer to become tender in Step 3.

MISO

Keeping a tub of miso in the fridge should be a habit. This fermented soybean paste adds tremendous flavor to soups, sauces, rubs, and marinades. It's easy to use and keeps forever. Always buy miso in paste form, not powdered or instant. You'll find it at many supermarkets and always at Japanese or Asian markets. The darker the miso, the more assertive the taste. White and yellow varieties are mild with a touch of sweetness (that's what I usually use for miso soup); red, brown, and black misos all taste a bit stronger, more tangy from the fermentation. You use them all the same way.

Chicken Soup with Ramen Noodles

Whether you use some kind of dried noodles or take the quick-cooking noodles from packaged ramen soup, the best bowl of chicken soup requires homemade broth and a bunch of fresh ingredients. The results here are way better than depending on the seasoning blend that comes in the package of ramen but still a fast and convenient dinner. **Serves 4**

Ingredients

3 or 4 boneless, skinless chicken thighs (about 12 ounces)

1 inch fresh ginger

3 tablespoons vegetable oil

Salt

¼ teaspoon red chile flakes

3 tablespoons soy sauce

3 cloves garlic

6 scallions

8 ounces ramen or somen noodles or 4 packages ramen soup

4 eggs

1 teaspoon sesame oil

Prep · Cook

☐ Thinly slice the chicken thighs.   ☐ Peel and mince 1 inch ginger.

1. Put 2 tablespoons vegetable oil in a large pot over medium-high heat. When it's hot, add the chicken and ginger and cook undisturbed until the chicken pieces brown and release easily from the pot, about 3 minutes. Sprinkle with a little salt and ¼ teaspoon red chile flakes.

2. Add 8 cups water and 3 tablespoons soy sauce and stir to scrape up any browned bits from the bottom of the pot.

    ☐ Peel and thinly slice 3 cloves garlic.

    ☐ Trim and chop the scallions, keeping the white and green parts separate.

3. When the soup comes to a boil, add the garlic and the white parts of the scallions. Adjust the heat so the broth bubbles steadily and cook, stirring once or twice, until the chicken is cooked through, 1 or 2 minutes.

4. Put a large skillet over medium-high heat for 1 minute. Add the noodles to the soup pot (discard the seasoning packets if there are any); break them apart with a fork if necessary and adjust the heat so the broth keeps bubbling gently. Cook, stirring occasionally, until just tender, 2 to 5 minutes, depending on the noodle.

5. Add 1 tablespoon vegetable oil to the skillet and swirl it to coat the bottom. Crack the eggs into the pan and turn the heat to low. Cover the pan and cook undisturbed until the whites are just set and the yolks are still runny, 3 or 4 minutes. Turn off the heat.

6. When the noodles and chicken are done, taste the broth and adjust the seasoning. Top each serving with a fried egg, a few drops of sesame oil, and some scallion greens.

• recipe continues →

Variations

Zucchini Soup with Ramen Noodles. Instead of the chicken, use 1½ pounds zucchini or any summer squash you like. Shred it on the large holes of a box grater or in the food processor with the grating disk (the bits of vegetable will melt into the broth). Cook it in the fat in Step 1, stirring occasionally, until the zucchini is almost dry (about the same amount of time as the chicken would take) before proceeding.

Sardine (or Mackerel) Soup with Ramen Noodles. With either of these canned fish comes big flavor. Instead of the chicken, use 2 cans sardines or mackerel (about 4 ounces each; for this purpose, water-packed is best). In Step 1 cook only the ginger in the oil; add the liquid from the canned fish to the pot. Wait to add the fish until after the noodles are cooked in Step 4. Then carefully lower the fish to the hot broth to heat before serving.

Beef Jerky Soup with Ramen Noodles. Instead of the chicken, use 4 ounces beef jerky. Snip it into thin strips with kitchen scissors; wait to add it until you add the water in Step 2. Cook until it softens, 3 to 5 minutes, then proceed.

Peanut Soup with Chicken and Collards

This West African–inspired soup demonstrates how easy it is to make peanuts and collards taste fantastic. And even though many traditional collard recipes call for long cooking, the greens are also delicious when cooked quickly, as they are here. **Serves 4**

Ingredients

2 tablespoons vegetable oil

4 to 6 boneless, skinless chicken thighs (about 1 pound)

1 large red onion

2 cloves garlic

1 inch fresh ginger

1 fresh hot green chile (like jalapeño)

1 cup peanut butter

1 tablespoon tomato paste

6 cups chicken or vegetable stock or water

Salt and pepper

1 small bunch collard greens (8 ounces)

¼ cup roasted peanuts

▢ Prep · **Cook**

1. Put 2 tablespoons vegetable oil in a large pot over medium-high heat.

   ▢ Cut the chicken into bite-sized chunks.

2. When the oil is hot, add the chicken and cook undisturbed until the pieces brown and release easily, 2 or 3 minutes. Continue cooking, stirring occasionally, until the meat is no longer pink, 2 to 3 minutes more.

   ▢ Trim, peel, halve, and slice the onion.

   ▢ Peel and chop 2 cloves garlic and 1 inch ginger.

   ▢ Trim the chile, remove the seeds if you like, and mince.

3. Add the onion to the pot and cook, stirring occasionally until softened, 2 or 3 minutes.

   ▢ Whisk together 1 cup peanut butter and ½ cup water in a small bowl until smooth.

4. Add the garlic, ginger, chile, and 1 tablespoon tomato paste to the pot. Cook, stirring until the mixture darkens and becomes fragrant, 1 to 2 minutes.

5. Add 6 cups stock or water, scraping up any browned bits from the bottom of the pot. Stir in the peanut butter mixture and sprinkle with salt and pepper. Bring the liquid to a boil.

   ▢ Trim the collards; slice the leaves in half along the stems, remove the thickest stems, then slice the leaves crosswise into thin ribbons.

● recipe continues →

6. When the soup boils, stir the collards into the soup and lower the heat so it bubbles gently. Cover and cook undisturbed until the greens soften and the chicken cooks through, 5 to 10 minutes.

   ☐ Chop ¼ cup peanuts or crush them on a cutting board with the flat side of a large knife.

7. Taste the soup and adjust the seasoning. Serve garnished with the peanuts.

Variations

Coconutty Peanut Soup with Chicken and Watercress. Substitute a yellow onion for the red, watercress for the collards, and 1 (14-ounce) can coconut milk for 2 cups of the stock. The watercress will take only 3 to 5 minutes to soften.

Cashew Soup with Chicken and Celery. Use cashew butter instead of the peanut butter and the tender heart and leaves from 1 bunch celery instead of the collards (save the outside celery stalks for another use). Sliced crosswise, you should have about 2 cups. Add them after the soup boils in Step 6 and let them cook until they are meltingly tender, 5 to 10 minutes.

Peanut Soup with Pork and Bok Choy. Use ground pork instead of the chicken, 1 bunch scallions instead of the red onion, bok choy instead of the collards, and 2 tablespoons soy sauce rather than the tomato paste. Add the soy sauce when you add the stock.

Sausage, Cannellini, and Kale Soup

Beans and greens are probably my all-time favorite combination, and they mix and match brilliantly. It's hard to top cannellini beans and hearty kale, seasoned with a bit of sausage and Parmesan cheese, but the variations aim high. **Serves 4**

Ingredients

2 tablespoons olive oil, plus more for garnish

8 ounces sweet or hot Italian sausage

3 cloves garlic

1 bunch kale (preferably lacinato; 1 pound)

3½ cups cooked or canned cannellini beans (two 15-ounce cans)

¼ teaspoon red chile flakes, or more to taste

Salt and pepper

6 cups vegetable or chicken stock or water

1 bay leaf

4 ounces Parmesan cheese (1 cup grated)

☐ Prep · Cook

1. Put 2 tablespoons olive oil in a large pot over medium heat.

   ☐ Cut the sausage into bite-sized chunks (kitchen shears are the handiest tool for this).

2. When the oil is hot, add the sausage and cook, stirring occasionally, until browned on most sides, 5 to 10 minutes.

   ☐ Peel and mince 3 cloves garlic.

   ☐ Trim and chop the kale.

   ☐ If you're using canned beans, rinse and drain them. Put 1 cup of the beans on a plate and mash them with a fork or potato masher until they're broken into bits.

3. When the sausage is browned, spoon off all but 2 tablespoons of the fat in the pan. Stir in the garlic and ¼ teaspoon red chile flakes, or more to taste. Cook, stirring until fragrant, 30 seconds or so. Add the kale, sprinkle with salt and pepper, and cook, stirring until it's coated with oil and just starting to wilt, a minute or two.

4. Add the mashed and whole beans, 6 cups stock or water, and 1 bay leaf. Bring the mixture to a boil, then adjust the heat so that it bubbles gently but steadily. Cook, stirring occasionally, until the broth thickens and the kale is fully tender, 10 to 20 minutes.

   ☐ Grate 1 cup Parmesan cheese.

5. Remove and discard the bay leaf. Taste and adjust the seasoning. Serve each bowl of soup drizzled with olive oil and sprinkled with cheese.

Variations

Merguez, Chickpea, and Chard Soup. Substitute merguez or other lamb and/or beef links for the Italian sausage. Instead of kale and cannellini beans, use any color chard and chickpeas. Try Manchego cheese instead of the Parmesan.

Andouille, Black-Eyed Pea, and Okra Soup. Spicy and smoky. Omit the Parmesan. Use andouille sausage. Substitute 1 pound okra for the kale; trim off the stem end and cut the pods into 1 or 2 pieces. To thicken the soup pleasantly without sliminess, cook the okra as directed for the greens in Steps 3 and 4 until it's quite tender and collapsed.

Lima Bean and Spinach Soup. You'll never miss the meat. Substitute frozen lima beans for the cannellinis and spinach for the kale. Instead of the sausage, chop 1 large white onion; cook it in the olive oil in Step 2, stirring occasionally, until it begins to color, about 10 minutes. In Step 4 don't add the spinach to the onions, just the lima beans, stock, and bay leaf. Cook until the beans begin to fall apart, 10 to 15 minutes, then run a potato masher through the soup to purée some but not all. Add the spinach and cook until it's just tender. Taste and adjust the seasoning, and serve.

THICKENING WITH BEANS

Mashing even a few beans in soup makes the texture thick and creamy. The starch released by the beans is water soluble, so it dissolves quickly, creating a viscosity similar to rich animal-based foods like butter and cream.

Broken Wonton Soup

You may not be up for filling and sealing wontons—even with packaged skins—on a busy weeknight. My solution: Deconstruct the whole thing and pull together homemade wonton-style soup in minutes. Be sure to check out the different directions you can go with the variations. **Serves 4**

Ingredients

8 cups chicken or vegetable stock

8 ounces shiitake mushrooms

2 cloves garlic

1 inch fresh ginger

3 scallions

12 ounces ground pork

1 egg

1 tablespoon soy sauce, plus more for serving

2 teaspoons sesame oil, plus more for serving

¼ teaspoon five-spice powder

Salt

1 (12- to 14-ounce) package wonton skins

Red chile flakes to taste (optional)

▫ Prep · **Cook**

1. Put 8 cups stock in a large pot over medium heat.

   ▫ Trim the tough parts off the mushroom stems and save for another use, like stock. Thinly slice the caps and add them to the pot.

   ▫ Peel and chop 2 cloves garlic and 1 inch ginger.

   ▫ Trim and chop the scallions, keeping the white and green parts separate.

2. Put the ground pork in a medium bowl; crack in the egg and add 1 tablespoon soy sauce, 2 teaspoons sesame oil, ¼ teaspoon five-spice powder, a sprinkle of salt, the garlic, ginger, and white parts of the scallions. Mix gently with a rubber spatula or your hands until just combined.

3. When the stock boils, adjust the heat so it bubbles steadily. With your fingers or 2 small spoons, pinch off and shape a walnut-sized piece of the pork mixture; drop it into the stock. Repeat until all the pork is used. Cook, adjusting the heat so the stock continues to bubble but not vigorously, until the meatballs firm up a bit, 1 to 2 minutes.

4. Separate 24 wonton skins (refrigerate or freeze what remains in the package for another use). Drop them into the pot, stirring carefully after every few to prevent them from sticking together. Cook until the meatballs are cooked through and the wonton skins are just tender, another minute or two. Taste and adjust the seasoning, adding more soy sauce if you like. Serve garnished with the scallion greens and a pinch of red chile flakes if you like. Pass more soy sauce and sesame oil at the table.

● recipe continues →

Variations

Broken Wonton Soup with Spicy Shrimp. Use thawed peeled shrimp instead of the pork. Pulse them in a food processor with the egg and seasonings in Step 2, adding a bit of chopped fresh green chile (like Thai), and continue with the recipe.

Broken Wonton Soup with Gingered Chicken. Substitute ground chicken for the pork (to grind your own, chop it in a food processor as in the previous variation); use an additional 2 inches ginger instead of the garlic.

Broken Wonton Soup with Silken Tofu and Watercress. A plant-based alternative. Omit the pork and egg. Trim 1 bunch watercress. Before adding stock to the pot in Step 1, trim and slice the shiitakes. Put 2 tablespoons vegetable oil in the pot over medium-high heat. Add the mushrooms, sprinkle with salt and pepper, and cook, stirring occasionally, until they're brown in places, 3 to 5 minutes. (You can prep the garlic, ginger, and scallions while they cook.) Add the five-spice powder, sesame oil, soy sauce, garlic, ginger, and scallion whites; stir a couple times, then immediately add the stock. When it comes to a boil, add the wonton skins and 24 ounces (2 bricks) soft silken tofu. Break it into large pieces with a wooden spoon as it cooks. When the tofu is hot and the wonton skins are tender, taste and adjust the seasonings. Serve garnished with the scallion greens and watercress.

MORE FUN WITH WONTON SKINS

If you're feeling even slightly ambitious, here are a few more ways to use store-bought wonton skins in this soup.

- **Make wonton cigars:** Don't add the pork mixture in Step 3. Instead, take the pinch of meat, put it at one pointed end of a skin, and roll the skin around it into a tube. Drop these wontons into the soup in Step 4. Give them 2 to 4 minutes to firm up and cook through.

- **Make fresh egg noodles:** Instead of dropping whole skins in the soup in Step 4, work in batches to stack and slice 24 wonton skins into short noodles, ½ inch wide or less.

- **Make a fried noodle garnish:** Cut a few extra wonton skins into thin strips and fry them in ½ inch vegetable oil in a skillet over medium-high heat, stirring almost constantly, until golden and crisp, just a minute or two. Drain on towels and sprinkle with salt. Sprinkle on top of the soup along with the scallion greens.

Korean-Style Beef Soup with Rice

A little bit like the rice porridges popular for breakfast throughout Asia, only much faster. To boost the flavor, I add an oil inspired by Korean flavors just before serving—the reverse of building a soup on a base of cooked aromatics and spices. The recipe calls for the Korean fermented soybean and chile paste called gochujang, which is now available in many supermarkets. It keeps in the fridge for months so you might consider buying it, even though the recipe doesn't call for a ton. For the heat you can substitute any dried chile flakes to taste (the not-too-hot, finely ground Korean gochugaru are an excellent option) and if you're feeling ambitious, add a tablespoon of miso or tahini to bolster the bottom notes in gochujang. **Serves 4**

Ingredients

3 tablespoons vegetable oil

1 pound boneless beef chuck

Salt

3 cloves garlic

8 cups beef or chicken stock or water

1 cup long-grain rice

2 tablespoons toasted sesame seeds

1 tablespoon gochujang or more to taste

1 tablespoon sesame oil, plus more for serving

3 tablespoons soy sauce, plus more for serving

1 tablespoon rice vinegar

4 scallions

6 celery stalks, plus any leaves

◻ Prep · **Cook**

1. Put 1 tablespoon vegetable oil in a large pot over high heat.

   ◻ Cut the beef into ½-inch chunks.

2. When the oil is nearly smoking, add the beef, sprinkle with salt, and cook, stirring once or twice until it browns in places, 3 to 5 minutes.

   ◻ Peel and mince 3 cloves garlic.

3. When the beef is browned, stir in the garlic and cook 30 seconds. Add 8 cups stock or water, 1 cup rice, and another pinch of salt. Bring to a boil and cook until the meat can be pierced with a fork, the rice is fully tender, and the liquid is cloudy, 15 to 20 minutes.

4. Put 2 tablespoons sesame seeds in a small saucepan over medium heat. Add the 1 tablespoon gochujang or ½ teaspoon red chile flakes, 1 tablespoon sesame oil, 2 tablespoons vegetable oil, 3 tablespoons soy sauce, and 1 tablespoon rice vinegar. Cook, stirring frequently, until the sauce becomes fragrant and hot but not sizzling, about 3 minutes.

   ◻ Trim and chop the scallions, keeping the white and green parts separate.

   ◻ Chop 6 celery stalks and any leaves, keeping them separate.

5. Toss the celery stalks into the soup pot and stir. Add the scallions and celery leaves to the pan with the sauce. Continue to cook and stir until the vegetables in the sauce soften, another couple minutes. Remove from the heat.

6. When the rice is fully cooked, add water if necessary to make it soupy again. Taste and add more salt if necessary, but remember the soup will also get a last-minute seasoning from the drizzling sauce. Serve, passing the warm drizzling sauce at the table.

Coconut-Beef Soup with Carrots

This quintessential chop-and-drop soup is inspired by the street food of Bangkok; it's sweet, hot, salty, and something you'll want to make again and again, especially if you try the variations. Serve it with rice noodles (page 495). **Serves 4**

Ingredients

1 pound boneless beef sirloin or rib-eye steak

4½ cups beef or chicken stock or water

2 inches fresh ginger

1 fresh hot green chile (like Thai), or to taste

2 lemongrass stalks (optional)

1 bunch fresh basil (preferably Thai)

1 (14-ounce) can coconut milk

5 medium carrots (1 pound)

1 lime

3 tablespoons fish sauce

1 teaspoon sugar

Salt and pepper

Prep · Cook

☐ Put the beef in the freezer.

1. Bring 4½ cups stock or water to a boil in a large pot.

   ☐ Peel and chop 2 inches of ginger.

   ☐ Trim and seed the chile; slice it crosswise into thin rounds.

   ☐ Trim 2 lemongrass stalks if you're using them; crush them on a cutting board with the flat side of a knife, and cut each into 3-inch pieces.

   ☐ Chop 1 cup basil leaves. Save the stems.

2. Add the ginger, chiles, lemongrass, and basil stems to the pot. When the liquid comes to a boil, adjust the heat so that it bubbles steadily but gently. Add the coconut milk; return the mixture to a steady bubble.

   ☐ Trim and peel the carrots; slice them crosswise into thin rounds.

   ☐ Halve the lime.

   ☐ Remove the beef from the freezer and slice it against the grain as thinly as you can.

3. Remove the lemongrass and basil stems from the pot with a slotted spoon; discard.

4. Add the carrots to the pot. Cook undisturbed until they begin to get tender, 2 to 3 minutes.

5. Add the beef to the pot and cook, stirring once and adjusting the heat so the liquid bubbles steadily, until just cooked through and the carrots are crisp-tender, 2 to 3 minutes.

6. Add 3 tablespoons fish sauce, 1 teaspoon sugar, and a sprinkle of salt and pepper. Squeeze the lime juice into the soup.

7. Stir in the basil leaves. Taste and adjust the seasoning. Serve.

Variations

Coconut-Squid Soup with Daikon. A gorgeous almost-white soup with basil leaves. Substitute daikon radish for the carrots; after trimming and peeling, slice it crosswise into coins and if they're big, cut them into half-moons. Use cleaned squid instead of the beef. There's no need to freeze it; just slice it crosswise into rings and separate the tentacles from the body. Add it to the soup when the carrots are crisp-tender; it's ready when the rings turn white and puff up a bit.

Coconut-Chicken Soup with Bean Sprouts and Snow Peas. Use 1 pound boneless, skinless chicken breasts or thighs. Freeze and slice as directed for the beef. The thighs will take 2 to 3 minutes more than the beef or chicken breasts to cook through. Substitute 8 ounces each snow peas and bean sprouts for the carrots. Add the bean sprouts in Step 4, and the snow peas with the chicken in Step 5.

Coconut Soup with Poached Eggs and Mustard Greens. Even faster. Omit the beef. Instead of the carrots, chop 1 pound mustard greens, or try tatsoi, mizuna, or other sharp greens; they'll cook in less than 3 minutes. After seasoning the soup in Step 6, maintain the soup at a steady bubble and carefully crack in 8 eggs. Cover and cook until the yolks are as runny as you like, 2 to 6 minutes. If they break and scramble, no big deal. Serve right away, scooping a couple eggs into each bowl.

Lamb Soup with Green Beans and Tomatoes

American-raised lamb is more widely available now than it used to be, and I'm glad. It's got a distinctive flavor that's actually quite mild, even though it smells stronger during cooking. That makes it perfect for an assertively spiced but balanced soup. If you don't like—or can't find—lamb, use ground beef, pork, or even chicken or turkey instead. **Serves 4**

Ingredients

2 tablespoons olive oil, plus more for serving

1 medium red onion

1 pound ground lamb

Salt and pepper

4 cloves garlic

1 tablespoon ground cumin

1 large (28-ounce) can diced tomatoes

3 cups chicken or vegetable stock or water

1 pound green beans

1 lemon

Several sprigs fresh parsley

☐ Prep · Cook

1. Put 2 tablespoons olive oil in a large pot over medium-high heat.

   ☐ Trim, peel, and chop the onion.

2. When the oil is hot, add the lamb and the onion, sprinkle with salt and pepper, and cook, stirring occasionally, until the lamb is browned and the onion is golden, 5 to 10 minutes. Spoon off all but 2 tablespoons of the fat in the pan.

   ☐ Peel and chop 4 cloves garlic.

3. Add 1 tablespoon ground cumin to the browned lamb and onion and cook, stirring until fragrant, 30 seconds or so. Add the garlic, cooking and stirring for another 30 seconds.

4. Add the tomatoes and their juice, scraping any browned bits off the bottom of the pot.

5. Add 3 cups stock or water. Bring the soup to a boil, then lower the heat so it bubbles steadily. Cook, stirring once in a while, until the tomatoes break up and the liquid thickens, 10 to 15 minutes.

   ☐ Trim the green beans and chop into 1-inch pieces. If you like your green beans on the silky side, add them to the soup as you chop them.

6. When the soup has thickened, stir in the green beans if you haven't already; adjust the heat so that the soup bubbles gently but steadily. Cover and cook undisturbed until the green beans are as tender as you like, 3 to 5 minutes.

• recipe continues →

☐ Zest the lemon. Refrigerate the fruit for another use.

☐ Strip the leaves from several parsley sprigs and chop.

7. When the green beans are ready, taste and adjust the seasoning. Serve sprinkled with the lemon zest and parsley, and pass olive oil at the table for drizzling.

Variations

Lamb Soup with Zucchini and Tomatoes. Instead of the green beans, trim 1 pound zucchini and cut them crosswise into ½-inch slices. Again, if you like the vegetables tender, add as you chop.

Curried Lamb Soup with Green Beans and Potatoes. Heartier. Omit the tomatoes. Substitute vegetable oil for olive oil and 2 tablespoons curry powder for the ground cumin. Increase the stock or water to 7 cups. Trim 2 large Yukon Gold potatoes, peel them if you like, chop them into ½-inch chunks, and add them with the stock in Step 5. Keep the lemon zest; instead of the olive oil and parsley, garnish with plain yogurt and chopped fresh mint.

Three Bean Soup with Tomatoes and Olives. Instead of the lamb, use 1¾ cups each cooked or canned kidney beans and chickpeas (one 15-ounce can each). Increase the olive oil to 3 tablespoons and cook the beans in Step 2 until they start to blister and break up a little, 3 to 5 minutes. Then proceed with the recipe.

Pasta and Noodles

t's tough to beat a bowl of noodles for comfort, flexibility, and speed. So naturally this is one of the biggest chapters in the book. Here are fairly traditional Italian-style recipes (only done faster) as well as personal favorites and noodle dishes inspired by Asian cuisines.

There are plenty of tomatoes among these recipes, both canned and fresh. And for a separate all-purpose tomato sauce and its variations, turn to page 492.

The only possible limitation is bringing a pot of water to boil. It's tempting to save time by skimping on water, but any time saved is then spent stirring the pasta and pulling it apart when it inevitably clumps together. Do yourself a favor: Fill your pot with ample water—a gallon per pound of pasta is about right—and spend the 20 minutes it takes to boil making the sauce.

Or consider this scenario: As soon as you get home from work, start the water and walk away. Say hi to your kids and change out of your work clothes. By the time you get back to the kitchen, you'll have a head start and time to spare to make salad.

Cacio e Pepe

Cheese and pepper—perhaps the most fundamental and basic of all Italian pastas. The cheese should be pecorino (from sheep), and good-quality pecorino Romano is increasingly available; if you can't find that, use real-deal Parmesan. And don't skimp on the pepper; if you can crack or lightly grind whole peppercorns, all the better. **Serves 4**

Ingredients

Salt

8 ounces pecorino Romano or Parmesan cheese (2 cups grated), plus more for serving

1 pound spaghetti or other long pasta

1 tablespoon black pepper, or more to taste

Prep · Cook

1. Bring a large pot of water to a boil and salt it.

   ☐ Grate 2 cups pecorino Romano or Parmesan.

2. When the water boils, add the pasta and cook, stirring occasionally. Start tasting after 5 minutes. When the pasta is tender but not mushy, drain it, reserving about 3 cups cooking water. Return the pasta to the pot and put over low heat.

3. Add the cheese, 1 tablespoon pepper, and enough cooking water to make it saucy (you may need only a cup or so). Toss, taste, and adjust the seasoning, then serve.

Variations

Buttery Cacio e Pepe. For an even richer version, add 4 tablespoons (½ stick) butter, softened, to the final dish.

Sort-of Alfredo. Omit the black pepper. Use Parmesan cheese instead of the pecorino if you like, for a milder taste. In Step 3, before adding any pasta water, add 1 cup cream and ¼ teaspoon ground nutmeg when you add the cheese. Let the cream coat the pasta and heat until steamy, then add pasta cooking water a little at a time until it's as saucy as you like.

Pasta with Mascarpone and Red Pepper. Sweet meets heat. Use 1 cup mascarpone cheese instead of the pecorino and a pinch of red chile flakes instead of the black pepper.

SALT PASTA WATER LIKE YOU MEAN IT

In order to season pasta properly and improve the way it cooks, the water in the pot should taste noticeably salty, almost like the ocean. If that seems like too much, remember that most is going to be drained off, and what remains will only help season the sauce. So be bold and try salting your pasta water by the palmful.

Mac and Cheese

Not to be confused with macaroni tossed in a milk-based cheese sauce, here you use the heat of the pasta to turn a load of cheese, a little milk, and some pasta cooking water into a rich and creamy version in a fraction of the time. While you set the table or toss a salad, the bread crumbs take a spin under the broiler to deliver the classic crisp topping. **Serves 4**

Ingredients

Salt

12 ounces cheddar, Gruyère, or Swiss cheese, or a combination (3 cups grated)

4 ounces Parmesan cheese (1 cup grated)

1 pound cut pasta (like elbows, shells, or orecchiette)

½ cup milk

4 tablespoons (½ stick) butter

Pepper

¾ cup bread crumbs

▢ Prep · Cook

1. Bring a large pot of water to a boil and salt it.

   ▢ Grate 3 cups cheddar, Gruyère, and/or Swiss cheese. Grate 1 cup Parmesan.

2. Turn the broiler to high; put the rack 4 inches from the heat.

3. When the water boils, add the pasta and cook, stirring occasionally. Start tasting after 5 minutes. When the pasta is barely tender and not quite edible, drain it and reserve some cooking water. Return the pasta to the pot.

4. Add the grated cheddar, Gruyère, and/or Swiss, ½ cup milk, 4 tablespoons butter, and a sprinkle of salt and pepper. Stir until the cheese melts, adding cooking water a tablespoon at a time to thin if necessary. The pasta should be almost fully tender; if not, keep cooking and stirring for another minute or two. Taste and adjust the seasoning.

5. Transfer the pasta to a 9 × 13-inch metal baking pan or rimmed baking sheet. Sprinkle the top with the Parmesan and ¾ cup bread crumbs. Broil until the cheese is bubbling and browned and the bread crumbs crisp, 2 to 5 minutes. Serve piping hot directly from the baking pan.

Variations

Mac and Parmesan. Familiar but different. Use all Parmesan instead of any other melting cheese.

Mac and Cheese and Tuna. Yes, this is tuna casserole—only cheesier. After stirring in the cheese and milk in Step 4, fold in 2 cans or jars (5 to 6 ounces each) drained olive oil–packed tuna.

Mac and Beans. Deliciously vegan. Omit the cheeses and milk. Substitute olive oil for the butter. While the pasta cooks, drain 2 (15-ounce) cans white beans (or use 3½ cups cooked beans); purée in a food processor with ¼ cup nutritional yeast, 2 cloves garlic, chopped, and just enough oat milk or pasta-cooking water to make a spoonable sauce. Use this to toss with the pasta in Step 4. Before broiling, sprinkle the top with ¾ cup bread crumbs.

Pasta with Broccoli Rabe and Ricotta

Stir a cup of ricotta cheese into hot pasta, add a splash of cooking water, and you've got a rich and creamy sauce that took you 30 seconds to make. Pleasantly bitter broccoli rabe is the perfect vegetable to cut through the richness of the cheese. **Serves 4**

Ingredients

Salt

3 tablespoons olive oil

1½ pounds broccoli rabe

Pepper

2 cloves garlic

¼ teaspoon red chile flakes

1 pound cut pasta (like elbows, penne, or ziti)

1 cup ricotta cheese (about half a 15-ounce container)

Prep · Cook

1. Bring a large pot of water to a boil and salt it.

2. Put 3 tablespoons olive oil in a large skillet over low heat.

   □ Trim and chop the broccoli rabe, separating any thick stems.

3. Raise the heat under the skillet to medium-high. Add any thick stems to the skillet and cook until they begin to soften, 3 to 4 minutes.

4. Add the leaves, a handful at a time if necessary to fit them in, and sprinkle with salt and pepper. Cook until just tender, 3 to 4 minutes.

   □ Peel and chop 2 cloves garlic; add them to the skillet along with ¼ teaspoon red chile flakes.

5. When the water boils, add the pasta and cook, stirring occasionally. Start tasting after 5 minutes. When the pasta is tender but not mushy, drain it, reserving about 1 cup cooking water. Return the pasta to the pot.

6. Add the broccoli rabe, 1 cup ricotta, a sprinkle of salt and pepper, and a splash of cooking water to make it saucy. Toss, taste, and adjust the seasoning, then serve.

Variations

Pasta with Sausage, Broccoli Rabe, and Ricotta. Before cooking the broccoli rabe, brown 8 ounces (2 links) chopped Italian sausage in the skillet over medium heat (kitchen shears are handy for chopping). Stir occasionally; this will take about 5 extra minutes. Remove the sausage from the skillet to make room for the broccoli rabe and spoon off all but 2 tablespoons of the fat. Proceed with the recipe, stirring the cooked sausage into the pasta in Step 6.

Pasta with Asparagus and Ricotta. With or without the sausage in the first variation. Use asparagus instead of broccoli rabe. After trimming, cut it into 1-inch pieces, separating and cooking any thick stems as described in Steps 3 and 4. The asparagus might take a little longer to cook in Step 4.

One-Pot Pasta Pesto with Cherry Tomatoes

Part pesto, part salsa cruda—and all rustic tomato sauce. Timed to come together in one pot without outrageous stirring. Basil is of course the classic pesto herb, but you can always substitute parsley or arugula; or use a combination, in which case a few mint leaves are a nice addition, too. To skip the tomatoes, simply double the pesto. **Serves 4**

Ingredients

8 tablespoons olive oil (½ cup)

Salt

1 pound bow ties or any cut pasta

1 large bunch basil

1 or 2 cloves garlic

4 ounces Parmesan cheese (1 cup grated)

2 tablespoons pine nuts

1 pint ripe cherry tomatoes

▢ Prep · Cook

▢ Put about a quart of water in a pitcher and have it handy by the stove.

1. Put 2 tablespoons olive oil in a large pot over medium-high heat. When it's hot, add the pasta and stir to coat in the oil. Add about 1 cup water and a big pinch of salt. Bring to a boil, then reduce the heat so the mixture bubbles gently. Cook, stirring frequently and adding more water ¼ cup at a time to keep the mixture saucy, until the pasta just begins to get tender, no more than 10 minutes. If it's almost tender before you are ready to add the pesto and tomatoes, turn off the heat.

   ▢ Strip 2 cups basil leaves from the sprigs. Put in a food processor.

   ▢ Peel 1 or 2 cloves garlic; add them to the food processor.

   ▢ Grate 1 cup Parmesan cheese.

2. Add 2 tablespoons pine nuts, 2 tablespoons olive oil, and a sprinkle of salt to the food processor. Process, streaming in another ¼ cup oil as you go and stopping to scrape down the sides as necessary, until the pesto is smooth.

   ▢ Halve the cherry tomatoes.

3. When the pasta is almost fully tender, return it to medium heat if necessary. Add the pesto, tomatoes, about half of the Parmesan, and a splash more water if necessary to make it saucy.

4. Cook, stir, and continue to add small amounts of water as necessary until the pasta is tender but still has some bite and the tomatoes are soft, just a couple minutes. Toss, taste, and adjust the seasoning. Serve hot or warm, passing the remaining Parmesan at the table.

Variation

One-Pot Pasta Pesto and Cherry Tomatoes with Burrata. The decadent fresh mozzarella that's almost liquid on the inside is perfect with this sauce. Cut about 6 ounces burrata cheese crosswise into 4 thick slices, careful not to let too much of the milky interior ooze out. Let the cheese slices sit at room temperature while you prepare the pasta, then just after serving, nestle a piece into each bowl of pasta.

Spaghetti with Garlicky Fresh Tomato Sauce

Save this recipe for peak summer when you have the juiciest ripe tomatoes. All other times use the recipe on page 492 or pop open one 28-ounce and one 15-ounce can diced tomatoes to make the sauce. **Serves 4**

Ingredients

Salt

2 tablespoons butter

2 tablespoons olive oil

4 large cloves garlic

5 or 6 large ripe tomatoes (2 pounds)

¼ cup white wine

Pepper

1 pound spaghetti

4 ounces Parmesan cheese (1 cup grated)

Several sprigs fresh basil

▢ Prep · Cook

1. Bring a large pot of water to a boil and salt it.

2. Put 2 tablespoons butter and 2 tablespoons olive oil in a large skillet over low heat.

   ▢ Peel and thinly slice 4 cloves garlic.

3. Add the garlic to the skillet and raise the heat to medium. Stir occasionally, and let the garlic flavor the fat without browning, about 5 minutes.

   ▢ Core and chop the tomatoes; begin adding them to the skillet as soon as the garlic is fragrant and soft.

4. Add ¼ cup white wine and a sprinkle of salt and pepper to the skillet. Bring to a boil, then adjust the heat so the sauce bubbles steadily. Cook, stirring occasionally, until the tomatoes break down, 10 to 15 minutes.

5. When the water boils, add the pasta and cook, stirring occasionally. Start tasting after 5 minutes.

   ▢ Grate 1 cup Parmesan cheese.

   ▢ Strip the leaves from several basil sprigs and chop.

6. When the pasta is tender but not mushy, drain it, reserving about 1 cup cooking water. Add the pasta to the sauce and turn the heat to medium-high. Add the Parmesan, basil, and a splash of cooking water if you want to make it saucier. Toss, taste, and adjust the seasoning, then serve.

Pasta with Spicy Eggplant and Tomato Sauce

Eggplant is the only vegetable that can be chewy, creamy, and silky at the same time, the ideal combination of textures for a simple pasta sauce. For crunch I like to sprinkle this dish with Fried Bread Crumbs (page 488). **Serves 4**

Ingredients

Salt

¼ cup olive oil

1 medium onion

2 large eggplants (about 1½ pounds)

2 cloves garlic

1 teaspoon red chile flakes

Pepper

1 large (28-ounce) can diced tomatoes

1 pound any cut pasta (like farfalle or rigatoni)

Several sprigs fresh basil

▫ Prep · Cook

1. Bring a large pot of water to a boil and salt it.

2. Put ¼ cup olive oil in a large skillet or large pot over medium-high heat.

    ▫ Trim, peel, and chop the onion.

3. When the oil is hot, add the onion and cook, stirring occasionally, until it begins to soften, about 3 minutes.

    ▫ Trim the eggplants and chop them into ½-inch pieces.

    ▫ Peel and chop 2 cloves garlic.

4. When the onion begins to soften, add the eggplant, garlic, 1 teaspoon red chile flakes, and a sprinkle of salt and pepper. Cook, stirring occasionally, until the eggplant is browned all over, 5 to 10 minutes.

5. When the eggplant is browned, add the diced tomatoes and their juice and adjust the heat so the mixture bubbles steadily but not vigorously. Cook, stirring occasionally, until the tomatoes start to break down and the eggplant is tender, 5 to 10 minutes.

6. When the water boils, add the pasta and cook, stirring occasionally. Start tasting after 5 minutes.

    ▫ Strip the leaves from several basil sprigs and chop.

7. When the pasta is tender but not mushy, drain it, reserving about 1 cup cooking water. Add the pasta to the sauce along with the basil and a splash of cooking water if the pasta looks dry. Toss, taste, and adjust the seasoning, then serve.

Broiled Rigatoni

All the flavors of a classic baked ziti but with a bigger, flatter noodle so more bubbling crust in way less time than my usual recipe. Crowd-pleasers don't come much easier than this. And of course you can always substitute ziti if you prefer. **Serves 4**

Ingredients

Salt

3 tablespoons olive oil, plus more for greasing the baking sheet

1 medium onion

2 cloves garlic

1 large (28-ounce) can crushed tomatoes

Pepper

1 pound rigatoni

8 ounces mozzarella cheese (preferably fresh)

4 ounces Parmesan cheese (1 cup grated)

▫ Prep · Cook

1. Bring a large pot of water to a boil and salt it.

2. Put 3 tablespoons olive oil in a large skillet over medium heat.

   ▫ Trim, peel, and chop the onion.

   ▫ Peel and chop 2 cloves garlic.

3. Add the onion and garlic to the oil and cook, stirring occasionally, until the onion softens, 3 to 5 minutes.

   ▫ Grease a rimmed baking sheet with olive oil.

4. Turn the broiler to high; put the rack 4 inches from the heat.

5. When the onion is soft, add the tomatoes, stir to combine, sprinkle with salt and pepper, and bring to a boil. Lower the heat so the sauce bubbles gently, and cook, stirring occasionally. Add a splash of pasta cooking water if the sauce is too thick to drop from a spoon.

6. When the water boils, add the pasta and cook, stirring occasionally. Start tasting after 5 minutes.

   ▫ Chop or grate 8 ounces mozzarella.

   ▫ Grate 1 cup Parmesan.

7. When the pasta is tender but not mushy, drain it and return it to the pot. Add the tomato sauce and half of the mozzarella and stir. Transfer the pasta to the baking sheet and spread it in an even layer. Top with the remaining mozzarella and the Parmesan.

8. Broil until the cheese is bubbling and browned and the top layer is crisp, 2 to 5 minutes. Let cool for a couple minutes before serving.

Spinach Carbonara

With the richness of eggs and Parmesan and the fresh bite of lightly cooked spinach, this recipe offers a hearty meatless alternative to more traditional pasta carbonara. (That's here, too; see the first variation.) You can replace the spinach with escarole, kale, mustard greens, chard, or broccoli rabe. Just cut the ones with large leaves and stems crosswise into ribbons and cook a little longer if necessary. **Serves 4**

Ingredients

Salt

3 tablespoons olive oil

1 pound spinach

2 cloves garlic

1 pound any long pasta

3 eggs

4 ounces Parmesan cheese (1 cup grated)

Pepper

□ Prep · Cook

1. Bring a large pot of water to a boil and salt it.

2. Put 3 tablespoons olive oil in a large skillet over low heat.

   □ Trim off any thick stems from the spinach.

3. Raise the heat under the skillet to medium-high. Cook the spinach, adding a handful at a time and stirring between batches, until the leaves are just wilted, about 5 minutes.

   □ Peel and chop 2 cloves garlic, adding them to the skillet as soon as you can (they'll cook with the spinach).

4. When the spinach is tender, turn off the heat.

5. When the water boils, add the pasta and cook, stirring occasionally. Start tasting after 5 minutes.

   □ Crack the eggs into a bowl.

   □ Grate 1 cup Parmesan cheese and add to the bowl; sprinkle with salt and lots of pepper. Whisk with a fork to combine.

6. When the pasta is tender but not mushy, drain it, reserving about 1 cup cooking water. Add the pasta to the spinach and pour in the egg mixture. Toss, adding a splash of cooking water if you want to make it saucier. Taste and adjust the seasoning, and serve.

Variations

More Traditional Pasta Carbonara. Omit the spinach. Instead, cook 8 ounces chopped guanciale (similar to other cured pork cuts, only this one comes from the jowls and is a special treat), pancetta, or bacon in the olive oil until crisp. Drain off some of the fat if you like—or not. Keep the garlic and proceed as directed.

Pasta with Asparagus and Eggs. Use cut pasta here, like orecchiette or fusilli. Substitute 1 pound asparagus for the spinach; trim and slice it on the diagonal into 1-inch lengths; chop the garlic at the same time, before cooking in Step 3. Start tasting after 3 minutes to capture one stage before your desired degree of doneness; then proceed.

Pasta with Mushrooms and Eggs. Instead of the spinach, trim and thinly slice 1 pound cremini mushrooms. Cook them in the olive oil until they're tender and begin to dry out, 10 to 15 minutes. Add the garlic and cook for a minute more before proceeding.

Linguine with Clams

Clams, butter, olive oil, garlic, and parsley make one of my all-time favorite pasta sauces. For a more elegant presentation, after the clams open, pluck out the meats and toss them with the pasta in Step 6 (and discard the shells). **Serves 4**

Ingredients

Salt

3 pounds littleneck, manila, or other small hard-shell clams

2 tablespoons olive oil

2 cloves garlic

1 teaspoon red chile flakes, or to taste

Pepper

1 pound linguine

Several sprigs fresh parsley

2 tablespoons butter

☐ Prep · Cook

1. Bring a large pot of water to a boil and salt it.

   ☐ Scrub the clams; discard any that don't close when you tap them.

2. Put 2 tablespoons olive oil in a large skillet over medium heat.

3. When the oil is hot, add the clams and ½ cup water and turn the heat to high. Cook, shaking the skillet occasionally, until the first few clams start to open, about 5 minutes.

   ☐ Peel and chop 2 cloves garlic.

4. When a few clams have opened, add the garlic and 1 teaspoon red chile flakes and sprinkle with pepper. Cover the skillet or pot and cook until all the clams open, 3 to 5 minutes. (You can discard those that remain tightly closed or gently pry them open with a butter knife to see if they release easily and look and smell normal.) Turn off the heat and leave covered.

5. When the water boils, add the pasta and cook, stirring occasionally. Start tasting after 5 minutes.

   ☐ Strip the leaves from several parsley sprigs and chop.

6. When the pasta is tender but not mushy, drain it, reserving about 1 cup cooking water. Add the pasta to the clams and turn the heat to medium-high. Add 2 tablespoons butter, the parsley, and a splash of cooking water to make it saucier. Toss, taste, and adjust the seasoning, adding more chile flakes if you like. Serve.

Variations

Chinese Egg Noodles with Clams and Fermented Black Beans. A couple ingredient changes and you get a fast spin on the classic dim sum dish. Start by soaking ¼ cup fermented black beans in ¼ cup rice vinegar and the chile flakes. Instead of the olive oil use vegetable oil; substitute dried Chinese egg noodles for the linguine. When you chop the garlic, also chop about 1 inch fresh ginger and add them to the skillet at the same time along with the fermented black beans. Instead of finishing with butter, use 2 teaspoons sesame oil; garnish with chopped scallions or cilantro.

Fideos with Shrimp, Tomatoes, and Peas

Fideos—short thin noodles, typically used in Spanish cooking—can be tricky to find at regular supermarkets. There's an easy fix: Just break up some angel hair pasta. Here the noodles are cooked almost risotto style, with shrimp and peas stirred in at the end. **Serves 4**

Ingredients

2 tablespoons olive oil

3 cloves garlic

1 pound fideos or angel hair pasta

½ teaspoon smoked paprika

½ cup white wine

1 (15-ounce) can diced tomatoes

Salt and pepper

12 ounces peeled shrimp

1½ cups frozen peas

☐ Prep · Cook

1. Put 2 tablespoons olive oil in a large skillet over medium heat.

   ☐ Peel and chop 3 cloves garlic.

2. Add the garlic to the oil and raise the heat a bit. Hold the fideos or angel hair over the skillet and break them into 1- or 2-inch pieces with your hands, dropping the pieces into the skillet as you go.

3. Toast the pasta, stirring frequently, until it is glossy with oil and slightly browned, about 5 minutes. Sprinkle with ½ teaspoon smoked paprika and stir. Add ½ cup white wine and the tomatoes and their juice. Sprinkle with salt and pepper and cook, stirring until the liquid evaporates and the tomatoes break down, 3 to 4 minutes. Adjust the heat so the mixture bubbles steadily but not vigorously.

4. Cook, stirring occasionally, until the pasta is pliable but not yet edible, 3 to 5 minutes.

   ☐ Rinse the shrimp under cold water to thaw them slightly if necessary; chop.

5. When the pasta is pliable, stir in the shrimp and 1½ cups frozen peas. Cook and stir until the peas are warmed through and the shrimp turn pink and cook through, 2 or 3 minutes. Taste and adjust the seasoning, and serve.

Variations

Fideos with Shrimp, Poblanos, and Corn. Omit the smoked paprika. Instead of the tomatoes, stem, seed, and thinly slice 2 poblano chiles. When you add them in Step 3, wait to add the wine until the chiles soften a little. Use frozen or fresh corn kernels instead of the peas.

Fideos with Chorizo, Tomatoes, and Cannellini. Omit the smoked paprika. Add 8 ounces chopped Spanish chorizo along with the garlic in Step 2. Substitute 1 (15-ounce) can cannellini beans or 2 cups cooked beans for the peas.

Pasta with Squid and Tomatoes

Squid is mild, cooks fast, and has a pleasant chew that's reminiscent of noodles. For anyone who hasn't tried it, pasta is an ideal introduction. The trick is to not overcook squid or it becomes tough. **Serves 4**

Ingredients

Salt

3 cloves garlic

12 ounces cleaned squid (whole or cut; frozen is fine)

1 small dried hot red chile

12 ounces cut pasta (like penne or ziti)

3 tablespoons olive oil

1 large (28-ounce) can whole peeled tomatoes

Pepper

Several sprigs fresh parsley

1 lemon

□ Prep · **Cook**

1. Bring a large pot of water to a boil and and salt it.

   □ Peel and chop 3 cloves garlic.

   □ Thaw the squid if necessary in a colander under cold running water. If the squid isn't sliced already, cut the bodies into rings; cut the tentacles (if you have them) in half if they're large.

   □ Chop the chile.

2. When the water boils, add the pasta and cook, stirring occasionally. Start tasting after 5 minutes.

3. Put 3 tablespoons olive oil in a large skillet over medium-high heat. When it's hot, add the garlic and cook until fragrant, about 1 minute.

4. Add the juice from the tomatoes to the skillet, followed by the tomatoes one at a time, breaking them up with your hand before you drop them in. Add the chile and a sprinkle of salt and pepper. Raise the heat to high and cook, stirring occasionally, until the mixture becomes saucy, 2 to 3 minutes.

   □ Strip the leaves from several parsley sprigs and chop.

   □ Cut the lemon into wedges.

5. When the pasta is tender but not mushy, drain it, reserving about 1 cup cooking water. Add the squid to the sauce and cook, stirring constantly, until it begins to turn opaque, about a minute. Add the pasta and parsley and a splash of cooking water if you want to make it saucier. Toss until the squid is tender and just cooked through, another minute or so. Taste and adjust the seasoning and serve with the lemon wedges.

Pasta with Brussels Sprouts, Chicken, and Blue Cheese

Talk about efficiency: The Brussels sprouts and chicken roast undisturbed while the pasta cooks, leaving you with the garnishes, setting the table, and pouring drinks. And cleanup is a breeze. **Serves 4**

Ingredients

Salt

1 pound Brussels sprouts

4 to 6 boneless, skinless chicken thighs (about 1 pound)

3 tablespoons olive oil

Pepper

4 ounces blue cheese (1 cup crumbled)

1 pound any cut pasta (like rigatoni or radiatore)

¼ cup balsamic vinegar

½ cup walnut pieces

▢ Prep · Cook

1. Heat the oven to 425°F. Bring a large pot of water to a boil and salt it.

   ▢ Trim the Brussels sprouts and halve them top to bottom; put them on one half of a rimmed baking sheet.

   ▢ Cut the chicken into bite-sized pieces and put them on the other half of the baking sheet.

2. Drizzle the Brussels sprouts and chicken with 3 tablespoons olive oil and toss, keeping them separated as best you can without worrying. Sprinkle with salt and pepper and transfer the pan to the oven.

3. Roast the Brussels sprouts and chicken undisturbed until they release from the pan easily, about 10 minutes. Toss with a spatula and continue roasting until the vegetables are tender, the chicken is no longer pink inside, and everything is browned, 3 to 5 minutes more. Remove from the oven.

   ▢ Crumble 1 cup blue cheese.

4. When the water boils, add the pasta and stir occasionally. Start tasting after 5 minutes. When the pasta is tender but not mushy, drain it, reserving about 2 cups cooking water.

5. Return the pasta to the pot over medium-low heat; add the Brussels sprouts and chicken. Pour about ½ cup of the reserved water into the baking sheet and scrape up any browned bits; transfer them to the pot along with the blue cheese, ¼ cup balsamic vinegar, ½ cup walnuts, and enough cooking water to make a sauce. Toss, taste, and adjust the seasoning, then serve.

Variations

Pasta with Chicken, Cabbage, and Gorgonzola. Instead of the Brussels sprouts, core 1 small head savoy or green cabbage (about 1 pound) and cut it into bite-sized chunks. Use cider vinegar instead of the balsamic and Gorgonzola for the blue cheese. Hazelnuts or pecans are a nice stand-in for the walnuts if you like.

Pasta with Chicken, Beets, and Goat Cheese. I like golden beets here, but red are good too. Substitute 1 pound beets for the Brussels sprouts; trim, peel, and chop them into bite-sized pieces. Instead of the blue cheese, use fresh goat cheese. Substitute the juice from 1 orange for the vinegar and pistachios for the walnuts.

Pasta with Chicken, Carrots, and Manchego. Simple substitutions: sliced carrots for the Brussels sprouts, grated Manchego cheese for the blue cheese, sherry vinegar for the balsamic, and almonds for the walnuts. Everything else stays the same.

Pasta with Chicken, Mushrooms, and Wine

One simple adjustment—use red wine in fall or winter, white in spring and summer—and the whole dish changes dramatically. The pieces of seared chicken and mushrooms have pleasantly similar chew; you can always increase the amount of either or both if you're feeding extra-hearty appetites. **Serves 4**

Ingredients

Salt

2 tablespoons olive oil

2 tablespoons butter

2 or 3 boneless, skinless chicken thighs or 1 boneless, skinless breast (12 ounces)

Pepper

1½ pounds button or cremini mushrooms

3 cloves garlic

¾ cup red or white wine

1 pound any cut pasta (like rigatoni or ziti)

Several sprigs fresh parsley

4 ounces Parmesan cheese (1 cup grated)

☐ Prep · **Cook**

1. Bring a large pot of water to a boil and salt it.

2. Put 1 tablespoon olive oil and 1 tablespoon butter in a large skillet or separate large pot over medium-high heat.

   ☐ Cut the chicken into ½-inch chunks.

3. Add the chicken to the oil and butter and sprinkle with salt and pepper. Cook undisturbed until the pieces brown and release easily, 2 to 3 minutes. Then cook, stirring occasionally, until the meat is no longer pink, 2 to 3 minutes.

   ☐ Trim and quarter the mushrooms.

4. When the chicken is no longer pink, transfer it to a plate with a slotted spoon. Add 1 tablespoon olive oil and 1 tablespoon butter to the skillet, then the mushrooms. Sprinkle with salt and pepper and cook, stirring occasionally until they soften, 5 to 10 minutes.

   ☐ Peel and chop 3 cloves garlic; add them to the mushrooms.

5. When the mushrooms are soft, return the chicken to the skillet, add ¾ cup wine, and scrape any browned bits off the bottom of the skillet. Let the wine bubble away until it reduces by about half. Turn the heat as low as it will go.

6. When the water boils, add the pasta and cook, stirring occasionally. Start tasting after 5 minutes.

   ☐ Strip the leaves from several parsley sprigs and chop.

   ☐ Grate 1 cup Parmesan cheese.

7. When the pasta is tender but not mushy, drain it, reserving about 1 cup cooking water. Add the pasta to the chicken and mushrooms and turn the heat to medium-high. Add the parsley, Parmesan, and a splash of cooking water if you want to make it saucier. Toss, taste, and adjust the seasoning, then serve.

Variations

Pasta with Chicken, Leeks, and Wine. Omit the garlic if you prefer. Substitute the white and light green parts of 2 large leeks, sliced and rinsed well, for the mushrooms. Cook the leeks, stirring occasionally until they are soft, 3 to 5 minutes. Substitute 3 sprigs fresh thyme for the parsley.

Pasta with Chicken, Eggplant, and Wine. Omit the butter and increase the olive oil to 4 tablespoons. Substitute 1½ pounds any kind of eggplant for the mushrooms. Peel the eggplant if you like and cut it into bite-sized pieces. Cook the eggplant in Step 4 until it's tender and browned in places, 5 to 10 minutes.

Pasta with Chicken, Fennel, and Wine. Omit the parsley. Substitute 1 large or 2 small fennel bulbs for the mushrooms. Trim the fennel and reserve the fronds; halve the bulb and slice thinly. Cook as directed, using the fronds for garnish.

Spaghetti and Drop Meatballs with Tomato Sauce

Stop rolling your meatballs. Instead, drop them like cookie dough from two spoons. It's faster, for one, and you won't risk overworking the meat, so they'll be more tender. For even more efficiency, I leave them alone to brown on the bottom of the pan while the tomato sauce comes together around them. **Serves 4**

Ingredients

Salt

2 tablespoons olive oil

12 ounces ground beef

6 ounces Parmesan cheese
(1½ cups grated)

1 bunch fresh parsley

¼ cup bread crumbs

1 egg

Pepper

1 large onion

3 cloves garlic

2 large (28-ounce) cans diced tomatoes

3 bay leaves

1 pound spaghetti

☐ Prep · Cook

1. Bring a large pot of water to a boil and salt it.

2. Put 2 tablespoons olive oil in a large skillet over medium-high heat.

   ☐ Put the ground beef in a medium bowl.

   ☐ Grate 1½ cups Parmesan cheese and add 1 cup to the bowl. Set aside the rest for serving.

   ☐ Chop ¼ cup parsley leaves and add to the bowl.

3. Add ¼ cup bread crumbs to the bowl, crack in the egg, and sprinkle with salt and pepper. Gently mix together until everything is just combined.

4. When the oil is hot, use 2 spoons to drop in rounds of the meatball mixture (without touching if you can help it). Once you've used up all the mixture, let the meatballs cook undisturbed until they're browned on the bottom and release easily, 5 to 6 minutes.

   ☐ Trim, peel, and chop the onion; scatter it around the meatballs.

   ☐ Peel and chop 3 cloves garlic; scatter them on the onions.

5. When the meatballs release from the pan easily, add the tomatoes and their juice to the skillet, along with 3 bay leaves and a sprinkle of salt and pepper. Stir gently to combine the meatballs with the sauce and scrape up any browned bits from the bottom of the pan. Adjust the heat so the mixture bubbles gently, then cover the skillet (by the time the pasta is cooked, the meatballs will be firm).

• recipe continues →

6. When the water boils, add the pasta and cook, stirring occasionally. Start tasting after 5 minutes. When the pasta is tender but not mushy, drain it, reserving about 1 cup cooking water. Return the pasta to the pot. Discard the bay leaves and spoon half of the sauce into the pasta pot, leaving the meatballs behind. Toss the pasta and sauce, adding a splash of cooking water if you want to make it saucier.

7. Transfer the pasta to a platter or serving bowls; top with the meatballs and some sauce. Serve, passing the remaining ½ cup Parmesan and sauce at the table.

Variations

Spaghetti and Pork Drop Meatballs with Tomato Sauce. Use ground pork instead of beef; add 1 tablespoon fennel seeds in addition to the parsley.

Spaghetti and Lamb Drop Meatballs with Tomato Sauce. Substitute ground lamb for the beef and 2 sprigs fresh rosemary for the parsley.

Spaghetti and Drop Chicken (or Turkey) Meatballs with Tomato Sauce. I prefer ground chicken in all cases, but I know others don't, so here's the option. Use ground chicken instead of beef and fresh basil instead of parsley.

Gooey Stovetop Lasagna

Egg roll wrappers are excellent stand-ins for fresh pasta sheets. Be sure to get the kind that are refrigerated, with a simple ingredient list that indicates they're minimally processed. With this method you don't even need to turn on the oven. **Serves 4**

Ingredients

4 large cloves garlic

Several fresh oregano sprigs or 1 tablespoon dried Italian seasoning

4 tablespoons olive oil

2 large (28-ounce) cans crushed tomatoes

Salt and pepper

4 ounces Parmesan cheese (about 1 cup grated)

2 eggs

2 cups ricotta cheese

4 ounces mozzarella cheese (preferably fresh)

16 egg roll wrappers

Prep · Cook

☐ Peel and chop 4 cloves garlic.

☐ If you're using fresh oregano, strip the leaves from several sprigs and chop about 2 tablespoons.

1. Put 2 tablespoons olive oil in a large skillet over medium-high heat. When it's hot, add the garlic and fresh oregano or 1 tablespoon Italian dried seasoning and cook, stirring until fragrant, about 1 minute.

2. Add the tomatoes and ½ cup water; sprinkle with salt and pepper. Bring the sauce to a boil, then adjust the heat so that it bubbles gently but steadily. Cook, stirring occasionally, while you prepare the filling.

   ☐ Grate 1 cup Parmesan cheese.

   ☐ Crack the eggs in a medium bowl; sprinkle with salt and pepper.

   ☐ Add the ricotta and ½ cup Parmesan to the eggs and whisk until smooth.

   ☐ If using fresh mozzarella cheese, tear it into bite-sized bits (or grate 1 cup low-moisture mozzarella).

   ☐ Separate the egg roll wrappers, count out 16, and restack them so they're handy. (Refrigerate or freeze any remaining in the pack.)

3. Remove the sauce from the heat and transfer about two-thirds to a medium saucepan over medium-low heat; cover and cook, stirring once or twice, until Step 5.

4. Carefully nestle 8 egg roll wrappers in the sauce in the skillet, overlapping them a little to fully cover the sauce and run up the sides about 1 inch. Spread the ricotta filling on top; cover with 8 wrappers, tucking the edges down inside the sides of the pan. Drizzle with 2 tablespoons olive oil.

● recipe continues →

5. Spoon on enough sauce to cover the top of the lasagna in a thin layer. Sprinkle on the mozzarella and ½ cup Parmesan. Return the skillet to medium heat; you want the sauce to bubble gently. Cover and cook undisturbed until the wrappers are tender and the filling is heated through, 4 to 5 minutes. Remove from the heat and let the lasagna set about 5 minutes. Cut into wedges and serve, passing the remaining sauce at the table.

Variations

Gooey Stovetop Spinach Lasagna. Before making the sauce, steam 5 ounces fresh spinach in the skillet over medium-high heat, covered, until softened, just a couple minutes. Drain in a colander while you make the sauce and filling. Squeeze the excess water out of the spinach, chop it, and add it to the ricotta filling before proceeding.

Gooey Stovetop Sausage Lasagna. Before making the sauce, cook 2 chopped hot or sweet Italian sausages (about 4 ounces each) in the skillet over medium-high heat, stirring frequently, until no longer pink, about 5 minutes. Transfer to towels to drain. Spoon off the fat and wipe out the skillet before making the sauce and proceeding. Add the sausage to the ricotta filling and finish as directed.

Gooey Stovetop White Lasagna. Rather decadent. Omit the tomatoes. Grate an extra 4 ounces mozzarella (1 cup). After cooking the garlic in the oil, add the oregano or Italian seasoning and 1½ cups half-and-half. Cook until steaming, then remove from heat. Build the lasagna in the skillet with the wrappers and ricotta filling, sprinkling 1 cup mozzarella on top of the filling before adding the final layer of wrappers. Scatter the remaining mozzarella and Parmesan over the top and drizzle with 1½ cups half-and-half. Cover and cook as described in Step 5. Garnish with chopped fresh chives.

Cool Peanut Noodles with Whatever You Have

"Whatever you have" is an invitation to clear the fridge of bits and pieces from meals gone by: cooked meat, chicken, shrimp, or vegetables; cubes of tofu; or things you'd happily eat raw like cucumbers, snow peas, bean sprouts, or celery hearts. After all, doesn't everything go well with peanut butter? And if you disagree—or want a change of pace—you can always substitute tahini, cashews, or sunflower seeds for the peanut butter. **Serves 4**

Ingredients

Salt

Stir-in ingredients: any combination of cooked meat, fish, or tofu, and/or any cooked or raw vegetables (3 to 4 cups total after chopping or shredding)

½ cup peanut butter

1 tablespoon sesame oil

1 tablespoon honey

3 tablespoons soy sauce

1 tablespoon rice vinegar

Dash of chile oil or hot sauce

Pepper

½ inch fresh ginger

12 ounces fresh or dried Chinese egg noodles

3 scallions

☐ Prep · Cook

1. Bring a large pot of water to a boil and salt it.

   ☐ Gather your stir-in ingredients from the fridge and chop or slice as needed.

2. Combine ½ cup peanut butter, 1 tablespoon sesame oil, 1 tablespoon honey, 3 tablespoons soy sauce, 1 tablespoon rice vinegar, a dash of chile oil or hot sauce, and a sprinkle of pepper in a large bowl.

   ☐ Peel and chop ½ inch ginger; add it to the bowl.

3. Whisk the sauce, thinning it with hot water until it has the consistency of heavy cream. Taste and adjust the seasoning.

4. When the water boils, add the noodles and cook, stirring occasionally. Start tasting after 3 minutes.

   ☐ Trim and chop the scallions.

5. When the noodles are tender but not mushy, drain them, rinse them under cold water until completely cool, then drain again. Add the noodles to the bowl with the sauce along with whatever you're stirring in and the scallions. Toss, taste, and adjust the seasoning, then serve.

Chile Noodles with Snow (or Sugar Snap) Peas and Crisp Pork

Why buy chile oil when it's so easy to make at home? Two ways to go: Dried chiles lend a smoky, toasted flavor, while fresh chiles produce a brighter-tasting oil. You can't go wrong either way. **Serves 4**

Ingredients

Salt

1 pound boneless pork shoulder or sirloin

5 tablespoons good-quality vegetable oil

5 dried red chiles (like pequin or arbol) or 3 fresh hot chiles (like Thai or serrano)

4 cloves garlic

1 inch fresh ginger

12 ounces snow (or sugar snap) peas

12 ounces udon noodles

Sesame seeds for garnish

Soy sauce for passing at the table

▢ Prep · Cook

1. Bring a large pot of water to a boil and salt it.

   ▢ Cut the pork into bite-sized pieces.

2. Put 1 tablespoon vegetable oil in a large skillet over medium-high heat. When it's hot, add the pork and sprinkle with salt. Cook undisturbed until the pieces brown and release easily from the pan, 3 to 5 minutes. Lower the heat to medium and continue to cook, stirring once or twice, until the pork crisps in places and is no longer pink inside, about 5 minutes more.

   ▢ If you're using dried chiles, leave them whole; if you're using fresh, slice them thinly.

   ▢ Peel 4 cloves garlic and 1 inch ginger and slice them both crosswise.

3. Transfer the pork to a plate with a slotted spoon. Add 4 tablespoons vegetable oil to the skillet and turn the heat to medium-low. Add the chiles, garlic, and ginger. Adjust the heat so that the oil bubbles ever so slightly, turning it down if anything starts to smell too toasted; let the flavors infuse the oil while you cook the noodles and peas.

   ▢ Trim the snow (or sugar snap) peas.

4. When the water boils, add the udon and cook, stirring occasionally. Start tasting after 3 minutes. When the noodles are almost tender, add the snow peas to the boiling water. Continue cooking until the noodles are tender but not mushy and the snow peas are softened but still crisp, just a minute or so.

• recipe continues →

5. Drain the noodles and snow peas, rinse them under cold water until they're room temperature, then drain again. Return the noodles and snow peas to the pot and add the pork. Pour the oil into the pot through a strainer (discard the solids if you like, or reserve them to pass at the table). Toss, taste, and adjust the seasoning. Garnish with the sesame seeds and serve, passing soy sauce at the table.

Variations

Chile Noodles with Gai Lan and Crisp Chicken. Gai lan is Chinese broccoli; good stand-ins are broccolini, mustard greens, and baby bok choy. Use 1 pound boneless, skinless chicken thighs instead of the pork and gai lan instead of the snow (or sugar snap) peas. (Chop it into 1-inch pieces.) The cooking times will be the same.

Chile Noodles with Snow (or Sugar Snap) Peas and Crisp Salmon. Substitute 1 pound salmon fillets for the pork. Leave the skin on if you like; it will crisp deliciously. Leave the fillets whole to start. In Step 2 cut the cooking time on both of the stages in half; break the salmon into big pieces with a spatula as it firms.

Chile Noodles with Carrot Ribbons and Crisp Edamame. Substitute a 10- or 12-ounce bag of frozen shelled edamame for the pork. Increase the total oil to 6 tablespoons, adding the extra tablespoon at the beginning of Step 2. Heat the oil over medium heat and as the edamame cook and crisp, mash them with the back of a spoon or a fork; they will be ready in about 5 minutes. Instead of the snow (or sugar snap) peas, trim and peel 2 carrots; use the peeler to continue cutting ribbons from the carrot, all the way down to the core. Add them to the noodles as described in Step 4.

Soba with Teriyaki Tofu

There's no need to buy bottled teriyaki sauce. The lightly sweetened soy sauce is a snap to make—and easy to adapt for noodles. Tofu loves the teriyaki treatment, emerging from searing and saucing with a wonderful glaze that's a delightful counterpoint to the assertive flavor of soba. **Serves 4**

Ingredients

Salt

2 tablespoons vegetable oil

1 brick firm tofu (14 to 16 ounces)

2 cloves garlic

1 inch fresh ginger

½ cup soy sauce

½ cup mirin or ¼ cup honey mixed with ¼ cup water

12 ounces soba noodles

4 scallions

Pepper

▢ Prep · Cook

1. Bring a large pot of water to a boil and salt it.

2. Put 2 tablespoons vegetable oil in a large skillet over medium-high heat.

   ▢ Pat the tofu dry; cut it into ½-inch cubes.

3. When the oil is hot, add the tofu and cook undisturbed until the tofu browns on the bottom and releases easily from the pan, about 5 minutes.

   ▢ Peel 2 cloves garlic and 1 inch ginger; chop them together.

4. When the tofu is browned on one side, use a spatula to stir it, scraping the pieces from the skillet if necessary. Add ½ cup soy sauce, ½ cup mirin or ¼ cup honey mixed with ¼ cup water, and the garlic and ginger to the skillet. Bring to a boil, then adjust the heat so that it bubbles gently.

5. When the water boils, add the soba and cook, stirring occasionally. Start tasting after 3 minutes.

   ▢ Trim and chop the scallions.

6. When the noodles are tender but not mushy, drain them, reserving about 1 cup cooking liquid. Add the soba to the skillet. Toss with the sauce, adding a little cooking water if necessary to coat the noodles. Be gentle to avoid breaking up the tofu. Taste and add a little salt and pepper if necessary. Serve garnished with the scallions.

Variations

Soba with Teriyaki Beef.
Substitute 12 ounces boneless beef sirloin or rib-eye, thinly sliced, for the tofu. Sear the beef on one side, without stirring, until the slices just lose their red color, then build the teriyaki sauce as directed.

Soba with Teriyaki Chicken.
Substitute 2 small boneless, skinless chicken breasts (about 12 ounces), thinly sliced, for the tofu. Sear the chicken on one side until it just loses its pink color, then build the teriyaki sauce as directed.

Soba with Teriyaki Pork. Use 12 ounces pork shoulder, thinly sliced, instead of the tofu. Stir-fry it in the oil in Step 3 until it just loses its pink color, then build the teriyaki sauce as directed.

SOY SAUCE, THE ULTIMATE SEASONING

Soy sauce, which is called "shoyu" in Japan and has been around for thousands of years, is made by fermenting soybeans and usually wheat with salt and bacteria. (Avoid anything that has more than those four ingredients.) Tamari usually contains only fermented soybeans without any wheat or with lesser amounts; if you must avoid wheat or gluten, be sure to check the label.

Depending on the brewing process, soy sauce will vary in color, saltiness, and intensity. Most versions come from Japan, China, and now the United States. All have the potential to make instant stocks and sauces simply with the addition of water. Any of them will do just fine in these recipes; I encourage you to try imported styles that might be unfamiliar. Just taste them first so you know what you're working with.

Curried Noodles with Shrimp and Sweet Potatoes

A one-pot meal that lands somewhere between sauced noodles and soup. This technique is a good one to learn and adapt: Start by building a fragrant broth with aromatics and spices, add vegetables and meat or seafood, then add noodles so they thicken the broth with their starch.
Serves 4

Ingredients

1 (14-ounce) can coconut milk

1 tablespoon curry powder

4 whole star anise

2 bay leaves

Salt

2 cloves garlic

1 inch fresh ginger

1 fresh hot green chile
(like serrano)

1 pound sweet potatoes

1 lime

Several sprigs fresh cilantro

12 ounces dried rice vermicelli

3 tablespoons fish sauce

12 ounces peeled shrimp

☐ Prep · Cook

1. Put 2 cups water in a large pot over medium-high heat. Add the coconut milk, 1 tablespoon curry powder, 4 whole star anise, 2 bay leaves, and a generous pinch of salt.

   ☐ Peel 2 cloves garlic and 1 inch ginger. Trim the chile; seed it if you like to reduce the heat. Chop them all together and add them to the pot.

   ☐ Peel the sweet potatoes, halve them lengthwise, and cut them into half-moons $\frac{1}{8}$ to $\frac{1}{4}$ inch thick. Add them to the pot.

2. Bring the mixture to a boil, then reduce the heat so the liquid bubbles steadily. Cook, stirring occasionally, until the sweet potatoes are barely tender, 6 to 8 minutes.

   ☐ Halve the lime.

   ☐ Chop several cilantro sprigs.

3. When the sweet potatoes are fully tender, add the rice noodles and stir. Squeeze in the lime juice and add 3 tablespoons fish sauce and the shrimp. Cook, stirring frequently and adding a little water if the mixture looks dry, until the noodles are tender and the shrimp turn pink and cook through, 2 to 5 minutes, depending on if they were frozen.

4. Fish out the star anise and bay leaves. Taste and adjust the seasoning. Serve garnished with the cilantro.

Variations

Curried Noodles with Chicken and Turnips. Use turnips instead of the sweet potatoes; peel them and cut into wedges. Substitute 4 boneless, skinless chicken thighs (about 12 ounces) for the shrimp. Chop the chicken into ½-inch pieces and add them to the pot along with the noodles in Step 3.

Lemongrass Noodles with Shrimp and Sweet Potatoes. Omit the bay leaves. Substitute two 3-inch pieces lemongrass stalks for the curry powder and 2 or 3 sprigs fresh basil for the star anise. Remove the lemongrass and basil before serving. Garnish with chopped basil leaves instead of the cilantro.

Curried Noodles with Pork and Daikon. Use daikon radish instead of the sweet potatoes. Instead of the shrimp, use 12 ounces boneless pork chops, cut into strips no more than ½ inch thick; it will take a couple minutes longer to cook in Step 3.

Noodles with Minty Scallion Sauce and Sliced Chicken

Quickly blanching scallions tames their heat and renders them silky—the perfect foundation for a sauce that features the sweet grassiness of mint. For other ingredients, see the variations. **Serves 4**

Ingredients

Salt

½ inch fresh ginger

1 small bunch fresh mint

1 bunch scallions

⅓ cup plus 2 tablespoons vegetable oil

1 tablespoon sesame oil

Pepper

12 ounces fresh or dried Chinese egg noodles

1 boneless, skinless chicken breast (about 12 ounces)

▢ Prep · Cook

1. Bring a large pot of water to a boil and salt it. Also bring a small saucepan of water to a boil.

2. Prepare a gas grill for direct cooking or turn the broiler to high; put the rack 4 inches from the heat.

   ▢ Peel and chop ½ inch ginger; put it in a food processor.

   ▢ Strip about ½ cup leaves from the mint sprigs. Put them in the food processor.

   ▢ Trim and chop the scallions.

3. When the small saucepan of water boils, add the scallions and cook for 1 minute. Drain; rinse under cold water until cool. Add them to the food processor.

4. Add ⅓ cup vegetable oil and 1 tablespoon sesame oil to the food processor along with a sprinkle of salt and pepper. Process, scraping down the sides and thinning the mixture with a splash of water if necessary, until it becomes a thick, smooth sauce. Transfer half of the sauce to a large bowl.

5. When the large pot of water boils, add the noodles and cook, stirring occasionally. Start tasting after 1 minute for fresh noodles or 3 minutes for dried. When the noodles are tender but not mushy, drain them, rinse them under cold water until completely cool, then drain again. Add the noodles to the bowl with the sauce and toss.

   ▢ Cut the chicken breast into 2 cutlets by working the knife parallel to the cutting board through the meat.

   ▢ Put the chicken cutlets on a rimmed baking sheet, rub with 2 tablespoons vegetable oil, and sprinkle both sides with salt and pepper.

6. When you're ready to cook, grill the chicken cutlets directly on the grates or broil them in the pan, turning once, until lightly browned on both sides and no longer pink inside, 2 to 5 minutes per side. Transfer the chicken to a clean cutting board and slice each cutlet crosswise into strips. Lay the chicken on top of the noodles, top with the remaining sauce, and serve.

Variations

Noodles with Spicy Scallion Sauce and Sliced Beef. Instead of the mint, use 1 bunch fresh cilantro; measure about 1 cup tender stems and leaves for the sauce. Trim and chop 1 fresh hot green jalapeño chile and add it to the food processor along with the ginger. Substitute 12 ounces skirt or flank steak for the chicken. Grill or broil it until a bit pinker inside than you like it, 2 to 5 minutes per side. Let it rest for 5 minutes before slicing.

Noodles with Peanutty Scallion Sauce and Sliced Chicken. Instead of the mint, add ½ cup peanut butter or roasted peanuts to the food processor. Since the sauce will be thick, you'll likely need a little extra water to make it spoonable.

Noodles with Fish and Lemony Scallion Sauce. Any firm white fish fillet works here, like catfish, rockfish, or cod. Instead of the mint, quarter a lemon and remove the seeds; add the whole thing to the food processor with the blanched scallions. Substitute 1 pound fish fillets for the chicken; cut the fish into 4 portions if necessary. Broil it on a rimmed baking sheet instead of grilling. It will take a little less time to cook, so check the inside for doneness frequently; it's ready when you can separate it into moist, barely opaque flakes. Serve it whole on top of the noodles.

Stir-Fried Noodles with Beef and Celery

Conventional wisdom for cooking stir-fries says you should prep all your ingredients first since once you start cooking, it all goes lightning-quick. But if you keep the ingredients to a few, as in this lo mein–style dish, you can prep as you go without, no sweat. **Serves 4**

Ingredients

Salt

3 tablespoons vegetable oil

12 ounces boneless beef sirloin or rib-eye

1 medium onion

3 celery stalks with leaves

1 lemon

2 tablespoons soy sauce

12 ounces dried Chinese egg or wheat noodles (or 8 ounces fresh)

☐ Prep · Cook

1. Bring a large pot of water to a boil and salt it.

2. Put 3 tablespoons vegetable oil in a large skillet or a separate large pot over medium-high heat.

   ☐ Slice the beef as thinly as you can.

3. When the oil is hot, add the beef and sprinkle with salt. Cook undisturbed until the pieces brown on the bottom and release easily from the pan, about 2 minutes. Stir once or twice, transfer the meat to a plate, leaving behind as much oil as possible, and remove the skillet or pot from the heat.

   ☐ Trim, peel, halve, and slice the onion.

   ☐ Trim and slice the celery; chop and save the leaves for garnish.

4. Return the skillet or pot to medium-high heat. Add the onion and celery and sprinkle with salt. Cook, stirring occasionally, until the onion begins to brown and the celery is just tender, 3 to 5 minutes.

   ☐ Halve the lemon.

5. When the vegetables are done, return the beef to the skillet or pot and add any accumulated juices. Squeeze in the lemon juice through a strainer or your fingers to capture the seeds; add 2 tablespoons soy sauce. Cook for 30 seconds to a minute, then turn off the heat.

6. When the water boils, add the noodles and cook, stirring occasionally. Start tasting after 2 minutes for fresh and 5 minutes for dried. When the noodles are tender but not mushy, drain them, reserving about 1 cup cooking water. Add the noodles to the skillet along with a splash of cooking water and turn the heat to medium-high.

7. Add the celery leaves and cook, tossing with tongs, until the noodles are coated with sauce. Taste and adjust the seasoning, and serve.

Variations

Stir-Fried Noodles with Beef and Bean Sprouts. Substitute 8 ounces bean sprouts for the celery. To keep them crunchy, instead of cooking them along with the onion, add them to the skillet when you return the beef in Step 5.

Stir-Fried Noodles with Tofu and Celery. Use 1 brick firm tofu (14 to 16 ounces) instead of the beef; blot it dry with towels. Cut the tofu into ½-inch cubes and cook it the same way as the beef in Step 3; it will take longer to brown and release, 5 or 6 minutes. Remove it from the skillet and proceed as directed.

Stir-Fried Japchae with Beef and Celery. A spicy Korean-style twist. Instead of the egg noodles, use sweet potato noodles; they take about the same time to cook as dried egg noodles. Replace the lemon juice and soy sauce with 2 tablespoons gochujang. Serve with cabbage or daikon kimchi if you like.

More Curried Noodles, with Chicken, Peppers, and Basil

Another vibrant, colorful curried noodle dish, this time inspired by a restaurant favorite often credited (mistakenly or not) to Singapore. And since rice vermicelli only require a quick soak to become tender, you can focus on the stir-frying part of the recipe. **Serves 4**

Ingredients

Salt

4 to 6 boneless, skinless chicken thighs (about 1 pound)

2 cloves garlic

1 inch fresh ginger

2 red bell peppers

12 ounces rice vermicelli

3 tablespoons vegetable oil

1 tablespoon curry powder

1 teaspoon sugar

1 tablespoon soy sauce, or more to taste

1 tablespoon fish sauce, or more to taste

1 bunch fresh basil (preferably Thai)

▢ Prep · Cook

1. Bring a medium saucepan of water to a boil and salt it.

   ▢ Cut the chicken into ½-inch chunks.

   ▢ Peel 2 cloves garlic and 1 inch ginger; chop them together.

   ▢ Core, seed, and slice the bell peppers.

2. When the water comes to a boil, add the noodles, stir once or twice, and turn off the heat. Let them steep until they're not quite fully tender, 3 to 5 minutes.

3. Put 3 tablespoons vegetable oil in a large skillet over medium-high heat. Add the chicken and cook undisturbed until the pieces brown and release easily, 2 to 3 minutes. Add the garlic and ginger and cook, stirring occasionally, until the meat is no longer pink, 2 to 3 minutes.

4. When the noodles are done, drain well, reserving some of the soaking liquid and shaking off as much excess water as you can.

5. Add 1 tablespoon curry powder and 1 teaspoon sugar to the chicken; cook until the curry powder is fragrant, about a minute. Add 1 tablespoon soy sauce, 1 tablespoon fish sauce, and the red bell peppers, and stir to combine.

   ▢ Chop or tear about 1 cup basil leaves.

6. When the peppers begin to soften and the chicken is cooked through, add the noodles and a splash of soaking liquid. Cook, tossing with tongs, until the noodles are tender and most of the liquid evaporates. Taste and adjust the seasoning, adding more fish sauce or soy sauce if you like. Stir in the basil and serve.

Rice and Grains

Rice and other grains are the human race's main source of calories; they have been staples since the beginning of agriculture. These foods aren't what we always consider as fast—but they can be.

A pot of white rice—universally eaten around the world—takes maybe 15 unattended minutes to cook and can be taken in infinite directions; bulgur, oats, farro, and couscous can all be on the table in 30 minutes or less. And if you prefer brown rice, which many people do for its high fiber and protein, see the hack on page 208 for how to adapt any of the recipes in this chapter.

A word on washing: I rinse all my grains in the pot before cooking, swirling and draining off a couple changes of water. It's not any residues that worry me; rinsing helps release some starch so the grains cook up fluffier.

Turning dishes that are typically considered sides into a meal isn't really a big deal. My secret? The fast techniques for cooking rice and grains resemble pasta more than pilaf: You cook the starchy thing in one pot while you prepare the vegetables, meat, and seasonings in a skillet simultaneously—then combine.

Fried Rice with Cabbage

The most versatile rice recipe ever—one you can use as a model for spontaneous lunch or dinner. While the rice bubbles away on the stove, you pull together a satisfying cabbage stir-fry. Then you've got a couple different choices for how you eat it. For times when you've got leftover rice already in the fridge, see the last variation. **Serves 4**

Ingredients

3 tablespoons vegetable oil, plus more if needed

1 tablespoon sesame seeds

1½ cups long-grain white rice

Salt

1 small head green or savoy cabbage (1 pound)

4 scallions

4 eggs

Soy sauce for serving

▢ Prep · Cook

1. Put 1 tablespoon vegetable oil in a medium saucepan over medium heat.

2. When the oil is hot, add 1 tablespoon sesame seeds, 1½ cups rice, and a sprinkle of salt. Cook, stirring frequently, until the rice is glossy and starting to color slightly, 3 to 5 minutes.

3. Add 3 cups water. Bring to a boil, then adjust the heat so the mixture bubbles gently but steadily. Cover and cook undisturbed until small craters appear on the surface, 10 to 15 minutes.

   ▢ Trim, core, and quarter the cabbage.

4. Put 2 tablespoons vegetable oil in a large skillet over low heat.

   ▢ Cut each cabbage quarter crosswise into thin ribbons.

5. Turn up the heat under the skillet to medium-high. Add the cabbage and sprinkle with salt. Cook, stirring occasionally, until the cabbage is lightly browned and crisp-tender (it should still have a little crunch), 3 to 5 minutes.

   ▢ Trim and chop the scallions.

6. Move the cabbage to one side of the skillet and add a drizzle of oil to the empty space if it looks dry. Crack the eggs into that space and cook, stirring constantly with a fork, until they're scrambled and set, a minute or two. Toss the eggs and cabbage together in the skillet and turn off the heat.

7. When small craters appear on the surface of the rice, tip the saucepan to see if any liquid remains. If so, re-cover and keep cooking until the rice is dry, checking every minute or two.

● recipe continues →

8. Add the cooked rice to the cabbage and eggs. Add the scallions and stir to combine. Taste and adjust the seasoning. Serve, passing soy sauce at the table. Or serve the stir-fry in bowls on top of the rice, garnished with the scallions.

Variations

Fried Rice with Bok Choy. Here, this vegetable delivers two distinct textures, crunchy stems and silky leaves. Substitute 1 pound bok choy for the cabbage; slice the stems and leaves crosswise into narrow ribbons and cook them the same way in Step 5.

Fried Rice with Tomatoes. Substitute 1 pound ripe tomatoes for the cabbage; core the tomatoes and chop in big chunks. Cook the tomatoes just until they start to release some of their juice but not so much that they break down into sauce, about 3 minutes. Then push them to the side and add the eggs as directed. If you like, garnish with chopped fresh cilantro or Thai basil along with the scallions.

Fried Rice with Leftover Rice. Works for the main recipe or either of the first two variations. If you have 3 to 4 cups leftover rice in the refrigerator—brown or white, long- or short-grain—use that instead of cooking a fresh batch. Skip Step 1. Toast the sesame seeds in a dry skillet over medium heat in Step 2, then transfer them to a small bowl. Add 2 tablespoons oil to the same skillet and raise the heat to high. Fry the rice until it sizzles and pops, just a minute or two. Transfer it to a large shallow bowl. Make the stir-fry in the skillet as described in Steps 5 and 6. Return the rice to the pan. Toss, taste, and adjust the seasoning. Garnish with the sesame seeds and serve.

SUBSTITUTING BROWN RICE FOR WHITE

Since brown rice takes about 45 minutes to cook—more than twice the time of its white counterparts—I don't call for any in this book. But with a bit of a head start, you can easily substitute brown rice in any recipe or variation here. First thing, bring a large pot of salted water to a boil like you would for pasta, then stir in the same quantity of brown rice as called for in the ingredient list. Adjust the heat so the water bubbles steadily; stir once more, then let it cook until the color lightens and the kernels begin to plump, about 12 minutes. Drain the rice thoroughly, then start the recipe as directed, using the semicooked brown rice instead of the raw white rice.

Reverse Risotto

Creamy risotto doesn't happen by itself. Or does it? I call it "reverse" because you wait until the very end to season and stir the rice. Though nothing about this technique is traditional, the results are quite similar to the classic: rice with a little bite, flavored with wine, Parmesan, saffron, and butter. **Serves 4**

Ingredients

1½ cups Arborio, Carnaroli, or other short-grain white rice

Salt

1 cup white wine (optional)

2 tablespoons olive oil

1 small onion or large shallot

Pinch of saffron threads or 1 teaspoon smoked paprika

4 ounces Parmesan cheese (1 cup grated), plus more for garnish

Several sprigs fresh parsley

2 tablespoons butter

▫ Prep · Cook

1. Put 1½ cups Arborio rice in a large pot with a pinch of salt, 1 cup white wine if you're using it, and 3 cups water (or 4 cups if you're not using wine). Bring to a boil. Reduce the heat so the liquid bubbles gently but steadily, cover, and cook undisturbed for 10 minutes.

2. Put 2 tablespoons olive oil in a medium skillet over low heat.

   ▫ Trim, peel, and chop the onion or shallot.

   ▫ Get about 1 cup water handy by the stove.

3. Turn up the heat under the skillet to medium-high and add the onion or shallot. Cook, stirring occasionally, until translucent, about 3 minutes. Lower the heat to medium and continue cooking until golden and slightly jammy, another 3 to 5 minutes. Add the saffron or smoked paprika and stir until fragrant, less than a minute, then turn off the heat.

4. Check the rice the first time after it's been cooking 10 minutes. It should be slightly firm and maybe no longer submerged. Add enough water to cover the rice by about ½ inch and stir, scraping up any that might be stuck to the bottom of the pot. Re-cover and continue cooking until the rice is creamy but still has a little bite, 2 to 5 minutes more.

   ▫ Grate 1 cup Parmesan cheese.

   ▫ Strip the leaves from several parsley sprigs and chop 2 tablespoons parsley leaves.

   ▫ Get 2 tablespoons butter handy.

● recipe continues →

5. When the rice is ready, add the seasonings from the skillet to the pot, along with the cheese and butter, and stir until melted. The risotto should be creamy but not mushy, and soupy enough to drop from the spoon like porridge. If not, add a little more water and continue to cook and stir another minute or so. Taste and adjust the seasoning. Serve, garnished with the parsley and more cheese.

Variations

Mushroom Reverse Risotto. Omit the saffron. To intensify the flavor, if you have some handy, rinse several slices dried porcini mushrooms, cut them into small pieces with kitchen scissors, and add them to the pot with the rice at the beginning of Step 1. Trim and slice 1 pound cremini mushrooms. Instead of the onion or shallot, chop 3 cloves garlic. In Step 2, use a large skillet. When the oil is hot, add the mushrooms, sprinkle with salt and pepper, and cook, stirring occasionally, until the mushrooms release their water. When the pan is almost dry again, add the garlic, lower the heat to medium, and cook, stirring once in a while, until the garlic softens, about 3 minutes before proceeding.

Reverse Risotto with Peas. Sure, you can use frozen peas, but this is way better. Omit the saffron. Trim 12 ounces sugar snap peas and chop them into pea-sized bits. Use a large skillet to cook the onions in Step 3. When they're ready, add the sugar snap peas and stir to coat in the oil before proceeding. Use chopped mint instead of the parsley.

Reverse Risotto with Anchovies and Chiles. Omit the saffron. Chop 4 cloves garlic and 1 or 2 fresh hot red or green chiles (like serrano or jalapeño) and cook them with the onion in Step 3. When the vegetables are soft and the onions jammy, add 4 to 6 oil-packed anchovy fillets (depending how intense you want the flavor). Continue to cook, stirring and mashing the anchovies and vegetables with a fork, until they form a loose paste. Then proceed. Garnish with the parsley or chopped fresh basil.

Rice, Beans, and Greens

Adding rice to the classic beans-and-greens equation—with a simple "backwards-pilaf" technique—takes the dish from soupy to fluffy. You can go with my suggestions or use whatever beans you have handy. One nuance: If you like your beans more intact than broken, cook the rice first, then toss the beans in with the cheese, just long enough to warm them.
Serves 4

Ingredients

1¾ cups cooked or canned cannellini beans (one 15-ounce can)

1½ cups long-grain white rice

Salt

2 cloves garlic

1 bunch greens (like escarole or lacinato kale; about 1 pound)

2 ounces Parmesan cheese (½ cup grated)

3 tablespoons butter

Pepper

☐ Prep · Cook

☐ If you're using canned beans, rinse and drain them.

1. Put the beans and 1½ cups rice in a large pot; add a big pinch of salt and enough water to cover by about an inch. Bring to a boil.

   ☐ Peel and slice 2 cloves garlic; add them to the pot.

2. When the liquid boils, adjust the heat so it bubbles steadily but not vigorously. Cover and cook undisturbed until the rice is tender but not mushy, 10 to 15 minutes.

   ☐ Trim the greens and cut the leaves and stems crosswise into ribbons.

   ☐ Grate ½ cup Parmesan.

3. When the rice is tender, stir in the greens with a large fork, adding more liquid if necessary to keep the grains from sticking to the bottom. Turn the heat to low, cover the pot, and let sit for 3 minutes. Tip the pot; if any liquid remains, re-cover and keep cooking until the rice is dry, checking every minute or two.

4. Stir in 3 tablespoons butter, the Parmesan, and some pepper with a fork to fluff the rice. Taste and adjust the seasoning, and serve.

Fast Rice Porridge with Chicken and Snow Peas

Jook is a traditional Chinese porridge made by simmering rice for hours until it breaks apart into a mass of silky starch. (And other cuisines have similar soupy rice traditions.) For a version made in only 30 minutes, I've developed a shortcut similar to the risotto on page 209, only served with vegetables and a little stir-fried meat on top. **Serves 4**

Ingredients

1½ cups long-grain white rice

6 cups chicken or vegetable stock or water

Salt

4 to 6 boneless, skinless chicken thighs (about 1 pound)

12 ounces snow peas

2 tablespoons vegetable oil

2 cloves garlic

1 inch fresh ginger

Pepper

3 scallions

Soy sauce for serving

Sesame oil for serving

▢ Prep · Cook

▢ Put 1½ cups rice in a food processor and pulse a few times to break up the grains.

1. Put the rice in a large pot with 6 cups stock or water and a pinch of salt; bring to a boil.

   ▢ Cut the chicken into ½-inch chunks.

   ▢ Trim the snow peas.

2. When the rice mixture boils, adjust the heat so it bubbles gently but steadily. Cover and cook, stirring a couple times, until the rice is very soft and its starch has thickened the liquid to the consistency of porridge, 15 to 20 minutes.

3. Put 2 tablespoons vegetable oil in a large skillet over medium-high heat. When the oil is hot, add the chicken and cook undisturbed until the pieces brown and release easily, 3 to 4 minutes. Then stir occasionally until the meat is no longer pink inside, about 3 minutes more.

   ▢ Peel 2 cloves garlic and 1 inch ginger; chop them together.

4. Add the garlic and ginger to the chicken and stir until fragrant, about a minute. Add the snow peas, sprinkle with salt and pepper, and cook, stirring occasionally, until they soften slightly, 3 to 4 minutes (they should still be mostly crunchy). Turn off the heat. Taste and adjust the seasoning.

   ▢ Trim and chop the scallions.

5. The rice should be soupy enough to drop easily from a spoon; if not, stir in some water. Taste and adjust the seasoning. Serve topped with the stir-fry and garnished with the scallions. Pass soy sauce and sesame oil at the table for drizzling.

Variations

Fast Rice Porridge with Beef and Bean Sprouts. If you've got it, use beef stock to cook the rice. Instead of chicken, thinly slice 1 pound beef sirloin against the grain; substitute 8 ounces bean sprouts for the snow peas. In Step 4, as soon as you stir in the bean sprouts, turn off the heat.

Fast Rice Porridge with Pork and Asparagus. Substitute 1 pound boneless pork chops or sirloin for the chicken and 1 pound asparagus for the snow peas. Trim the asparagus and cut into 1-inch pieces. The cooking times will be about the same.

Fast Rice Porridge with Tofu and Spicy Cabbage. Instead of the chicken, use two 12- or 14-ounce bricks extra-firm silken tofu, cut into cubes. Instead of stir-frying it in Step 3, lay it on top of the rice after checking it in Step 5 and return the pot lid to let the tofu heat through. Substitute 1 pound napa cabbage, chopped, for the snow peas (if you have extra, save it for another time). Just before turning off the heat in Step 4, add ½ teaspoon red chile flakes (or more or less to taste) and 1 tablespoon rice vinegar.

Hoppin' John with Collards

Rice and beans appear a few different ways in the South. This Carolina classic comes together in a flash with my chop-and-drop method. To make it a one-pot meal, I also add collards, which would usually be slow simmered with pork or ham and served on the side. **Serves 4**

Ingredients

1½ cups long-grain white rice

4 ounces slab bacon (without the rind) or 6 to 8 slices thick-cut bacon

1 medium onion

3 cloves garlic

2 sprigs fresh thyme

1 small bunch collard greens (about 12 ounces)

1¾ cups cooked or canned black-eyed peas (one 15-ounce can)

Red chile flakes to taste

Salt and pepper

☐ Prep · Cook

1. Put 1½ cups long-grain white rice and 3½ cups water in a large pot; bring to a boil.

   ☐ Chop the bacon; add it to the rice.

   ☐ Trim, peel, and chop the onion; add it to the pot.

   ☐ Peel and chop 3 cloves garlic; add them to the pot.

   ☐ Strip the leaves from 2 thyme sprigs; chop and add to the pot.

   ☐ Trim the collards of any tough stems. Stack the leaves and fold them in half along the stem, then cut crosswise into thin ribbons; add them to the pot.

   ☐ If you're using canned black-eyed peas, rinse and drain them. Add the black-eyed peas to the pot.

2. When the mixture boils, season with some red chile flakes, a pinch of salt, and pepper to taste. Adjust the heat so the mixture bubbles gently but steadily.

3. Cover and cook until the rice is tender and the liquid is absorbed, 15 to 20 minutes. Taste and adjust the seasoning. Fluff with a fork and serve.

Variations

Hoppin' John with Andouille and Okra. More like jambalaya. Instead of the bacon, use 4 ounces chopped andouille sausage or tasso ham (about ½ cup). Substitute 1 pound okra for the collards; trim the tops but leave the pods whole (they won't get as slimy).

Hoppin' John with Celery and Ham. I love the way the celery gets a little silky when it's cooked this way. Instead of the bacon, use 4 ounces chopped ham (about ½ cup). Substitute 1 pound celery hearts for the collards; chop across the stalks as thinly as you can (reserve the leaves for garnish).

Hoppin' Succotash. Now it's vegetarian. Omit the bacon. Substitute frozen lima beans for the black-eyed peas and green beans for the collards. Trim and cut the green beans into 1-inch pieces, adding them to the pot after the onions and garlic, along with the lima beans. Add 1 cup fresh or frozen corn kernels once the rice is tender in Step 3.

Rice Bowl with Sausage and Fennel

In the Japanese tradition of chirashi, bowls of sushi rice have all sorts of ingredient combinations scattered on top. This one is not at all Japanese but is inspired by that concept, and the flavors can go in all sorts of directions; see the variations. **Serves 4**

Ingredients

1½ cups short-grain white rice

Salt

2 tablespoons olive oil, plus more for drizzling (optional)

1 pound hot or sweet Italian sausage links

2 medium fennel bulbs (about 1 pound)

Pepper

1 or 2 lemons for serving (optional)

Several sprigs fresh basil

Red chile flakes to taste

□ Prep · Cook

1. Put 1½ cups rice in a medium saucepan; add a big pinch of salt and water to cover by about an inch. Bring to a boil.

2. Put 2 tablespoons olive oil in a large skillet over medium heat.

   □ Cut the sausages into slices; add them to the skillet.

   □ Trim and halve the fennel, chopping some of the fronds for garnish. Thinly slice the bulbs and add to the skillet.

3. Sprinkle the sausage and fennel with salt and pepper and cook, stirring occasionally, until the sausage is browned and the fennel is soft, 10 to 15 minutes.

   □ Quarter and seed the lemons.

4. When the rice mixture boils, adjust the heat so it bubbles steadily but not vigorously. Cover and cook undisturbed until small craters appear on the surface of the rice, 10 to 15 minutes.

   □ Strip the leaves from several basil sprigs and chop.

5. When small craters appear, tip the saucepan to see if any liquid remains. If so, re-cover and keep cooking until the rice is sticky and no water remains, checking every minute or two.

6. Serve the rice with the sausage and fennel spooned over the top. Garnish with the basil, fennel fronds, and a sprinkle of red chile flakes and serve. Pass olive oil and lemon wedges at the table if you like.

● recipe continues →

Variations

Rice Bowl with Chorizo and Pineapple. Pleasantly sweet, tart, and spicy. Substitute fresh Mexican-style chorizo for the Italian sausage and 1 small pineapple for the fennel. Trim the top and bottom from the pineapple, then working downward on the fruit, slice away the skin. Cut the flesh from the core and chop it into bite-sized pieces. Proceed as directed. Use cilantro instead of the basil, and serve with ½ cup crumbled queso fresco and lime wedges instead of extra olive oil and the lemon.

Rice Bowl with Brats, Onions, and Pickles. Omit the cheese and lemon. Use bratwurst instead of the Italian sausage and 2 sliced white onions instead of the fennel. After the onions soften in Step 3, add 1 cup sliced bread-and-butter pickles and some of their brine to the skillet. Garnish the bowls with fresh chopped dill instead of basil.

Rice Bowl with Lamb and Eggplant. Instead of the Italian sausage, use 1 pound ground lamb. After it browns, sprinkle with 2 teaspoons ground cumin, ½ teaspoon ground cinnamon, and salt and pepper. Substitute 1 pound eggplant for the fennel; trim, leave the skin on if you like, and cut into 1-inch cubes. When you add the eggplant in Step 3, add ½ cup water. Garnish with crumbled feta instead of the Parmesan and chopped mint instead of the basil; serve with the lemon wedges.

Quinoa Pilaf with Pistachios, Chickpeas, and Apricots

You won't find many pilafs with this spectrum of textures: toasted nuts for crunch, chewy dried fruit, and creamy chickpeas—all with the unique pop of quinoa in every bite. And swapping these components is simple, so use what you have and what you like. I find it faster to make pilafs in a large (12-inch) deep skillet since there's more surface area. You'll need a tight-fitting lid. If your skillet doesn't come with one, cover it with foil or use a large pot with a lid. **Serves 4**

Ingredients

3 tablespoons olive oil

½ cup shelled pistachios

1¾ cups cooked or canned chickpeas (one 15-ounce can)

1½ cups quinoa

Salt and pepper

½ cup dried apricots

1 bunch fresh parsley

1 lemon

Prep · Cook

1. Put 2 tablespoons olive oil in a large skillet over medium heat.

   □ Chop ½ cup nuts.

2. Add the nuts and cook, shaking the skillet occasionally, until lightly browned and fragrant, 2 or 3 minutes. Transfer them to a plate with a slotted spoon; add 1 tablespoon olive oil to the pan.

   □ If you're using canned chickpeas, rinse and drain them. Lightly mash the chickpeas with a fork.

   □ Put 1½ cups quinoa in a strainer and rinse under running water for about a minute; shake it to drain well.

3. Stir the quinoa into the hot oil with a sprinkle of salt and pepper. Cook, stirring occasionally, until the quinoa is glossy and coated with oil, about 2 minutes.

   □ Chop ½ cup dried apricots.

4. When the quinoa is glossy, stir in the chickpeas, apricots, and 4 cups water. Bring to a boil, then adjust the heat so the liquid bubbles gently. Cover and cook undisturbed until small craters appear on the surface, 15 to 20 minutes.

   □ Chop ½ cup parsley.

   □ Grate the zest of a lemon (reserve the lemon for another use).

5. When small craters appear on the surface of the quinoa, tip the skillet to see if any liquid remains. If so, re-cover and keep cooking until the quinoa is dry and a light ring appears around the kernels, checking every minute or two. When it's ready, turn off the heat, add the parsley, lemon zest, and reserved nuts; fluff with a fork. Taste and adjust the seasoning, and serve.

Variations

Quinoa Pilaf with Almonds, Black Beans, and Raisins. I prefer golden raisins here, but either kind is fine. Substitute almonds for the pistachios, black beans for the chickpeas, and raisins for the apricots. Add ½ teaspoon ground cinnamon to the quinoa in Step 4 before adding the black beans. Garnish with fresh cilantro instead of parsley and lime zest instead of lemon.

Quinoa Pilaf with Pecans, Cannellini, and Dates. Substitute pecans for the pistachios, cannellini beans for the chickpeas, and dates for the apricots. Garnish with fresh mint instead of parsley.

Quinoa Pilaf with Peanuts, Edamame, and Prunes. Use vegetable oil instead of olive oil. Substitute peanuts for the pistachios, frozen shelled edamame for the chickpeas, and prunes for the apricots. Add ½ teaspoon five-spice to the quinoa in Step 4 before adding the edamame. Garnish with 2 chopped scallions instead of the parsley, and pass sesame oil and soy sauce for drizzling at the table.

STOCK VERSUS WATER

Cooking grains in plain water, especially when fat, seasonings, and other ingredients are also in play, will never be bland. If you happen to have a stock with complementary flavors handy in the fridge or freezer—or feel like making some first (see page 489)— then by all means use it instead. But I never bother with boxed or canned stock.

Smoky Bulgur with Eggplant and Feta

Here's what happens when you cross a pilaf with tabbouleh: You get well-seasoned vegetable-and-herb–spiked rice with all the brightness of salad. Eat this hearty hybrid hot, at room temperature, or out of the fridge the next day. It also makes a stellar contribution to potlucks and picnics. Try this recipe with any summer squash or bell peppers; other cheeses like ricotta salata or Manchego are terrific too. **Serves 4**

Ingredients

¼ cup olive oil

2 medium or 3 or 4 small eggplants (about 1 pound)

1 medium red onion

Salt and pepper

1 cup bulgur (medium grind)

2 cloves garlic

¼ cup tomato paste

1 teaspoon smoked paprika

1 teaspoon ground cumin

1 bunch fresh parsley

4 ounces feta cheese (1 cup crumbled)

☐ Prep · **Cook**

1. Bring 2 cups water to a boil in a medium saucepan.

2. Put ¼ cup olive oil in a large skillet over medium-high heat.

   ☐ Trim and chop the eggplants into ½-inch pieces; add to the skillet.

   ☐ Trim, peel, and chop the onion; add to the skillet.

3. Sprinkle with salt and pepper and cook, stirring occasionally, until the vegetables are brown in places and soft, 10 to 15 minutes.

4. When the water comes to a boil, add the bulgur and a pinch of salt. Stir, cover, and remove from the heat. Let it sit until you're ready to assemble the dish.

   ☐ Peel and chop 2 cloves garlic; add to the skillet and stir.

5. When the vegetables are browned and soft, stir in the tomato paste, 1 teaspoon smoked paprika, and 1 teaspoon ground cumin. Cook, stirring frequently, until fragrant, about 2 minutes. Check the bulgur. It should be tender but still have some bite; if it hasn't absorbed all the water, drain it in a strainer.

   ☐ Chop ½ cup parsley leaves.   ☐ Crumble 1 cup feta cheese.

6. When the bulgur is tender—and drained if necessary—add it to the skillet along with the feta, and fluff with a fork. Taste and adjust the seasoning. Serve garnished with the parsley.

Oats for Dinner, Four Ways

Take steel-cut oats in a savory direction—with vegetables, fruits, nuts, even canned fish or anything you like, really—and you've got a one-dish meal with an unbeatable fluffy creaminess. The generously seasoned cooking liquid adds yet another dimension with deep background flavors. **Serves 4**

Ingredients

¼ cup olive oil

1 large leek

1½ cups steel-cut oats

¼ teaspoon ground nutmeg

Salt and pepper

1 bunch chard

1 orange

½ cup walnuts

▢ Prep · **Cook**

1. Put ¼ cup olive oil in a large pot over low heat.

   ▢ Trim and chop the white and light green parts of the leek; put it in a colander under cold water to rinse away any grit. Drain.

2. Add the leek to the pot and raise the heat to medium-high. In a minute or two, when the water has evaporated and the leek sizzles, add 1½ cups oats and ¼ teaspoon ground nutmeg, and sprinkle with salt and pepper. Cook, stirring often, until the leek begins to soften but not brown, about 2 minutes. Lower the heat to medium-low.

   ▢ Trim the chard; separate the center ribs and leaves; chop the ribs, add them to the pot, and stir.

   ▢ Halve the orange and squeeze the juice into the pot through a strainer or your fingers to catch the seeds.

3. Add 3 cups water to the pot and bring to a boil. Reduce the heat so the liquid bubbles gently but steadily. Cover and cook undisturbed for 10 minutes.

   ▢ Stack the chard leaves and slice them into thin ribbons.

   ▢ Chop the walnuts as finely as you can manage.

4. Tip the pot: If there's no water, add another ½ cup. Stir in the chard ribbons with a fork. Return the lid and cook, checking once or twice to make sure the oats aren't sticking to the bottom of the pot, until the oats are tender and the water is absorbed, another 5 to 10 minutes. Taste and adjust the seasoning. Add the walnuts, fluff with a fork, and serve.

● recipe continues →

Variations

Oats with Broccoli and Cheddar for Dinner. Use the juice of 1 lemon instead of the orange juice. Substitute 1 pound broccoli for the chard; trim and chop the florets and stems into ½-inch pieces. Add them in Step 4 as directed for the chard leaves. Instead of the walnuts, grate 1 cup sharp cheddar cheese (preferably white); add it and fluff with a fork before tasting for seasoning in Step 4.

Oats with Sharp Greens and Fried Eggs for Dinner. Substitute ¼ cup balsamic vinegar for the orange juice. Instead of the chard, use 1 pound assertive greens like radicchio, watercress, or dandelion greens (alone or in combination). Trim and chop them, then add in Step 4 as directed for the chard leaves. While the oats and greens are finishing at the end of Step 4, fry 4 or more eggs as described on page 483.

Oats with Spinach and Sardines for Dinner. Inspired by an iconic dish from southern Spain. Instead of the orange juice, increase the water in Step 3 to 3½ cups and add ½ cup raisins. Substitute 10 ounces spinach for the chard. Trim it if necessary, but leave the leaves whole. Add it in Step 4 as directed for the chard leaves. Substitute pine nuts for the walnuts and top each serving with several small oil-packed smoked sardines (from 2 cans or jars, about 4 ounces each).

Quinoa Puttanesca with Parmesan Cheese

Noodle casseroles like mac and cheese and baked ziti are beloved, yet grain casseroles still haven't hit the mainstream. This recipe sets the example: Start with something familiar—here, a classic Italian pasta sauce—and adapt it for grains. **Serves 4**

Ingredients

Salt

2 tablespoons olive oil

2 cloves garlic

3 or 4 anchovies

½ cup pitted black olives

2 tablespoons capers

½ teaspoon red chile flakes

1 large (28-ounce) can diced tomatoes

Pepper

1½ cups quinoa

6 ounces Parmesan cheese (1½ cups grated)

Several sprigs fresh basil

□ Prep · Cook

1. Bring a medium saucepan of water to a boil and salt it. Put 2 tablespoons olive oil in a large skillet over medium heat.

   □ Peel 2 cloves garlic; chop them together with 3 or 4 anchovies.

   □ Pit ½ cup olives if necessary and chop them too.

2. Add the garlic, 3 or 4 anchovies, and ½ cup olives to the oil along with 2 tablespoons capers and ½ teaspoon red chile flakes. Turn the heat to medium-high and cook, stirring, for a minute.

3. Add the tomatoes and their juice and sprinkle with pepper. (Wait to add salt until later.) Cook, stirring occasionally, until the tomatoes break down and thicken the sauce, 10 to 15 minutes.

   □ Put 1½ cups quinoa in a strainer and rinse under running water for about a minute; shake it to drain well.

4. When the water boils, add the quinoa. Adjust the heat so it bubbles steadily, and stir occasionally. Start tasting after 7 minutes; you're looking for the kernels to pop and go from gritty to fluffy.

5. Turn the broiler to high; put the rack 4 inches from the heat.

   □ Grate 1½ cups Parmesan.

   □ Strip the leaves from several basil sprigs and chop or tear them.

6. When the quinoa is tender and rings appear around the outside of the kernels, drain it through a strainer, reserving some cooking water. Add the quinoa to the skillet along with ½ cup of the Parmesan and a splash of cooking water if you want to make it saucier. Taste and adjust the seasoning, adding more chile flakes if you like.

● recipe continues →

7. Transfer the mixture to a broiler-proof baking dish (or use the skillet if it doesn't have a wooden or plastic handle). Scatter the remaining Parmesan on top and broil until the cheese is bubbling and golden, 2 to 3 minutes. Scatter the basil over the top and let the dish cool for a few minutes to set, then serve.

Variations

Quinoa Puttanesca with Ricotta. Instead of the mozzarella, use 2 cups whole milk ricotta (one 15-ounce container). You can season it with ¼ teaspoon ground nutmeg if you like. In Step 7, drop tablespoons of the cheese on top of the quinoa, spread it around a little with the back of the spoon, and broil as directed.

Lemony Farro with Mascarpone. Lighter and super-bright tasting. Omit the tomatoes, anchovies, olives, mozzarella, and Parmesan. Grate the zest from a lemon and juice the fruit, removing the seeds. Substitute farro for the quinoa and add the lemon juice to the cooking water; the cooking time should be about the same as for the quinoa for pleasantly chewy not gummy kernels. Instead of the mozzarella, use mascarpone; stir the lemon zest into the cheese. In Step 7, drop tablespoons of the cheese on top of the farro, spread it around a little with the back of the spoon, and broil as directed. Garnish with chives instead of basil if you like.

Zucchini Rice with Parmesan. Omit the tomatoes, anchovies, olives, and mozzarella. Use long-grain white rice instead of quinoa; the cooking time will be about the same. Double the amount of Parmesan to 8 ounces (2 cups grated). Trim and grate 1 pound zucchini (2 medium). Instead of making the puttanesca sauce in Steps 2 and 3, cook the zucchini with the garlic in the oil, stirring until it releases water and the pan dries, about 10 minutes. Add half the cheese to the skillet in Step 6 and use what remains to scatter over the rice and zucchini before broiling. Garnish with fresh chopped dill instead of basil.

Masa and Rajas

With masa harina—the flour ground from lime-treated ground corn that's used to make tortillas—you get tamale flavors minus the fuss. Instead of steaming in individual corn husks, a quick masa dough steams as one big cake in a covered skillet, with the added benefit of a crisp crust on the bottom and a poufy top. Finish with a stir-fry of poblanos (rajas means "slices" or "slits" and refers to the shards of poblano chile), onions, and a touch of cream.
Serves 4

Ingredients

1½ cups masa harina

¾ teaspoon baking powder

Salt and pepper

5 tablespoons vegetable oil

1 large onion

4 poblano chiles

2 cloves garlic

½ cup cream, or more to taste

☐ Prep · **Cook**

1. Combine 1½ cups masa harina, ¾ teaspoon baking powder, a sprinkle of salt and pepper, and 1 tablespoon vegetable oil in a medium bowl. Stir to combine into a coarse meal. Add 1½ cups warm water and stir to make a thick batter.

   ☐ Trim, peel, and chop the onion.

   ☐ Trim, core, seed, and slice the poblanos.

2. Put 2 tablespoons vegetable oil in a large skillet over medium-high heat.

   ☐ Peel and slice 2 cloves garlic.

3. When the oil is hot, add the onion, poblanos, and garlic and sprinkle with salt and pepper. Cook, stirring occasionally, until the vegetables are soft, 8 to 12 minutes.

4. Put 2 tablespoons vegetable oil in another large skillet over medium-high heat. When it's hot, add the masa batter, spreading it into an even layer (about ½ inch thick) with a rubber spatula or a big spoon. Cover the skillet and cook, adjusting the heat so the edge barely sizzles, until the cake is crisp on the bottom and slightly puffed up and firm on the top, 5 to 10 minutes. When the cake is done, remove the pan from the heat.

5. When the vegetables are soft, stir in ½ cup cream and cook until it reduces slightly, a minute or two. Taste and adjust the seasoning. To serve, cut the cake into 4 or 8 wedges and spoon the poblano mixture over the top.

● recipe continues →

Variations

Masa and Rajas with Chicken. Before adding the vegetables, slice 4 boneless, skinless chicken thighs (about 12 ounces) and cook them in the hot oil undisturbed until they brown and release easily, 2 to 3 minutes. Sprinkle with salt and pepper, then continue to cook, stirring occasionally until the meat is no longer pink, 2 to 3 minutes more. Remove the chicken from the skillet, then cook the vegetables. Stir the chicken back in along with the cream in Step 5.

Masa and Rajas with Beef. Before adding the vegetables, cut 8 ounces beef sirloin steak against the grain into slices as thin as you can. Cook them in the hot oil undisturbed until they brown and release easily, 2 to 3 minutes. Sprinkle with salt and pepper, stir, then transfer the steak to a plate. Cook the vegetables. Stir the steak back in along with the cream in Step 5.

Masa and Rajas with Chorizo. Before adding the vegetables, cook 8 ounces fresh Mexican-style chorizo (squeezed from the casing if necessary) in the hot oil, stirring once in a while, until crisp and lightly browned, about 5 minutes. Transfer the chorizo to a plate with a slotted spoon and drain off all but 2 tablespoons of the fat before proceeding. Stir it back in along with the cream in Step 5.

Farro with Cannellini and Tuna

The distinctively nutty flavor and chewy texture of farro reminds me of wheat berries—only it cooks much more quickly, especially when you boil it like pasta. And the sturdy kernels make the perfect base for lots of stir-ins, starting with the winning Mediterranean combination of tuna and cannellini beans. **Serves 4**

Ingredients

Salt

¼ cup olive oil

1 lemon

1 small red onion

3½ cups cooked or canned cannellini beans (two 15-ounce cans)

1 (6-ounce) jar or (5-ounce) can tuna packed in olive oil

¼ cup capers

1½ cups farro

1 bunch fresh parsley

Pepper

▢ Prep · Cook

1. Bring a medium pot of water to a boil and salt it.

   ▢ Put ¼ cup olive oil in a large bowl.

   ▢ Halve the lemon; squeeze the juice into the bowl through a strainer or your fingers to catch the seeds.

   ▢ Trim, peel, halve, and slice the onion; add it to the bowl.

   ▢ If you're using canned beans, rinse and drain them. Add the beans to the bowl.

2. Add the tuna (with its oil) to the bowl along with ¼ cup capers (with or without any brine).

3. When the water boils, add the farro and cook, stirring occasionally. Start tasting after 10 minutes. You want it tender but not mushy.

   ▢ Chop ½ cup parsley leaves and add it to the bowl.

4. When the farro is ready, drain it. Add it to the bowl, sprinkle with salt and pepper, and toss. Taste and adjust the seasoning, and serve.

Bulgur Pilaf with Edamame and Bok Choy

This recipe demonstrates how well bulgur—which is partially cooked cracked wheat—works with all sorts of flavor profiles. Instead of steeping this bulgur in plain water, you get all the other ingredients and seasonings going in a big pot first, then let the grains steep and soak in all that flavor while you set the table. **Serves 4**

Ingredients

⅓ cup vegetable oil

1 medium red onion

1 inch fresh ginger

Salt and pepper

One 10- or 12-ounce bag frozen shelled edamame (about 2 cups)

1½ pounds bok choy

1 cup bulgur (medium grind)

1 lemon

Soy sauce for serving

▢ Prep · Cook

1. Put ⅓ cup vegetable oil in a large pot over medium heat.

   ▢ Trim and peel 1 medium onion, halve it lengthwise, and slice it thinly. Drop it in the pot.

   ▢ Peel 1 inch ginger and chop it; drop it in the pot.

2. Sprinkle the onion and ginger with salt and pepper and cook, stirring occasionally, until they're soft, about 5 minutes.

   ▢ Rinse 2 cups edamame in a colander under warm water to thaw them a little, then add to the pot with the onions and ginger.

   ▢ Trim 1½ pounds bok choy and cut the leaves from the stems; chop the stems and add them to the pot.

   ▢ Chop the leaves; leave them on the cutting board.

3. Cook the vegetables and edamame, using a fork or potato masher to break up the beans and bok choy stems, until everything is soft and fragrant, about 5 minutes. Add 1 cup bulgur and a little more salt. Stir until the mixture sizzles and the grain is glossy, another minute or two.

4. Add 3 cups water and bring to a boil. Scatter the bok choy leaves on top, cover the pot, and turn off the heat. Let the pilaf sit undisturbed until the bulgur is tender, 10 to 15 minutes.

   ▢ Halve the lemon.

5. When the bulgur is tender, squeeze in the lemon juice through a strainer or your fingers to catch the seeds; fluff the pilaf with a fork. Taste and adjust the seasoning. Serve, passing soy sauce at the table.

• recipe continues →

Bulgur Pilaf
with Tempeh
and Spinach

Variations

Bulgur Pilaf with Fava Beans and Chard. Simple substitutions: Olive oil for the vegetable oil; 2 or 3 cloves garlic for the ginger; fava beans for the edamame; chard instead of bok choy. Season with the lemon juice and pass balsamic vinegar at the table instead of the soy sauce.

Bulgur Pilaf with Tempeh and Spinach. Instead of the edamame, crumble 8 ounces tempeh (1 block) into the pot with the onions and ginger in Step 2. Substitute spinach for the bok choy; wait to add it until after the water comes to a boil in Step 4.

Bulgur Pilaf with Crab and Peppers. Substitute 2 bell peppers, any color, for the bok choy. Use olive oil instead of the vegetable oil and substitute 3 cloves garlic for the ginger. Replace the edamame with about 6 ounces lump crabmeat (about ¾ cup); add it after the vegetables soften in Step 3, along with as many chopped fresh red chiles, like Thai or serrano, as you like. Chop the bell peppers and add them after the water comes to a boil in Step 3. Season with lime instead of lemon juice and toss in ¼ cup chopped fresh parsley just before serving.

Couscous Helper

Maybe you have eaten Hamburger Helper, the skillet main course from a box where all you add is the meat. My version, made with real ingredients and equally easy, starts with the flavors of Morocco, then takes a couple detours in the variations. **Serves 4**

Ingredients

4 tablespoons olive oil

1 large red onion

12 ounces ground beef

Salt and pepper

3 cloves garlic

2 oranges

2 teaspoons ground cumin

½ teaspoon ground cinnamon

1 cup couscous (white or whole wheat)

Several sprigs fresh parsley

▢ Prep · Cook

1. Put 2 tablespoons olive oil in a large skillet over medium-high heat.

   ▢ Trim, peel, and chop the onion.

2. When the oil is hot, add the ground beef and onion, sprinkle with salt and pepper, and cook, stirring occasionally, until the beef is browned and the onions are golden, 5 to 10 minutes.

   ▢ Peel and chop 3 cloves garlic.

   ▢ Halve the oranges and squeeze them through a strainer or your fingers to capture the seeds and get ½ cup juice; refrigerate any remaining fruit.

3. When the beef is browned and the onions are golden, stir in the garlic, 2 teaspoons ground cumin, ½ teaspoon ground cinnamon, and 1 cup couscous. Cook, stirring until the spices are fragrant and the couscous is lightly toasted, a minute or two.

4. Add the orange juice and 1 cup water, bring to a boil, then cover and turn off the heat. Let steep until the couscous is tender and the liquid is absorbed, about 5 minutes, a couple minutes more for whole wheat.

   ▢ Strip the leaves from several parsley sprigs and chop.

5. When the couscous is ready, add the parsley and 2 tablespoons olive oil and fluff with a fork. Taste and adjust the seasoning and serve right away.

Variations

Couscous Helper with Five-Spice. Substitute vegetable oil for the olive oil, ground pork for the beef, and yellow onion for red. Instead of the ground cumin and cinnamon, use 2 teaspoons five-spice powder. For the liquid, use 1½ cups chicken stock or water with a dash of soy sauce mixed in. Garnish with scallions and some sesame oil instead of the parsley and olive oil.

Couscous Helper with Fennel Seeds and Parmesan. Substitute ground chicken for the beef, 1 tablespoon fennel seeds for the ground cumin, and ½ teaspoon red chile flakes for the ground cinnamon. For the liquid, use 1¼ cups chicken stock or water and ¼ cup white wine. Garnish with basil instead of parsley and up to 1 cup grated Parmesan.

Couscous Helper with Spiced Lamb. Substitute vegetable oil for the olive oil, ground lamb for the beef, and yellow onion for red. Instead of the ground cumin and cinnamon, use 1 tablespoon garam masala. For the liquid, use 1 (14-ounce) can coconut milk (reduced-fat is okay here). Garnish with chopped scallions or cilantro and some chopped pistachios instead of the parsley and olive oil.

Couscous Paella with Chicken and Zucchini

The technique of letting couscous cook in a hot oven with boneless chicken and vegetables is akin to how you cook paella, especially when you finish by crisping the bottom on the stove. Not with the same slow-cooking ingredients as traditional versions, maybe, but quite delicious. **Serves 4**

Ingredients

3 tablespoons olive oil

4 to 6 boneless, skinless chicken thighs (about 1 pound)

Salt and pepper

1 pound zucchini (2 medium)

3 cloves garlic

1 teaspoon smoked paprika

1½ cups chicken stock or water

1 cup couscous (white or whole wheat)

1 bunch fresh parsley

1 lemon

▢ Prep · **Cook**

1. Heat the oven to 450°F. Put 3 tablespoons olive oil in a large ovenproof skillet over medium-high heat.

2. When the oil is hot, add the chicken, sprinkle with salt and pepper, and cook undisturbed until it browns and releases from the pan, about 3 minutes. Turn and brown on the other side, about another 3 minutes.

   ▢ Trim the zucchini and halve them lengthwise; slice crosswise ¼ inch thick.

   ▢ Peel and chop 3 cloves garlic.

3. Transfer the chicken to a cutting board. Add the zucchini and garlic to the skillet with the smoked paprika; stir and scrape up any browned bits. Add 1½ cups stock or water. Adjust the heat so the mixture bubbles steadily but not vigorously. Cover and cook until the zucchini is quite tender, about 5 minutes.

   ▢ Slice the chicken thinly (it's okay if it's still pink in spots).

4. Bring the mixture in the skillet to a boil. Stir in 1 cup couscous and a sprinkle of salt. Shake the pan so it forms an even layer; if necessary, add enough water to just submerge the couscous. Scatter the chicken on top, drizzle with the accumulated juices, and transfer the skillet (uncovered) to the oven.

   ▢ Trim and chop ¼ cup parsley leaves.

   ▢ Cut the lemon into wedges.

● recipe continues →

5. Cook until the couscous is tender, the liquid has evaporated, and the couscous and chicken are starting to brown on top, 5 to 10 minutes. Taste and adjust the seasoning.

6. Transfer the pan to the stove over medium-high heat. Serve hot or warm, garnished with the parsley and lemon wedges.

Variations

Couscous Paella with Chicken and Fennel. Omit the parsley. Substitute 2 large fennel bulbs, trimmed and sliced, for the zucchini. They won't quite break apart like the zucchini, but they will get tender and silky and add a ton of flavor. Reserve and chop some of the fennel fronds for garnish.

Warm-Spiced Couscous Paella with Chicken and Peppers. Substitute 2 red bell peppers for the zucchini; trim, core, and slice them top to bottom. When you add them to the skillet in Step 3, along with the paprika, add 1 teaspoon ground cumin, ½ teaspoon ground cinnamon, and ¼ teaspoon ground allspice. Cook, stirring constantly, for a minute until fragrant before adding the stock or water and proceeding.

Couscous with Chicken and Peas and Carrots. Shave up to 10 minutes off the time by using frozen peas and carrots instead of the zucchini; plus it's good in a nostalgic way. Omit the zucchini. Cook the garlic in the oil for just a minute in Step 3. Use 2 to 3 cups peas and carrots, depending on how vegetable-y you want the paella. Add them after stirring in the couscous and water; top with the chicken and put the skillet straight in the oven.

Shrimp over Grits

This sublime Southern classic is easy to make relatively quickly with the same slurry method I use for polenta (see page 243)—that is, mixing the grits with a little water before cooking to make a smooth paste. It's a little trick that helps you avoid lumps *and* lots of stirring. While the grits cook, you make the lively sauce on the adjacent burner so you can keep an eye on everything at the same time. **Serves 4**

Ingredients

1 cup grits (preferably stone-ground)

1¼ cups milk

Salt

4 ounces andouille sausage or tasso (½ cup chopped)

1 medium onion

2 tablespoons butter

2 cloves garlic

2 celery stalks with leaves

1 green bell pepper

Pepper

2 large ripe tomatoes or 1 (15-ounce) can diced tomatoes

1 pound peeled shrimp

▢ Prep · Cook

1. Put 1 cup grits in a large saucepan with 1 cup water and whisk to form a smooth slurry. Whisk in 1¼ cups milk and a pinch of salt and set the pot over medium-high heat. Bring to a boil.

   ▢ Get another 3 cups water handy.

   ▢ Chop 4 ounces andouille or tasso.

   ▢ Trim, peel, and chop the onion.

2. Put 2 tablespoons butter in a large skillet over medium-high heat. Add the meat and cook, stirring frequently, until it browns in places, about 3 minutes. Stir in the onion and lower the heat to medium. Cook, stirring occasionally, until the onion is golden and soft, 5 to 10 minutes.

   ▢ Peel and mince 2 cloves garlic; add them to the skillet.

   ▢ Trim and chop 2 celery stalks; save any leaves for garnish. Add the celery to the skillet.

3. When the grits come to a boil, lower the heat to medium and cook, whisking frequently and adding more water a little at a time to prevent lumps and to keep the mixture somewhat soupy. Expect to add another 1½ to 2½ cups water and to cook 15 to 20 minutes before the grits are ready. You want them tender, thick, and creamy with just a little grittiness; the mixture will pull away from the side of the pot when you stir.

   ▢ Core, seed, and chop the bell pepper; add it to the skillet.

4. Sprinkle the meat and vegetables with salt and pepper and cook, stirring occasionally, until they soften, 5 to 10 minutes.

• recipe continues →

□ Core and chop the fresh tomatoes. (Or drain the canned tomatoes and reserve the juice for another use.)

5. When the vegetables are soft, stir in the fresh tomatoes (or the drained canned tomatoes) and cook, stirring once or twice, until they begin to release their juice or break down if canned, 3 to 4 minutes. Add the shrimp, sprinkle with salt and pepper, and cook, stirring occasionally, until they turn pink and cook through, 2 to 5 minutes, depending on whether they were frozen.

6. Taste the grits and the sauce and adjust the seasoning. To serve, spoon the shrimp mixture over the grits and garnish with the celery leaves.

Variations

Creamy Shrimp over Grits. Stir ¼ cup cream into the sauce right before adding the shrimp in Step 5.

Shrimp over Polenta. A couple switches and the dish veers toward Italy. Use sweet or hot Italian sausage or prosciutto instead of the andouille and medium-grind cornmeal instead of the grits. Cook the sausage a little longer in Step 2 so that it's browned and no longer pink. Spoon off all but 2 tablespoons of the fat before proceeding.

Eggs over Grits or Polenta. Immediately after stirring the shrimp into the sauce in Step 5, adjust the heat under the sauce so it bubbles gently. Make 4 indentations in the sauce with the back of a spoon; crack an egg into each. Cover the skillet and cook until the eggs are as jiggly or firm as you like them (the shrimp will be cooked by that time), and carefully lift one out with each serving.

Polenta with Sausage and Mushrooms

I can't think of much that's cozier than a dish of creamy Parmesan polenta topped with a meaty sauté of Italian sausage and mushrooms. Except maybe eating it on the couch in front of a glowing fire. **Serves 4**

Ingredients

1 cup cornmeal (medium-grind)

½ cup milk, plus more if needed

Salt

4 tablespoons olive oil, plus more if needed

1 pound sweet or hot Italian sausage

1 medium red onion

1½ pounds cremini mushrooms

Pepper

Several sprigs fresh parsley

4 ounces Parmesan cheese (1 cup grated)

▫ Prep · Cook

1. Put 1 cup cornmeal in a large saucepan with 2 cups water and whisk to form a smooth slurry. Whisk in ½ cup milk and a pinch of salt. Set the pot over medium-high heat. Bring to a boil.

   ▫ Get another 3 cups water handy.

2. Put 2 tablespoons olive oil in a large skillet over medium-high heat.

   ▫ Chop the sausage or remove the meat from the casings and break it up.

3. Add the sausage to the skillet and cook, stirring occasionally, until it starts to brown, 3 to 5 minutes.

4. When the polenta comes to a boil, lower the heat to medium. Cook, whisking frequently; add more water a little at a time to prevent lumps and to keep the polenta somewhat soupy. Expect to add another 1½ to 2½ cups water and a little more milk (for richness) and to cook 15 to 20 minutes before the polenta is ready. You want the grains tender and the polenta thick and creamy with just a little grittiness; the polenta should pull away from the side of the pot when you stir.

   ▫ Trim, peel, and chop the onion; add it to the skillet.

   ▫ Trim and slice the mushrooms; add them to the skillet as you work.

5. Sprinkle the mushrooms with salt and pepper. Cook, stirring occasionally and adding more olive oil if the skillet gets too dry, until the sausage is browned and the mushrooms are tender, 8 to 12 minutes. Add ¼ cup water and scrape up any browned bits to make a little sauce. Taste and adjust the seasoning.

   ▫ Strip the leaves from several parsley sprigs and chop.

   ▫ Grate 1 cup Parmesan cheese.

• recipe continues →

6. When the polenta is done, stir in the Parmesan, 2 tablespoons olive oil, and lots of pepper. Taste and adjust the seasoning. Serve topped with the sausages, mushrooms, and sauce, garnished with the parsley.

Variations

Polenta with Chicken and Asparagus. Substitute 1 pound boneless, skinless chicken thighs for the sausages; cut them into ½-inch chunks. Instead of the mushrooms, trim 1 pound asparagus and cut it into 1-inch pieces. Cook the chicken until it loses its pink color, then add the asparagus and continue cooking until the asparagus is just tender and the chicken is cooked through, 5 to 6 minutes. Garnish with 1 tablespoon chopped fresh tarragon instead of the parsley if you like and finish with a squeeze of lemon juice.

Polenta with Sausage and Fennel. Omit the parsley. Instead of the mushrooms, trim and thinly slice 2 medium fennel bulbs; reserve some of the fronds to use for garnish.

Polenta with Pancetta, Escarole, and Romano. Substitute 4 ounces chopped pancetta for the sausage and cook it as described in Step 3; it might take a little longer to brown and crisp. Instead of the mushrooms, trim and chop 1 large head escarole. When you cook it in Step 5, add ¼ cup water and cover the skillet so it steams and softens quickly, but wait to add salt. Instead of the Parmesan, add grated pecorino Romano cheese (which is saltier than Parmesan) to the polenta in Step 6; taste and adjust the seasoning of the vegetables and pancetta just before serving.

Millet with Curried Cauliflower

Sometimes millet can be stubborn and take longer than you think it should to cook; sometimes it doesn't. So figure this might run a hair over 30 minutes—but with the gorgeous sunshine color and satisfying texture, it's a vegan meal you won't want to miss. **Serves 4**

Ingredients

1 cup millet

Salt

½ large head cauliflower (about 12 ounces)

2 inches fresh ginger

2 tablespoons vegetable oil

4 scallions

1 cup cashews

1 bunch fresh cilantro

2 limes

2 tablespoons curry powder

1 (14-ounce) can coconut milk (reduced-fat is okay)

▢ Prep · Cook

1. Put the millet in a medium saucepan with a pinch of salt and enough water to cover by 1 inch. Bring to a boil.

   ▢ Trim the cauliflower, and chop into bite-sized pieces, stem and all. (You should have 3 to 4 cups.)

   ▢ Peel and chop 2 inches ginger.

2. Put 2 tablespoons vegetable oil in a large skillet over medium heat. Add the cauliflower and ginger and cook, stirring occasionally, until the cauliflower browns in places, about 5 minutes.

   ▢ Slice the scallions, keeping the white and green parts separate.

3. When the millet comes to a boil, adjust the heat to a steady bubble. Cover and cook, stirring once or twice, until it's tender, about 20 minutes.

   ▢ Chop 1 cup cashews.

   ▢ Trim and chop 1 cup cilantro leaves and tender stems.

   ▢ Halve 1 lime; quarter the other.

4. Add the white parts of the scallions and 2 tablespoons curry powder to the cauliflower. Cook and stir until fragrant, about 1 minute. Stir in the coconut milk and most of the cashews; adjust the heat so the liquid bubbles gently. Cook, stirring once in a while, until the sauce thickens and the cauliflower is very tender, another 5 to 10 minutes. Squeeze in the juice from the halved lime. If the curry is ready before the millet is, cover and turn off the heat.

5. Taste and adjust the seasoning in the millet and the curry. Serve them together, garnished with the remaining cashews, the cilantro, and lime wedges.

Pozole and Pork Chops

A super-hearty stew based on hominy—aka pozole. This form of corn has been processed with calcium hydroxide (essentially lye) to remove the outer germ and bran and make it more digestible. The flavor is corny in the same way tortillas are. Since in its dried form it can take up to 4 hours to cook—usually not feasible for weeknights—I often turn to good-quality canned hominy; look for as few ingredients on the label as possible. You can substitute boneless chicken thighs or sirloin steak for the pork; cook the first longer and the second less time. Or make a meatless version by using 1 can (or about 2 cups cooked) pinto beans.
Serves 4

Ingredients

2 tablespoons olive oil

4 bone-in pork chops
(1 inch thick or less;
1½ pounds)

Salt and pepper

1 medium red onion

3 cloves garlic

½ head green cabbage
(about 12 ounces)

1 tablespoon chili powder

1 cup chicken or vegetable
stock or water

1 (15-ounce) can hominy
(2 cups)

4 radishes

Several sprigs fresh cilantro

Sour cream for garnish

□ Prep · Cook

1. Put 2 tablespoons olive oil in a large skillet or large pot over medium-high heat. When the oil is hot, add the pork chops and sprinkle with salt and pepper. Cook, turning once, until browned on both sides, 3 to 5 minutes per side.

   □ Trim, peel, and chop the onion.   □ Peel and chop 3 cloves garlic.

2. When the pork chops are browned on both sides, remove them from the skillet to a plate and add the onion and garlic. Cook, stirring occasionally, until the onion softens, 2 to 3 minutes.

   □ Trim, core, and quarter the cabbage. Cut each quarter crosswise into wide ribbons.

3. When the onion softens, add 1 tablespoon chili powder and cook, stirring once or twice, until fragrant, a minute or two. Sprinkle with salt and pepper and stir in 1 cup stock or water.

   □ Drain and rinse the hominy; add it to the skillet.

4. Nestle the pork chops into the hominy mixture, drizzle with any accumulated juices, and adjust the heat so the liquid bubbles steadily but not vigorously. Cover and cook until the cabbage and pork chops are tender, 5 to 10 minutes.

   □ Trim and thinly slice 4 radishes.   □ Chop several cilantro sprigs.

5. Taste and adjust the seasoning. Serve the stew in shallow bowls with the radishes, cilantro, and sour cream for garnish at the table.

• recipe continues →

Variations

Chicken Pozole. Substitute 4 to 6 boneless, skinless chicken thighs (about 1 pound) for the pork chops. Brown them on both sides just as you would the pork and proceed as directed, only slice them crosswise after browning in Step 2 so they're in pieces when you return them to the stew to finish cooking.

Pozole with Sliced Steak. Instead of the pork chops, sear 1½ pounds skirt, flank, or sirloin steak in Step 1; cut them into pieces that fit comfortably in the skillet. Adjust the heat so they cook without burning; turn once or twice until they're one stage more rare than you ultimately want them. Transfer to a cutting board and tent loosely with foil to rest while you finish the pozole. Just before serving, slice the steak thinly against the grain and pour any accumulated juices into the stew. Top bowls of pozole with the sliced steak and garnish.

Pozole with Pinto Beans. Vegan if you substitute toasted pepitas (hulled green pumpkin seeds) for the sour cream garnish. Omit the pork chops. When the oil is hot, go directly to cooking the onions and garlic in Step 2. Rinse and drain 2 (15-ounce) cans pinto beans or use 3½ cups cooked beans with some of their liquid, and add them with the hominy.

Vegetable Mains

Most days I go all day without eating animal protein, then I take a "less-meatarian" approach to eating vegetables at dinner. Here they move to the center of the plate, spanning a variety of cooking methods and occasionally including small amounts of chicken, fish, beef, or pork. So you'll be satisfied even though you're eating on the light side.

That said, any eggs, nuts, or bacon can also be omitted or replaced with beans, tofu, or more vegetables. Be sure to check out the variations for some ideas. To round out your meal, consider making something from the Snacks chapter, or bulk up the vegetable factor by adding a side of vegetables (page 498). Bread and a salad are always appropriate. As are noodles (page 493), potatoes (page 503), or grains (page 496).

Vegetables do require more prep work than other ingredients. After that, the cooking moves along quickly. Delicious, nourishing, and filling, vegetables really should be the cornerstone of our diets; if you're not already heading in that direction, this chapter offers a well-rounded repertoire to help point the way.

Broiled Caprese

The summer salad we love made all hot and bubbling in the broiler. The ratio of cheese to tomatoes to basil is flexible, depending on your taste and what you have on hand. My favorite way to eat this—or any of the variations that follow—is meatless, either with a hunk of sturdy bread or on top of buttered rice, pasta, or egg noodles (see the recipes on pages 496 and 493).
Serves 4

Ingredients

5 or 6 large ripe tomatoes (about 2 pounds)

Olive oil for drizzling

12 ounces fresh mozzarella cheese

Salt and pepper

1 bunch fresh basil

2 tablespoons balsamic vinegar

▫ Prep · **Cook**

1. Turn the broiler to high; put the rack 4 inches from the heat.

   ▫ Core the tomatoes; slice crosswise into rounds about ½ inch thick; put them on a rimmed baking sheet. Drizzle with some olive oil.

   ▫ Slice the mozzarella about the same thickness.

2. Sprinkle the tomatoes with salt and pepper and lay the mozzarella on top. (You may have to cut some of the cheese slices in half.) Drizzle with a little more olive oil and broil until the cheese is bubbling and browned, about 5 minutes.

   ▫ Strip about ½ cup leaves from the basil sprigs.

3. Remove from the broiler and drizzle with 2 tablespoons balsamic vinegar. Garnish with the basil and serve.

Variations

Broiled Blue Cheese Peaches.
Substitute 4 large peaches for the tomatoes; halve them through the stem end and remove the pits. Use 8 ounces crumbled blue cheese (about 2 cups) instead of the mozzarella. Broil the peach halves cut side down until the skin softens, about 5 minutes. Then turn them and proceed with the recipe from Step 2.

Broiled Tomato Rarebit (Without the Bread).
Substitute grated cheddar cheese (about 3 cups) for the mozzarella, 2 tablespoons chopped fresh chives for the basil, and malt or cider vinegar for the balsamic.

Sweet Pepper Queso Fundido

Mexico's answer to fondue is usually served as a snack or appetizer, often with a garnish of creamed poblano chiles (called rajas), mushrooms, or chorizo. Bulked up with vegetables and served with something for dipping, I call it a dinner without any leftovers. **Serves 4**

Ingredients

3 tablespoons olive oil

3 large red bell peppers (about 1 pound)

2 cloves garlic

Salt and pepper

12 ounces Jack, Oaxaca, or low-moisture mozzarella cheese (3 cups grated)

Several sprigs fresh cilantro

2 limes for serving

12 to 16 corn tortillas or a big bag of tortilla chips for serving

▫ Prep · Cook

1. Turn the broiler to high; put the rack 4 inches from the heat.

2. Put 3 tablespoons olive oil in a medium broiler-proof skillet over medium-high heat.

   - ▫ Core, seed, and slice the bell peppers.
   - ▫ Peel and chop 2 cloves garlic.

3. Add the bell peppers and garlic to the skillet, sprinkle with salt and pepper, and cook, stirring occasionally, until the peppers soften, 5 to 10 minutes.

   - ▫ Grate 3 cups cheese.
   - ▫ Quarter the limes.
   - ▫ Chop the leaves and tender stems from several cilantro sprigs.
   - ▫ Divide the tortillas into 2 stacks, wrap each in foil, and put them in the oven while the broiler heats.

4. When the peppers are soft, turn off the heat, add the cheese to the skillet, and toss so the peppers are well distributed throughout.

5. Broil until the cheese is bubbling and browned, 2 to 3 minutes. Garnish with the cilantro and serve with the tortillas or chips and lime wedges.

Variations

Summer Squash Queso Fundido. Now's the time to try something other than zucchini, like pattypan or yellow squash. Substitute 1 pound squash for the peppers; trim and grate them. In Step 3 cook them with the garlic, stirring frequently, until they release water and begin to turn golden in places. This might take a little more than 10 minutes. Proceed with Step 4.

Spinach Queso Fundido. Use a large pot instead of a skillet; set it over medium heat. Substitute 1 pound spinach for the peppers; frozen is fine. After adding it in Step 3, cover the pot and cook, stirring once or twice, until the spinach is soft (or thawed and heated through), about 5 minutes. Proceed.

Eggplant Steaks with Fresh Tomato Sauce

Grilling or broiling the eggplant lends smokiness to this spin on eggplant Parmesan. And the quick, garlicky sauce is hard to beat. If roma (plum) tomatoes are riper than other options, use them. **Serves 4**

Ingredients

6 tablespoons olive oil, plus more as needed

4 or 5 large ripe tomatoes (about 1½ pounds)

4 cloves garlic

Salt and pepper

2 or 3 large eggplants (about 2 pounds)

1 bunch fresh basil

4 ounces Parmesan cheese (1 cup grated)

☐ Prep · **Cook**

1. Prepare a grill for direct cooking or turn the broiler to high; put the rack 4 inches from the heat.

2. Put 2 tablespoons olive oil in a medium skillet over medium heat.

   ☐ Core and chop the tomatoes; add them to the skillet as you go.

   ☐ Peel and chop 4 cloves garlic; add them to the skillet.

3. Sprinkle the tomatoes with salt and pepper and cook, stirring occasionally, until they begin to break down, 8 to 10 minutes.

   ☐ Trim the eggplants and slice them crosswise into 1-inch-thick rounds.

   ☐ Put the eggplant on a rimmed baking sheet and rub both sides with 4 tablespoons olive oil; sprinkle with salt and pepper.

4. Grill the eggplant directly on the grates or broil in the pan, turning once or twice and brushing with more oil if it looks dry, until tender and browned on both sides, about 10 minutes total.

   ☐ Chop ½ cup basil leaves.   ☐ Grate 1 cup Parmesan.

5. When the tomatoes start to break down, turn off the heat. Taste and adjust the seasoning.

6. As the eggplant slices become tender and browned on both sides, transfer them to a platter; spoon the tomato sauce over all. Sprinkle the Parmesan over the top, garnish with the basil, and serve.

Glazed Brussels Sprouts with Peanuts

A Vietnamese-style glaze breathes sweet and spicy life into crisp-tender Brussels sprouts—or any other sturdy vegetable, like carrots or butternut squash. An abundance of peanuts makes the dish more satisfying, though there's no shortage of vegetables here. Or see the variations for other protein ideas. Serve any of them over a bowl of rice or rice noodles (see pages 496 and 495). **Serves 4**

Ingredients

2 tablespoons good-quality vegetable oil

2 pounds Brussels sprouts

Salt and pepper

1 large clove garlic

1 fresh hot chile (like Thai or jalapeño), or more to taste

2 limes

2 tablespoons fish sauce

2 teaspoons sugar

1 cup raw or roasted peanuts

Several sprigs fresh cilantro

▫ Prep · Cook

1. Put 2 tablespoons vegetable oil in a large skillet over low heat.

   ▫ Trim the bottoms and outer leaves from the Brussels sprouts.

2. Raise the heat under the skillet to medium-high and add the Brussels sprouts along with a light sprinkle of salt and lots of pepper. Stir a couple times until they sizzle, then add ⅓ cup water and adjust the heat so it bubbles gently.

3. Cover and cook, stirring once or twice, until the Brussels sprouts are a little shy of tender, 5 to 10 minutes depending on their size.

   ▫ Peel 1 clove garlic. Trim the chile. Chop them together and transfer to a small bowl.

   ▫ Halve the limes; squeeze the juice into the bowl.

   ▫ Add 2 tablespoons fish sauce, 2 teaspoons sugar, and ⅓ cup water to the bowl and stir to combine.

4. Check the Brussels sprouts after about 5 minutes. When you can barely pierce one with a fork, remove the cover, add the lime juice–fish sauce mixture and the peanuts, and raise the heat to high. Cook, stirring just a few times, until the liquid reduces to a thick glaze and the color of the vegetables and nuts darkens a bit, 2 to 3 minutes.

   ▫ Chop several cilantro sprigs.

5. Taste and adjust the seasoning. Sprinkle with the cilantro and serve hot or warm.

● recipe continues →

Variations

Glazed Brussels Sprouts with Cashews. Substitute raw or roasted cashews for the peanuts.

Glazed Brussels Sprouts with Chicken, Beef, or Pork. A perfect use for leftovers. Depending on how much cooked meat you have handy, you can either omit the nuts or reduce them to ½ cup. The goal is to get to 2 cups pulled or chopped plainly cooked chicken, beef, or pork alone or in combination with the peanuts or cashews. Add it with the lime juice–fish sauce mixture in Step 4.

Glazed Brussels Sprouts with Tofu. Keep the nuts, or omit them if you prefer. Before starting, cut 1 brick firm tofu (14 to 16 ounces) into ½-inch cubes. Increase the oil to 3 tablespoons. Add the tofu to the skillet in Step 4 along with the sauce. Be careful stirring so the tofu doesn't crumble too much.

BRAISING AND GLAZING

The technique in this recipe—which I call "braising and glazing"—is an excellent and versatile way to quickly cook firmer vegetables like Brussels sprouts, winter squash, parsnips, or other roots like beets, parsnips, and carrots. The braising part consists of nothing more than simmering the vegetables with a little water and oil or butter in a covered skillet until they are nearly tender—the steam from the liquid helps get this done fairly quickly. Then you uncover the pot, add seasonings if you haven't already, and turn the heat to high so the liquid becomes a glaze and the vegetables become fully tender.

Unstuffed Cabbage

The most onerous part about making stuffed cabbage is precooking, filling, and rolling the cabbage leaves—essentially everything but the cooking. So let's just cut to the chase, shall we? **Serves 4**

Ingredients

1 large head savoy or green cabbage (about 2 pounds)

2 tablespoons olive oil, plus more for drizzling

2 cloves garlic

1 cup Israeli couscous (or whole wheat couscous)

1 (15-ounce) can diced tomatoes

2 teaspoons smoked paprika

Salt and pepper

1 bunch fresh parsley

☐ Prep · **Cook**

☐ Carefully cut the core from the cabbage, leaving the head intact; peel away 12 outer leaves. (It's okay if they tear a little.) Refrigerate the remaining cabbage for another use.

☐ If the cabbage leaves have thick stems, cut them out.

1. Rub 1 tablespoon olive oil in the bottom of a large skillet. Line the pan with the cabbage leaves, overlapping them to get good coverage.

   ☐ Peel and chop 2 cloves garlic; put them in a medium bowl.

2. Add 1 cup Israeli couscous, 1 tablespoon olive oil, the tomatoes and their juice, 2 teaspoons smoked paprika, and a sprinkle of salt and pepper to the bowl. Stir to combine.

3. Spread the couscous mixture over the top of the cabbage; add 1 cup water and bring to a boil. Reduce the heat to a gentle bubble. Cover and cook until the cabbage and couscous are tender and most of the liquid is absorbed, 10 to 15 minutes.

   ☐ Strip about ¼ cup parsley leaves from their stems.

4. When the cabbage and couscous are tender, taste and adjust the seasoning of the filling. Drizzle the top with a little more olive oil and garnish with the parsley. To serve, cut portions with a spatula or spoon and scoop the cabbage out from the bottom.

● recipe continues →

Variations

Unstuffed Cabbage with Spicy Sausage. A more filling meal. Before lining the skillet with the cabbage, brown 2 hot Italian sausage links or about 8 ounces (1 cup) loose sausage meat in the skillet, breaking them up as they cook. This will take 5 to 10 extra minutes. Transfer the meat to a large bowl and spoon off the fat, wipe out the skillet, and start from Step 1. In Step 2, add the garlic and remaining stuffing ingredients to the bowl with the cooked sausage and proceed.

Unstuffed Cabbage with Bulgur. I like to garnish this with a mixture of fresh mint and parsley and serve it with a dollop of yogurt. Substitute medium-grind bulgur for the couscous. You'll probably need to cook the filling an extra 5 minutes in Step 3. Add a couple tablespoons water if necessary to keep the cabbage from burning.

Unstuffed Cabbage with Crumbled Chickpeas. Use either the main recipe or either of the preceding variations. Instead of the couscous, rinse and drain 2 (15-ounce) cans chickpeas, or use 3½ cups cooked. In Step 2, mash them with a fork or potato masher in a large, flat-bottomed bowl with the garlic until the beans break up and crumble. Then add the remaining ingredients and finish the recipe.

SAVOY CABBAGE

I love this versatile, long-storing variety of cabbage—grab it whenever you see it. Like green and red cabbages, savoy comes in a tightly packed head, only the leaves are curly and slightly less firm; the flavor is a little milder too. So it's perfect for salads and slaws and has a supple texture when cooked.

Potato Rösti with Warmed Apples

Potato pancakes with applesauce make an indulgent but somehow light meal, and they're a lot more accessible when you cook one giant pancake instead of many little ones. This recipe is based on what they do in Switzerland, where rösti are beloved. To make this heartier, top with fried or poached eggs or ribbons of cold-smoked salmon and sour cream. Or serve it as dinner for two instead of four. I'm happiest with something green on the side like a salad or spinach. **Serves 4**

Ingredients

2 pounds russet or Yukon Gold potatoes

Salt and pepper

3 tablespoons olive oil, plus more as needed

2 tablespoons butter

3 medium apples (about 1 pound)

¼ teaspoon ground cardamom

Sour cream or crème fraîche for serving (optional)

Prep · **Cook**

◻ Peel the potatoes if you like. Shred them in a food processor with a grating disk or by hand with a box grater.

◻ Drain the potatoes well in a colander or strainer, wringing them dry in kitchen towels to squeeze out as much moisture as possible.

◻ Sprinkle with salt and pepper and toss.

1. Put 3 tablespoons olive oil in a large skillet (preferably carbon steel or nonstick) over medium-high heat.

2. Spread the potatoes in the skillet and press them down with a spatula. Cook undisturbed until the bottom of the cake releases easily and is crisp, 5 to 10 minutes. Adjust the heat as it cooks so you hear it sizzle without smelling burning; you'll need to lift the edge carefully with a spatula to check the progress.

3. Put 2 tablespoons butter in a large pot over medium heat.

   ◻ Core the apples and cut them into thin slices.

4. When the butter has melted, add the apples, ¼ teaspoon ground cardamom, a sprinkle of salt, and ⅓ cup water. Cook, stirring occasionally and adding more water if the mixture gets too dry, until the apples soften and start to fall apart, 10 to 15 minutes.

5. When the first side of the rösti is browned, slide it onto a plate, top the potatoes with another plate, upside down, and carefully invert the two. Add a little more olive oil to the pan, then slide the potatoes back in. Continue to cook, adjusting the heat if necessary, until the second side is browned, 5 to 10 minutes. To serve, cut the rösti into wedges; top with the warmed apples and a dollop of sour cream or crème fraîche if you like.

Squash Gratin with Toasted Hazelnuts

Cream works magic on grated vegetables, turning them into a luxurious, velvety treat, especially wonderful with a crunchy, cheesy topping. The trick is to spread the vegetables in a thin layer for quick cooking. Double the recipe, increase the time in the oven, and you've got a vegetarian star of the Thanksgiving table. **Serves 4**

Ingredients

1 large butternut or other winter squash (2 to 2½ pounds)

3 sprigs fresh sage

2 tablespoons olive oil

Salt and pepper

1 cup cream

1 cup shelled hazelnuts

4 ounces Parmesan (1 cup grated)

▢ Prep · Cook

1. Heat the oven to 450°F.

    ▢ Cut the squash in half lengthwise, trim and peel it, scoop out and discard the seeds, and cut the flesh into chunks. Shred the squash in a food processor with a grating disk (by far the easier method) or by hand with a box grater. You should have about 6 cups; refrigerate the rest for another use.

    ▢ Strip the leaves from 3 sage sprigs and chop.

2. Put the squash in a 9 × 13-inch baking dish. Add the sage, 2 tablespoons olive oil, and a sprinkle of salt and pepper. Toss to coat, then spread in an even layer. Pour 1 cup cream over the top.

3. Cover the baking dish with foil and bake until the squash is tender and the cream is bubbling and thick, 10 to 15 minutes.

    ▢ Chop 1 cup hazelnuts; put them in a medium bowl.

    ▢ Grate 1 cup Parmesan; add it to the bowl and toss.

4. When the squash is tender, uncover the dish and sprinkle the Parmesan and nuts over the top. Return the baking dish to the oven and bake uncovered until the topping is lightly browned, about 5 minutes more. Let cool for at least 2 or up to 10 minutes before serving.

Variations

Turnip Gratin with Toasted Pecans. Instead of the squash, use turnips; trim and peel them before grating. Substitute a pinch of ground nutmeg for the sage, pecorino Romano for the Parmesan, and pecans for the hazelnuts.

Celery Root Gratin with Toasted Bread Crumbs. Replace the squash with celery root; trim and peel it before grating. Instead of the sage, chop ¼ cup fresh dill; wait to use it as a final garnish after baking. Let Gruyère stand in for the Parmesan. Toss the cheese with 1 cup bread crumbs (preferably fresh, page 488) and use that for the topping in Step 4.

Cauliflower "Polenta" with Mushrooms

Polenta, the Italian cousin to our cornmeal mush or grits, is a creamy vehicle for all sorts of saucy toppings. (See the recipes on pages 241 and 243.) A well-seasoned alternative based on super-soft cauliflower increases your vegetable intake without decreasing your pleasure.
Serves 4

Ingredients

4 tablespoons olive oil

Salt

1 pound button or cremini mushrooms

Pepper

1 large head cauliflower (about 2 pounds)

1 large shallot

2 sprigs fresh rosemary

4 ounces Parmesan or pecorino Romano cheese (1 cup grated)

2 tablespoons butter, or more to taste

⬚ Prep · **Cook**

1. Put 2 tablespoons olive oil in a large skillet over medium-low heat. Put 2 cups water and a big pinch of salt in a large pot over high heat.

   ⬚ Trim and slice the mushrooms. Add them to the skillet as you work.

2. Sprinkle the mushrooms with salt and pepper and raise the heat to medium. Cook, stirring occasionally, until tender and lightly browned, about 15 minutes.

   ⬚ Trim and halve the cauliflower. With the flat side on the cutting board, chop each half into small bits. Add the cauliflower to the pot of water as you work.

3. Bring the cauliflower to a boil, then lower the heat so the water bubbles steadily. Cook, stirring occasionally, until the cauliflower is quite tender and the liquid thickens, 10 to 12 minutes. If the mixture becomes too dry and sticks, add more water ¼ cup at a time.

   ⬚ Trim, peel, and slice the shallot.

   ⬚ Strip the leaves from 2 rosemary sprigs and chop.

4. When the mushrooms are lightly browned, add 2 tablespoons olive oil and the shallot and rosemary. Cook, stirring until fragrant, about 2 minutes. Remove from the heat.

   ⬚ Grate 1 cup Parmesan.

5. When the cauliflower breaks down and looks like porridge, remove it from the heat. Use a potato masher or immersion blender to purée it in the pot. Add 2 tablespoons butter and the Parmesan and return it to medium-low heat. Cook, stirring and adding water if necessary to

● recipe continues →

make the cauliflower steamy and loose enough to drop from a spoon like polenta. (If the mixture is too soupy, raise the heat and let some liquid bubble away for a couple minutes.) Taste and add more butter or salt if you like; keep warm.

6. Return the mushrooms to medium heat until they sizzle. Spoon the cauliflower "polenta" into bowls, top with the mushrooms, and serve.

Variations

Chianti Cauliflower "Polenta" with Mushrooms. Magenta polenta! Instead of using water to cook the cauliflower in Steps 1 and 3, substitute Chianti or another fruity red wine.

Cauliflower "Polenta" with Zucchini. Instead of the mushrooms, trim 1 pound zucchini; slice crosswise into thin coins. Use ¼ cup chopped fresh parsley instead of the rosemary if you like. Cook and season the vegetables as you would the mushrooms.

Mashed Potatoes with Mushrooms or Zucchini. Works with either the mushrooms in the main recipe or the previous variation. Substitute peeled baking potatoes like russets for the cauliflower. After cooking, mash by hand with a fork or potato masher—don't use an immersion blender or they will get gummy. They may need 10 minutes more cooking time, depending on how small you chop them.

BUTTON VERSUS CREMINI MUSHROOMS

The second are darker, slightly firmer—and usually more expensive—than the first. So what's the difference between common button mushrooms and increasingly common cremini (which are in fact baby portobellos)? They're interchangeable in recipes, though cremini usually don't release quite as much liquid during cooking, so the pan might dry out more quickly. For a more robust flavor and appearance, go the cremini route; for milder mushroom taste and a more supple texture, choose button mushrooms. Both have edible stems, so all you need to do is trim off the toughest bits at the bottom.

Stuffed Poblanos with Black Beans and Cheese

Stuffed poblano recipes usually have you wrangling with fragile roasted peppers, struggling to keep them intact. That's too much work for most nights. (Though if you want to do it, see the instructions for roasting and peeling peppers on page 501). Treat 'em more like normal stuffed bell peppers and suddenly the process is manageable. **Serves 4**

Ingredients

8 large poblano chiles

1 cup cooked or canned black beans (from one 15-ounce can)

1 small red onion

1 bunch fresh cilantro

4 ounces Manchego or Jack cheese (1 cup grated)

Salt and pepper

2 tablespoons olive oil

2 limes

Sour cream or Mexican crema for serving

▢ Prep · Cook

1. Turn the broiler to high; put the rack 6 inches from the heat (or as far away as you can).

   ▢ Cut a slit down the length of each poblano and carefully pry each one open just wide enough to remove the seeds (and later to stuff them).

   ▢ If you're using canned beans, rinse and drain them; put 1 cup in a medium bowl (and refrigerate the rest for another use).

   ▢ Trim, peel, and chop the onion; add it to the bowl.

   ▢ Chop about ½ cup cilantro leaves and tender stems. Reserve 2 tablespoons for garnish and add what remains to the bowl.

   ▢ Grate 1 cup Manchego or Jack cheese and add it to the bowl.

2. Sprinkle the stuffing with salt and pepper and stir to combine.

3. Using your fingers, gently fill the poblanos with the bean stuffing. When all the peppers are stuffed, put them on a rimmed baking sheet, rub with 2 tablespoons olive oil, and sprinkle with salt and pepper.

4. Broil, turning occasionally to avoid burning, until the peppers are soft and lightly charred on all sides and the cheese is melted, 10 to 15 minutes.

   ▢ Cut the limes into wedges.

5. When the peppers are done, put them on plates or a platter, and garnish with the reserved cilantro. Pass the sour cream or crema and lime wedges at the table.

Sweet Potato Flautas

Stuffing and rolling tortillas for an everyday dinner is one thing. But deep-frying them usually puts them in the territory of weekend fare. Turns out you can get some of the same shattering crunch on flautas by brushing them with oil and broiling. Then the crisp tortillas give way to a perfectly almost-creamy filling. **Serves 4**

Ingredients

3 tablespoons olive oil, plus more as needed

2 pounds sweet potatoes

Salt and pepper

6 scallions

1 fresh hot green chile (like serrano)

Twelve 8-inch flour tortillas

Sour cream for serving

Salsa for serving

◻ Prep · Cook

1. Turn the broiler to high; put the rack 4 inches from the heat. Put 3 tablespoons olive oil in a large skillet over low heat.

   ◻ Peel the sweet potatoes; shred them in a food processor with a grating disk or by hand with a box grater.

2. Put the sweet potatoes in the skillet with ½ cup water, sprinkle with salt and pepper, and raise the heat to medium-high. Cook, stirring occasionally, until they begin to soften and lighten in color, 8 to 10 minutes. Add 1 or 2 more tablespoons oil if they start to stick to the skillet.

   ◻ Trim and chop the scallions.

   ◻ Trim and chop the chile.

3. When the sweet potatoes begin to lighten in color, add the scallions and chile. Cook, stirring frequently, until the potatoes are tender but not mushy, 2 to 3 minutes. Spoon about ¼ cup of the sweet potatoes onto each of 12 tortillas. Roll them up tightly, leaving the ends open; brush the outsides generously with olive oil. As you work, transfer the flautas to a rimmed baking sheet seam side down so they stay closed.

4. Broil until the tops are browned and crisp, 2 to 3 minutes. Turn and brown the other side, about 2 minutes. Watch them so the tortillas don't burn. Serve hot, passing sour cream and salsa at the table.

• recipe continues →

Variations

Potato and Chorizo Flautas. Substitute 1½ pounds russet or Yukon Gold potatoes for the sweet potatoes. Wait to add any oil to the skillet; in Step 1, cook 8 ounces fresh Mexican-style chorizo over medium-high heat (if using meat in casing or tubes, first squeeze the meat out of the casing into the pan). Stir frequently until browned, about 5 minutes. Transfer to a plate with a slotted spoon. Cook the potatoes in the pan drippings as described in Steps 2 and 3, adding olive oil only if needed. Return the chorizo to the skillet. Toss, taste, and adjust the seasoning before filling the flautas.

Sweet Potato and Pork Flautas. Use just 1½ pounds sweet potatoes. Wait to add oil to the skillet; start by cooking 8 ounces ground pork over medium-high heat, stirring frequently until browned, about 5 minutes. Transfer to a plate with a slotted spoon. Cook the sweet potatoes in the pan drippings as described in Steps 2 and 3, adding olive oil only if needed. Return the pork to the skillet. Toss, taste, and adjust the seasoning before filling the flautas.

Potato and Cheese Flautas. I like the crumbly texture of queso fresco here, but if you want something that melts more, use asadero or Jack cheese. Substitute 1½ pounds russet or Yukon Gold potatoes for the sweet potatoes. Crumble 8 ounces queso fresco into the skillet in Step 3 before filling the flautas.

Potato and Spinach Saag

Saag, an Indian stew of spinach and aromatics, develops a luxurious flavor and texture from simmering with ghee (a kind of toasted clarified butter) and sometimes cream. To quicken the pace while retaining as much of that silkiness as possible, I go with straight butter and more cream. The potatoes lend their starch to the sauce, which thickens it even further. You'll want some kind of rice (page 496) or bread to sop it up. **Serves 4**

Ingredients

Salt

1½ pounds russet or Yukon Gold potatoes

1½ pounds spinach

2 tablespoons butter

1 inch fresh ginger

2 cloves garlic

1 fresh hot green chile (like serrano)

1 tablespoon garam masala or curry powder

Pepper

1¼ cups cream

▫ Prep · Cook

1. Put a large pot filled halfway with water over high heat; salt it.

   ▫ Peel the potatoes and cut them into ½-inch cubes, adding them to the pot as you work.

2. Cover the pot, bring to a boil, and cook, stirring once or twice, until the potatoes are tender enough to pierce with a fork but not mushy, 5 to 15 minutes.

   ▫ Trim and chop the spinach, including the stems.

3. Put 2 tablespoons butter in a large skillet over medium-low heat.

   ▫ Peel 1 inch ginger and 2 cloves garlic; trim the chile. Chop them all together.

4. Add the ginger, garlic, and chile to the skillet and turn the heat to medium-high. Cook, stirring frequently, until the aromatics soften, about 2 minutes. Add 1 tablespoon garam masala or curry powder and a sprinkle of salt; stir until fragrant, less than a minute. Add the spinach a handful at a time if necessary so there's room as it cooks, and sprinkle with salt and pepper. Cook, stirring occasionally, until the spinach is soft and most of the water boils off, about 5 minutes.

5. When the potatoes are ready, drain them in a colander, reserving about 1 cup cooking liquid. Return the potatoes to the pot, add the spinach mixture, and turn the heat to medium. Add 1¼ cups cream. Stir to combine and heat until steaming without coming to a boil, just a minute or two; add some of the reserved potato cooking water if the saag looks dry. Taste and adjust the seasoning, and serve.

● recipe continues →

Variations

Mushroom and Spinach Saag.
This saag comes together in
one pot. Substitute 1 pound
trimmed and quartered
button mushrooms for the
potatoes. Skip Steps 1 and 2.
In Step 3, put the butter in a
large pot. When it melts, add
the mushrooms, and cook,
stirring occasionally, until they
release their liquid and start
to darken, 5 to 10 minutes.
Then pick up the recipe at the
beginning of Step 4 when you
add the aromatics.

Tofu and Spinach Saag. Even
faster than the main recipe,
and you only need the one
large pot. Use 2 bricks firm
or extra-firm tofu (14 or
16 ounces each) instead of
the potatoes. Cut into 1-inch
cubes. Use the large pot to
cook the spinach sauce, then
add the tofu in Step 5. Cook,
stirring once or twice, until the
tofu warms through and the
sauce thickens, just a couple
minutes after adding the tofu.

Paneer and Spinach Saag.
If you can't find paneer, the
Indian fresh cheese, substitute
feta (which is a little saltier)
or farmer cheese or fresh
mozzarella (which are milkier).
Substitute 1 pound paneer for
the potatoes; cut it into ½-inch
cubes. Use a large pot to cook
the spinach sauce; add the
cheese in Step 5. Cook, stirring
once or twice, until the paneer
warms through and the sauce
thickens, just a couple minutes.

CREAMY SAUCES MADE FROM GREENS

Stir a creamy liquid into slightly overcooked
sautéed greens and instantly they become a
hearty sauce. Cream is most familiar for this (as
in creamed spinach), but coconut milk, yogurt,
tahini thinned with a little water, or puréed silken
tofu—or any combination of these—will all
provide that thick, rich base into which the greens
can just melt away. My ratio is 1½ pounds greens
to 1 to 2 cups creamy base, with the option to
add some water if the sauce threatens to get too
thick. Once the greens are tender and the creamy
component is added, the sauce is ready to serve,
but simmering the sauce for a bit allows all the
flavors to meld and gives you the opportunity to
cook something else, like potatoes or chopped
chicken or fish fillets, directly in it. Note that very
delicate greens like arugula and spinach will melt
into a sauce almost instantly. Collards and other
sturdy greens will take longer to get to the same
stage or will retain some crunch if you pull them
off the heat early.

Seared Zucchini with Pita and Olives

Think of a cross between fattoush (the Lebanese pita salad) and ratatouille (the Mediterranean summer stew)—and a world of possibilities emerges. Though the main recipe calls for zucchini, you can substitute cubed eggplant or sliced red bell pepper for some or all of it. **Serves 4**

Ingredients

Four 8-inch pitas

4 tablespoons olive oil

3 or 4 medium zucchini (1½ pounds)

Salt and pepper

2 cloves garlic

1 large (28-ounce) can whole peeled tomatoes or 6 ripe roma (plum) tomatoes

½ cup green or black olives

1 bunch fresh parsley

▢ Prep · Cook

1. Heat the oven to 350°F. Put the pitas on a rimmed baking sheet, brush with 1 tablespoon olive oil, and put in the oven (it's okay that it isn't heated yet). Bake, turning once, until crisp, about 15 minutes.

2. Put 3 tablespoons olive oil in a large skillet over medium-high heat.

    ▢ Trim the zucchini and cut it into coins about ¾ inch thick.

3. When the oil is hot, put the zucchini in the skillet in a single layer, working in batches to avoid overcrowding. Sprinkle the zucchini with salt and pepper, and cook undisturbed until browned on the bottom and just softened, 3 to 5 minutes. Transfer them to a plate and repeat with the remaining zucchini.

    ▢ Peel and chop 2 cloves garlic.   ▢ If you're using fresh tomatoes, core and chop them.

4. When all the zucchini are cooked and out of the skillet, add the garlic and tomatoes (with the juice from the can). Cook, stirring occasionally with a spatula to break up the canned tomatoes, until the liquid comes to a boil. Return the zucchini to the skillet, reduce the heat to a steady bubble, and cook, stirring once or twice, until the stew thickens, about 5 minutes.

    ▢ Pit ½ cup olives if necessary.   ▢ Chop ½ cup parsley leaves.

5. When the pitas are ready, add the olives to the skillet and stir. Then break or tear in the pita, and turn off the heat. Toss to combine, taste, and adjust the seasoning. Garnish with the parsley and serve.

Scrambled Broccoli with Parmesan and Lemon

Somewhere between scrambled eggs and a broccoli frittata falls what I call "vegetable scramble." The main recipe pairs the hearty richness of eggs and Parmesan with the bright punch of lemon juice. See the first variation for an interpretation with Chinese flavors. Then use the other variations—or whatever looks best at the market—to keep the concept rolling.
Serves 4

Ingredients

2 tablespoons olive oil, plus more if needed

1 large head broccoli (about 1½ pounds)

8 eggs

1 lemon

4 ounces Parmesan cheese (1 cup grated), plus a little more for garnish

Salt and pepper

▢ Prep · Cook

1. Put 2 tablespoons olive oil in a large skillet over medium-high heat.

   ▢ Trim the broccoli and chop the florets and tenderest stems into bite-sized pieces.

2. Add the broccoli to the skillet along with ⅓ cup water. Cook, stirring occasionally, until the broccoli is just tender and the skillet is dry, 5 to 6 minutes.

   ▢ Crack the eggs into a medium bowl.

   ▢ Grate the lemon zest into the bowl, then halve the lemon.

   ▢ Grate 1 cup Parmesan and add to the bowl.

3. Sprinkle the eggs with salt and lots of pepper and beat with a fork or whisk until evenly colored. When the broccoli is just tender and the pan is dry (there should still be some oil visible; if not, add some), turn the heat to low and pour in the egg mixture.

4. Cook, stirring occasionally, until the eggs are just set, 3 to 5 minutes. Using a strainer or your fingers to catch the seeds, squeeze as much lemon juice as you like over the top, then finish by grating on more cheese. Taste and adjust the seasoning, and serve.

Variations

Scrambled Broccoli with Soy Sauce and Lime. Omit the Parmesan cheese. Use regular broccoli or Chinese broccoli (gai lan), tatsoi, mizuna, or another Asian green. Substitute 1 tablespoon good-quality vegetable oil and 1 tablespoon sesame oil for the olive oil, 2 limes for the lemon, and add 2 tablespoons soy sauce as a last-minute drizzle.

Scrambled Asparagus, Two Ways. Following either the main recipe or the first variation, substitute 1½ pounds asparagus, trimmed and cut into 1-inch pieces. The cooking time and water required should be the same.

Scrambled Green Beans, Two Ways. Following either the main recipe or the first variation, substitute 1½ pounds green beans, trimmed and cut into 1-inch pieces. Increase the water to ½ cup and increase the cooking time by a couple minutes in Step 2.

EGGS TO THE RESCUE

If you ever have simply cooked or assorted raw vegetables in the fridge and feel uninspired, turn to eggs. Scrambled, poached, or fried (see page 483), they are ready in a flash and can make cooked vegetables, rice, noodles, or grains—which might otherwise feel like a side dish—into something far more substantial. I like to keep hard-boiled eggs handy in the fridge to crank up salads or sandwiches. Or stir raw eggs into the pan while you're cooking or fry or poach them in a separate pan, serve on top, and dinner is done.

Bok Choy Pancake with Soy Dipping Sauce

Korean pa jun (or pajeon) are crisp pancakes filled with scallions or other vegetables and sometimes seaweed, kimchi, and/or bits of meat. This is a lot like that, only thicker and loaded with vegetables like a frittata. Turning it is undeniably tricky the first time you try, so if you've got a broiler-proof skillet, you can skip that step and pop it under a hot broiler in the pan for a few minutes to set the top. Or use the batter to make 3- or 4-inch pancakes and cook in batches, adding oil to the skillet as needed. It won't take much longer. **Serves 4**

Ingredients

3 tablespoons good-quality vegetable oil, plus more if needed

1 large head bok choy (1½ pounds)

Salt and pepper

1 egg

¾ cup flour, plus more if needed

1 teaspoon sesame oil

¼ cup soy sauce

¼ cup rice vinegar

1 teaspoon sugar

□ Prep · Cook

1. Put 3 tablespoons vegetable oil in a large skillet (preferably cast iron, carbon steel, or other nonstick) over medium heat.

   □ Trim the bok choy; cut or pull off the leaves and thinly slice the stems.

2. Add the stems to the skillet and raise the heat to medium-high. Cook, stirring occasionally, until they start to soften, 3 to 5 minutes.

   □ Cut the bok choy leaves into thin ribbons.

3. Add the leaves, a little salt, and some pepper to the skillet. Cook, stirring occasionally, until the leaves wilt and the stems are nearly tender but still have some crunch, 3 to 4 minutes. Remove from the heat.

4. Meanwhile, in a large bowl, combine the egg, ¾ cup flour, 1 teaspoon sesame oil, and ½ cup water. Add a pinch of salt and pepper and whisk until smooth. It should have the consistency of thin pancake batter; if it doesn't, add more water or flour as necessary.

5. When the bok choy is done, stir it into the batter. Put a thin film of vegetable oil in the skillet if it's dry and put it back over medium-high heat. When it's hot, pour in the batter and spread it into an even layer with a spatula. Adjust the heat so the pancake sizzles without burning. Cover and cook undisturbed until the edges crisp and the batter sets, 4 to 8 minutes.

6. In a small bowl, whisk together ¼ cup soy sauce, ¼ cup rice vinegar, 1 teaspoon sugar, and ½ cup water.

• recipe continues →

7. Peek to see if the pancake is browned on the bottom, then loosen it with a spatula. To turn, cover the pancake with an unrimmed baking sheet and invert the skillet, being careful to avoid any hot pan drippings. (I usually do this over the sink or a cutting board.)

8. Slide the pancake off the baking sheet back into the skillet and cook until the second side is crisp and the pancake is no longer raw in the center (use a paring knife to cut into it and peek), another 3 to 5 minutes. Transfer the pancake to a cutting board. Cut it into wedges or squares and serve with little bowls of the dipping sauce.

Variations

Bean Sprout Pancake with Soy Dipping Sauce. Instead of the bok choy, use 12 ounces bean sprouts (about 3 cups) and 1 thinly sliced medium shallot. Cook the shallot as you would the stems in Step 2 and the bean sprouts as the leaves in Step 3. The rest of the recipe stays the same.

Scallion-Crab Pancake with Citrusy Dipping Sauce. Instead of the bok choy, use 2 bunches scallions. Cut the white parts into inch-long pieces and slice the green tops; keep them separate. Cook the white parts as you would the bok choy stems in Step 2 and the green tops as the leaves in Step 3. Add 8 ounces lump crabmeat (about 1 cup) to the batter in Step 4. For the dipping sauce, use a mixture of lemon or lime and orange juices for the rice vinegar.

Carrot-Edamame Pancake with Miso Dipping Sauce. Substitute 1 pound carrots and 1 cup frozen shelled edamame for the bok choy. Trim and grate the carrots; stir-fry them and the edamame at the same time in the hot oil as described in Steps 2 and 3. Stir frequently; they both should be soft in about 5 minutes. Assemble the pancake batter and cook as described. For the dipping sauce, whisk together ¼ cup white or yellow miso, 1 tablespoon Dijon mustard, and ½ cup water.

Celery Root Tempura
With or Without Shrimp

Root vegetables make the best tempura—crisp on the outside and perfectly creamy on the inside. And though it can be a tad messy, deep-frying is a super-fast way to cook. If you like shrimp, fry up some of those too. Both go well with this unorthodox but delicious dipping sauce. **Serves 4**

Ingredients

Ice cubes

3 eggs

2½ cups flour

Salt

2 pounds celery root

8 or 12 extra-large peeled shrimp (optional)

Good-quality vegetable oil for deep-frying

½ cup mayonnaise

2 tablespoons soy sauce

Wasabi powder or dry mustard, to taste

☐ Prep · Cook

☐ Combine 2 cups cold water and 1 or 2 cups ice in a large bowl and let it sit for a minute.

☐ Separate 3 eggs; put the yolks in another large bowl; discard the whites or save for another use.

1. Measure out 2 cups of the ice water (without the ice) and add it to the yolks along with 1½ cups flour and a big pinch of salt. Beat the mixture lightly; the batter should be lumpy and very thin.

☐ Trim and peel the celery root; cut it into thin disks or sticks (not so big that you can't eat a piece in a few bites).

☐ If you're using shrimp, rinse with cold water, then pat them dry with towels.

2. Put at least 2 inches vegetable oil in a large pot over medium heat (you want the oil to get to 350°F).

3. Whisk together ½ cup mayonnaise, 2 tablespoons soy sauce, and a pinch of wasabi to taste.

☐ Put 1 cup flour in a shallow bowl for dredging.

☐ Line a plate with towels.

4. When a pinch of flour sizzles in the oil but doesn't burn, begin coating pieces of celery root and shrimp in the flour, then dipping them in the batter. Fry in batches, adjusting the heat to maintain the oil temperature and turning once if necessary, until each piece is golden, 3 to 5 minutes. As they finish, transfer the tempura to the towels to drain; sprinkle with salt if you like. Serve right away with the sauce. Continue frying and eating as you go until there's nothing left.

• recipe continues →

Variations

Sweet Potato Tempura With or Without Shrimp. Substitute 2 large sweet potatoes (any color or type) for the celery root.

Kohlrabi Tempura With or Without Shrimp. The mild cabbage flavor is delicious with this dipping sauce. Substitute 1½ pounds kohlrabi for the celery root.

Chips and Fish. Instead of the celery root, use either 1½ pounds sweet potatoes or Yukon Gold potatoes. Instead of the shrimp, cut 1 pound firm white fish (like cod, catfish, or halibut) into big pieces; it will take a couple minutes more than the shrimp to crisp and cook through. Add chopped dill pickles and a tablespoon of Dijon mustard to the sauce to make a Japanese-style tartar sauce.

EATING AROUND THE STOVE

It's no secret that the kitchen is always the center of the party. Why not celebrate any night and gather around the stove—or if you're lucky, a comfy center island—for dinner? It's casual, sure, and also practical: There's nothing quite like nibbling on something piping hot, crunchy, and crisp while you're watching the next batch bubble away in the pot. And since you cut out the middle plate, it's easy and fast too. So the next time you crave tempura (or its ilk), pull up a barstool, slide into the breakfast nook, or prop yourself up against a counter and dig in.

Braised Cabbage and Sauerkraut With or Without Ham

When you treat sauerkraut like an ingredient rather than just a condiment and braise it with ham, dill, and beer, everything tastes as if you've been cooking for hours. The fresh cabbage tempers the intensity of the kraut while adding a little crunch. The mustard is your call, but I can't imagine skipping it. Plain boiled or baked potatoes are also perfect, assuming you don't have soft pretzels lying around. **Serves 4**

Ingredients

2 tablespoons good-quality vegetable oil

8 ounces smoked ham steak

1 large onion

1 pound sauerkraut

1 small head savoy cabbage (about 1 pound)

1 bunch fresh dill

2 bay leaves

Salt and pepper

2 cups water or beer

Mustard for serving (optional)

☐ Prep · Cook

1. Put 2 tablespoons vegetable oil in a large pot over medium-high heat.

   ☐ Cut the ham into bite-sized pieces.

2. Add the ham to the pot and cook, stirring occasionally, until it's browned in spots, about 5 minutes.

   ☐ Trim, peel, halve, and slice the onion.

   ☐ Rinse and drain the sauerkraut.

3. Add the onion to the pot and cook, stirring occasionally, until it softens, 3 to 5 minutes.

   ☐ Trim, quarter, core, and slice the cabbage.

   ☐ Chop ⅓ cup dill leaves and tender stems.

4. When the onion softens, add the sauerkraut, cabbage, and dill, along with 2 bay leaves, a sprinkle of salt and pepper, and 2 cups water or beer (or a combination). Bring the liquid to a boil, then adjust the heat so that it bubbles steadily.

5. Cover and cook, stirring occasionally and adding more liquid if the mixture gets too dry, until the cabbage is tender and most of the liquid is gone, 8 to 12 minutes.

6. Remove the bay leaves from the pot. Taste and adjust the seasoning. Garnish with the dill and serve with mustard on the side if you like.

Variations

Braised Cabbage, Sauerkraut, and Smoked Sausage. Instead of the ham, use chopped smoked sausage (like Polish sausage) or even Spanish chorizo.

Braised Cabbage, Kimchi, and Tofu. If you can get your hands on smoked tofu, this is the time to use it. Substitute 1 brick firm tofu (14 to 16 ounces), cubed, for the ham, kimchi for the sauerkraut, and cilantro for the dill. Serve this spicy combo in a deep bowl with simply cooked rice (page 496), rice noodles (page 495), or boiled sliced rice cakes (tteokgukyong-tteok).

Braised Cabbage, Pickles, and Potatoes. Instead of the ham, cut 1 pound Yukon Gold potatoes into bite-sized pieces. Brown them the same way as described in Step 2. Replace the sauerkraut with several large dill pickles (about 1 cup chopped or sliced, with at least 2 tablespoons of their juice). Instead of rinsing and draining them, include a little of their juice to taste along with the beer.

COOKING WITH BEER

Plenty of recipes call for wine as an alternative to water or stock for deglazing, braising, and making sauce. So why not cook more with beer? It has a better flavor than store-bought stocks and might even be handier, assuming you have some in your fridge. (Flat beer is fair game for cooking too.) Leave the intricacies of beer flavors to the experts and just use what you like to drink, knowing that lagers and wheat beers will produce a lighter, fruitier liquid or sauce; porters will add richness; and stouts will impart deep caramelized flavors.

Pan-Seared Corn With or Without Pork

Skillet-charred fresh corn kernels are fantastic. But you can easily combine them with crisp bits of pork shoulder and the boldness of chiles for something more substantial. With frozen corn, this comes together even faster; figure you'll need 3 to 4 cups (two 10-ounce bags). Serve with chopped salad in the same bowl (page 487) and you have a meal. **Serves 4**

Ingredients

2 tablespoons olive oil

1 pound ground pork

Salt and pepper

4 large ears fresh corn

1 fresh hot green chile (like jalapeño), or more to taste

2 teaspoons chili powder

1 lime

1 bunch fresh cilantro (optional)

□ Prep · Cook

1. Put 2 tablespoons olive oil in a large skillet (preferably cast iron) over medium-high heat.

2. Add the pork to the skillet, sprinkle with salt and pepper, and cook, stirring once or twice, until the pork is brown and crisp, 5 to 10 minutes. (If you're not ready to proceed to Step 3 before the pork is ready, turn the heat under the pork to low.)

   □ Husk the corn and cut the kernels off the cobs. (If using frozen, no need to thaw it.)

   □ Trim and chop the chile.

3. When the pork has browned, transfer it to a bowl with a slotted spoon; sprinkle it with the chili powder and toss. Spoon off all but 2 tablespoons of the fat from the skillet, add the corn and chile to the pan, return it to medium-high heat, and sprinkle with salt and pepper. Cook, shaking the pan occasionally and keeping the corn in as much of a single layer as possible, until the kernels are well browned on at least one side, 5 to 10 minutes.

   □ Halve the lime.

   □ If you're using cilantro, chop ½ cup leaves and tender stems.

4. When the corn is ready, return the pork to the skillet and cook, stirring a couple times until it heats through, 1 or 2 minutes more. Squeeze the lime juice over the top, garnish with the cilantro if you like, and serve.

Variations

Pan-Seared Succotash.
Instead of the meat, use 2 cups frozen lima beans; no need to thaw them. They'll sear a couple minutes faster than directed for the pork. Reduce the corn to 3 ears or 3 cups frozen kernels. Keep the chile if you like and add 1 chopped red bell pepper at the same time in Step 3; give it a little extra time to soften and heat through before returning the lima beans to the skillet.

Super-Soft Green Beans
With or Without Bacon

As wonderful as barely cooked, perfectly crisp-tender green beans are, sometimes you want them soul food–style: super-soft and silky like only stewing will make them. Bacon and beer send this over the top. Perfect with plain rice (page 496), egg noodles (page 493), saltines, or corn bread if you happen to have some handy. Other vegetables to try this way: broccoli florets, broccolini, or sliced fennel. **Serves 4**

Ingredients

2 tablespoons olive oil

4 to 6 slices bacon (optional)

1 large onion

2 cloves garlic

2 pounds green beans

1 large (28-ounce) can diced tomatoes

1½ cups beer (1 regular 12-ounce can or bottle, as light or full bodied as you like)

Salt and pepper

4 scallions

☐ Prep · **Cook**

1. Put 2 tablespoons olive oil in a large pot over medium heat.

   ☐ Chop the bacon if you're using it and add it to the skillet.

   ☐ Trim, peel, and chop the onion; add it to the skillet.

   ☐ Peel and chop 2 cloves garlic; add them to the skillet.

2. Cook, stirring occasionally and adjusting the heat so the fat sizzles, until the bacon (if you're using it) is crisp and the onion is golden and soft, 5 to 10 minutes.

   ☐ Trim the green beans.

3. Spoon off all but 2 tablespoons fat if you cooked bacon and add the green beans to the pot along with the tomatoes and their juice, 1½ cups beer, and a sprinkle of salt and pepper. Bring the liquid to a boil, then adjust the heat so it bubbles vigorously. Cover and cook until the tomatoes break down into a thick sauce and the green beans are very tender, 15 to 20 minutes.

   ☐ Trim and chop the scallions.

4. When the beans are virtually falling apart, taste and adjust the seasoning. Garnish with the scallions and serve.

Beans and Tofu

like many people around the world, I eat more beans than any other single form of protein. And fortunately, more Americans are doing the same. Not only are beans a low-fat, low-calorie source of quality protein and fiber, but they're versatile. Whether they're canned or dried, they almost never go bad, and they're relatively inexpensive. Most important, legumes are a crop that is beneficial to grow, meaning they actually add to, rather than deplete, soil nutrients.

There was a time not long ago when I called tofu a tough sell. Not anymore. Thanks to increased availability, more choices of textures and types, and tons of innovative recipes, home cooks are regularly incorporating tofu into their meals. So instead of thinking of tofu as a meat replacement, try using it as you would dairy. For all these reasons, there are many more tofu recipes and variations in this book than there were in the first edition. Check the index to find them all.

Back to beans for one technical note: With the exception of a handful of recipes that call for frozen beans, the ingredient lists offer the option of canned or home-cooked from dried. So if you're happy with the convenience of canned, go for it. But I encourage you to try the master recipe on page 505 every now and then.

Hot and Sour Black Beans with Bok Choy

Turns out when you marinate black beans in a flavorful liquid for even a few minutes, they take on the characteristics of their fermented and dried counterparts minus the intensity. If you come across black soybeans, snap 'em up, but ordinary black beans are just fine. The variations show how to substitute leftover beef or chicken for the beans. And of course you can use different beans or even cubes of tofu. Serve with rice or noodles to make a meal.
Serves 4

Ingredients

3½ cups cooked or canned black beans (two 15-ounce cans)

2 tablespoons soy sauce

2 tablespoons rice vinegar

1 tablespoon sesame oil

1 teaspoon sugar

½ teaspoon red chile flakes, or more to taste

Pepper

3 tablespoons good-quality vegetable oil

1 large head bok choy (1½ pounds)

2 cloves garlic

Salt if needed

☐ Prep · Cook

☐ If you're using canned beans, rinse and drain them. Put the beans in a medium bowl.

1. Add 2 tablespoons soy sauce, 2 tablespoons rice vinegar, 1 tablespoon sesame oil, 1 teaspoon sugar, ½ teaspoon red chile flakes, and a good amount of pepper. Toss to combine.

2. Put 3 tablespoons vegetable oil in a large skillet over medium heat.

   ☐ Trim the bok choy and chop it crosswise into thin ribbons.

3. Add the bok choy to the skillet and raise the heat to medium-high. Cook, stirring occasionally, until it starts to soften, 3 to 5 minutes.

   ☐ Peel and chop 2 cloves garlic.

4. Add the garlic to the bok choy. Cook, stirring occasionally, until the leaves are completely tender but the stems still have some crunch, 3 to 4 minutes.

5. Stir in the beans and all of the marinade and cook, stirring to combine, just until the beans are warmed through, 3 to 4 minutes. Taste and adjust the seasoning, and serve.

● recipe continues →

Variations

Lemony Chickpeas with Kale. Omit the sugar. Substitute chickpeas for the black beans, a sprinkle of salt for the soy sauce, olive oil for the sesame oil, lemon juice for the rice vinegar, and olive oil for the vegetable oil. Use kale instead of bok choy.

Hot and Sour Chicken with Bok Choy. Perfect when you have leftover simply seasoned roast or grilled chicken. Instead of the beans, use plainly cooked chopped or pulled chicken breast or thigh meat; 1 to 2 cups (8 to 12 ounces) is all you need. Remove the meat from the bones and any skin if necessary and shred or chop the meat into bite-sized pieces; add it to the marinade in Step 1.

Hot and Sour Beef with Asparagus. You can use any plainly cooked cut: roast beef, grilled steak, or even cooked ground meat; 1 to 2 cups (8 to 12 ounces) is plenty. Remove any bones if necessary and shred or chop the meat into bite-sized pieces; add it to the marinade in Step 1. Instead of the bok choy, use asparagus. Trim, then slice diagonally, trying to keep the thickness as even as possible. To avoid overcooking, wait to add the asparagus and garlic together in Step 4 and reduce the cooking time to about a minute for thin spears and 2 minutes for thick ones before proceeding with Step 5; then check frequently for the degree of doneness you like.

Beans and Greens

Most of my books include some spin on this irresistible and simple combination. I'm leaving this recipe wide open for you to choose the type of beans and greens. The timing and cues will remain almost the same. Cook this following the directions for intact beans. Or if you've got a little extra time and crave a softer stew, let the beans and greens bubble gently, adding more stock or water if the pan gets too dry, until the vegetables are meltingly tender and the beans begin to break apart, up to 45 minutes. **Serves 4**

Ingredients

1½ pounds spinach, kale, collards, escarole, chard, or broccoli rabe

2 tablespoons olive oil, plus more for drizzling

Salt

1 small onion

2 cloves garlic, or more to taste

3½ cups cooked or canned beans (two 15-ounce cans, any kind)

1 cup vegetable stock or water, plus more as needed

Pepper (optional)

▢ Prep · Cook

▢ Trim and chop the greens, keeping any thick stems separate.

1. Put 2 tablespoons olive oil in a large pot over medium-high heat. When it's hot, add any chopped stems to the pot and cook until they begin to soften, 3 to 4 minutes. Sprinkle with salt.

   ▢ Peel and halve the onion; slice it thinly. Add it to the pot.

   ▢ Peel and chop 2 cloves garlic.

   ▢ If you're using canned beans, rinse and drain them.

2. When the stems begin to soften, add the chopped greens, in batches if necessary to fit them in. Stir in the garlic, beans, and 1 cup stock or water.

3. Cook, stirring occasionally and adding more liquid if the mixture starts to look dry, until the beans are warmed through and the greens are just soft: 3 to 4 minutes for spinach; 4 to 5 minutes for escarole, chard, or broccoli rabe; 5 to 6 minutes for kale or collards.

4. Taste and adjust the seasoning, adding lots of pepper if you like. Serve drizzled with some olive oil.

• recipe continues →

Variations

Beans and Broccoli. Butter beans are terrific here. For contrasting textures, use as much of the broccoli stems as possible. Instead of the greens, trim 1½ pounds broccoli, keeping the tender florets and stems separate. Slice the stems crosswise as thinly as you can manage. Follow the directions, substituting the stems for the greens stems and the florets for the leaves.

Beans and Cauliflower. An excellent place for chickpeas or fava beans. Substitute 1 medium head cauliflower (1½ pounds) for the greens. Trim the ends and any leaves; chop the florets and the tenderest parts of the stem into bite-sized bits. Add it all to the pot in Step 1.

Beans and Beans. Slightly green-tinted frozen lima beans or flageolets are lovely in this combo. Instead of the greens, trim 1½ pounds green beans (or yellow wax beans for that matter). Follow the directions, adding the beans as directed for the stems in the main recipe.

Beans and Sausage (with Greens, Broccoli, Cauliflower, or Beans). Use any bean here and any sausage. Some ideas: cannellini beans with Italian sausage links; black beans and fresh Mexican-style chorizo; frozen lima beans and chicken sausage. Two or 3 links (8 to 12 ounces) is all you need. Reduce the olive oil to 1 tablespoon. Before doing anything, cut the sausage into bite-sized bits while you heat the oil as described in Step 1 (kitchen shears are handy for this step). Cook the sausage, stirring frequently, until it's no longer pink (or red in the case of fresh chorizo) and browns in places, 5 to 10 minutes. Proceed with the recipe, picking up later in Step 1 with adding the greens stems.

White Beans and Fresh Tomatoes with Parmesan Toast

A bright summertime stew, perfect for under- or overripe seasonal tomatoes. Thick slices of Parmesan-topped toast answer the call for something crusty and crunchy to dip into it. And when fresh tomatoes aren't happening, see the last variation. **Serves 4**

Ingredients

3 tablespoons olive oil, plus more for drizzling

1 small onion

3 or 4 cloves garlic

3 or 4 large ripe tomatoes

Salt and pepper

3½ cups cooked or canned any white beans (two 15-ounce cans)

4 thick slices any rustic bread

½ cup white wine or water

1 cup chicken stock, vegetable stock, or water, plus more if needed

4 ounces Parmesan cheese (1 cup grated)

Several sprigs fresh basil

☐ Prep · Cook

1. Turn the broiler to high; put the rack 4 inches from the heat. Put 3 tablespoons olive oil in a large skillet or large pot over medium heat.

   ☐ Trim, peel, and chop the onion.

   ☐ Peel and chop 3 or 4 cloves garlic.

2. Add the onion and garlic to the skillet and cook, stirring occasionally, until the onion softens, 3 to 5 minutes.

   ☐ Core and chop the tomatoes.

3. Add the tomatoes to the skillet and sprinkle with salt and pepper. Cook, stirring occasionally, until the tomatoes release some juice, about 5 minutes.

   ☐ If you're using canned beans, rinse and drain them.

   ☐ Put 4 slices bread on a rimmed baking sheet.

4. When the tomatoes begin to soften, add ½ cup white wine or water and let it bubble until evaporated. Add 1 cup stock or water, the beans, and a sprinkle of salt and pepper. Bring to a boil, then adjust the heat so it bubbles gently but steadily.

5. Cook, stirring occasionally and adding more liquid if the mixture gets too dry, until the tomatoes break down and the beans soften, 10 to 15 minutes.

   ☐ Grate 1 cup Parmesan cheese.

   ☐ Strip the leaves from several basil sprigs and chop.

● recipe continues →

6. Drizzle both sides of the bread with a little olive oil. Broil until the tops are golden, a minute or two. Turn the bread; sprinkle the untoasted sides with the Parmesan. Continue broiling until the cheese is bubbling and browned, another minute or two.

7. When the tomatoes and beans are as thick or as soupy as you like, taste and adjust the seasoning. Divide among 4 bowls, scatter the basil over the top, drizzle with olive oil, and serve with the Parmesan toast.

Variations

White Beans and Fennel with Manchego Toast. Omit the basil. Use Manchego cheese instead of the Parmesan. Substitute 2 medium fennel bulbs for the tomatoes. After trimming the bottoms, remove and chop the stalks, reserving some of the fronds for garnish; halve, core, and slice the bulb. Add the fennel to the skillet in Step 4 with the wine or water before proceeding.

Pinto Beans and Fresh Tomatoes with Cheesy Tortillas. Substitute good-quality vegetable oil for the olive oil, pinto beans for the white beans, and beer for the white wine. Instead of bread, use four 6-inch flour or corn tortillas; they'll toast in an instant under the broiler, so watch them. After turning, sprinkle the tops with grated cheddar or Jack cheese instead of Parmesan. Garnish with cilantro instead of basil.

Wintertime Beans and Tomatoes. Works for the pinto bean variation too. Omit the 1 cup stock or water. Instead of fresh tomatoes, use 1 large (28-ounce) can whole peeled tomatoes. If you don't feel like chopping them, there's no need: After you add them and their juice in Step 3, break them up as you stir. Proceed with the recipe or variation.

Stir-Fried Curried Chickpeas with Two-Tone Potatoes

Crisp spiced chickpeas are one of the most satisfying snack foods, too good to confine to nibbling. So let's add them to grated root vegetables for a hearty stir-fry, which benefits exponentially from the extra crunch and seasoning. Serve with flatbread. **Serves 4**

Ingredients

4 tablespoons good-quality vegetable oil

3½ cups cooked or canned chickpeas (two 15-ounce cans)

12 ounces russet or Yukon Gold potatoes

12 ounces sweet potatoes

2 cloves garlic

1 inch fresh ginger

1 tablespoon curry powder

Salt and pepper

1 bunch fresh cilantro

2 limes

□ Prep · Cook

1. Put 2 tablespoons vegetable oil in a large skillet over medium-high heat.

   □ If you're using canned chickpeas, rinse and drain them.

2. Add the chickpeas to the skillet and cook, stirring or shaking the pan occasionally, until they are golden and crisp, 10 to 15 minutes.

   □ Trim and scrub the potatoes; trim and peel the sweet potatoes. Shred both in a food processor with a grating disk or by hand with a box grater.

   □ Peel 2 cloves garlic and 1 inch ginger; chop them together.

3. When the chickpeas are golden and crisp, add 1 tablespoon curry powder and a sprinkle of salt and pepper. Cook, stirring, until the curry powder is fragrant, a minute or two. Transfer the chickpeas to a plate.

4. Add 2 tablespoons vegetable oil to the skillet along with the garlic and ginger. Cook, stirring, until they're fragrant, 30 seconds to 1 minute.

5. Add the shredded potatoes and sweet potatoes, stirring them around to coat in whatever curry powder was left behind. Cook, stirring occasionally, until the vegetables are tender and lightly browned, 8 to 12 minutes.

   □ Chop 1 cup cilantro leaves and tender stems.

   □ Cut the limes into wedges.

6. When the vegetables are ready, stir in the cilantro and the chickpeas. Taste and adjust the seasoning, and serve with the lime wedges.

Variations

Spicy Stir-Fried Chickpeas with Sweet Potatoes. Use 1½ pounds sweet potatoes and omit the russets or Yukon Golds. Substitute 1 or 2 chopped fresh hot green chiles for the ginger and 2 teaspoons ground cumin for the curry powder.

Stir-Fried Curried Chickpeas with Celery Root. Instead of the potatoes and sweet potatoes, trim, peel, and grate about 2 pounds celery root. Everything else stays the same.

Curried Chickpeas with Two-Tone Potatoes. Not quite soup but definitely more soupy. Works with the other variations above too. Follow the directions through Step 4. After stir-frying the vegetables in Step 5, add another tablespoon curry powder and stir until fragrant. Pour in 1 (14-ounce) can coconut milk (full- or reduced-fat as you like) and stir with a fork until bubbling; then add the chickpeas and cilantro.

Red Beans and Cabbage in Buttery Tomato Sauce

Combine the soft, silky texture of braised cabbage with beans and tomatoes, build in a little richness with butter, all while the pleasant sharpness of ginger lingers in the background. Sounds like a stew that cooked all afternoon, right? The beauty is how everything comes together simultaneously. Rice is the natural accompaniment, though quinoa is nice too. Start quinoa before beginning the recipe; for white rice, wait until you add the tomatoes. **Serves 4**

Ingredients

4 tablespoons (½ stick) butter

2 inches fresh ginger

1 large (28-ounce) can diced tomatoes

1 small head savoy or green cabbage (1 pound)

3½ cups cooked or canned red beans (two 15-ounce cans)

Salt and pepper

□ Prep · Cook

1. Put 2 tablespoons butter in a large pot over medium heat.

   □ Peel and chop 2 inches ginger.

2. Add the ginger to the pot and cook, stirring occasionally, until fragrant, a minute or two. Add the tomatoes and their juice and turn the heat to medium-high.

   □ Trim, core, quarter, and chop the cabbage; add it to the pot as you go.

   □ If you're using canned beans, rinse and drain them.

3. Add the beans to the pot. Add ½ cup water, sprinkle with salt and pepper, and stir to combine.

4. Lower the heat so the liquid bubbles steadily and cook, stirring occasionally and adding more liquid if the mixture gets too dry, until the tomatoes break down, the cabbage becomes tender, and the beans get creamy, 10 to 15 minutes.

5. Stir in 2 tablespoons butter. Taste and adjust the seasoning, and serve.

Variations

Black-Eyed Peas and Okra in Buttery Tomato Sauce. Substitute 1 pound okra, trimmed and cut crosswise into 1-inch pieces, for the cabbage. If you don't like the slimy texture of okra, you can add a little more liquid to the pot and simmer the mixture partially covered until the okra more or less melts into the sauce, about an hour.

Beans and Cabbage in Creamy Vegan Tomato Sauce. Works for the main recipe or the other variation. Substitute olive oil for the butter. Use 1 cup oat or soy milk instead of the water in Step 3.

Lima Bean and Zucchini Gratin with Rye Crumbs

The starchiness of beans makes them perfect for the cheesy casseroles known as "gratins." If you don't fancy—or have—rye bread, whole wheat is a good alternative. And instead of dragging out the food processor, you can use good-quality panko and save a couple minutes.
Serves 4

Ingredients

4 tablespoons (½ stick) butter

2 or 3 medium zucchini (about 1 pound)

¼ cup red wine vinegar

Salt and pepper

2 slices rye bread (a little stale is fine)

4 ounces Gruyère cheese (1 cup grated)

3 cups frozen lima beans

1 tablespoon Dijon mustard

▫ Prep · Cook

1. Turn the broiler to high; put the rack 6 inches from the heat. Put 4 tablespoons butter in a large broiler-proof skillet over low heat.

   ▫ Trim the zucchini and cut into 1-inch chunks.

2. Turn the heat under the skillet to medium-high and add the zucchini to the butter along with ¼ cup red wine vinegar and a sprinkle of salt and pepper. Cook, stirring occasionally, until the zucchini has softened, 8 to 10 minutes.

   ▫ Tear 2 slices rye bread to pieces into a food processor, then pulse into coarse crumbs.

   ▫ Grate 1 cup Gruyère cheese.

3. When the zucchini is tender, stir in 3 cups lima beans and 1 tablespoon Dijon mustard. Cook, stirring occasionally, until the lima beans are warmed through, 2 to 3 minutes. Taste and adjust the seasoning.

4. Spread the mixture evenly in the skillet, sprinkle with the cheese, and scatter the bread crumbs over the top.

5. Broil until the cheese is bubbling and browned and the bread crumbs are crisp. Let it cool for a minute or two, then serve.

Black Bean Chili

Caramelizing onions with bell pepper, tomato paste, garlic, and spices sets the stage for a shortcut vegetarian chili. A few simple substitutions—including the option to add meat—quickly change everything. For even more flavor, substitute a 12-ounce bottle of beer for 1½ cups of the water in Step 3. Serve this chili with warmed tortillas or chips, rice (page 496), or corn bread if you've got some. It's also good tossed with pasta (page 493).
Serves 4

Ingredients

1 onion

2 cloves garlic

¼ cup olive oil

1 red bell pepper

3½ cups cooked or canned black beans (two 15-ounce cans)

⅓ cup tomato paste

1 tablespoon chili powder

1 teaspoon ground cumin

1 teaspoon smoked paprika

1 bunch fresh cilantro

4 ounces queso fresco (1 cup crumbled; optional)

▫ Prep · Cook

▫ Trim, peel, and chop the onion.

▫ Peel and chop 2 cloves garlic.

1. Put ¼ cup olive oil in a large pot over medium-high heat. When the oil is hot, add the onion and garlic and cook, stirring occasionally, until they soften, about 3 minutes.

   ▫ Core, seed, and chop the bell pepper and add it to the pot.

   ▫ If you're using canned beans, rinse and drain them.

2. Add ⅓ cup tomato paste, 1 tablespoon chili powder, 1 teaspoon ground cumin, and 1 teaspoon smoked paprika to the vegetables. Cook, stirring, until the mixture darkens and becomes fragrant, 1 to 2 minutes.

3. Add 3 cups water, stirring to scrape up any browned bits. Add the beans. Adjust the heat so the mixture simmers gently but steadily and cook until it thickens, about 5 minutes.

   ▫ Chop 1 cup cilantro leaves and tender stems.

   ▫ Crumble the queso fresco if you're using it.

4. When the chili is ready, taste and adjust the seasoning. Serve, garnished with the cilantro and queso fresco.

● recipe continues →

Variations

White Bean Green Chili. Use 1 (11-ounce) can crushed or whole tomatillos instead of the tomato paste and navy beans instead of black beans. Substitute 1 large or 2 small poblano chiles for the bell pepper. Reduce the water to 2 cups. If using whole tomatillos, before adding the beans in Step 3, use a potato masher to break them up. Keep the garnish or sprinkle with pepitas (hulled green pumpkin seeds) before serving.

Pinto Bean Chili. Substitute pinto beans for the black beans and use a green bell pepper instead of red. Grated cheddar cheese and chopped green onion make good garnish options. Everything else stays the same.

Meaty Black, White, or Pinto Bean Chili. Works for the main recipe or the first two variations. Reduce the olive oil to 2 tablespoons. Before you prep the onion and garlic, heat the oil in the pot and cook up to 1 pound any ground meat or Mexican-style chorizo (removed from the casing). Stir occasionally until the meat browns in places, about 5 minutes. Then add the onions and garlic and proceed with the recipe.

Zingy Edamame and Cabbage Stir-Fry

The seasoning for this stir-fry will remind you of kimchi, spreading its salty-sweet-spicy-tangy flavors onto crisp-tender edamame. The Korean red pepper paste gochujang is now available at many supermarkets, but if you can't find it or want to cook from your pantry, red chile flakes or a few dashes of sriracha will add the heat. A little sesame oil will bring the nuttiness. Rice is the obvious accompaniment, though any simply cooked grain is welcome. **Serves 4**

Ingredients

2 tablespoons good-quality vegetable oil

4 cloves garlic

1 inch fresh ginger

Salt and pepper

1 medium head savoy or napa cabbage (1½ pounds)

3 tablespoons gochujang, or more to taste

3 tablespoons soy sauce

2 tablespoons rice vinegar

1 tablespoon sugar

3 cups frozen shelled edamame (12 ounces)

2 scallions

☐ Prep · Cook

1. Put 2 tablespoons vegetable oil in a large skillet or large pot over low heat.

   ☐ Peel 4 cloves garlic and 1 inch ginger; chop them together.

2. Raise the heat under the skillet to high.

   ☐ Trim, core, quarter, and chop the cabbage; add it to the skillet and stir as you work.

3. Continue to stir and cook the cabbage until it softens enough to fit in the skillet. Add the garlic and ginger and cook, stirring, until fragrant, just a minute or so. Reduce the heat to medium.

4. Stir in 3 tablespoons gochujang, 3 tablespoons soy sauce, 2 tablespoons rice vinegar, and 1 tablespoon sugar. Cook, stirring occasionally, until the cabbage is softened and coated in the sauce, 5 to 10 minutes.

   ☐ Put the edamame in a colander and rinse under cold water.

   ☐ Trim and chop the scallions.

5. Add the edamame to the cabbage and cook, stirring a couple times, until they're warmed through, 2 to 3 minutes. Taste and adjust the seasoning. Garnish with the scallions and serve.

• recipe continues →

Variations

Edamame and Broccoli Stir-Fry with Miso. Instead of the gochujang, use white, yellow, or red miso (the darker the color, the more intense the flavor). Instead of the cabbage, use about 1 pound broccoli; after trimming, cut into florets and slice the stems into ¼-inch-thick coins. You might not need all the soy sauce, so add it 1 tablespoon at a time in Step 4 and taste as you go.

Edamame and Asparagus Stir-Fry with Miso. Follow the preceding variation, substituting asparagus for the broccoli. Trim the tough ends, and cut into 1-inch pieces.

Edamame and Pork Stir-Fry with Cabbage (or Broccoli or Asparagus). Adds some heft to the main recipe or either of the previous variations. Add 8 ounces boneless pork loin or sirloin, cut into bite-sized pieces. In Step 1, when the oil is hot but not quite smoking, add the pork and sprinkle it with salt and pepper. Cook undisturbed until the pieces release from the pan, about 1 minute. Then cook, stirring occasionally, until browned, 3 to 5 minutes, before proceeding with the recipe.

BBQ Lima Beans with Collards

Let's talk about the difference between frozen lima beans (which are green) and butter beans (which are white and usually come canned or dried). They're both limas. The green are smaller and technically immature, so they tend to be pleasantly mealy and have a hint of herbaceousness. Butter beans can be the size of your thumb and are super creamy and, well, buttery. Both take well to simmering in barbecue sauce, so feel free to substitute cooked or canned butter beans for the frozen limas in this recipe. **Serves 4**

Ingredients

2 tablespoons olive oil

4 slices bacon

1 medium onion

2 cloves garlic

1 large or 2 small bunches collard greens (1 pound)

1 cup ketchup

¼ cup cider vinegar

1 tablespoon molasses

1 tablespoon Dijon mustard

1 tablespoon Worcestershire sauce

Salt and pepper

3 cups frozen lima beans (12 ounces)

Bottled hot sauce for serving

▢ Prep · Cook

1. Put 2 tablespoons olive oil in a large pot over medium-high heat.

   ▢ Chop the bacon and add it to the pot.

2. Cook, stirring, until the bacon begins to curl and sizzle, a minute or two.

   ▢ Trim, peel, and chop the onion.

   ▢ Peel and mince 2 cloves garlic.

3. Add the onion and garlic to the bacon and cook, stirring occasionally, until the onion softens and the bacon loses its flabbiness, about 5 minutes.

   ▢ Trim the toughest stems from the collard greens; chop the collards into bite-sized pieces.

4. Add 1 cup ketchup, ¼ cup cider vinegar, 1 tablespoon molasses, 1 tablespoon Dijon mustard, and 1 tablespoon Worcestershire sauce. Sprinkle with salt and pepper, add 1 cup water, and stir to combine.

5. Add the lima beans and collards to the pot and cook, stirring occasionally, until the liquid boils. Adjust the heat to maintain a steady bubble, cover, and cook, stirring once in a while and adding water if the stew looks dry, until the beans and greens become tender, 10 to 15 minutes. Taste and adjust the seasoning. Serve with hot sauce.

White Bean and Ham Gratin

A hurry-up "cassoulet" with ham and cannellini beans instead of the duck, sausage, and traditional flageolets. The idea is to pull together a quick braise, top it with crisp bread crumbs, run it under the broiler, and serve. The variations are equally excellent in the smokiness department, though there's nothing at all traditional about them. **Serves 4**

Ingredients

¼ cup olive oil, plus more for drizzling

1 medium red onion

2 cloves garlic

8 ounces boneless ham steak or other thickly cut ham

3½ cups cooked or canned cannellini beans (two 15-ounce cans)

1 lemon

1 or 2 sprigs fresh tarragon or 2 teaspoons dried herbes de Provence

¼ cup white wine or water

Salt and pepper

½ cup bread crumbs

▫ Prep · Cook

1. Turn the broiler to high; put the rack 6 inches from the heat. Put ¼ cup olive oil in a large broiler-proof skillet over medium-high heat.

   ▫ Trim, peel, halve, and slice the onion.

   ▫ Peel and mince 2 cloves garlic.

2. Add the onion and garlic to the oil and cook, stirring occasionally, until the onion softens, 3 to 5 minutes.

   ▫ Chop the ham into bite-sized pieces.

   ▫ If you're using canned beans, rinse and drain them.

   ▫ Grate the zest from the lemon; refrigerate the fruit for another use.

   ▫ If you're using fresh tarragon, strip the leaves from 1 or 2 sprigs and chop.

3. Stir in the ham, beans, tarragon or 2 teaspoons herbes de Provence, lemon zest, ¼ cup white wine or water, and a sprinkle of salt and pepper. Cook and stir just until the liquid evaporates, about a minute.

4. Spread the mixture evenly in the skillet, scatter the bread crumbs over the top, and drizzle with a little olive oil.

5. Broil until the beans are hot and bubbling and the bread crumbs are crisp, 3 to 5 minutes. Let sit for a minute or two, then serve.

Variation

White Bean and Smoked Fish Gratin. Instead of the ham, use 8 ounces smoked salmon (first choice is the flaky hot-smoked kind, though lox is fine too) or smoked trout or whitefish. Instead of the tarragon, chop ¼ cup fresh dill.

Fast Feijoada

Feijoada (pronounced fay-JWA-da) is the national dish of Brazil, a one-pot stew of beans and cured meats that inspires rhapsodies, arguments, memories, and other passions. This totally inauthentic version employs canned black beans—or your own home-cooked beans—and a little smoked sausage to cut way back on the cooking time yet still hit the high notes. Ditto with the fast spins on other iconic international bean dishes that follow. All go well with simply cooked rice (page 496) or buttery toasted bread. **Serves 4**

Ingredients

2 tablespoons good-quality vegetable oil

1 large onion

3 cloves garlic

8 ounces linguiça or kielbasa sausage

3½ cups cooked or canned black beans (two 15-ounce cans)

2 dried hot red chiles (like chile de árbol), or more to taste

1 cup chicken stock, vegetable stock, or water

Salt and pepper

☐ Prep · Cook

1. Put 2 tablespoons vegetable oil in a large pot over medium-high heat.

   ☐ Trim, peel, and chop the onion.

   ☐ Peel and chop 3 cloves garlic.

2. Add the onion and garlic to the oil and cook, stirring occasionally, until the onion softens, 3 to 5 minutes.

   ☐ Cut the sausage into bite-sized chunks.

3. Add the sausage to the pot and cook, stirring occasionally, until it browns and crisps in places, about 10 minutes.

   ☐ If you're using canned beans, rinse and drain them.

   ☐ Trim the dried chiles; seed them if you like and chop.

4. Stir in the beans, chiles, and 1 cup stock or water. Bring to a boil, then adjust the heat so the mixture bubbles steadily but not vigorously.

5. Cook, stirring occasionally, until the liquid mostly disappears, 5 to 10 minutes. Taste and add some salt and pepper, stir again, and serve.

Variations

Fast New Orleans–Style Red Beans. Use andouille sausage instead of the linguiça and red kidney beans instead of black beans. Substitute 1 green bell pepper and a pinch of cayenne for the dried chiles. Core, seed, and chop the bell pepper while the onions and garlic are cooking in Step 2; add it with the sausage in Step 3.

Fast Tuscan-Style White Beans with Rosemary. Omit the sausage, or use sweet Italian sausage if you like. After chopping, cook the sausage until no longer pink in Step 3. Instead of the chiles, strip the leaves from 2 sprigs fresh rosemary and chop; add the rosemary in Step 4 just before the beans and stir until fragrant. Pass grated Parmesan cheese at the table.

Fast Refried Beans. Meatless unless you choose to use lard instead of the vegetable oil. Either way, increase the quantity of fat to ¼ cup. Omit the sausage. Substitute pinto beans for the black beans. Cook in a large skillet, adding the beans as soon as the onions soften in Step 2. As the beans heat, stir constantly, gradually adding 1 cup water and mashing them with a potato masher until the texture is as lumpy or smooth as you like.

THICKNESS, QUICKLY

To make any bean stew thicker, hold back up to 1 cup of the beans, put them on a plate, and break them apart with a fork or a potato masher. Then add them to the beans in the pot. The starches released by the broken beans will add body to the liquid so you don't have to spend time boiling it off or waiting for the bean skins to break on their own.

Toasted Shell Beans with Cherry Tomatoes

First choice here in the frozen shell bean department are green favas, which are sort of bumpy and hooked into a pronounced kidney shape. They split lengthwise easily, and their interiors veer toward a pleasant grittiness. They're perfect lightly browned this way—almost like nuts. Finding them, however, can be a fickle endeavor. Lima beans, edamame, and even black-eyed peas are good substitutes. Serve this over rice (page 496) or thick slices of bread, or toss with pasta (page 493) or torn salad greens. **Serves 4**

Ingredients

3 cups frozen green fava or other shell beans (12 ounces)

4 tablespoons olive oil, plus more for drizzling

2 large shallots

2 pints ripe cherry or grape tomatoes

Salt

1 bunch fresh parsley

½ cup white wine or water

Pepper

Prep · Cook

1. Heat the oven to 425°F. Put 3 cups frozen fava beans on a rimmed baking sheet and drizzle with 2 tablespoons olive oil. Toss to coat, then spread them into a single layer. Don't wait for the oven to reach 425°F; just put the pan in. Roast the favas, turning them with a spatula once or twice, until they're browned and crunchy in places, 15 to 20 minutes.

   - Peel the shallots and slice thinly crosswise; separate the rings as best you can. (It's fine if they're not perfect.)
   - Trim any tough stem ends from the tomatoes.

2. Put 2 tablespoons olive oil in a large skillet over medium heat. When it's hot, add the shallots and sprinkle with salt. Cook, stirring frequently, until they soften and turn golden, about 10 minutes. Transfer them all (every bit if you can) to a small plate with a slotted spoon; turn the heat to high.

   - Chop ½ cup parsley.

3. When the oil is smoking hot, add the tomatoes and sprinkle with salt. As the tomatoes sputter and start to darken in spots, adjust the heat to medium; shake the pan occasionally for even browning until they split and release some juice, about 5 minutes. Add the wine and stir to scrape up any browned bits from the bottom of the skillet. Keep cooking and stirring until the tomatoes soften and the liquid thickens, another minute or two.

4. As soon as the fava beans are ready, remove them from the oven and sprinkle with just a little salt and pepper. Stir the tomatoes into the favas along with the shallots and parsley. Taste and adjust the seasoning. Serve hot or at room temperature, drizzled with more olive oil.

recipe continues →

Variations

Blistered Whole Fava Beans and Cherry Tomatoes. It's a kitchen miracle when you discover that the whole fava bean—yes, the gnarly pods full of skin-on beans that hit stores and markets in spring and early summer—is edible. Better than that, it's delicious. Figure about 2 pounds whole fava beans serves 4. Turn the oven on, then trim the beans by cutting almost through the toughest end and pulling the string down the length of the bean (similar to stringing sugar snap or snow peas). Cut off any black bits and scrub well. Toss the pods with the oil and roast as described in Step 1; they'll take about the same amount of time. Continue with the recipe. When the beans are fork-tender and golden in places, chop them crosswise into bite-sized pieces and stir them into the skillet with the tomatoes. Substitute fresh mint for the parsley if you like.

Roasted Mature Fava Beans with Cherry Tomatoes. These are the large brown fava beans common to all parts of the Mediterranean and Middle East. You rarely see either the canned or dried kind in supermarkets, so when you see 'em—sometimes labeled "foul" or "ful"—grab some. (Or try a Mediterranean grocery.) Follow the main recipe, substituting 3½ cups cooked or rinsed and drained canned beans for the green favas. They won't get crunchy but will develop a golden crust. Use fresh dill or parsley to finish—your choice, as is a dollop of yogurt.

Roasted Cannellini with Cherry Tomatoes. Follow the main recipe. Substitute 1 cup (at least) whole fresh basil leaves for the parsley. Substitute 3½ cups cooked or canned cannellini beans for the favas. They won't get crunchy but will develop a golden crust. Either drizzle with more olive oil or shave some Grana Padano or pecorino Romano cheese on top before serving.

Chickpea Hash with Tahini Sauce

Imagine breaking fried falafel into bits, then crisping it another time for good measure—only with this method there's no bubbling oil, just a hot oven, a skillet, and some olive oil. Whether you make the main recipe or one of the variations, the serving suggestions remain the same: Scatter across torn greens, stuff into a flatbread sandwich, or feature in a rice or couscous bowl. **Serves 4**

Ingredients

¼ cup olive oil

1 onion

Salt and pepper

3 cloves garlic

1 lemon

½ cup tahini

½ cup boiling water

3½ cups cooked or canned chickpeas (two 15-ounce cans)

1 teaspoon baking soda

1 bunch fresh parsley

1 tablespoon ground cumin

1 teaspoon ground coriander

Aleppo pepper or cayenne, to taste

Prep · Cook

1. Put ¼ cup olive oil in a large skillet over medium heat.

   ☐ Trim, peel, and chop the onion.

2. Add the onion to the oil, sprinkle with salt and pepper, and cook, stirring occasionally, until it's soft and turning golden, 5 to 10 minutes.

3. Bring ½ cup water to a boil in a small saucepan.

   ☐ Peel and chop 3 cloves garlic. Put 1 teaspoon of the chopped garlic in a small bowl; add what remains to the onion and stir.

   ☐ Halve the lemon.

4. While the aromatics cook, make the sauce: Add ½ cup tahini to the garlic in the bowl along with ½ cup boiling water; squeeze in the juice from both lemon halves through a strainer or your fingers to catch the seeds. Sprinkle with salt and whisk until smooth. Taste and adjust the seasoning. The mixture will thicken a little as it cools.

   ☐ If you're using canned chickpeas, rinse and drain them.

5. Transfer the aromatics to a small bowl with a slotted spoon, leaving behind as much oil as possible. Return the skillet to medium-high heat and add the chickpeas and 1 teaspoon baking soda. Stir, then crush about half the chickpeas with a fork or potato masher. Cook, stirring occasionally and scraping up any browned bits, until the chickpeas are crisp, 5 to 10 minutes.

   ☐ Chop 1 cup parsley leaves.

● recipe continues →

6. Return the onion mixture to the skillet. Add 1 tablespoon ground cumin, 1 teaspoon ground coriander, and Aleppo or cayenne pepper to taste, and stir until fragrant, less than a minute. Remove from the heat, add the parsley, and toss to combine. Taste and adjust the seasoning. Serve hot or at room temperature with the tahini sauce.

Variations

Chickpea Hash with Chile-Almond Sauce. Omit the Aleppo pepper or cayenne. Substitute almond butter for the tahini. Chop 1 small hot red chile, or more to taste, and add it to the sauce in Step 4. Everything else stays the same.

Chickpea Hash with Sumac Tomatoes. Perfect for peak summer. Sumac is the ground berry of a shrub grown throughout the world. If you have sumac—which has an underlying tartness—omit the lemon altogether. If you can't find it, use the zest of the lemon that you juice. Omit the tahini and boiling water. To make the sauce in Step 4, core and chop 2 or 3 large ripe tomatoes and add them to the garlic. Sprinkle the tomatoes with some salt and pepper and 1 to 2 teaspoons sumac (to taste) or the lemon zest and toss to combine. For the herbs, use any combination of fresh dill, cilantro, parsley, and/or mint and stir them into the tomatoes instead of the hash in Step 6.

Black-Eyed Pea Hash with Cucumber Yogurt. Omit the tahini and boiling water. Substitute good-quality vegetable oil for the olive oil, black-eyed peas for the chickpeas, and fresh cilantro for the parsley. To season the hash, use 1 tablespoon curry powder and 1 teaspoon garam masala instead of the ground cumin and coriander. To make the sauce in Step 4, peel, seed, and chop 1 large cucumber and combine it with 1 cup Greek or other thick yogurt (preferably full-fat). Add the lemon juice and garlic, sprinkle with a little salt, and stir until combined.

Red Lentils and Fennel over Toasted Flatbread Triangles

I'm hesitant to call this a dal. Though the slightly soupy consistency is similar to some of the traditional Indian legume dishes, the spins are decidedly improvisations. The cold butter helps make the lentils creamy; for a vegan version, go for the oil option. Plain rice is a common accompaniment to dals; here I suggest toasted flatbread triangles for a crunchy base that softens as you eat. You have lots of options: pita, lavash, naan, chapati, even flour tortillas. Whole grain bread is encouraged, as is a salad or simply cooked vegetable alongside. **Serves 4**

Ingredients

1½ cups dried red lentils

2 inches fresh ginger

3 or 4 cloves garlic

1 or 2 large fennel bulbs (about 1 pound)

1 tablespoon yellow or brown mustard seeds (or 1 tablespoon whole grain mustard)

½ teaspoon ground cardamom

¼ teaspoon ground cloves

1 ancho or other mild dried chile, or red chile flakes to taste

4 to 8 flatbreads (See the headnote for kinds; the number depends on their size)

2 tablespoons cold butter or good-quality vegetable oil, plus more for brushing (optional)

Salt and pepper

□ Prep · Cook

□ Rinse 1½ cups red lentils in a colander under cold water, picking through for anything that looks odd.

1. Heat the oven to 425°F.

2. Put the lentils in a large pot and add water to cover by about an inch. Bring to a boil, then adjust the heat so it bubbles steadily. You're going to be adding seasonings to the pot as you prepare them.

   □ Peel 2 inches ginger and 3 or 4 cloves garlic, and chop them together; add to the pot.

   □ Trim and halve the fennel, reserving some of the fronds for garnish. Chop the bulb and tender stalks into bite-sized pieces and add them to the pot.

3. Add 1 tablespoon mustard seeds or mustard, ½ teaspoon ground cardamom, ¼ teaspoon ground cloves, and 1 chile to the pot. Cover and cook, stirring occasionally and adding just enough water to keep the lentils from sticking, until they soften and fall apart, about 20 minutes.

   □ Cut the flatbreads into triangles of any size and spread them out on a rimmed baking sheet. Brush them with a little vegetable oil if you like, but it's not necessary.

   □ Chop or tear the reserved fennel fronds.

• recipe continues →

4. Put the baking sheet in the oven and toast the flatbread, turning once if the bread is thick, until crisp, 5 to 10 minutes depending on the type. Spread them out on a serving platter or put in individual shallow bowls.

5. When the lentils have broken down and thickened the liquid, add some salt and pepper and stir in 2 tablespoons butter or vegetable oil. Remove the chile; if you'd like, break the flesh and seeds apart and stir them back into the pot. (Or just leave the chile out.) Taste and adjust the seasoning. Garnish with the fennel fronds and serve over the flatbread.

Variations

Red Lentils and Celery over Toasted Flatbread Triangles. A hint of crispness, just enough to be interesting. Instead of the fennel, use 3 or 4 celery stalks from the heart (with leaves reserved for garnish if possible). When you're doing the chop-and-drop prep in Step 2, slice the celery and add it to the pot with the lentils. Everything else stays the same.

Red Lentils with Zucchini over Toasted Flatbread Triangles. Instead of the fennel, use about 1 pound zucchini. When you're doing the chop-and-drop prep in Step 2, trim the zucchini, cut into bite-sized pieces, and add to the pot with the lentils.

Split Peas with Green Beans over Toasted Flatbread Triangles. Substitute green or yellow split peas for the red lentils and 1 pound green or yellow wax beans for the fennel. When you're doing the chop-and-drop prep in Step 2, trim the beans, cut them into 1- to 2-inch pieces, and add to the pot.

Stir-Fried Tofu and Carrots

A stir-fry in two parts: Get the tofu started right away, then turn your attention to prepping and sauce. (Or you can use any grated root vegetables or chopped green beans or sugar snap peas.) Staying busy will prevent you from messing with the tofu and causing it to stick and crumble. Rice vermicelli, Chinese egg noodles, bean threads, japchae (sweet potato starch) noodles, or glass (mung bean) noodles are all good ways to round out the meal, as is good old rice. **Serves 4**

Ingredients

3 tablespoons good-quality vegetable oil, plus more as needed

2 bricks firm tofu (14 to 16 ounces each)

Salt and pepper

1 pound carrots (4 or 5 medium)

2 cloves garlic

1 fresh hot green chile (like serrano)

3 tablespoons soy sauce

2 teaspoons sugar

2 teaspoons sesame oil

Sesame seeds for garnish

▫ Prep · **Cook**

1. Put 3 tablespoons vegetable oil in a large skillet over medium heat.

   ▫ Cut the tofu into 1-inch cubes.

2. Add the tofu to the skillet (it's okay if the pieces are crowded), sprinkle with salt and pepper, and cook until the bottoms are golden and crisp and release from the pan, about 5 minutes. Use a spatula to stir once they release. Cook, stirring once in a while, to crisp and brown as many sides as possible, another 5 minutes or so.

   ▫ Trim the carrots and grate them with the biggest holes of a box grater.

   ▫ Peel 2 cloves garlic; trim the chile. Chop them together and put them in a small bowl.

3. When the tofu is as crisp as you want, remove it from the pan and increase the heat to medium-high. Add a little more vegetable oil to thinly film the bottom of the pan. Add the carrots, sprinkle with salt and pepper, and cook, stirring occasionally, until they brown in places, about 3 minutes.

   ▫ Add ½ cup water, 3 tablespoons soy sauce, 2 teaspoons sugar, and 2 teaspoons sesame oil to the bowl with the garlic and chile. Whisk to combine.

4. When the carrots are lightly browned, return the tofu to the skillet and pour over the sauce. Stir gently with a spatula, tossing until the sauce thickens a bit to coat everything, and heat. Taste and adjust the seasoning. Serve sprinkled with sesame seeds.

Pan-Fried Tofu with Peanut Sauce and Scallions

If you think you don't like tofu, try letting it sizzle in hot oil until golden and then serving it with a savory dipping sauce—then we'll talk. Serve this over cooked rice or noodles, on a bed of steamed vegetables or salad greens, or simply with sliced cucumbers, tomatoes, or radishes. **Serves 4**

Ingredients

Good-quality vegetable oil for frying

2 bricks firm tofu (14 to 16 ounces each)

1 clove garlic

½ inch fresh ginger

Salt

½ cup peanut butter

1 tablespoon soy sauce

1 tablespoon rice vinegar

2 teaspoons sesame oil

3 scallions

□ Prep · Cook

1. Put about an inch of vegetable oil in a large skillet over medium heat until just shimmering. Keep an eye on it; at the first sign of smoke, carefully remove the pan from the heat until you're ready to proceed.

   □ Cut each brick of tofu in half along its equator, then cut each of those halves into 2 triangles; pat them dry with a paper towel. You'll end up with 4 pieces for each brick.

   □ Peel 1 clove garlic and ½ inch ginger; chop them together and put them in a small bowl.

   □ Line a plate with towels.

2. When the vegetable oil is ready, test a piece of tofu; if it sizzles without immediately darkening, the temperature is right (adjust the heat accordingly). Fry the tofu triangles in batches, turning for the first time when they release, after about 3 minutes. Continue cooking and turning until the pieces are golden brown and puffed, about 3 minutes more. As each batch is finished, remove the pieces with a slotted spoon to drain on the prepared plate; sprinkle with salt.

3. While you're cooking the tofu, add ½ cup peanut butter, 1 tablespoon soy sauce, 1 tablespoon rice vinegar, and 2 teaspoons sesame oil to the bowl. Whisk to combine, adding enough hot water to turn it into a pourable sauce. Taste and add salt if you like.

   □ Trim and chop the scallions.

4. When all the tofu is fried, pile it on a platter, scatter the scallions over the top, and serve the peanut sauce on the side for dipping.

Variations

Pan-Fried Tofu with Orange Sauce. This sauce is more like a dipping or marinating sauce. Instead of the peanut butter, use the juice of 3 oranges (about 1 cup). Everything else stays the same.

Pan-Fried Tofu with Pistachio-Coconut Sauce. Substitute 1 cup pistachios for the peanut butter, the juice of 1 lime (about 2 tablespoons) for the soy sauce and rice vinegar, and ¼ cup coconut milk for the sesame oil. While the vegetable oil is heating, put the sauce ingredients in a blender and purée, adding more coconut milk as needed to reach the consistency you like. Garnish with chopped fresh cilantro instead of the scallions.

Pan-Fried Tofu with Spaghetti and Tomato Sauce. Putting tofu to the versatility test. This takes a little longer but is totally worth the wait. Omit the garlic, ginger, peanut butter, soy sauce, rice vinegar, sesame oil, and scallions. Use olive oil for frying. Bring a large pot of salted water to a boil. Start by making one of the tomato sauces on page 492. Cut the tofu into 1-inch cubes instead of triangles and pan-fry as directed. Transfer the fried tofu cubes to the sauce as they finish cooking. Cook 1 pound spaghetti as described on page 493. Drain the spaghetti when it is ready, reserving 1 cup cooking liquid in case you want to thin the sauce; then toss everything together, taste and adjust the seasoning, and serve.

PRESSING TOFU

Just as packaged pressed tofu has much of the water squeezed out to give it a firmer texture, regular tofu can be subjected to the same process to make it drier and firmer. This takes a little extra time, of course, and you won't achieve nearly the same consistency as commercial pressed tofu, but it does make a difference. Cut the brick of tofu (firm and extra-firm are sturdiest) in half through its equator. Put the halves on a clean kitchen towel and cover them with another towel, or use several layers of towels above and below. Put something moderately heavy on top so the tofu bulges at the sides slightly but doesn't get crushed or cracked. Wait for 20 to 30 minutes, or longer if you have time, changing the towels if they become saturated. The longer you press it, the more liquid it will release and the drier and easier to handle the tofu will be, but even the few minutes that it takes to get your other ingredients ready will make a difference.

Tofu and Cauliflower à la Suvir

A quick braise based on a Chinese-Indian dish known as "Manchurian cauliflower" made famous by my friend (and phenomenal chef) Suvir Saran. I've been doing different interpretations for years, since the ketchup-based sauce is amazing with virtually everything. Serve in a rice or grain bowl or stuffed into sub rolls. **Serves 4**

Ingredients

5 tablespoons good-quality vegetable oil

1 brick firm tofu (14 to 16 ounces)

Salt and pepper

1 small head cauliflower (about 1 pound)

2 cloves garlic

1 cup ketchup

½ teaspoon cayenne

Prep · Cook

1. Put 3 tablespoons vegetable oil in a large skillet over medium-high heat.

   ☐ Cut the tofu into 1-inch cubes.

2. Add the tofu to the skillet (it's okay if the pieces are crowded), sprinkle with salt and pepper, and cook until the bottoms are golden and crisp and release from the pan, about 5 minutes. Use a spatula to stir once they release. Cook, stirring once in a while, to crisp and brown as many sides as possible, another 5 minutes or so.

   ☐ Trim and halve the cauliflower and cut out the toughest part of the stalk. Break or chop the rest into bite-sized pieces.

   ☐ Line a plate with towels.

3. When the tofu is ready, transfer it to the towels with a slotted spoon. Add 2 tablespoons oil and the cauliflower to the skillet, sprinkle with salt and pepper, and raise the heat to high. Cook undisturbed until the florets sizzle, about 3 minutes.

   ☐ Peel and mince 2 cloves garlic.

4. Stir the cauliflower; let cook undisturbed until lightly browned in places, another 2 to 3 minutes.

5. Add the garlic to the skillet along with 1 cup ketchup and ½ teaspoon cayenne. Cook, stirring, until the ketchup starts to bubble and caramelize around the edges of the skillet.

6. Return the tofu to the skillet and toss to coat with the sauce; add a splash of water if the mixture needs to be thinner for better coverage.

7. Turn the heat to medium, cover, and cook until the tofu is warmed through and the cauliflower is tender, 2 to 3 minutes. Taste and adjust the seasoning and serve.

Microwave-Steamed Tofu with Baby Bok Choy and Miso Drizzle

Call the microwave into action for this simple dish where you stir-fry greens, make a quick sauce, and then steam the tofu to serve with everything else on top, sort of like a savory sundae. As for the tofu—I'm leaving the texture up to you. All varieties of silken and "regular" tofu work here the same way. The softer kind you eat with a spoon; firm tofus, with a fork. **Serves 4**

Ingredients

2 tablespoons good-quality vegetable oil

3 or 4 scallions

2 inches fresh ginger

3 or 4 cloves garlic

Salt

Several individual baby bok choy (about 1½ pounds)

¼ cup red or brown miso

2 teaspoons sesame oil

Pepper

24 to 32 ounces soft silken or soft "regular" tofu (two 12-, 14-, or 16-ounce packages)

☐ Prep · Cook

1. Put 2 tablespoons vegetable oil in a large skillet over medium-low heat.

   ☐ Trim and slice the scallions, keeping the white and green parts separate; add the white parts to the skillet and reserve the green parts for garnish.

   ☐ Peel 2 inches ginger and 3 or 4 cloves garlic; chop them together. Add them to the skillet and stir.

2. Raise the heat under the skillet to medium-high and sprinkle in some salt. Cook, stirring occasionally, until the aromatics sizzle and are soft and browned in places, 3 to 5 minutes.

   ☐ Trim the bok choy and cut it into wedges.

3. Combine ¼ cup miso and 2 teaspoons sesame oil in a small bowl with ½ cup hot tap water; whisk until smooth. Taste and add a little salt and pepper if you like.

   ☐ If you're using firm tofu, cut it into 4 portions.

4. Add the bok choy to the skillet with ¼ cup water and cook, stirring occasionally, until the leaves soften, 3 to 5 minutes.

5. Put the tofu in a microwave-safe bowl, cover, and cook on high until steaming hot, about 3 minutes depending on your machine.

6. Add another ¼ cup water if the pan looks dry, and cook, stirring almost constantly, until the stems become tender, just a minute or two. Transfer the tofu and bok choy to plates or a platter, drizzle with the miso sauce, and garnish with the scallion greens.

● recipe continues →

Variations

Steamed Tofu and Mustard Greens with Miso Drizzle. Instead of the bok choy, use red or green mustard greens— or turnip greens, beet greens, or kale, for that matter.
You only need to separate the stems from the leaves if they're a lot firmer; otherwise just add everything to the skillet in Step 4 and turn off the heat when they're tender. White or yellow miso is nice here since the mustard greens are more intensely flavored than bok choy.

Steamed Tofu and Cabbage with Chile Drizzle. Substitute napa cabbage for the bok choy. Instead of the miso sauce, put 2 tablespoons good-quality vegetable oil and the 2 teaspoons sesame oil in a small saucepan over medium heat. When it shimmers, remove from the burner and add a pinch of red chile flakes. To make it a little hot and sour, carefully stir in 1 tablespoon rice vinegar before proceeding.

Steamed Tofu and Watercress with Lemon Drizzle. Substitute watercress for the bok choy. For the sauce, start by following the chile variation, only instead of adding the chile flakes, add the zest and juice of 1 lemon.

TOFU AND STICKING

Patience is required to keep tofu from sticking to your cookware unless you have nonstick skillets and baking sheets. And even then you want to wait for the pieces to cook evenly over medium or medium-high heat and form a crisp crust so they will release easily. Having a thin film of fat in the pan helps. When baking tofu, lining the baking sheet with parchment paper assures success.

Tofu Scramble with Tomatoes and Basil

The thing about scrambling tofu with vegetables—just as you'd do with eggs (see page 483)—is that it seems less like breakfast, more like a stir-fry. Toss this with pasta or noodles, spoon over rice or other grains, stuff into burritos or tacos, or fold into pitas. Or yeah, serve it with a side of hash browns. It's that kind of meal. Some ingredient notes: The turmeric helps make the tofu look more like eggs and adds a teeny bit of flavor, but you can skip it. As you'll see once you try this technique a couple times, you can swap in all sorts of seasonal vegetables. And for a smoother texture, see the last variation. **Serves 4**

Ingredients

3 tablespoons olive oil

2 or 3 large ripe tomatoes (about 1 pound)

Salt and pepper

1 bunch fresh basil

1½ pounds firm tofu (from two 14- or 16-ounce packages)

½ teaspoon ground turmeric (optional)

1 lemon

□ Prep · **Cook**

1. Put 2 tablespoons olive oil in a large skillet over medium-high heat.

   □ Core and chop the tomatoes, adding them to the skillet as you go.

2. Once all the tomatoes are in the pan, sprinkle with salt and pepper. Cook, adjusting the heat so they sizzle and stirring once in a while, until they release their water and start to stick to the skillet, 5 to 10 minutes.

   □ Strip 1 cup leaves from the basil sprigs; tear them a little if you like or leave them whole.

   □ Drain the tofu and pat it dry. (Refrigerate any extra tofu for another use.)

3. When the tomatoes are fairly dry, add 1 tablespoon olive oil to the skillet. When it's hot, crumble in the tofu and sprinkle with ½ teaspoon ground turmeric if you're using it and more salt. Cook, stirring occasionally, until the tofu is steaming, 3 to 5 minutes.

   □ Cut the lemon into wedges.

4. Turn off the heat and fold in the basil. Taste and adjust the seasoning. Serve hot or at room temperature, with the lemon wedges.

● recipe continues →

Variations

Tofu Scramble with Bell Peppers and Chiles. Instead of the tomatoes, core, seed, and chop 2 bell peppers (any color) and 1 poblano or other, hotter, chile. They will take a bit less time than the tomatoes to become tender and won't release much water, so be prepared to add the tofu a little sooner. Substitute fresh cilantro for the basil (use a mixture of leaves and tender stems, packed tight in the measuring cup) and 2 limes for the lemon.

Tofu Scramble with Eggplant. Use fresh dill or basil here—your choice. Instead of the tomatoes, use 1 pound eggplant; peel it if you like and cut it into bite-sized chunks. Increase the olive oil to ¼ cup and add it all in Step 1. The eggplant will take about the same time as the tomatoes to become tender but won't release any water, so keep an eye on it to avoid burning.

Creamy Tofu Scramble with Tomatoes and Basil, Bell Peppers and Chiles, or Eggplant. Amazing custardy, egglike texture if you take a little extra time to purée the tofu before starting. (Simply using silken tofu won't work as well.) Follow the main recipe or the previous two variations. Before beginning, crumble the tofu into a food processor. Add a sprinkle of salt and the ground turmeric if you're using it, and let the machine run for a minute or so. Stop to scrape down the sides of the work bowl with a rubber spatula and repeat until the tofu is smooth. When the vegetables are ready in Step 3, stir in the tofu and reduce the heat to medium-low. Stir a couple times, scraping the bottom of the pan, until the tofu is steaming, then turn off the heat and fold in the herbs.

Wispy, Crispy Tofu and Sugar Snap Peas with Quick-Pickled Cucumbers

Be prepared for some crunch coming at you—from all angles. Something happens to crumbled tofu when you coat it in hot oil on the stove, then transfer the pan to the oven and stir once or twice. Stray bits flatten and get crunchy—yes, wispy—in a way that not even deep-frying can achieve. Once you make tofu like this, you'll find all sorts of ways to eat it. The brined and dilled cucumbers add even more crunch. **Serves 4**

Ingredients

¼ cup good-quality vegetable oil

1½ pounds firm tofu (from two 14- or 16-ounce packages)

½ cup rice vinegar

Salt

1 or 2 cucumbers (about 1 pound)

1 pound sugar snap peas

Several sprigs fresh dill

Pepper

▢ Prep · **Cook**

1. Heat the oven to 450°F. Put ¼ cup vegetable oil in a large ovenproof skillet over medium-high heat.

2. When the oil is hot, crumble in the tofu and let it sizzle for about a minute. Stir with a spatula a couple times to coat in the oil (it's okay if it sticks a little), then transfer the skillet to the oven. Cook undisturbed while you prepare the sugar snap peas and pickle; figure you'll check in about 20 minutes.

3. Put ½ cup rice vinegar in a small saucepan with ½ cup water and a pinch of salt. Bring the brine to a boil, then turn off the heat.

   ▢ Trim and peel the cucumber, split it lengthwise, and scoop out the seeds. Chop the cucumber as finely as you can manage and put it in a medium bowl.

4. Pour the brine over the cucumber, stir, and transfer to the freezer to quick-chill.

   ▢ Trim the stem end from the sugar snap peas, pulling down the flat side to remove the thick string.

   ▢ Chop several dill sprigs; you'll need 2 to 3 tablespoons.

5. Check the tofu. It should be turning golden and crisp and starting to look wispy. Use a spatula to toss the pieces in the hot oil, breaking them up and scraping the bottom. Return the tofu to the oven to finish crisping, another 3 to 5 minutes.

● recipe continues →

6. Remove the cucumbers from the freezer and stir in the dill. Taste and add more salt and some pepper if you like.

7. When the tofu is ready, carefully remove the skillet from the oven. Add the sugar snap peas and sprinkle lightly with salt. Stir to combine with the tofu and coat in oil as they sizzle. (The idea is to barely cook them.) Taste and adjust the seasoning. Serve hot or at room temperature with the pickled cucumber.

Variations

Wispy, Crispy Tofu and Asparagus with Quick-Pickled Red Onions. A couple simple substitutions: Instead of the sugar snap peas, trim 1 pound asparagus; doesn't matter if it's thick or thin. Slice the spears thinly at a diagonal so that the pieces are no more than ½ inch thick, leaving the tips whole. Pickle thinly sliced red onions instead of the cucumbers. Use fresh chives instead of dill. Everything else stays the same.

Wispy, Crispy Tofu and Carrots with Quick-Pickled Scallions. Substitute 1 pound carrots for the sugar snap peas. After trimming and peeling, slice them at a diagonal into thin coins. Use 1 bunch scallions (the larger the better) instead of the cucumber; trim the ends and slice them thinly. You won't need the dill.

Wispy, Crispy Tofu and Chard with Quick-Pickled Shallots. Instead of the sugar snap peas, trim and chop 1 bunch chard (any color). Pickle a few large shallots instead of the cucumber; trim and peel them, then slice crosswise and separate the rings. Dill is good here, but you don't need it.

Seafood

Fish and shellfish are the fastest-cooking animal proteins. Seafood comes in such a wide variety of flavors and textures that you could cook it every day without getting bored.

Don't let the complexities of buying fish be a deterrent. Yes, the global market is complicated, and making sustainable choices is more important than ever for the future of seafood. But you have three things going in your favor: Supermarkets and other fish retailers are more attuned to these issues and can be of some help; I provide guidance and a resource for more information on page 340; and the recipes and variations in this chapter are written in a general way so that you can use virtually any species. Ordering fish online is also an option.

Given that seafood is much more expensive than it was thirty years ago when I started writing about it, the quantities in the following recipes are adjusted for realistic portions, and there are almost always vegetables or other components included. The result is all-inclusive dishes that only need some noodles, rice, whole grain bread, or greens to round them out into a meal.

Salmon and Asparagus with Buttery Bread Crumbs

Since wild salmon fillets and medium or thin asparagus spears take the same time to broil, they're a natural sheet-pan dinner. Another thing they have in common? They're even better with butter and crunchy bread crumbs. A simple salad is all you need on the side or maybe nothing at all. **Serves 4**

Ingredients

6 tablespoons butter

1 large bunch thin asparagus (1 pound)

1 pound salmon fillets, preferably wild caught

Salt and pepper

1 cup bread crumbs

1 lemon

□ Prep · Cook

1. Turn the broiler to high; put the rack 4 inches from the heat.

   □ Cut 4 tablespoons of the butter into bits. Or if it's softened, just unwrap for dabbing.

   □ Trim the tough bottoms from the asparagus.

   □ Cut the salmon into 4 portions.

2. Put the salmon and asparagus on a rimmed baking sheet, skin side up, dab with bits of butter, and sprinkle with salt and pepper.

3. Broil undisturbed for 5 minutes. Carefully turn the salmon and shake the pan to roll the asparagus. Return the baking sheet to the broiler and cook until the salmon is cooked as you like and the asparagus is tender and browned in places. (No more than 5 additional minutes for medium to medium-well salmon, and less if you like your salmon closer to medium-rare.)

4. While the salmon and asparagus cook, put the remaining 2 tablespoons butter in a medium skillet over medium-high heat. When it's hot, add the bread crumbs, sprinkle with salt and pepper, and stir gently to coat the crumbs with the butter. Cook, stirring frequently and adjusting the heat to avoid burning, until the crumbs are golden and crisp, 3 to 5 minutes.

   □ Cut the lemon into wedges.

5. When the salmon and asparagus are done, sprinkle the bread crumbs over the top. Serve with the lemon wedges.

Broiled Fish with Fresh Salsa

This recipe is a template for one of my favorite ways to eat all kinds of fish and shellfish: paired with salsa based on fresh seasonal produce. The list of possibilities is long: cod, rockfish, catfish, bass, or halibut, for starters. Thin fish fillets, scallops, peeled shrimp, and squid rings and tentacles are other options for this technique. All will cook several minutes quicker than thick fish fillets, so check them earlier than directed in the recipe. For salsa ideas, take advantage of summer melons, berries, or peaches and other stone fruit, or go with pineapple, citrus, mango, or papaya in winter and apples or pears in the fall. **Serves 4**

Ingredients

2 or 3 large ripe tomatoes (about 1 pound)

1 small onion

1 fresh hot red or green chile (like Anaheim or jalapeño), or more to taste

1 lemon

Salt and pepper

1 pound any thick fish fillets or steaks

2 tablespoons olive oil

1 small bunch fresh basil, dill, cilantro, or chives

◻ Prep · Cook

1. Turn the broiler to high; put the rack 4 inches from the heat.

   ◻ Core and chop the tomatoes; put them in a medium bowl.

   ◻ Trim, peel, and chop the onion; add it to the bowl.

   ◻ Trim and mince the chile; add it to the bowl.

   ◻ Halve the lemon; squeeze the juice through a strainer into the bowl, removing the seeds. Sprinkle with salt and pepper and stir. If you want the salsa cold, put it in the freezer while you cook the fish.

2. When the broiler is hot, cut the fish into 4 portions and put on a rimmed baking sheet. Drizzle with 2 tablespoons olive oil and sprinkle with salt and pepper.

   ◻ Chop ½ cup herb leaves.

3. Broil the fish undisturbed for 5 minutes. Carefully turn it and return the baking sheet to the broiler. Cook until the fish is just opaque at the center (nick with a small knife and peek inside to check), usually no more than 5 minutes more.

4. Add the herbs to the salsa and toss. Taste and adjust the seasoning. Serve the fish with the salsa on top, on the side, or underneath.

Pan-Seared Tuna with Ginger-Scallion Snow Peas

Tuna is pricey and can be iffy, quality- and environmentally-wise. So when you can get your hands on a sustainable variety and it's gorgeous—brightly colored, the flake tight rather than gaping, and it doesn't look slick or shiny—it's time to sear it to eat rare on a bed of gingery vegetables. If you want rice on the side, start that first. **Serves 4**

Ingredients

1 pound tuna steaks
(1 to 1½ inches thick)

3 tablespoons good-quality vegetable oil

Salt

2 inches fresh ginger

4 scallions

1 pound snow peas

3 tablespoons soy sauce, plus more to taste

Sesame seeds for garnish (optional)

▫ Prep · Cook

1. Put a large skillet over high heat.

   ▫ Put the tuna on a plate and rub it all over with 2 tablespoons vegetable oil. Sprinkle with salt.

2. When the skillet is smoking hot, add the tuna and cook, turning once, until it's browned on both sides but still quite rare in the center, 2 to 4 minutes per side, depending on the thickness. (Nick with a small knife and peek inside to check for doneness.) Transfer the tuna to a cutting board.

   ▫ Peel and chop 2 inches ginger.

   ▫ Trim 4 scallions and slice, keeping the white and green parts separate.

3. Put the skillet over medium heat. Add 1 tablespoon vegetable oil, followed by the ginger and the white parts of the scallions. Cook, stirring occasionally, until the scallions are soft, about 3 minutes.

   ▫ Trim the stem end of the snow peas, pulling on the tough string running down the flat side to remove it. Cut the snow peas in half on the diagonal.

4. Add 3 tablespoons soy sauce to the skillet along with ¼ cup water. When it starts to bubble, add the snow peas. Cook, stirring frequently, until the snow peas are tender and glossy and the liquid has mostly evaporated, 2 to 3 minutes. Remove from the heat; taste and adjust the seasoning, adding more soy sauce if desired.

   ▫ Slice the tuna thinly against the grain.

● recipe continues →

5. Serve the snow peas with the tuna slices on top. Pour the remaining pan juices into a small bowl, add more soy sauce and a little water, and stir in the sesame seeds if you're using them. Garnish with the scallion greens and serve with the sauce on the side.

Variations

Pan-Seared Tuna with Tomatoes. Omit the water. Use about 1½ pounds cored, chopped ripe tomatoes or whole ripe cherry tomatoes instead of the snow peas. In Step 4 add the tomatoes with the soy sauce, stirring frequently until they release their liquid and the sauce reduces a bit; this will take another 3 to 5 minutes. Garnish with chopped fresh Thai basil (if you have it) instead of the sesame seeds.

Pan-Seared Tuna with Spinach. Omit the water. Substitute 1 pound spinach for the snow peas. Trim off any thick stems and rinse well. Add it in batches while stirring to make room in the pan.

Pan-Seared Tuna with Watercress. Substitute 1 or 2 bunches watercress for the snow peas. Trim any tough ends; if the stems are long, chop the bunches in half. Add in Step 4 and cook as described in the main recipe.

MAKING THE SUSHI GRADE

You may have heard the phrase *sushi grade* used to describe fish that is fit to consume raw. In fact, there's no such designation. Nor is so-called fresh tuna an indication of quality, since the best has almost always been frozen. As with buying any seafood, the best option is to find a source you trust; the people working there should be able to steer you in the right direction. If not, or if you feel unsure about anything, then keep looking until you find the right place to buy fish.

Chopped Raw Tuna with Daikon and Peanuts

Seasoned raw fish—inspired by poke (pronounced poke-AY), an iconic Hawaiian dish—requires no cooking, obviously. My fast take is salty, spicy, slightly sweet, and easily adaptable to other vegetables and nuts. Be sure to get the tuna from a reliable source and check that it really does look good enough to eat. If raw fish doesn't float your boat, try the variation with poached fish, or substitute canned tuna. Though a scoop of this is more like sushi than salad, you could serve it on a bed of cooked or raw greens, plain cooked rice or grains, in a sandwich or wrap, or with chips or fried wonton skins as an appetizer. **Serves 4**

Ingredients

1 lemon

¼ cup mayonnaise

3 tablespoons soy sauce

2 teaspoons sesame oil

Sriracha or other hot sauce to taste

1 pound tuna loin or steak

½ small daikon radish or other radishes (about 8 ounces)

4 scallions

⅓ cup roasted peanuts

Salt and pepper

▢ Prep · Cook

▢ Halve the lemon and squeeze the juice into a large bowl through a strainer or your fingers to catch the seeds.

1. Add ¼ cup mayonnaise, 3 tablespoons soy sauce, and 2 teaspoons sesame oil to the bowl and stir. Stir in sriracha to taste.

   ▢ Cut the tuna into ½-inch chunks. Add to the bowl of sauce.

   ▢ Peel the daikon radish if that's what you're using. Chop the radish(es) into ½-inch bits; add to the bowl.

   ▢ Trim and chop the scallions; add them to the bowl.

   ▢ Chop ⅓ cup peanuts and add them to the bowl.

2. Toss to combine. Taste and add salt and pepper to taste. Serve right away, or chill in the freezer for a few minutes.

Variation

Chopped Poached Fish with Daikon and Peanuts. Takes a few extra minutes. Use tuna or any thick fish fillet you like. Start by putting 1 inch water in a large saucepan with a big pinch of salt and a bay leaf if you have it. Bring the water to a boil, lower in the fish, cover, and remove from the heat. Let the fish poach while you get everything else ready, about 10 minutes; check to make sure it's cooked through and return to a quick boil if necessary. Transfer the fish to a plate with a slotted spoon to drain it; break it into chunks with a fork, removing any bones and skin. Pop the plate in the freezer for a couple minutes to chill the fish a bit, then toss it with the sauce.

Smoky Shrimp Scampi

Lots of garlic and olive oil, smoked paprika, parsley, and lemon juice make the best bath a shrimp could ever ask for. Scampi is a perennial favorite that works as a main dish when tossed with rice or pasta or simply spooned over thick slices of toasted bread. Or serve hot or cold on toothpicks as an appetizer. **Serves 4**

Ingredients

⅓ cup olive oil, or more as needed

4 cloves garlic

1 bunch fresh parsley

1½ pounds peeled medium shrimp

Salt and pepper

1½ teaspoons smoked paprika

1 lemon

☐ Prep · Cook

1. Put ⅓ cup olive oil in a large skillet over low heat. There should be enough to cover the bottom of the pan; don't skimp.

   ☐ Peel and chop 4 cloves garlic.

   ☐ Chop ½ cup parsley leaves.

   ☐ If the shrimp are frozen, rinse under cold water to thaw; drain well.

2. Add the garlic, shrimp, a sprinkle of salt and pepper, and 1½ teaspoons smoked paprika to the skillet. Toss to coat and turn the heat to medium-high. Cook, gently shaking the skillet once or twice, until the shrimp turn pink on one side, about 2 minutes.

   ☐ Halve the lemon; cut one half into 4 wedges.

3. Turn the shrimp and add half of the chopped parsley. Cook, shaking the pan again until the shrimp are pink all over and just cooked through, about 2 minutes more. (It's okay to cut into one to check.)

4. Squeeze the juice from the lemon half through a strainer or your fingers into the pan and cook for another 30 seconds. Taste the sauce and adjust the seasoning. Garnish with the remaining parsley and lemon wedges and serve.

• recipe continues →

Variations

Smoky Scallop "Scampi." Use sea scallops in place of shrimp. Before Step 2, heat the oil over high heat. Wait to add the garlic, paprika, and parsley until directed here. Put the scallops in the hot oil in a single layer and cook until they are seared on the bottom and release from the pan, about 2 minutes. Turn, then sprinkle the cooked side with the paprika, add the garlic to the pan, and lower the heat to medium. Cook undisturbed until the scallops are pearly in the middle, about another 2 minutes. Proceed with Step 4, using all the parsley for garnish before serving.

Smoky Squid "Scampi." Substitute squid for the shrimp. It should be cleaned, with the bodies cut into rings and the tentacles separated. (Frozen is fine; rinse it under cold water to thaw a bit.) After adding the squid in Step 2, cook and stir until just opaque, 1 to 3 minutes, depending on whether it was still frozen. Stir in all the parsley and the lemon juice and serve right away.

Smoky Chicken "Scampi." Use 2 large boneless, skinless chicken breasts (1½ pounds) instead of the shrimp; cut them into strips or chunks about ½ inch across. Fresh oregano is a good herb here; if you go that route, you'll only need a couple tablespoons. Add it all at once in Step 3.

SUSTAINABLE SEAFOOD

Buying seafood is more complicated than cooking it. Fish comes to our supermarkets and specialty stores from all over the world. Some is wild, and some is farmed; some is abundant, and some is depleted; some is caught in ways that protect the environment, and some is caught in ways that destroy it. And the status of different species, farming methods, and wild fisheries changes all the time. Reputable retailers do their best to keep up. But when you're staring at the fish counter trying to decide what to make for dinner, you might need more help. The Monterey Bay Aquarium Seafood Watch is an invaluable resource to help you purchase fish with confidence and a clear conscience. Download the app to your phone or visit their website at seafoodwatch.org.

Stir-Fried Shrimp with Tomatoes, Eggs, and Scallions

This is shrimp embellished big time. So much so that you've got to do most of the prep before firing up the stove to keep up with the fast-paced stir-frying. If you're cooking a pot of white rice or noodles on the side—always a good idea—make that your first move. Or for a change, warm some corn or flour tortillas and pile this into tacos or burritos. **Serves 4**

Ingredients

2 eggs

Salt and pepper

1 inch fresh ginger

2 cloves garlic

4 scallions

2 or 3 ripe tomatoes

2 tablespoons good-quality vegetable oil

1 pound peeled shrimp

1 tablespoon sesame oil

Soy sauce for serving

☐ Prep · Cook

☐ Crack 2 eggs into a medium mixing bowl, sprinkle with salt and pepper, and whisk to combine.

☐ Peel 1 inch ginger and 2 cloves garlic and chop them together.

☐ Trim 4 scallions and separate the white and green parts. Cut the whites into 1-inch chunks; slice the green parts and reserve them separately.

☐ Core and chop the tomatoes.

1. Put 2 tablespoons vegetable oil in a large skillet over high heat. Add the shrimp, sprinkle with salt and pepper, and cook, stirring once or twice, until the outsides are pink and the centers are firm and opaque, 2 to 5 minutes, depending on the size and whether they were frozen. Transfer from the skillet to a plate with a slotted spoon, leaving as much oil as possible in the pan.

2. Reduce the heat under the skillet to medium-high. Add 1 tablespoon sesame oil, the ginger, garlic, and scallion whites, and stir a few times. When they start to sizzle, add the tomatoes. Cook, stirring occasionally, until they release their liquid and the pan begins to dry again, about 5 minutes.

3. Add the eggs and shrimp to the skillet and cook, stirring almost constantly, until the eggs thicken and the shrimp are warm again, about 3 minutes. Turn off the heat.

4. Add the scallion greens and stir a couple times to combine. Taste and adjust the seasoning. Serve, passing soy sauce at the table.

Buffalo Shrimp

Toss something in hot sauce and butter, serve it with something blue cheese-y—like this chunky cross between salad and sauce we'll call a relish—and it'll inevitably be pretty great. Even things that aren't chicken wings. Try this over rice, thick slices of toast, or stuffed into corn or flour tortillas, topped with a big spoonful of the celery–blue cheese relish. **Serves 4**

Ingredients

3 celery stalks

4 ounces blue cheese (1 cup crumbled)

½ cup mayonnaise

2 tablespoons cider vinegar

Salt and pepper

4 tablespoons (½ stick) butter

Hot sauce of choice to taste, plus more for serving

1 pound peeled shrimp

Prep · Cook

1. Turn the broiler to high; put the rack 4 inches from the heat.

    - Trim and chop 3 celery stalks; put them in a medium bowl. Save any leaves for garnish.

    - Crumble 1 cup blue cheese; add to the bowl.

2. To make the relish, add ½ cup mayonnaise to the bowl along with 2 tablespoons cider vinegar and a sprinkle of salt and pepper. Taste and adjust the seasoning.

3. Melt 4 tablespoons butter in a rimmed baking sheet under the broiler as it heats; watch it carefully so the butter doesn't burn.

4. Carefully remove the baking sheet from the broiler. Add up to a few shakes of hot sauce to the melted butter, depending on what kind you're using and how much you like the heat. Carefully put the shrimp on the baking sheet, sprinkle with a little salt and pepper, and toss to coat in the sauce.

5. Return the baking sheet to the broiler and cook the shrimp, shaking the pan once or twice, until they are pink, golden in places, and opaque at the center, 2 to 5 minutes, depending on their size and whether they were frozen.

6. Transfer the shrimp to a serving bowl and pour the pan juices over all. Pass the blue cheese relish and a bottle of hot sauce at the table.

recipe continues →

Variations

Buffalo Shrimp with Rémoulade. Instead of the celery, trim, peel, and grate about 8 ounces celery root (you'll want 1 cup grated). Substitute 2 tablespoons Dijon mustard for the blue cheese.

Buffalo Shrimp with Blue Cheese Slaw. Instead of the celery, trim, peel, and grate about 8 ounces green cabbage from the tenderest part of the heart (you'll want 1 cup grated). Everything else stays the same.

Buffalo Cauliflower. Works with the main recipe and both previous variations but takes a little more time. Instead of the shrimp, use 1 medium head cauliflower (about 1½ pounds). Cut the florets in large pieces from the core and stem (reserve those parts for another use if you like). Put the rack 6 inches from the heat for long-distance broiling. Coat the cauliflower in the melted butter as described in Step 3 and spread it out on the baking sheet. In Step 4, broil the cauliflower, shaking the pan once or twice, until it's crisp-tender and browned in places, about 5 minutes. Serve with the sauces as described.

Black Pepper Scallops and Broccoli

The contrast between the sweetness of scallops and the little bit of spice is alluring, especially when you treat them in this unusual way—cut into nuggets and dusted with flour and seasonings, blasted in hot oil, and tossed with crisp-tender broccoli. A bed of rice is the natural choice for serving. But for a change, consider using this to top rice noodles or egg noodles and heating some stock in a small pot to pour over everything for a super-fast soup.
Serves 4

Ingredients

¼ cup good-quality vegetable oil, plus more as needed

1 pound sea scallops

2 tablespoons flour

Salt and pepper

1 large head broccoli (1½ pounds)

1 inch fresh ginger

2 cloves garlic

½ cup chicken stock or water

2 tablespoons soy sauce

◻ Prep · Cook

1. Put ¼ cup vegetable oil in a large skillet over low heat.

   ◻ Pat the scallops dry and cut them into quarters; put them in a bowl. Add 2 tablespoons flour, a sprinkle of salt, and lots of pepper (like a teaspoon or more if you're a fan) and toss to coat.

2. Raise the heat under the skillet to high. When the oil is hot, add the scallops and cook, turning once or twice, until they are golden and crisp all over, 3 to 5 minutes. Transfer the scallops to a plate with a slotted spoon and remove the skillet from the heat.

   ◻ Trim the broccoli; break or cut off the florets and thinly slice the stems.

3. Add more oil to the skillet if it's dry and return it to high heat. Add the broccoli and sprinkle with just a little salt. Cook, stirring occasionally, until the broccoli is bright green and glossy and beginning to brown, 3 to 5 minutes.

   ◻ Peel 1 inch ginger and 2 cloves garlic; chop them both together.

4. Add the garlic and ginger to the broccoli and stir a couple times. Add ½ cup stock or water and 2 tablespoons soy sauce. Continue to cook, stirring frequently, until most of the liquid has evaporated and the broccoli is tender, another minute or two.

5. Return the scallops to the skillet and turn off the heat. Toss a couple times to coat them lightly with the sauce and heat through. Taste and adjust the seasoning, and serve.

Salmon with Gingery Greens

A pile of just-wilted greens makes a perfect bed for steaming fish, providing enough moisture to cook it through without scorching or drying out. I call for salmon here since its flavor stands up to the ginger and assertive greens. But really any thick fillet or steak is equally good—only the flavor balance shifts toward the vegetables. **Serves 4**

Ingredients

3 tablespoons butter

1 bunch kale or collard greens (1 pound)

2 inches fresh ginger

Salt and pepper

½ cup vegetable stock or water

4 thick salmon steaks or fillets (1½ pounds)

☐ Prep · Cook

1. Put 3 tablespoons butter in a large skillet over low heat.

   ☐ Trim and chop the kale or collards, separating any thick stems from the leaves and chopping everything into bite-sized pieces.

2. Raise the heat to medium-high. Add any thick stems to the skillet and cook, stirring occasionally, until they begin to soften, about 3 minutes.

   ☐ Peel and chop 2 inches ginger.

3. Add the ginger to the skillet, along with the leaves of the greens a handful at a time, stirring after each addition if necessary, until they all fit in. Sprinkle with salt and pepper. Cover and cook until the greens are just soft, 3 to 5 minutes.

4. Add ½ cup stock or water, lay the salmon on top of the greens, and sprinkle with salt and pepper.

5. Lower the heat to medium, cover, and cook for no more than 10 minutes for medium to medium-well, and less if you like your salmon closer to medium-rare. Taste and adjust the seasoning, and serve.

Variations

Salmon with Garlicky Greens. Use 4 cloves garlic instead of the ginger. Everything else stays the same.

Salmon with Gingery Creamed Corn. An unexpectedly good combination, especially when corn is in season. Substitute 4 cups fresh or frozen corn kernels for the greens. (If using fresh, you'll need to cut them from 4 to 6 ears.) Skip Step 2, but prepare the ginger as directed. In Step 3, cook the ginger and corn in the hot butter long enough for them to soften a little, just a minute or two. In Step 4, instead of the stock, use 1 cup cream.

Salmon with Gingery Creamed Peas. Follow the directions for the variation above, using fresh or frozen peas instead of the corn.

Thin (or Thick) Fish Fillets with Orange-Glazed Carrots

One skillet delivers main dish and vegetable, each taking a buttery, fruity, and pleasantly sweet turn in the pan and ending up on the same platter. It's a model for all sorts of combinations, starting with the three utterly different variations. To substitute thick fillets or steaks, cook over medium heat in Step 3 for a couple minutes longer on each side, peeking inside to assess doneness. **Serves 4**

Ingredients

6 tablespoons (¾ stick) butter

1 pound carrots

1 teaspoon sugar

2 sprigs fresh thyme

Salt and pepper

1 orange

1 pound thin fish fillets, like sole or trout

1 bunch fresh parsley

½ cup white wine or water

▢ Prep · Cook

1. Put 2 tablespoons butter in a large skillet over medium-low heat.

   ▢ Trim, peel, and slice the carrots into coins about ¼ inch thick.

2. Raise the heat to medium-high. When the butter foams, add the carrots, 1 teaspoon sugar, 2 sprigs thyme, ¼ cup water, and a sprinkle of salt and pepper. Cook, stirring occasionally, until the carrots are crisp-tender, about 5 minutes.

   ▢ Grate the zest from the orange.

   ▢ Halve the orange.

   ▢ Cut the fish into 4 portions and sprinkle with salt and pepper.

3. Leaving the thyme sprigs behind, transfer the carrots to a serving platter or plates. Add 2 tablespoons butter to the skillet. When the butter melts and the foam subsides, add the fish and sprinkle with salt and pepper. Cook until it's golden on the bottom, about 2 minutes. Turn and cook until the fish is opaque and flakes easily with a fork, just a minute or so more. Carefully put the fish on top of the carrots.

   ▢ Chop ¼ cup parsley leaves.

4. Squeeze the orange into the skillet through a strainer or your fingers to catch the seeds and add the zest. Return the skillet to high heat. Add ½ cup wine or water and a sprinkle of salt and pepper. Let the liquid reduce a bit, then remove the thyme sprigs. Whisk in 2 tablespoons butter. Pour the sauce over the fish and carrots, garnish with the parsley, and serve.

• recipe continues →

Variations

Thin (or Thick) Fish Fillets with Tomato Sauce. Instead of the carrots, use 1 pound ripe tomatoes in season, cored and chopped, or 1 large (28-ounce) can diced tomatoes and their juice. No need to add water in Step 2, but do add the sugar, as it helps balance the acidity and richness. Wipe out the pan before cooking the fish; you might need a little more butter. Instead of the parsley, garnish with ½ cup chopped fresh basil if you like.

Thin (or Thick) Fish Fillets with Dilly Potatoes. Omit the thyme. Instead of the carrots, trim 1½ pounds Yukon Gold or fingerling potatoes and chop them into ½-inch pieces. When you cook them in Step 2, add 1 cup milk along with the water, reduce the heat to medium-low, and cover in between stirs. They'll take another 5 minutes or so. When they're ready, mash them in the skillet with the back of a spoon or spatula. Wipe out the pan before cooking the fish; you might need a little more butter. Substitute fresh dill for the parsley; if you like, add it to the potatoes before transferring them to a platter or plates.

Lemony Thin (or Thick) Fish Fillets with Asparagus. Substitute 1 pound asparagus for the carrots. After trimming, slice them as thinly as you like at a diagonal. They'll cook faster than the carrots. Instead of the orange, zest ½ lemon and add the juice and zest to the sauce as described in Step 4. Garnish with chopped fresh chives instead of parsley if you like.

Fish Steaks with Salsa Verde

A piquant sauce is perfect with sturdy fish steaks. The photograph shows salmon with fresh tomatillos lightly cooked into a pretty green sauce. You could mix and match tomatoes or olives with cod, mackerel, or halibut. Tortillas—flour or corn—are the ideal companion so you can savor all the sauce. **Serves 4**

Ingredients

4 tablespoons olive oil

1 onion

1 poblano chile

1½ pounds fresh tomatillos (8 to 12, depending on their size) or 1 large (28-ounce) can tomatillos

2 cloves garlic

1 lime

Salt and pepper

2 to 4 fish steaks (depending on their size; about 1 pound)

☐ Prep · Cook

1. Turn the broiler to high; put the rack 6 inches from the heat. Put 2 tablespoons olive oil in a medium skillet over medium-high heat.

   ☐ As you prep each, add it to the skillet:

   ☐ Trim, peel, and chop the onion.

   ☐ Trim, core, seed, and chop the poblano.

   ☐ If you're using fresh tomatillos, husk, trim, and chop them. No need to chop the canned; just add them and their juice.

   ☐ Peel and chop 2 cloves garlic.

   ☐ Halve the lime; squeeze in the juice.

2. Sprinkle the sauce mixture with salt and pepper and cook, stirring occasionally, until the tomatillos break down and thicken the sauce, about 10 minutes.

3. Put the fish steaks on a rimmed baking sheet and pat them dry. Sprinkle with salt and pepper and drizzle with 2 tablespoons olive oil.

4. Broil the fish until the tops of the steaks are sizzling and opaque, 3 to 5 minutes depending on the thickness. (If you're cooking tuna steaks and you want them more rare to medium-rare, check inside for doneness now; it might be time to take them from under the broiler.) Turn and repeat on the other side. Nick with a small knife to peek inside to check doneness; everything but tuna should be juicy and just opaque at the center.

5. When the sauce has thickened, taste and adjust the seasoning. Serve the fish and salsa together, drizzled with any juices from the baking sheet.

Thick Fish Fillets and Chickpea Stew

They might not seem to go well together, but beans and fish are one of my favorite combinations. Try this hearty stew with chickpeas and spinach—or the variation that includes squid—and you'll agree. Plus everything comes together in a single skillet. Any thick white fish fillet, like cod, halibut, or rockfish, that is sturdy enough to hold its own with the flavor and texture of beans will work perfectly. A hunk of bread is really all you need on the side. **Serves 4**

Ingredients

3 tablespoons olive oil

1 onion

3 cloves garlic

1 pound spinach

1¾ cups cooked or canned chickpeas (one 15-ounce can)

2 teaspoons smoked paprika

Salt and pepper

1 cup chicken or vegetable stock or water

1 pound thick white fish fillets, like halibut or cod

Several sprigs fresh parsley

☐ Prep · Cook

1. Put 3 tablespoons olive oil in a large skillet over medium-high heat.

    ☐ Trim, peel, and chop the onion and put it in the skillet.

    ☐ Peel and chop 3 cloves garlic and add them to the skillet.

2. Cook, stirring occasionally, until the onion softens, 3 to 5 minutes.

    ☐ Trim off any thick stems from the spinach and chop the leaves.

    ☐ If you're using canned chickpeas, rinse and drain them.

3. When the onion softens, add 2 teaspoons smoked paprika and cook, stirring, until fragrant, about a minute.

4. Add the spinach, in batches if necessary to fit it all in the pan. Stir in the chickpeas and sprinkle with salt and pepper. Cook, stirring frequently, just until the spinach softens.

5. Add 1 cup stock or water. Sprinkle the fish with salt and pepper and lay it on top of the spinach and chickpeas. Adjust the heat so the mixture bubbles steadily but not vigorously.

6. Cover the skillet; cook until a thin-bladed knife inserted into the thickest part of the fish meets little resistance, 5 to 10 minutes. Or nick with a small knife and peek inside to see if it's done.

    ☐ Strip the leaves from several parsley sprigs and chop.

7. When the fish is ready, break it into big chunks with a fork. Taste the spinach and adjust the seasoning. Serve garnished with parsley.

Variations

Thick Fish Fillets and Cannellini Stew. Substitute 1 tablespoon chopped fresh rosemary for the smoked paprika, escarole for the spinach, and cannellini beans for the chickpeas.

Thick Fish Fillets and Black-Eyed Pea Stew. A great variation for catfish. Substitute 1 pound okra for the spinach; trim the ends but leave the pods whole. Instead of chickpeas, use black-eyed peas, either canned or frozen. Two cups or so chopped ripe tomatoes (or a 15-ounce can diced, and their juice) are a natural addition but not necessary. If you go that route, add them after the okra in Step 4.

Squid and Bean Stew. Use any bean plus the vegetables and seasoning from the main recipe or the previous variations. Instead of the fish, use 1½ pounds cleaned squid (cut into rings and tentacles; frozen is fine). It will cook much more quickly in Step 6; start checking after 2 minutes; frozen squid will take a minute or two longer. You're looking for it to turn white and opaque but not curl around the edges too much.

Miso-Glazed Thick Fish Fillets and Mushrooms

Fish fillets roast relatively fast, by coincidence in just the right amount of time it takes to whip up a quick sauce for a final glazing. Halibut (as shown in the photo), cod, bass, and catfish are all good choices here. And I like salmon or bluefish like this too. Serve the fillets and mushrooms over plain rice (page 496), drizzled with the reserved glaze. **Serves 4**

Ingredients

1½ pounds button or cremini mushrooms

2 tablespoons good-quality vegetable oil

Salt and pepper

½ cup miso (preferably dark)

¼ cup packed brown sugar

2 tablespoons butter

1 pound thick fish fillets

4 scallions

▢ Prep · **Cook**

1. Heat the oven to 450°F.

   ▢ Trim and quarter the mushrooms.

2. Put the mushrooms on a rimmed baking sheet, drizzle with 2 tablespoons vegetable oil, and sprinkle with salt and pepper. Roast undisturbed until the mushrooms sizzle and release some liquid, about 10 minutes.

3. While the mushrooms roast, combine ½ cup miso, ¼ cup brown sugar, 2 tablespoons butter, and ¼ cup water in a small saucepan over medium heat. Cook, stirring occasionally, until the sugar dissolves and the butter melts, about 5 minutes; turn off the heat.

   ▢ Cut the fish into 4 portions if you like.

   ▢ Trim and chop the scallions.

4. Lower the oven to 375°F. Stir the mushrooms with a spatula and make room on the baking sheet for the fish. Put the fish directly on the baking sheet; return to the oven and roast undisturbed for 10 minutes.

5. Spoon about half the miso glaze over the fish and mushrooms and cook until the fish is done and the glaze is lightly caramelized, another 3 to 5 minutes. (Peek inside with a sharp knife; it should flake a little and be opaque but still juicy.) Garnish with the scallions; serve with the remaining glaze on the side.

• recipe continues →

Variations

Miso-Glazed Fish Fillets and Parsnips. Substitute parsnips for the mushrooms. Trim and peel them, then cut them at a diagonal into ½-inch slices.

Hoisin-Glazed Fish Fillets and Shiitakes. Substitute ½ cup hoisin sauce for the miso, 2 tablespoons soy sauce for the sugar, and rice vinegar for the water. Use 12 ounces shiitake mushrooms instead of button or cremini; trim off and discard the stems and halve the caps.

Teriyaki-Glazed Fish Fillets and Sweet Potatoes. Instead of the mushrooms, peel and grate 1½ pounds sweet potatoes. Use ½ cup soy sauce instead of the miso; add 1 tablespoon each chopped fresh ginger and garlic to the glaze.

FISH ROASTS

Extra-thick fish steaks and fillets—anything around 2 inches, and especially the triangular fillets or steaks from large fish like swordfish—qualify as roasts. There are two ways to roast a big piece of fish: Either cook it in a 450°F oven from beginning to end, or sear it on one side in an ovenproof skillet to form a crust, turn, and finish it in the oven. Both are usually fast, 15 to 20 minutes. Instead of slicing them thinly against the grain like meat, cut or break them into portions.

Fish Kebabs over Minty Bulgur

A quick-cooking whole grain with Mediterranean-inspired seasoning makes a simple and satisfying bed for grilled or broiled fish kebabs. Be sure to choose a fish that's thick and sturdy like halibut, cod, salmon, or swordfish so it stands up to the skewers and cooking. If you're nervous about that, use the two-skewer method described after the recipe or go for the broiling method. Whole wheat couscous is another good option. **Serves 4**

Ingredients

1 lemon

1 bunch fresh mint

1 small red onion

¾ cup green olives

¼ cup olive oil, plus more for brushing the fish

Pepper

1 cup bulgur (any grind)

Salt

1 pound thick fish fillets or steaks

Prep · Cook

1. Bring 2½ cups water to a boil in a large saucepan.

   ☐ If you're using wooden skewers, soak 4 of them in water.

2. Prepare a grill for direct cooking or turn the broiler to high; put the rack 4 inches from the heat.

   ☐ Halve the lemon; squeeze the juice into a large bowl through a strainer or your fingers to catch the seeds.

   ☐ Strip 1 cup leaves from the mint sprigs, chop, and add them to the bowl.

   ☐ Trim, peel, and chop the onion. Pit ¾ cup olives if necessary and chop them. Add both to the bowl.

   ☐ Add ¼ cup olive oil and pepper to the bowl (I like a lot here but you might not) and stir to combine. Transfer ¼ cup of the dressing to a small bowl.

3. Add 1 cup bulgur to the boiling water with a large pinch of salt, stir, cover, and remove from the heat. Fine-grind bulgur will become tender in 10 to 15 minutes, medium in 15 to 20, and coarse in 20 to 25.

4. Cut the fish into 2-inch chunks and thread them onto the skewers on a large rimmed baking sheet. Brush the fish with a little olive oil and sprinkle with salt and pepper.

5. Grill the kebabs directly on the grates or broil in the pan until the side facing the heat source sizzles and browns, 2 to 5 minutes. Turn and cook the other side until the fish is tender but not dry and done as much as you want, another couple minutes.

• recipe continues →

6. When the bulgur is tender, drain it in a strainer, pressing out any excess water with a spoon. Add it to the large bowl with the dressing and toss to combine. Taste and adjust the seasoning.

7. To serve, spoon the bulgur onto plates or a platter, top with the kebabs, and drizzle the reserved dressing on top.

Variations

Fish Kebabs over Basil Farro. Substitute farro for the bulgur, fresh basil for the mint, and ½ cup raisins plus ¼ cup pine nuts for the olives. In Step 1, put the farro and water in the pot at the same time, add some salt, and bring to a boil. Reduce the heat so the liquid bubbles steadily, cover, and cook until the farro is tender, about 20 minutes. Proceed with the recipe while the farro is cooking. If you like, grate a little Parmesan into the farro after you stir it into the sauce.

Shrimp Kebabs over Tomato Bulgur. Use fresh mint, basil, or parsley as the herb and 2 large ripe tomatoes, cored and chopped, instead of the olives. Substitute 1½ pounds peeled large shrimp for the fish; thaw them first under cold running water if they're frozen. In Step 5 the shrimp will take as little as half the cooking time to become pink outside and opaque at the center—figure 1 or 2 minutes a side.

Chicken Kebabs over Seasoned Bulgur or Farro. Works for the main recipe or the first variation. Use 1 pound boneless, skinless chicken thighs instead of the fish steaks. They'll take longer to cook, 5 to 7 minutes per side, depending on how big you cut the pieces.

TWO SKEWERS, ONE KEBAB

Whether you're threading skewers with fish, meat, or vegetables, inserting two through each kebab will make them a lot easier to turn on the grill or under the broiler. They'll also have a better chance of cooking evenly, and they definitely won't spin around. (That's a function of the protein shrinking as it cooks.) Two parallel skewers may take a few extra seconds threading time but will ultimately make cooking a lot easier and more efficient.

Steamed Mussels with Garlicky Mayonnaise

The difference between this mussels recipe and the clams that follow is the amount of liquid involved. So instead of ending up with a lot of broth, here you get a concentrated brine to stir into seasoned mayonnaise for a fabulous drizzle sauce. (See page 362 for more about how to substitute clams.) You still need lots of bread, preferably toasted. **Serves 4**

Ingredients

2 to 3 pounds mussels

2 tablespoons olive oil

4 to 6 cloves garlic

¾ cup mayonnaise

1 lemon

Salt and pepper

Prep · Cook

☐ Scrub the mussels under cold water; discard any that don't close when you tap them.

1. Put 2 tablespoons olive oil in a large pot over medium heat.

   ☐ Peel 4 to 6 cloves garlic and slice thinly.

2. Add the garlic to the oil and cook, stirring occasionally, until it sizzles, just a minute or two.

   ☐ Put ¾ cup mayonnaise in a small heatproof bowl.

   ☐ Halve the lemon and squeeze the juice into the mayonnaise through a strainer or your fingers to catch the seeds; whisk to combine.

   ☐ Get a large strainer handy; line it with cheesecloth if you have it.

3. Add the mussels to the pot, turn the heat to high, and cover the pot. Cook, shaking the pot occasionally, until they all (or nearly all) open, 5 to 10 minutes. (You can discard those that remain tightly closed or gently pry them open with a butter knife to see if they release easily and look and smell normal.) Transfer the mussels to a serving bowl.

4. Strain the liquid remaining in the pan through the strainer into the mayonnaise mixture; whisk until smooth. Taste and add salt and pepper. Drizzle the mayonnaise sauce over the mussels and serve.

Variations

Mussels with Miso Mayonnaise. Omit the garlic and lemon and skip Step 2. Before you cook the mussels in Step 3, add ¼ cup white or yellow miso to the mayonnaise and whisk until smooth. Continue with the recipe.

Mussels with Dijon Mayonnaise. Before you cook the mussels in Step 3, add 2 tablespoons Dijon mustard to the mayonnaise and whisk until smooth. Taste and add more if you like. Continue with the recipe.

Clams with Chorizo and Cherry Tomatoes

A big pot of steamed clams is so inviting. No matter what goes in there with them, the broth makes for fantastic dunking, so be sure to serve with crusty bread. Or pour everything over rice or noodles. See page 362 if you want to use mussels in the main recipe or any of the variations. **Serves 4**

Ingredients

4 to 5 pounds littleneck or other small hard-shell clams

2 tablespoons olive oil

4 ounces Spanish chorizo

4 cloves garlic

1 pint ripe cherry tomatoes

1 cup white wine

Pepper

1 bunch fresh parsley

Salt

☐ Prep · Cook

☐ Scrub and rinse the clams under cold water; discard any that don't close when you tap them; let them drain in a colander.

1. Put 2 tablespoons olive oil in a large pot over medium-high heat.

   ☐ Chop 4 ounces chorizo; add it to the pot.

   ☐ Peel and thinly slice 4 cloves garlic; add them to the pot.

2. Cook the chorizo and garlic, stirring occasionally, until the garlic is golden, 2 to 3 minutes.

3. When the garlic is golden, add the clams, tomatoes, 1 cup white wine, and a sprinkle of pepper. Adjust the heat so the liquid bubbles steadily, cover, and cook, shaking the pot occasionally, until the clams have opened, 5 to 10 minutes. (You can discard those that remain tightly closed or gently pry them open with a butter knife to see if they release easily and look and smell normal.)

   ☐ Chop ⅓ cup parsley leaves.

4. Taste the broth and add a little salt if necessary. Serve in shallow bowls, garnished with the parsley.

• recipe continues →

Variations

Clams Steamed in Coconut Broth with Wakame. A delicious bright green seaweed that's super-convenient when you find the instant kind that doesn't require long soaking. Omit the chorizo and tomatoes. Add ¼ cup instant or regular wakame seaweed; if using regular, you'll need to break it up with kitchen scissors or pulse in a food processor. Substitute good-quality vegetable oil for the olive oil, 2 inches ginger, peeled and minced, for the garlic, 1 (14-ounce) can coconut milk for the wine, and fresh cilantro for the parsley. In Step 2, cook the ginger, stirring occasionally, in the hot oil for a couple minutes until it plumps and softens, then add the coconut milk and adjust the heat so it gently bubbles. If you're using regular wakame, add it at the same time as the clams. If you're using instant wakame, wait until you taste the broth and add the parsley in Step 4.

Steamed Clams with Fermented Black Beans. Terrific served over a bed of steamed Asian greens like tatsoi, mizuna, Chinese broccoli (gai lan), or bok choy. Instead of the chorizo, use ¼ cup fermented black beans. When you prep the garlic, also peel 1 inch fresh ginger and trim 2 scallions; chop them all together. Cook them with the fermented black beans in Step 2. Substitute water for the wine and cilantro for the parsley. Just before serving, drizzle with some soy sauce and a few drops of sesame oil.

Steamed Clams with Tarragon and Cream. This combination gives the dish a French bistro twist. Omit the chorizo. Use butter instead of olive oil and 2 shallots instead of the garlic. Add ½ cup cream along with the wine and garnish with 1 tablespoon chopped fresh tarragon instead of parsley.

SWAPPING MUSSELS AND CLAMS

As far as I'm concerned, these are interchangeable in all recipes. Since clam shells weigh a lot more than mussel shells, you'll need about half as much weight of mussels when adapting a clam recipe and twice the weight called for when substituting clams in a mussel recipe. Mussels also tend to open a bit faster than clams, but if they've got beards, they take more effort to clean, so the extra time shifts to the front end with prep. Both need a good rinse and light scrub. One significant benefit of mussels is that they are usually less expensive.

Chicken

For several decades now in America, chicken has been king of the animal proteins. It cooks quickly and takes well to all kinds of seasonings and cooking methods. This chapter focuses on only the fastest methods and cuts, so there are mostly recipes here for boneless, skinless breasts and thighs.

But I promise you won't be bored. There are lots of different flavor profiles in the mix; the variations play with swapping ingredients and venture into ideas for using other poultry and meats, seafood, or vegetarian protein options. There's even some turkey and duck thrown in for good measure.

By far the most common mistake people make is to overcook chicken. The fastest cut—boneless, skinless chicken breasts—is also the leanest and the quickest to dry out, and the thickness and sizes vary wildly. So check the interior frequently—the easiest way is to nick a piece with a knife and peek—and remove pieces from the heat as they're done. And for this reason I frequently recommend using thigh cutlets; the dark meat is a little fattier, more flavorful, and more forgiving to cook. There's more about checking for doneness on page 371.

Broiled Chicken Breasts with Avocado Salsa

The simplest technique, especially if you can find precut cutlets. Otherwise, making them yourself is easy and fast once you give up the idea that you have to pound them super-thin. Since garlic burns easily under the broiler, the nifty trick here delivers tons of flavor without having charred bits. **Serves 4**

Ingredients

2 large boneless, skinless chicken breasts (1½ pounds) or 1½ pounds chicken cutlets

2 tablespoons olive oil

2 teaspoons paprika

Salt and pepper

2 cloves garlic

2 avocados

1 small red onion

1 cup ripe cherry tomatoes

1 lime

1 jalapeño chile, or more to taste

Several sprigs fresh cilantro

▫ Prep · Cook

1. Turn the broiler to high; put the rack 4 inches from the heat.

   ▫ If you're using whole breasts, cut each in half horizontally to make 2 thin cutlets. Press down on each with the heel of your hand to flatten them a little.

2. Put the cutlets on a rimmed baking sheet, rub with 2 tablespoons olive oil, and sprinkle with 2 teaspoons paprika and some salt and pepper.

3. Broil, turning once, until lightly browned on both sides and just cooked through, 2 to 5 minutes per side.

   ▫ Peel and halve 2 cloves garlic.

   ▫ Halve and pit the avocados, cut the flesh into cubes, and scoop it out of the skin into a medium bowl.

   ▫ Trim, peel, and chop the onion; add it to the bowl.

4. Rub the browned cutlets all over with the raw garlic and put them on plates or a platter. Discard what's left of the garlic.

   ▫ Halve 1 cup cherry tomatoes; add them to the bowl.

   ▫ Halve the lime.

   ▫ Trim and halve the jalapeño, remove the seeds if you like, chop, and add to the bowl of salsa.

   ▫ Chop several cilantro sprigs; add to the salsa.

5. Squeeze the lime juice into the salsa and sprinkle with salt and pepper; stir to combine. Taste and adjust the seasoning. Spoon the salsa over the top of the chicken and serve.

Sautéed Chicken Cutlets with Lemon Pan Sauce

We sometimes forget how good this classic French technique is, even with plain water instead of wine. I've changed up the ingredients in the variations, so you can use thin or thick fish fillets or boneless pork chops as the protein. The cooking time will vary: fish takes less than chicken and pork a minute or two more on each side. All you need is a pile of simply cooked vegetables and sliced baguette to round out the meal. **Serves 4**

Ingredients

2 large boneless, skinless chicken breasts (1½ pounds) or 1½ pounds chicken cutlets

2 tablespoons olive oil, plus more as needed

1 cup flour

Salt and pepper

1 bunch fresh parsley

1 lemon

1 cup white wine or water

2 tablespoons cold butter

◻ Prep · Cook

◻ If you're using whole breasts, cut each in half horizontally to make 2 thin cutlets. Press down on each with the heel of your hand to flatten them a little.

1. Heat the oven to 200°F and put an ovenproof platter on the middle rack. Put 2 tablespoons olive oil in a large skillet over medium-high heat.

   ◻ Put 1 cup flour on a plate and stir in a pinch of salt.

   ◻ Sprinkle the chicken with a little salt and pepper on both sides.

2. When the oil is hot, dredge the chicken cutlets in the flour on both sides, one at a time; shake off the excess. As you flour each cutlet, add it to the skillet.

3. Cook the cutlets, adjusting the heat so they sizzle but don't burn, until the bottoms are browned, 3 to 4 minutes. (You may need to rotate them before turning to promote even cooking.) Turn and cook on the other side until browned and no longer pink inside but still juicy, another 3 to 4 minutes.

4. As each cutlet is done, transfer it to the platter in the oven to keep warm; continue cooking the remaining cutlets, adding more oil to the skillet if needed to keep the bottom coated with a thin film.

   ◻ Chop ¼ cup parsley leaves.

   ◻ Grate the zest from the lemon; halve the lemon.

5. When all the cutlets are cooked and warming in the oven, add 1 cup wine or water (or a combination) to the skillet. Cook, scraping the bottom of the pan occasionally, until the liquid is reduced by about half, a minute or two. Lower the heat to medium-low.

6. Add the butter and lemon zest, squeeze in the lemon juice through a strainer or your fingers to catch the seeds, and stir in the parsley. Cook, swirling the pan and whisking to melt the butter. Taste and adjust the seasoning. Pour the sauce over the cutlets and serve.

Variations

Sautéed Chicken Cutlets with Orange Sauce. Instead of the lemon, use a small orange. If you have access to satsumas, mandarins, tangerines, or other small sweet citrus, use that. Substitute fresh mint for the parsley.

Sautéed Chicken Cutlets with Balsamic Pan Sauce. Instead of the lemon, add ¼ cup balsamic vinegar. Substitute fresh basil for the parsley and add lots of black pepper to the sauce.

Sautéed Chicken Cutlets with Mushroom Pan Sauce. Omit the lemon. Trim and chop 8 ounces cremini mushrooms. Substitute red wine for white if you like. After you remove the last cutlet, in Step 5 add the mushrooms to the skillet and cook, stirring occasionally, until they release their water and start to get tender, 3 to 5 minutes. Then add the wine and finish the sauce. Substitute fresh chives for the parsley if you like.

7 Ways to Vary Any Pan Sauce in This Recipe

Add any of the following to the pan sauce in Step 6, alone or in combination, to your taste:

1. Minced garlic, fresh ginger, or chiles
2. Chopped fresh rosemary, sage, thyme, or oregano
3. Capers
4. A pinch of saffron
5. Curry powder, chili powder, or your favorite spice blend
6. Chopped pitted olives
7. Mashed anchovies

Fastest Chicken Parm

One of the most popular recipes from the first edition, this spin on the classic couldn't be easier. Instead of dredging and pan-frying, just broil the components in two stages. Throw together a green salad on the side and you'll be all set. **Serves 4**

Ingredients

5 tablespoons olive oil

3 ripe tomatoes
(about 1 pound)

2 large boneless, skinless chicken breasts (1½ pounds) or 1½ pounds chicken cutlets

Salt and pepper

8 ounces fresh mozzarella cheese

2 ounces Parmesan cheese (½ cup grated)

1 cup bread crumbs

▢ Prep · Cook

1. Turn the broiler to high; put the rack 6 inches from the heat. Put 2 tablespoons olive oil on a rimmed baking sheet and spread it around; put the baking sheet under the broiler while it heats.

   ▢ Core and slice the tomatoes.

   ▢ If you're using whole breasts, cut each in half horizontally to make 2 thin cutlets. Press down on each with the heel of your hand to flatten them a bit.

2. Carefully remove the baking sheet from the broiler. Put the chicken cutlets on the pan and sprinkle with salt and pepper. Top with the tomato slices and broil until the chicken is no longer pink in the center, 5 to 10 minutes, rotating the pan if necessary for even cooking.

   ▢ Tear 8 ounces fresh mozzarella cheese into bits about the size of peas.

   ▢ Grate ½ cup Parmesan cheese.

   ▢ Combine 1 cup bread crumbs with the mozzarella and Parmesan in a medium bowl.

3. When the chicken is cooked through, remove the baking sheet from the broiler. Sprinkle the tomatoes with the bread crumb and cheese mixture, and drizzle with 3 tablespoons olive oil.

4. Return the baking sheet to the broiler and cook until the bread crumbs and cheese are browned and bubbling, 2 to 4 minutes. Serve right away.

Variations

Fastest Eggplant Parm.
Instead of the chicken, trim, then slice 2 large eggplants (about 1½ pounds) crosswise 1 inch thick. After the baking sheet is hot, in Step 2 spread out the eggplant slices, but do not top them with the tomatoes. Sprinkle with salt and pepper and turn to coat them in some oil, adding a little more if they look dry. Broil until softened and browned in places, 3 to 5 minutes. Turn, then top with the tomato slices and proceed with the recipe from the end of Step 2.

Roasted Chicken and Portobellos with Black Olive Vinaigrette

Tapenade meets vinaigrette and becomes a sauce for high-heat roasted chicken and portobellos. So many options for how to serve the results: on sub rolls, chopped and tossed with pasta, or layered on a pile of greens. **Serves 4**

Ingredients

2 large portobello mushrooms (about 1 pound)

Salt and pepper

8 tablespoons olive oil

2 large boneless, skinless chicken breasts (1½ pounds) or 1½ pounds chicken cutlets

½ cup black olives

1 clove garlic

Several sprigs fresh parsley

3 tablespoons red wine vinegar

▢ Prep · Cook

1. Heat the oven to 450°F. Put 2 rimmed baking sheets on racks inside.

   ▢ Remove the mushroom stems if there are any and slice the caps crosswise about ½ inch thick.

2. Carefully remove one of the pans from the oven and add the mushrooms. Sprinkle with salt and pepper, drizzle with 2 tablespoons olive oil, and toss with tongs. Spread the mushrooms out in a single layer (it's okay if they aren't all lying flat). Transfer to the oven and cook until they release some liquid and begin to brown, 5 to 10 minutes.

   ▢ If you're using whole breasts, cut each in half horizontally to make 2 thin cutlets. Press down on each with the heel of your hand to flatten them a little.

3. Remove the second pan from the oven, drizzle with 1 tablespoon olive oil, and spread out the chicken cutlets. Sprinkle with salt and pepper and smear the tops with another tablespoon olive oil. Put the pan back in the oven and roast until the chicken begins to turn opaque, about 5 minutes.

   ▢ Pit ½ cup black olives if necessary and chop. Put them in a small bowl.

   ▢ Peel and chop 1 clove garlic; add it to the bowl.

   ▢ Strip the leaves from several parsley sprigs and chop; add them to the bowl.

4. Turn the chicken and toss the mushrooms. Return them to the oven to roast until the mushrooms are darkened and the chicken is only slightly pink at the center, 5 to 10 minutes.

5. To finish the vinaigrette, add 3 tablespoons red wine vinegar and 4 tablespoons olive oil to the bowl; stir with a fork to combine. Taste and add salt and pepper if you like.

6. When the chicken and mushrooms are ready, divide them among plates. Serve drizzled with the vinaigrette.

Variations

Chicken and Butternut Squash with Green Olive Vinaigrette. Omit the parsley. Instead of the mushrooms, peel and seed 1½ pounds butternut squash; cut it into ½-inch cubes (save the rest for another use—or just buy 1 pound fresh or frozen cubed squash). Substitute green olives for the black. Instead of red wine vinegar, use the juice of 1 lemon in the vinaigrette.

Chicken and Zucchini with Basil Vinaigrette. Instead of the mushrooms, trim 1 pound zucchini; slice them lengthwise into planks about ½ inch thick. Instead of the olives and parsley, chop 1 cup fresh basil leaves for the vinaigrette.

Roast Chicken and Cabbage with Peanut Sauce. Instead of the mushrooms, trim and core 1 small or ½ large head cabbage (about 1 pound); slice it into ribbons about ½ inch wide. Substitute roasted peanuts for the black olives and cilantro for the parsley. Instead of red wine vinegar, use the juice of 2 limes in the vinaigrette.

CHECKING CHICKEN FOR DONENESS

The U.S. Department of Agriculture officially recommends cooking chicken to 165°F, which all but guarantees dried-out white meat. And getting an accurate read on thin pieces can be tricky with most thermometers. You can always use a small knife to nick and peek inside the thickest section.

When you make the cut, you want the juices to be visible and clear, not pink; the meat should be opaque. The tiniest trace of pink is okay if you plan on leaving it in the hot pan, keeping it warm in the oven, or warming it in sauce before serving, since it will continue to cook before you get it to the table. For bone-in pieces, cut right down to the bone, while for boneless chicken make sure you can see into the middle of the thickest part.

Poached Chicken and Asparagus with Lemon Aïoli

I'm always looking for excuses to eat mayonnaise. Here's a semifancy dinner that combines two techniques in one pot: While the chicken poaches in herbed water, asparagus steams on top. And yes, both components pair well with this lemony shortcut aïoli. **Serves 4**

Ingredients

2 lemons

2 large boneless, skinless chicken breasts (1½ pounds)

3 sprigs fresh thyme

2 bay leaves

1 tablespoon black peppercorns (optional)

Salt

1 bunch asparagus (1 pound)

1 clove garlic

½ cup mayonnaise

Pepper

Prep · Cook

☐ Trim 1 lemon and slice it thinly.

1. Put the chicken in a large pot with 2 cups water, 3 thyme sprigs, 2 bay leaves, 1 tablespoon black peppercorns if you're using them, and a sprinkle of salt. Scatter the lemon slices into the water and turn the heat to high.

2. When the liquid comes to a boil, lower the heat so it bubbles steadily but not vigorously and turn the chicken. Cover and cook until the chicken is opaque and just cooked through, 10 to 15 minutes.

   ☐ Trim the asparagus and peel the ends of thick spears if you like.

   ☐ Peel and chop 1 clove garlic; add it to a small bowl.

   ☐ Halve the other lemon; squeeze the juice into the bowl through a strainer or your fingers to catch the seeds.

3. Ten minutes after you covered the chicken, check it by cutting into the thickest part. It should be slightly firm and still pink at the center. If it's not there yet, re-cover and check again in a couple minutes.

4. If using thick asparagus, layer it on top of the chicken and re-cover the pot. If the asparagus spears are thin, wait to add them after the chicken cooks for another 3 minutes. The idea is to have the chicken just barely pink at the thickest part when the asparagus is tender but still has a little crunch, usually about 5 minutes more; check both once or twice in that time. If the chicken finishes first, transfer it to a cutting board.

   ☐ To finish the aïoli, add ½ cup mayonnaise to the bowl with the lemon juice and garlic and sprinkle with salt and pepper; whisk to combine.

• recipe continues →

5. When the asparagus is done, put it on a serving plate. Cut the chicken against the grain into long diagonal slices; transfer them to the plate. Serve the chicken and asparagus with the aïoli on the side.

Variations

Poached Chicken and Carrots with Grapefruit Mayonnaise. Instead of the asparagus, trim 1 pound carrots and quarter or halve them lengthwise so they're no more than ½ inch thick. Substitute ½ grapefruit for the lemon.

Poached Chicken Cutlets and Red Peppers with Smoked Paprika Mayonnaise. Omit the lemon and garlic. Replace the asparagus with 2 large red bell peppers. After trimming, coring, and seeding, cut them into thick slices; they'll take a little less time to cook. Add 1 teaspoon smoked paprika to the mayonnaise in Step 4.

Poached Chicken and Baby Bok Choy with Soy Sauce Mayonnaise. Instead of the thyme, cut 1 inch fresh ginger (peel and all) into coins and add it to the poaching liquid. Substitute 1 pound baby bok choy for the asparagus. Trim and halve them before adding to the pot in Step 4. Instead of the garlic and lemon in the sauce, whisk 2 tablespoons soy sauce into the mayonnaise in Step 4.

Totally Shortcut Chicken Tagine

It takes a long time and many ingredients to make a proper tagine. But you can infuse a few key North African spices into a quick chicken-and-chickpea braise, serve it over couscous with maybe a salad on the side, and be happy with taking a total shortcut for a weeknight.
Serves 4

Ingredients

3 tablespoons olive oil, plus more for drizzling

4 to 6 boneless, skinless chicken thighs (about 1 pound)

Salt and pepper

1¾ cups cooked or canned chickpeas (one 15-ounce can)

1 lemon

2 teaspoons ground cumin

1 teaspoon ground coriander

½ teaspoon ground cinnamon

¼ teaspoon Aleppo pepper or cayenne, plus more to taste

1 (15-ounce) can diced tomatoes

Several sprigs fresh parsley

Prep · Cook

1. Put 3 tablespoons olive oil in a large skillet over medium heat.

    ☐ Cut the chicken thighs into bite-sized chunks.

2. Raise the heat to medium-high. When the oil is hot, add the chicken, sprinkle with salt and pepper, and cook undisturbed until the pieces sizzle and release easily from the skillet, 3 to 5 minutes.

    ☐ If you're using canned chickpeas, rinse and drain them.

    ☐ Halve the lemon.

3. Stir the chicken with a spatula to scrape up any browned bits. Sprinkle with 2 teaspoons ground cumin, 1 teaspoon ground coriander, ½ teaspoon ground cinnamon, and ¼ teaspoon Aleppo pepper or cayenne. Stir a couple more times. Add the chickpeas and the tomatoes and their juice, and squeeze in the juice from the lemon through a strainer or your fingers to catch the seeds. Stir to combine.

4. Adjust the heat so the mixture bubbles steadily but gently. Cook, stirring once or twice, until the chicken is cooked through, about 10 minutes. If the sauce sticks to the pan while stirring, add 1 or 2 tablespoons water.

    ☐ Strip the leaves from several parsley sprigs and chop.

5. Taste and adjust the seasoning. Serve right away, garnished with the parsley and a drizzle of olive oil.

Chicken Marsala with Lots of Mushrooms

Chicken Marsala is an old-school Italian restaurant favorite that doesn't need much in the way of tweaking. This version increases the mushrooms, since their earthiness balances the sweet sauce brilliantly. Either boiled small potatoes or plain egg noodles (page 493) would be excellent on the side. If Marsala—which is a fortified wine—isn't to your taste, other options follow, including two that are nonalcoholic. **Serves 4**

Ingredients

2 large boneless, skinless chicken breasts (1½ pounds) or 1½ pounds chicken cutlets

4 tablespoons (½ stick) butter

2 tablespoons olive oil, plus more as needed

1 cup flour

Salt and pepper

1½ pounds button or cremini mushrooms

Several sprigs fresh parsley

¾ cup Marsala wine

1 cup chicken stock, vegetable stock, or water

▢ Prep · Cook

1. Heat the oven to 200°F and put an ovenproof platter on the middle rack.

    ▢ If you're using whole breasts, cut each in half horizontally to make 2 thin cutlets. Press down on each with the heel of your hand to flatten them a little.

2. Put 2 tablespoons butter and 2 tablespoons olive oil in a large skillet over medium-high heat.

    ▢ Put 1 cup flour on a plate and stir in a pinch of salt.

    ▢ Sprinkle the chicken with a little salt and pepper on both sides.

3. When the butter is foaming, dredge the chicken cutlets in the flour on both sides, one at a time; shake off the excess. As you finish each cutlet, add it to the skillet.

4. Cook the cutlets, adjusting the heat so they sizzle but don't burn, until the bottoms are browned, 3 or 4 minutes. (You might need to rotate them on the first side to promote even browning.) Turn and cook on the other side until browned and cooked through, another 3 or 4 minutes.

    ▢ Trim and slice the mushrooms.

5. As each cutlet is done, transfer it to the platter in the oven to keep warm; continue cooking the remaining cutlets, adding more oil to the skillet if needed to keep the bottom coated with a thin film.

6. When all of the cutlets are in the oven, add more oil to the skillet if it's dry, then add the mushrooms. Sprinkle with salt and pepper and cook, stirring occasionally, until the mushrooms are tender and the pan is beginning to dry out, 8 to 12 minutes.

    ▢ Strip the leaves from several parsley sprigs and chop them.

7. Add ¾ cup Marsala and 1 cup stock or water to the pan; raise the heat to high and let the liquid bubble away until it thickens a bit. Add 2 tablespoons butter and stir until it melts. Taste and adjust the seasoning. Pour the sauce over the cutlets, garnish with the parsley, and serve.

Variations

Chicken with Red Wine Sauce and Mushrooms. Instead of the Marsala, use a dry red wine. Since it's not nearly as sweet, feel free to substitute wine for the stock or water too.

Chicken with Coconut Curry Sauce and Shiitakes. A twirl of rice noodles is the way to go here. Substitute 1 (14-ounce) can coconut milk (reduced fat is fine) for the Marsala and stock or water. If you're using shiitake mushrooms, before slicing them, trim and discard the stems or save them for stock. When the mushrooms are done in Step 6, stir in 2 tablespoons curry powder before adding the coconut milk. Instead of the parsley, stir in ½ cup chopped fresh cilantro just before serving.

Chicken with Apple Cider Sauce and Turnips. Back to boiled potatoes or egg noodles for this one. Substitute 1½ cups apple cider for the Marsala and stock, and turnips for the mushrooms. After trimming, cut the turnips into thin wedges; if the greens look good, chop and add them too. Garnish with chopped fresh chives.

THE FORMULA FOR VEGETABLES AND PAN SAUCE

Use this recipe as a model for turning pan-cooked meat—like the chicken breasts here, or chicken thighs, pork chops, or not-too-thick sirloin steak—into a meal. After you remove the meat from the skillet, add a little extra butter or oil to the pan, followed by chopped vegetables like sliced zucchini or cabbage, carrot coins or sticks, snow or sugar snap peas, chopped greens, or chunks of asparagus—whatever you've got handy. When the vegetables are as tender as you like, either remove them and make the sauce or leave them in the skillet and integrate them.

Stir-Fried Chicken and Chard

It might not be the most common green used in stir-fries, but chard takes well to high heat and has a ton of flavor. The leaves soften quickly and acquire wonderful singed brown spots (especially in a cast-iron or carbon-steel skillet), while the little bits of the stems form a crunchy counterpoint. Try serving this with soba noodles for something different. **Serves 4**

Ingredients

4 tablespoons good-quality vegetable oil

6 to 8 boneless, skinless chicken thighs (about 1½ pounds)

Salt and pepper

1 inch fresh ginger

2 cloves garlic

4 scallions

1 bunch chard (about 1 pound)

2 tablespoons soy sauce, or more to taste

Sesame oil for serving

Prep · Cook

1. Put 2 tablespoons vegetable oil in a large skillet over medium-high heat.

    □ Slice the chicken into ½-inch strips or chop into bite-sized pieces.

2. Add the chicken to the skillet, sprinkle with salt and pepper, and cook undisturbed until it sizzles and releases easily from the pan, about 3 minutes. After that, stir occasionally until it loses its pink color and browns in places, another 5 to 10 minutes.

    □ Peel 1 inch ginger and 2 cloves garlic; chop them together.

    □ Trim and chop the scallions, keeping the white and light green parts separate from the dark green tops.

    □ Rinse and trim the chard, keeping everything but the toughest stem ends. Cut the leaves across the stem into ribbons as wide or thin as you like.

3. When the chicken is done, add the ginger, garlic, and white and light green parts of the scallions. Cook, stirring, until fragrant, about a minute. Transfer the chicken mixture to a bowl.

4. Add 2 tablespoons vegetable oil to the skillet and turn the heat to high. Add the chard, a handful at a time if necessary to fit it in, and sprinkle with salt and pepper. Cook until the leaves soften and begin to brown slightly, 5 to 7 minutes.

5. Return the chicken mixture to the skillet; add 2 tablespoons soy sauce and ½ cup water and stir until most of the liquid evaporates before turning off the heat. Taste and adjust the seasoning. Garnish with the scallion greens and serve, passing sesame oil at the table.

• recipe continues →

Variations

Stir-Fried Chicken and Okra with Fresh Chiles. Trust me: Keep the soy sauce—it goes well with the okra, which is miraculously un-slimy with this cooking method. Instead of the ginger, trim and slice 1 or 2 hot red chiles (like Thai or serrano, seeded if you like) and add them with the garlic and scallions in Step 3. Substitute 1 pound okra for the chard; trim the ends and slice in half lengthwise. When you add them to the skillet in Step 4, try to put them cut side down. It's okay if the pan is crowded or they don't quite fit in a single layer.

Stir-Fried Chicken and Kale. Substitute any kind of kale for the chard. Instead of the soy sauce, add the zest and juice of 1 small orange or other citrus like tangerine or satsuma (if they're really small, use 2; be sure to remove any seeds). Everything else stays the same.

Stir-Fried Chicken and Mustard Greens. Sharper, for sure; use either green or purple leaves. Substitute either for the chard. Everything else stays the same.

Stir-Fried Chicken and Green Beans. Use the flavorings in the main recipe or either of the first two variations. Substitute 1 pound green beans for the chard. Trim the stem ends and cut the beans into 1- or 2-inch pieces.

Stir-Fried Chicken and Broccoli with Black Bean Sauce

Once you start incorporating fermented black beans into your stir-fries, you might not ever stop. They're made from black soybeans that have been salted and cured so they become soft and develop nuanced flavors of soy sauce, legumes, and brininess. Serve this with a scoop of rice or toss with Chinese egg noodles. **Serves 4**

Ingredients

2 tablespoons fermented black beans

2 tablespoons white wine or water

2 tablespoons soy sauce

1 teaspoon sugar

4 tablespoons good-quality vegetable oil

6 to 8 boneless, skinless chicken thighs (about 1½ pounds)

Salt and pepper

1 inch fresh ginger

4 cloves garlic

3 scallions

1 small head broccoli (about 1 pound)

1 tablespoon rice vinegar

☐ Prep · Cook

1. Combine 2 tablespoons fermented black beans, 2 tablespoons white wine or water, 2 tablespoons soy sauce, and 1 teaspoon sugar in a small bowl.

2. Put 2 tablespoons vegetable oil in a large skillet over medium-high heat.

   ☐ Slice the chicken into ½-inch strips or chop into bite-sized pieces.

3. Add the chicken to the skillet, sprinkle with salt and pepper, and cook undisturbed until it sizzles and releases easily from the pan, about 3 minutes. After that, stir occasionally until it loses its pink color and browns in places, another 5 to 10 minutes.

   ☐ Peel 1 inch ginger and 4 cloves garlic; chop them together.

   ☐ Trim and chop the scallions, keeping the white and light green parts separate from the dark green tops.

   ☐ Trim the broccoli. Break or chop it into florets slightly bigger than bite-sized; peel the stem if you like and slice it into coins.

4. When the chicken is done, add the ginger, garlic, and white and light green parts of the scallions to the skillet. Cook, stirring until fragrant, about a minute. Transfer the chicken mixture to a bowl.

5. Add 2 tablespoons vegetable oil to the skillet and raise the heat to high. Add the broccoli and cook, stirring occasionally, until it browns slightly, 3 to 5 minutes. Add ¼ cup water, cover the skillet, and cook until the broccoli is just tender, another 2 to 3 minutes.

• recipe continues →

6. Return the chicken mixture to the skillet with the broccoli. Add the fermented black bean mixture and 1 tablespoon rice vinegar, tossing to coat everything with the sauce. Turn off the heat. Taste and adjust the seasoning. Garnish with the scallion greens and serve.

Variations

Stir-Fried Chicken and Broccoli with Tomato-Soy Sauce. For a nontraditional tomatoey glaze. Increase the soy sauce to 3 tablespoons. Substitute 2 tablespoons tomato paste for the fermented black beans, stirring well in Step 1 to create a smooth sauce.

Stir-Fried Chicken and Cauliflower with Black Bean Sauce. Substitute 1 small head cauliflower (1 pound) for the broccoli. Chop it into bite-sized pieces.

Stir-Fried Asparagus with Black Bean Sauce. Substitute 1 pound asparagus for the broccoli. After trimming, cut it diagonally into 1-inch pieces. In Step 5 reduce the total cooking time to 3 to 5 minutes.

FIRE UP ANOTHER SKILLET

You can shave off a couple minutes stir-fry time by cooking the vegetables and meat simultaneously in two skillets. This works especially well when you have help in the kitchen to do prep and clean up. (Otherwise the time saved is a wash.) Just be sure to swirl a little water in the empty pan and drizzle the pan drippings into the other skillet when you combine components. You don't want to sacrifice one drop of flavor.

Sesame Chicken and Snow Peas

There are times when you want a slightly sweet, slightly thick stir-fry sauce—almost like gravy. Sesame chicken is one of those dishes. Before you begin, start a pot of rice or set water to boil for noodles. Once you get going on the directions, the recipe comes together before you know it. **Serves 4**

Ingredients

3 tablespoons sesame seeds

4 tablespoons good-quality vegetable oil

4 to 6 boneless, skinless chicken thighs (about 1 pound)

Salt and pepper

1 inch fresh ginger

2 cloves garlic

1 lemon

2 tablespoons cornstarch

1 pound snow peas

3 tablespoons soy sauce

2 teaspoons honey

◻ Prep · Cook

1. Put 3 tablespoons sesame seeds in a large dry skillet over medium-high heat. Cook, shaking the pan frequently, until the seeds are lightly browned and fragrant, 2 to 3 minutes. Transfer them to a small bowl.

2. Put 2 tablespoons vegetable oil in the skillet over medium-high heat.

   ◻ Slice the chicken into ½-inch strips or chop into bite-sized pieces.

3. Add the chicken to the skillet, sprinkle with salt and pepper, and cook, stirring occasionally, until the chicken loses its pink color and is cooked through, 5 to 10 minutes.

   ◻ Peel 1 inch ginger and 2 cloves garlic; chop them together.

   ◻ Halve the lemon.

   ◻ Whisk together 2 tablespoons cornstarch and ⅓ cup water in a small bowl.

4. Transfer the cooked chicken to a bowl. Add 2 tablespoons vegetable oil to the skillet along with the ginger, garlic, and snow peas. Cook, stirring occasionally, until the snow peas are slightly tender but still have some crunch, 2 to 3 minutes.

   ◻ Squeeze the lemon juice into the cornstarch mixture through a strainer or your fingers to catch the seeds. Add 3 tablespoons soy sauce and 2 teaspoons honey and whisk to combine.

5. When the snow peas are slightly tender but still have some crunch, return the chicken to the skillet. Add the cornstarch mixture and all but 2 teaspoons of the sesame seeds. Cook, stirring constantly, until the chicken and snow peas are coated in a thick sauce, no more than 1 minute. Taste and adjust the seasoning. Garnish with 2 teaspoons sesame seeds and serve.

Curried Chicken and Cauliflower with Apricot Relish

Yogurt-and-curry–marinated chicken thighs and cauliflower roast while you prepare a dried apricot relish brightened with ginger. Colorful and full of different textures in every bite. Serve with rice, Israeli couscous, or warmed flatbreads. **Serves 4**

Ingredients

4 tablespoons good-quality vegetable oil

2 cups yogurt

2 tablespoons curry powder

Salt and pepper

1 small head cauliflower (1 pound)

4 to 6 boneless, skinless chicken thighs (about 1 pound)

1 small red onion or large shallot

1 inch fresh ginger

1 cup dried apricots (about 6 ounces)

1 bunch fresh cilantro

¼ cup cider vinegar

□ Prep · **Cook**

1. Heat the oven to 450°F. Grease a rimmed baking sheet with 2 tablespoons vegetable oil.

2. Put 2 cups yogurt and 2 tablespoons vegetable oil in a large bowl. Add 2 tablespoons curry powder and a sprinkle of salt and pepper and whisk to combine.

   □ Trim the cauliflower and break or chop it into small florets. Add them to the bowl and toss to coat.

3. Fish the florets out of the marinade with a slotted spoon, shaking to let as much of the marinade as possible drop back into the bowl. Spread out the florets on half of the baking sheet in a single layer.

   □ Cut the chicken into large chunks. Add them to the marinade and toss to coat.

4. Transfer the chicken to the other half of the baking sheet the same way you did the cauliflower. Discard any marinade left in the bowl. Put the baking sheet in the oven and roast undisturbed for 15 minutes.

   □ Trim, peel, and chop the onion or shallot and put it in a small bowl.

   □ Trim, peel, and chop 1 inch ginger; add it to the bowl.

   □ Chop 1 cup dried apricots; add them to the bowl.

   □ Chop ½ cup cilantro tender stems and leaves; add them to the bowl.

5. Add ¼ cup cider vinegar to the relish with a sprinkle of salt and pepper, and stir to combine. Taste and adjust the seasoning.

● recipe continues →

6. Stir the chicken and cauliflower, keeping them on their separate sides. Return the pan to the oven and cook until the chicken is no longer pink inside and the cauliflower can be easily pierced with a fork, another 5 to 10 minutes. Serve the chicken and cauliflower with the apricot relish.

Variations

Curried Chicken and Squash with Apricot Relish. Instead of the cauliflower, peel and seed 1 small butternut squash; cut it into 1-inch chunks. Marinate and roast it as described in the recipe.

Curried Chicken and Eggplant with Cilantro-Mint Relish. Instead of the cauliflower, trim 1 or 2 large or several small eggplants (about 1 pound). Peel if you like, then cut into 1-inch cubes. Marinate and roast as described in the recipe. Instead of the apricots, chop a small bunch of fresh mint (about 1 cup) for the relish.

Rosemary Chicken and Cauliflower with Tomato Relish. Substitute 2 tablespoons chopped fresh rosemary for the curry powder in the marinade. Instead of the apricots, core and chop 5 or 6 ripe plum tomatoes. Use balsamic vinegar instead of cider vinegar and fresh basil or parsley instead of the cilantro.

Provençal Chicken

I'm a sucker for the flavors of Provence; olives, capers, garlic, and tomatoes are the makings of this hearty country stew. When I'm not in a hurry, I make it with bone-in parts and pay attention to browning the skin and all that. On busy weeknights, this recipe requires blissfully less focus. Serve with sliced baguette or buttered cannellini beans. And be sure to check out the photo of this dish that appears opposite the title page. **Serves 4**

Ingredients

4 tablespoons olive oil

4 to 6 boneless, skinless chicken thighs (about 1 pound)

Salt and pepper

2 or 3 medium zucchini (about 1 pound)

3 ripe tomatoes (1 pound)

½ cup black olives (any kind)

2 tablespoons capers

4 cloves garlic

2 sprigs fresh thyme

½ cup white wine or water

Several sprigs fresh basil

▢ Prep · **Cook**

1. Put 2 tablespoons olive oil in a large skillet or large pot over medium-high heat.

   ▢ Cut the chicken into large chunks.

2. Add the chicken to the skillet, sprinkle with salt and pepper, and cook, stirring occasionally, until it loses its pink color and is just cooked through, 5 to 10 minutes.

   ▢ Trim the zucchini and cut them into bite-sized chunks.

   ▢ Pit ½ cup black olives if necessary and halve or chop.

   ▢ Core and chop the tomatoes.

   ▢ Drain 2 tablespoons capers.

3. Transfer the chicken to a bowl. Add 2 tablespoons olive oil to the skillet. Add the zucchini, sprinkle with salt and pepper, and cook, stirring occasionally, until it is browned in spots, about 5 minutes.

   ▢ Peel and chop 4 cloves garlic; add to the skillet.

   ▢ Strip the leaves from 2 thyme sprigs and chop.

4. Add the tomatoes to the skillet along with the olives, capers, thyme, ½ cup wine or water, and lots of pepper. Scrape any browned bits from the bottom of the pan, then return the chicken and any accumulated juices to the skillet.

5. Adjust the heat so the mixture bubbles steadily but not vigorously. Cook, stirring once or twice, until the tomatoes break down and the chicken finishes cooking, 5 to 10 minutes.

   ▢ Strip the leaves from several basil sprigs and chop.

6. When the stew is ready, taste and adjust the seasoning. Garnish with the basil and serve.

Charred Chicken and Pita with Gyro Fixings

Gyros—those meaty, saucy wraps—get soggy fast. So why not assemble them at the table? Serve the components on a couple platters, and let everyone make sandwiches or devour them however they like. **Serves 4**

Ingredients

6 to 8 boneless, skinless chicken thighs (about 1½ pounds)

3 tablespoons olive oil

1 teaspoon ground cumin

½ teaspoon ground turmeric

Salt and pepper

1 lemon

1 cup yogurt

¼ cup mayonnaise

1 head iceberg lettuce

2 medium ripe tomatoes

1 small red onion

Four 8-inch pitas (with or without pockets)

☐ Prep · Cook

1. Turn the broiler to high; put the rack 4 inches from the heat. Put the chicken on a rimmed baking sheet; drizzle with 2 tablespoons olive oil and sprinkle with 1 teaspoon ground cumin, ½ teaspoon ground turmeric, and a sprinkle of salt and pepper. Toss to coat the chicken in the oil and spices, then spread it out in a single layer.

2. Broil the chicken, turning once, until lightly charred on both sides and just cooked through, 5 to 10 minutes per side.

   ☐ Halve the lemon and squeeze the juice into a small bowl through a strainer or your fingers to catch the seeds.

3. Add 1 cup yogurt, ¼ cup mayonnaise, and a sprinkle of salt and pepper to the bowl with the lemon juice. Stir to combine; taste and adjust the seasoning.

   ☐ Core and chop the lettuce; pile it on one end of a serving plate.

   ☐ Slice the tomatoes; add them to the serving plate.

   ☐ Trim, peel, halve, and thinly slice the onion; add it to the platter (or a large cutting board).

4. Transfer the chicken to a cutting board and let it cool for a minute or two.

5. Put the pitas on a clean rimmed baking sheet, brush all over with 1 tablespoon olive oil, and broil, turning once, until browned or even slightly charred on both sides, 2 to 5 minutes total.

6. Slice or chop the chicken and serve on the board with the onions or put it on a separate plate. Serve the chicken and fixings with the pitas and the sauce.

● recipe continues →

Variations

Charred Chicken and Tortillas with Taco Fixings. Substitute 1 tablespoon chili powder for the ground turmeric, 8 flour tortillas for the pita, lime for the lemon, and 1 cup crumbled queso fresco for the yogurt. Serve with sliced avocado, salsa, and hot sauce.

Charred Chicken and Crusty Bread with Hero Fixings. Substitute 2 teaspoons dried oregano for the ground cumin and turmeric, split sub rolls for the pita, 3 tablespoons red wine vinegar for the lemon juice, and ½ cup olive oil for the mayonnaise and yogurt. Substitute romaine for the iceberg lettuce. If you have any olives or spicy pickled peppers, add them to the spread too.

Charred Chicken and Brown Rice Bowls with Hippy Fixings. Figure around 45 minutes unless you have about 4 cups cooked brown rice already in the fridge. Before doing anything, make a batch of brown basmati rice as described on page 497. Season the chicken and make the sauce as described in the main recipe or any of the variations. Instead of the lettuce, rinse 1 to 2 cups microgreens and slice a couple avocados. Let everyone assemble their own bowls.

Chicken Stroganoff

Yes, you can enjoy the richness of this 1960s darling—including beef, pork, and vegetarian spins—on a weeknight. Buttered egg noodles (page 493) are the usual accompaniment, but I also like it spooned on top of steamed spinach or chard. **Serves 4**

Ingredients

3 tablespoons butter

1 medium onion

1 pound button or cremini mushrooms

Salt and pepper

4 to 6 boneless, skinless chicken thighs (about 1 pound)

2 tablespoons tomato paste

1 cup chicken stock or water

1 tablespoon Dijon mustard

1 bunch fresh dill

½ cup sour cream

☐ Prep · **Cook**

1. Put 3 tablespoons butter in a large skillet over medium heat.

   ☐ Trim, peel, and chop the onion.   ☐ Trim and slice the mushrooms.

2. Add the onion and mushrooms to the skillet, sprinkle with salt and pepper, and raise the heat to medium-high. Cook, stirring occasionally, until the onion and mushrooms are soft, about 10 minutes.

   ☐ Cut the chicken into large chunks.

3. Add the chicken and 2 tablespoons tomato paste to the skillet, sprinkle with salt and pepper, and cook, stirring occasionally, until the mixture is sizzling, just a minute or two.

4. Add 1 cup stock or water and 1 tablespoon Dijon mustard. Adjust the heat so the mixture bubbles steadily but not vigorously. Cover and cook, stirring once in a while, until the chicken is cooked through, 5 to 10 minutes.

   ☐ Chop ½ cup dill leaves and tender stems.

5. When the chicken is cooked through, stir in ½ cup sour cream and turn off the heat. Taste and adjust the seasoning. Serve right away, garnished with dill.

Variations

Beef Stroganoff. Substitute boneless beef sirloin or rib-eye steak for the chicken; slice it thinly across the grain. It'll probably take a few minutes less to cook and is best if it's still a little pink inside.

Pork Stroganoff. Use boneless pork loin or sirloin instead of the chicken; cut it into bite-sized chunks. It'll take about the same time to cook as the chicken.

All-Mushroom Stroganoff. Omit the chicken and use vegetable stock or water if you'd like. Increase the mushrooms to 2 pounds—or add 4 to 8 ounces of another kind, like shiitakes (in which case you'll need to trim away all but the tenderest part of the stems).

Jerk-Inspired Chicken and Onions

In addition to being easy and insanely flavorful, this dish—which takes cues from the iconic Jamaican grilled chicken—will reacquaint you with all the worthy and underused spices in your cupboard. Once the spice paste comes together, all you have to do is toss it with a mess of chicken and sliced onions and broil away, which gives you a stretch to whip up a side, like a salad or simply cooked vegetables. If you want to serve it with rice, start that first. **Serves 4**

Ingredients

1 clove garlic

½ inch fresh ginger

1 teaspoon dried thyme

1 teaspoon ground allspice

1½ teaspoons paprika

¼ teaspoon cayenne, or more to taste

1 teaspoon sugar

3 tablespoons good-quality vegetable oil

Salt and pepper

2 large onions

6 to 8 boneless, skinless chicken thighs (about 1½ pounds)

▢ Prep · Cook

1. Turn the broiler to high; put the rack 6 inches from the heat.

   ▢ Peel 1 clove garlic and ½ inch ginger; chop them together. Put them in a small bowl.

2. Add 1 teaspoon dried thyme to the bowl along with 1 teaspoon ground allspice, 1½ teaspoons paprika, ¼ teaspoon cayenne, 1 teaspoon sugar, 3 tablespoons vegetable oil, and a sprinkle of salt and pepper. Stir into a paste.

   ▢ Trim, peel, halve, and slice the onions thickly.

3. Put the onions and chicken thighs on separate halves of a rimmed baking sheet. Rub the spice paste on everything, starting with the onions. (Getting your hands messy is the best way.) Spread everything in a single layer.

4. Broil, turning the chicken once and tossing the onions occasionally, until the chicken is browned and cooked through and the onions are browned and tender, 10 to 15 minutes total. Serve the chicken and onions together, hot or at room temperature.

Variations

Chicken and Scallions with Five-Spice Powder. Substitute 2 tablespoons five-spice powder for the thyme, allspice, paprika, cayenne, and sugar, and 2 bunches scallions (trimmed only) for the onions.

Chicken and Onions with Za'atar. Substitute 2 tablespoons za'atar for the thyme, allspice, paprika, cayenne, and sugar. Use olive oil instead of vegetable oil.

Lemon-Pepper Chicken and Onions. Use 1½ tablespoons grated lemon zest and lots of black pepper instead of the thyme, allspice, paprika, cayenne, and sugar. Use olive oil instead of vegetable oil.

Chicken and Peppers with Black Bean Sauce

Mole, the iconic Mexican sauce, is made in many versions in several colors, from golden and green to red and black (*mole amarillo*, *mole verde*, *mole rojo*, or *mole negro* in Spanish). Some might include upward of thirty ingredients, taking hours to prepare and years to perfect. For the fast kitchen, my versions are obviously super-scaled back, but they're also super-flavorful. That's because my trick for braising quickly is to turn to the broiler, an ideal tool for browning meat while you simmer a sauce on the stove. Serve with a stack of warm corn tortillas and a salad. **Serves 4**

Ingredients

3 bell peppers (any color)

4 large or 6 small bone-in, skin-on chicken thighs (about 2 pounds)

Salt and pepper

2 tablespoons vegetable oil

3½ cups cooked or canned black beans (two 15-ounce cans)

2 ounces dark chocolate

2 cloves garlic

¾ cup almonds or peanuts or a combination

1 tablespoon chili powder

1 teaspoon ground cumin

½ teaspoon ground cinnamon

1 cup chicken stock or water, plus more as needed

1 lime

Several sprigs fresh cilantro

▢ Prep · Cook

1. Turn the broiler to high; put the rack 4 inches from the heat.

   ▢ Core, seed, and quarter the bell peppers.

2. Put the chicken and peppers on a rimmed baking sheet, sprinkle all over with salt and pepper; turn the chicken skin side up and drizzle with 2 tablespoons vegetable oil. Broil until the chicken skin begins to brown, 8 to 10 minutes.

   ▢ If you're using canned beans, rinse and drain them. Put the beans in a blender.

   ▢ Break 2 ounces dark chocolate into the blender.

   ▢ Peel and crush 2 cloves garlic with the flat side of a knife; add them to the blender.

3. Add ¾ cup almonds or peanuts to the blender along with 1 tablespoon chili powder, 1 teaspoon ground cumin, ½ teaspoon ground cinnamon, 1 cup stock or water, and a sprinkle of salt and pepper. Blend, stopping to scrape down the sides once or twice, until smooth.

4. Pour the sauce from the blender into a large skillet. Add more stock or water if it looks thicker than you like and bring to a boil. Adjust the heat so that it bubbles gently but steadily until the chicken is ready.

5. Nestle the peppers and the browned chicken skin side up into the sauce along with any juices from the baking sheet. Adjust the heat so the sauce bubbles steadily, cover the skillet, and cook undisturbed until the chicken is no longer pink at the bone, about 15 minutes.

   ☐ Cut the lime into wedges.

   ☐ Chop several cilantro sprigs.

6. When the chicken is ready, taste the sauce and adjust the seasoning. Garnish with cilantro and lime wedges and serve.

Variations

Chicken and Peppers with Pumpkin Seed Sauce. Use hulled green pumpkin seeds (pepitas) instead of the nuts.

Chicken and Peppers with Tomatillo Sauce. Omit the chocolate. Replace the black beans with 1½ pounds husked and chopped tomatillos or 1 large (28-ounce) can (about 4 cups).

Chicken and Peppers with Tomato-Chocolate-Chipotle Sauce. Instead of the black beans, use 1 large (28-ounce) can whole peeled tomatoes and their juice. In addition to the chili powder, add 1 or 2 canned chipotle chiles with some of their adobo.

Peanutty Chicken Thighs with Crisp Bean Sprouts

Boneless thighs get the broil-and-baste treatment with a peanut sauce that you whip up while the broiler heats. Crisp stir-fried bean sprouts provide a light, refreshing bed for the tender chicken. Since there's plenty of sauce and some pan drippings, cooked rice or pad Thai–style rice noodles are perfect to serve underneath for tossing at the table. **Serves 4**

Ingredients

1 clove garlic

½ inch fresh ginger

½ cup peanut butter

2 tablespoons soy sauce

¼ cup hot tap water, plus more as needed

4 to 6 boneless, skinless chicken thighs (about 1 pound)

4 tablespoons good-quality vegetable oil

Salt and pepper

1 pound bean sprouts (3 to 4 cups)

4 scallions

□ Prep · Cook

1. Turn the broiler to high; put the rack 4 inches from the heat.

    □ Peel 1 clove garlic and ½ inch ginger; chop them together. Put them in a medium bowl.

2. Add ½ cup peanut butter, 2 tablespoons soy sauce, and ¼ cup hot water to the bowl. Stir in more hot water by the tablespoon until the sauce is as smooth as you like. Reserve half the sauce in a separate small bowl for serving.

3. Rub the chicken with 2 tablespoons vegetable oil and sprinkle with salt and pepper. Broil the first side until the thighs are opaque and starting to brown, about 5 minutes. Turn and repeat with the other side, another 3 to 5 minutes.

4. Put 2 tablespoons vegetable oil in a large skillet over medium-high heat.

    □ Rinse the bean sprouts in a colander and shake them dry.

    □ Trim and chop the scallions, keeping the white and green parts separate.

5. Add the bean sprouts and scallion whites to the skillet, sprinkle with salt and pepper, and cook, stirring occasionally, until the sprouts are slightly softened but still crunchy, 2 to 4 minutes. If the pan starts to get dry while they cook, add a couple tablespoons water.

6. As soon as the bean sprouts are ready, remove the skillet from the heat. After broiling the second side of the chicken, turn and brush with some peanut sauce. Broil until the sauce is caramelized, just a couple minutes. Turn the chicken and repeat on the other side, using all the sauce left in the medium bowl.

7. When the chicken is done, tuck the pieces into the bean sprouts. Drizzle with the reserved peanut sauce and any pan juices from the baking sheet, garnish with scallion greens, and serve.

Variations

Peanutty Chicken Thighs with Crisp Cabbage. Instead of the bean sprouts, use 1 small green or savoy cabbage (about 1 pound). Trim, core, and quarter the cabbage; cut each quarter crosswise into thin ribbons before proceeding.

BBQ Chicken Thighs with Crisp Red Cabbage and Red Onion. Omit the peanut butter. Substitute 1 cup good-quality store-bought or homemade barbecue sauce for the peanut sauce, 1 small head red cabbage for the bean sprouts (cut it as described in the previous variation), and 1 thinly sliced red onion for the scallions, and add them all with the cabbage in Step 5.

Peanutty or BBQ Chicken Breasts with Crisp Cabbage or Bean Sprouts. Follow the main recipe or either of the previous variations, only substitute 2 large boneless, skinless chicken breasts (about 1½ pounds) for the thighs. Cut each in half horizontally to make 4 thin cutlets. Cook the same way, only expect the time under the broiler at every stage to be half what is directed for the thighs.

Chile Chicken and Bubbling Cheese

A little like nachos only in reverse: You use chips or warm tortillas to scoop through the cheese and get to the toppings. Or if you plan ahead a little, you can spoon all the gooey goodness over rice or baked potatoes (if you have some extra time—or leftovers). **Serves 4**

Ingredients

3 tablespoons good-quality vegetable oil

1 pound ground chicken

Salt and pepper

1 onion

3 cloves garlic

3 poblano chiles

2 medium ripe tomatoes

2 teaspoons ground cumin

12 ounces Oaxaca cheese or low-moisture mozzarella (1½ cups grated)

1 lime

Several sprigs fresh cilantro

Tortilla chips or warm flour or corn tortillas for serving

□ Prep · Cook

1. Heat the oven to 450°F. Put 3 tablespoons vegetable oil in a large ovenproof skillet over medium-high heat.

2. Add the chicken to the skillet while it heats. Sprinkle with salt and pepper.

    □ Trim, peel, and chop the onion; add it to the skillet.

3. Cook, stirring frequently, until the chicken browns in places and the onion softens, about 5 minutes.

    □ Peel and chop 3 cloves garlic; add to the skillet and stir.

    □ Trim, core, seed, and slice the poblanos.

    □ Core and chop the tomatoes.

4. When the chicken and onions are ready, spoon off all but 2 tablespoons fat. Add the chiles and tomatoes to the skillet. Sprinkle in 2 teaspoons ground cumin and a little more salt and pepper. Cook, stirring occasionally, until the chiles are soft and the tomatoes release some juice, 3 to 5 minutes.

    □ Grate 1½ cups Oaxaca or mozzarella cheese.

5. Taste the chile-chicken mixture and adjust the seasoning. Scatter the cheese on top and transfer the skillet to the oven. Bake until the cheese is bubbling, 5 to 10 minutes.

    □ Quarter the lime.   □ Chop several cilantro sprigs.

6. Remove the skillet from the oven, garnish with cilantro, and serve with chips or tortillas and lime wedges.

Braised and Glazed Chicken and Leeks

If you braise meat and vegetables in very little liquid, there's enough to generate steam for cooking but not so much that you need to spend time reducing it for a sauce at the end. Just toss in a little butter to thicken it, and you're all set. **Serves 4**

Ingredients

1 tablespoon olive oil

4 large or 6 small bone-in, skin-on chicken thighs (about 2 pounds)

Salt and pepper

3 or 4 large leeks (about 1½ pounds)

½ cup white wine or water

½ cup chicken stock or water

2 tablespoons butter

▢ Prep · Cook

1. Put 1 tablespoon olive oil in a large skillet or large pot over medium-high heat.

   ▢ Pat the chicken thighs dry and sprinkle the skin with salt and pepper.

2. When the oil is hot, add the chicken skin side down and season the other side with salt and pepper. Cook undisturbed until the skin is browned and releases easily from the pan, about 10 minutes. Turn and cook the bottom for a couple minutes, then transfer the pieces to a plate with a slotted spoon.

   ▢ Trim the leeks and halve them lengthwise; cut the white and light green parts into 2-inch pieces. Rinse in a colander under cold water to remove grit; drain.

3. Pour off some of the fat from the skillet if you like; return the skillet to medium-high heat. Add ½ cup wine and ½ cup stock or water to the skillet, scraping any browned bits from the bottom. Add the leeks and sprinkle with salt and pepper.

4. Return the chicken to the pot skin side up, pouring in any accumulated juices from the plate. Adjust the heat so the mixture bubbles steadily but gently. Cover and simmer until the chicken is no longer pink at the bone and the leeks are tender, about 15 minutes.

5. Transfer the chicken to a clean plate with the slotted spoon. Add 2 tablespoons butter to the skillet and stir to melt; taste and adjust the seasoning and serve the chicken on top of the leeks.

Variations

Braised and Glazed Chicken and Shallots. Substitute about 1 pound shallots for the leeks; trim the ends and slice them thickly.

Braised and Glazed Chicken and Brussels Sprouts. Use 1 pound Brussels sprouts instead of the leeks. Trim the bottoms and halve the sprouts if they're big.

Braised and Glazed Chicken and Parsnips. Use parsnips instead of the leeks—or half and half! Trim and peel the parsnips, then cut into bite-sized chunks.

Chicken and Ricotta Sausage over Broccoli Rabe

The best thing about making your own chicken sausage is the many ways you can customize it. Assuming you start with ground meat—and are okay with making patties instead of stuffing into casings—time isn't even an issue. The flatness of the patties lets the meat cook fast while allowing the edges to crisp. All you need alongside is thick slices of Italian bread or split rolls. **Serves 4**

Ingredients

4 tablespoons olive oil

1 or 2 bunches broccoli rabe (about 1½ pounds)

Salt and pepper

4 cloves garlic

Several sprigs fresh basil

2 ounces Parmesan cheese (½ cup grated)

½ cup ricotta cheese

1 pound ground chicken

□ Prep · Cook

1. Put 2 tablespoons olive oil in a large skillet over low heat.

   □ Trim the broccoli rabe; split the stems as necessary to make stalks no more than ½ inch thick.

2. Raise the heat to medium-high. Add the broccoli rabe to the skillet, sprinkle with salt and pepper, and cook, stirring occasionally, until it softens and turns dark green, 5 to 10 minutes.

   □ Peel and chop 4 cloves garlic; add half to the skillet while the rabe is cooking; put the other half in a large bowl.

   □ Strip the leaves from several basil sprigs and chop; add to the garlic in the bowl.

3. As soon as the broccoli rabe is ready, remove the skillet from the heat. Use tongs to transfer the greens to a bowl; tent with foil if you want to keep them warm.

   □ Grate ½ cup Parmesan; add it to the garlic and basil.

4. Add ½ cup ricotta, the ground chicken, and a sprinkle of salt and pepper to the bowl. Mix gently with your hands to combine.

5. Put 2 tablespoons olive oil in the skillet over medium-high heat.

6. Gently shape the meat into 8 patties about ½ inch thick, adding them to the skillet as you go. Cook, turning once, until the patties are browned on both sides and the inside is no longer pink, 4 or 5 minutes per side. Serve the patties on top of the broccoli rabe.

• recipe continues →

Variations

Chicken and Feta Sausage over Spinach. Use spinach instead of the broccoli rabe, mint instead of the basil, ¼ cup chopped pitted kalamata olives instead of the Parmesan cheese, and crumbled feta instead of the ricotta. The spinach will take about half the time to cook as the broccoli rabe.

Chicken and Blue Cheese Sausage over Chard. Substitute any color chard for the broccoli rabe, separating the stems and leaves as in the main recipe. Use parsley instead of the basil and crumbled blue cheese instead of the ricotta.

Maple Chicken Apple Sausage over Red Cabbage. Substitute 1 medium head red cabbage for the broccoli rabe, 2 tablespoons chopped fresh sage for the basil, 1 tablespoon maple syrup for the Parmesan cheese, and ½ cup chopped dried apples for the ricotta. The cabbage will take a little more time to wilt than the broccoli rabe. A splash of cider vinegar during cooking is a nice touch.

The Best Turkey Burgers

Since ground turkey is so mild and lean, it usually needs a leg up. I bring these burgers to life by incorporating a sort-of sofrito—a cooked-down mixture of green pepper, onions, garlic, and tomato paste—that contributes flavor and moisture. **Serves 4**

Ingredients

4 tablespoons good-quality vegetable oil, plus more as needed

1 green bell pepper

1 large onion

2 cloves garlic

1 tablespoon tomato paste

1½ pounds ground turkey

Salt and pepper

4 hamburger buns for serving (optional)

▢ Prep · **Cook**

1. Put 2 tablespoons vegetable oil in a large skillet over medium heat.

    - ▢ Core, seed, and chop the bell pepper. Trim, peel, and chop the onion. Peel 2 cloves garlic.

    - ▢ Chop the vegetables together as finely as you can manage; it's okay if the pieces are uneven.

2. Raise the heat to medium-high and add the chopped vegetables and 1 tablespoon tomato paste. Cook the sofrito, stirring occasionally, until the vegetables soften and the tomato paste darkens, 3 to 5 minutes.

3. Put the turkey in a large bowl. When the sofrito is ready, add it to the turkey. Sprinkle with salt and pepper and mix gently with a rubber spatula just enough to incorporate the sofrito.

4. Wipe out the skillet, add 2 tablespoons vegetable oil, and return the pan to medium-high heat.

5. Gently shape the meat into 4 patties, adding them to the skillet as you go. Cook undisturbed until the bottoms of the burgers brown and release easily, 3 to 5 minutes. Turn and repeat on the other side, cooking and turning as necessary until the center is no longer at all pink (peek inside with a sharp knife), about another 5 minutes.

6. While the burgers cook, split and toast the buns if you're using them. Serve the burgers on the buns or plain, with your favorite condiments.

Variations

The Best Chipotle-Turkey Burgers. Instead of the bell pepper and tomato paste, add 1 or 2 (or more!) mashed canned chipotle chiles and no more than 1 tablespoon of their adobo to the onion and garlic in Step 2.

The Best Olive-Turkey Burgers. Instead of the bell pepper, add ¼ cup pitted kalamata olives; chop them with the onion and garlic.

The Best Turkey-Anchovy Burgers. I promise you won't even know the anchovies are there except for the savory flavor they leave in their wake. Substitute 3 or 4 oil-packed anchovies for the bell pepper; chop them with the onion and garlic.

Seared Duck Breast with Fruit Sauce

Duck breasts are low effort, high flavor. They cook in their own delicious fat until the skin is irresistibly crisp. Add a quick fruit pan sauce, and there's no easier or faster restaurant-style main dish. They are most commonly found frozen, so plan a day or so in advance and let them thaw in the fridge. **Serves 4**

Ingredients

4 boneless, skin-on duck breasts (about 1½ pounds)

Salt and pepper

1 shallot

2 cups blackberries (frozen are fine)

2 sprigs fresh thyme or 1 teaspoon dried

2 tablespoons butter

Prep · Cook

1. To score the duck skin, make a few slices across the skin on each breast, cutting down into the fat but not the meat (about ¼ inch deep). Sprinkle both sides with salt and pepper.

2. Put the breasts skin side down in a large skillet over medium-low heat. Cook undisturbed until much of the fat has rendered and the skin is crisp, 8 to 12 minutes.

   ☐ Trim, peel, and chop the shallot.   ☐ Trim the thyme sprigs.

   ☐ Chop the blackberries into bits.

3. When the duck skin is crisp, turn the breasts and cook until the duck is done to your liking, 2 to 4 minutes for rare (deep pink in the middle when you cut into it and peek from the back side) or cook it a little longer if you prefer it more done. Transfer the breasts to a plate and tent with foil to keep warm.

4. Pour off all but 1 tablespoon of the rendered duck fat—save it in the fridge for roasting potatoes if you want—and put the skillet over medium heat. Add the shallot and thyme and cook for a minute, then stir in the blackberries and sprinkle with salt and pepper.

5. Cook, stirring occasionally, until the berries break down and the mixture gets saucy, about 5 minutes. Stir in 2 tablespoons butter and any juices that have accumulated around the duck; taste and adjust the seasoning. Remove the thyme sprigs if you used them.

6. Leave the duck breasts whole or slice crosswise about ½ inch thick if you like and spoon the sauce over the top or serve it on the side.

recipe continues →

Variations

Seared Duck Breast with Mango-Ginger Sauce. Takes several minutes longer to prepare the mango, but the sauce will be a little creamier. Substitute 1 mango for the berries and 2 inches fresh ginger, peeled and chopped, for the shallots. Cut the mango up into smaller bits.

Seared Duck Breast with Plum-Rosemary Sauce. Terrific for the transition from summer to fall when plums are at their best; if possible, use the oval Italian-style prune plums. Substitute 1 pound fresh plums for the berries and 2 sprigs fresh rosemary for the shallot. Pit the plums and chop them into small bits, skin and all. Strip the leaves from the rosemary sprigs and chop them too. Wait to add the rosemary until you add the plums in Step 4.

Seared Duck Breast with Cherry Sauce. Frozen are fine. Substitute 2 cups sweet cherries for the berries; pit them if necessary.

Meat

Like for so many other Americans, my meat-eating habits have changed in the decade since the first edition of this book was published. Beef, pork, and lamb still appeal to me, but I pay more attention to where the meat comes from and how the animals were raised, and I eat less of it—and less frequently.

That means meat has moved even farther from the center of the plate, from a two- or even three-time daily habit to a few meals a week, and always with an abundance of vegetables. We obviously want to enjoy every bite—but that doesn't necessarily mean we want to labor over cooking it.

These recipes help you do all that. Some cooking methods and cuts of meat are already associated with fast cooking, while tricks like slicing pork or lamb shoulder thin for quick braising, or stir-frying the vegetables in the same pan you browned the meat in, save cleanup time while developing good flavor. And the variations now offer lots of vegan and vegetarian options for meals when you don't want any meat at all.

Juicy Steak with Mustard Spinach

Skillet, steak, spinach: That's all you need for this phenomenal spin on two steak-house classics. Increase the quantity of steak to 1½ pounds if you'd like a larger serving; you may need to cook it in two batches, but the process is so fast, you'll have plenty of time. The mustard may seem like a lot, but it mellows in the sauce; if you're still worried, try one of the variations. **Serves 4**

Ingredients

1 pound boneless beef rib-eye, sirloin, or strip steak (1 to 1½ inches thick)

Salt and pepper

1 tablespoon olive oil

1 pound spinach

1 shallot

2 tablespoons Dijon mustard

¼ cup white wine or water

2 tablespoons butter

☐ Prep · Cook

1. Put a large skillet over high heat. Pat the steak dry with a paper towel and sprinkle both sides with salt and pepper. Cut the steak if necessary so it will fit in the skillet.

2. When the skillet is smoking hot, add 1 tablespoon olive oil, and immediately add the steak. Cook until it browns and releases easily from the pan, 2 to 5 minutes, depending on the thickness. Turn and repeat on the other side, nicking it with a small knife after another minute to check the inside; you want it one shade pinker than desired.

   ☐ Trim and chop the spinach, discarding any thick stems.

   ☐ Trim, peel, and slice the shallot.

3. When the steak is done, transfer it to a cutting board with tongs. Lower the heat to medium-high. Add the shallot, 2 tablespoons Dijon mustard, ¼ cup white wine or water, and 2 tablespoons butter. Stir until the butter melts, then add handfuls of spinach, stirring until there's room in the pan to add more.

4. Sprinkle the spinach with salt and pepper and cook, stirring occasionally, until it is tender and coated with the sauce, 2 to 3 minutes. Taste and adjust the seasoning. Slice the steak against the grain and serve with the spinach, drizzled with any juices from the cutting board.

Variations

Juicy Steak with Creamy Spinach. Omit the wine or water, shallot, and butter; use 1 cup cream and a pinch of ground nutmeg when you cook the spinach.

Juicy Steak with Garlicky Chard. Omit the mustard. Substitute chard for the spinach (keep the stems separate after trimming and chop them), red wine for white, and 2 or more cloves garlic for the shallots. Before adding the chard leaves to the skillet in Step 2, cook the stems by themselves to soften a bit, just a minute or two.

Steak, Lettuce, and Herb Wraps

A little like Thai-style beef salad, only deconstructed so you can eat it with your hands. Here's the strategy: Make a quick dipping sauce while the steak grills, then lay out herbs and lettuce leaves and let everyone assemble their own wraps. I like to have rice on the table for each person to add to the filling or put on the plate to capture the drippings. **Serves 4**

Ingredients

1 pound beef flank steak or skirt steak

Salt and pepper

3 limes

1 fresh hot red chile
(like Thai bird; optional)

¼ cup peanuts

¼ cup fish sauce

1 tablespoon packed brown sugar

2 large heads Boston lettuce

1 bunch fresh mint

1 bunch fresh cilantro

1 bunch fresh Thai or regular basil

□ Prep · Cook

1. Prepare a grill for direct cooking or turn the broiler to high; put the rack 4 inches from the heat. Put the steak on a rimmed baking sheet, blot it dry with a paper towel, and sprinkle both sides with salt and pepper.

2. Grill the steak directly on the grates or broil in the rimmed baking sheet, turning once or twice, until it is charred on both sides but still a bit pinker inside than you like it, 5 to 10 minutes total.

   □ Halve 2 of the limes and squeeze the juice of one into a small bowl.

   □ Cut the remaining lime in wedges and reserve.

   □ Trim and mince the chile if you're using it. Chop ¼ cup peanuts. Add both to the lime juice.

3. Add ¼ cup fish sauce, ½ cup water, and 1 tablespoon brown sugar to the bowl. Stir to combine; taste and add salt and pepper if you like.

4. When the steak is done, transfer it to a cutting board.

   □ Remove the leaves from the lettuces, trimming the bottoms as necessary but leaving the leaves intact. Rinse, then gently dry them with towels (or in a spinner).

   □ Strip leaves from the mint, cilantro, and basil bunches until you have about 1 cup each. (Or you can leave the tender herb sprigs and tops intact if you'd like.)

5. Thinly slice the steak against the grain. Put it on a serving platter and drizzle with any accumulated juices. On another platter, pile the lettuce on one side and the herbs on the other.

6. Serve with the dipping sauce in individual bowls, with the remaining lime wedges on the side. To eat, nestle some steak and herbs in a lettuce leaf, roll, and dip into the sauce.

• recipe continues →

Variations

Tofu and Herb Lettuce Wraps with Thai-Style Dipping Sauce. Substitute 1½ bricks firm tofu (21 to 24 ounces) for the steak. Before cooking the tofu in Step 2, cut the bricks lengthwise in half, then crosswise into planks about ½ inch thick. (Reserve the extra half-brick for another use.) Sprinkle the tofu with salt and pepper and coat it generously with 2 tablespoons good-quality vegetable oil. Tofu will take a little longer than steak to brown and form a crust, so give it a few minutes more on each side. Everything else stays the same.

Chicken and Basil Lettuce Wraps with Parmesan Vinaigrette. Totally different with some simple substitutions. Substitute chicken tenders for the steak, ½ cup grated Parmesan cheese for the peanuts, ¼ cup balsamic vinegar for the fish sauce and brown sugar, and 1 bunch fresh basil (1 cup whole leaves) for all the herbs. Omit the chile. The chicken will probably cook a couple minutes faster, depending on how thick the tenders are; nick with a small knife to make sure the insides are no longer pink. Everything else stays the same.

Salmon and Dill Lettuce Wraps with Lemony Crème Fraîche. Use salmon fillet instead of the steak, 1 cup crème fraîche instead of the peanuts and brown sugar, the juice and zest of 1 lemon instead of the fish sauce, and 1 bunch fresh dill (1 cup leaves and tender stems) for the herbs. Omit the chile. The fish will probably cook in about the same time as the steak; nick with a small knife to make sure the inside is no longer raw. Everything else stays the same.

Caramel Stir-Fried Beef and Green Beans

Beef braised in caramel flavored with fish sauce is a staple of Vietnamese cooking. The sauce can be streamlined for a quick stir-fried version, bubbling down to a sweet-salty coating for beef and green beans in minutes. Rice is the classic accompaniment, but I also like this over steamed broccoli, bok choy, or Asian greens like tatsoi or gai lan (Chinese broccoli). **Serves 4**

Ingredients

1 pound boneless beef sirloin, flank, or rib-eye steak

½ cup sugar

3 shallots

1 inch fresh ginger, or more to taste

1 fresh hot green or red chile (like Thai or serrano)

1 pound green beans

1 tablespoon fish sauce, or more to taste

Pepper

Several sprigs fresh cilantro

1 lime

☐ Prep · Cook

☐ Put the beef in the freezer.

1. Put ½ cup sugar in a large skillet over medium-low heat. Cook, shaking the pan occasionally, until the sugar becomes liquid and darkens slightly, 5 to 7 minutes. (Be sure to keep an eye on the skillet so the caramel doesn't burn while you prep the vegetables.)

   ☐ Trim, peel, and thinly slice the shallots.

   ☐ Peel 1 inch ginger. Trim the chile; seed it if you like. Chop the ginger and chile together.

   ☐ Trim the green beans.

2. As soon as the sugar begins to darken, remove the pan from the heat and carefully add 1 cup water and 1 tablespoon fish sauce. Stir in a big pinch of pepper and return the skillet to medium heat. It's okay if some of the caramel seizes up; scrape any hard bits into the liquid, where they will dissolve as you cook.

3. Add the shallots, ginger, chile, and green beans to the sauce. Cook, stirring occasionally, until the vegetables begin to soften, 3 to 5 minutes. Remove the pan from the heat.

   ☐ Remove the beef from the freezer and slice it against the grain as thinly as you can.

4. Return the skillet to medium heat and add the steak. Cook, stirring occasionally, until it's still a little pink at the center (or more well done if you like) and the caramel has thickened and coats the beef and green beans, about 3 minutes. Return the beans and aromatics to the skillet and toss to combine.

• recipe continues →

Caramel Stir-Fried Beef and Green Beans, continued

☐ Cut the tenderest stems from several cilantro sprigs but leave them whole.

☐ Cut the lime into wedges.

5. Taste and adjust the seasoning, adding more fish sauce if you like. Serve with cilantro and lime wedges.

Variations

Orange Caramel Stir-Fried Pork and Green Beans. Substitute boneless pork loin or sirloin for the beef and orange juice for the fish sauce. When you taste and adjust the seasoning in Step 5, add salt or soy sauce to taste.

Soy Caramel Stir-Fried Beef and Peppers. Substitute soy sauce for the fish sauce and green bell peppers for the green beans; after trimming, coring, and seeding, slice the peppers lengthwise into strips.

Caramel Stir-Fried Butternut Squash with Spicy Peanuts. Totally meat free. Instead of the beef and green beans, trim, peel, and seed about 2 pounds butternut squash and cut it into bite-sized chunks. Add it to the skillet in Step 3 and cook, stirring once in a while, until you can easily pierce it with a fork, 5 to 10 minutes. While the squash is cooking, chop 1 cup roasted peanuts with 1 or 2 fresh red chiles (like Thai or serrano); chop the cilantro. Toss the peanuts, chiles, and cilantro together and use that for garnish.

Steak and Vegetables with Chimichurri

Chimichurri, the tangy fresh herb sauce of Argentina, is best known as a sidekick for steak, but it's one of those things that's great with everything. So here's a recipe that shows how you can drizzle it on, well, everything. This is truly a one-dish meal, though you'll probably want some bread on the side for swooshing around on your plate. **Serves 4**

Ingredients

1 pound boneless beef sirloin, rib-eye, or strip steak (or steaks), about 1 inch thick

8 ounces Yukon Gold potatoes

1 large onion

2 red bell peppers

10 tablespoons olive oil, plus more as needed

Salt and pepper

2 bunches fresh parsley

1 bunch fresh cilantro

3 cloves garlic

2 tablespoons sherry vinegar

½ teaspoon red chile flakes, or to taste (optional)

▫ Prep · Cook

1. Turn the broiler to high; put the rack 4 inches from the heat.

   ▫ Blot the steak(s) dry with a paper towel.

   ▫ Peel the potatoes if you like and cut them crosswise into thin rounds.

   ▫ Trim, peel, and slice the onion into rounds.

   ▫ Trim, core, seed, and quarter the bell peppers.

2. Toss the vegetables with 2 tablespoons olive oil and sprinkle with salt and pepper. Spread them out in a single layer on a rimmed baking sheet. Put the steak(s) on another baking sheet or in a broiler-proof skillet and sprinkle with salt and pepper.

3. Broil the vegetables first, tossing with a spatula a couple times, until they're tender and browned in spots, 10 to 15 minutes.

   ▫ Strip 2 cups leaves from the parsley bunches. Pull 1 packed cup cilantro sprigs from the bunch.

   ▫ Peel 3 cloves garlic.

4. Put the herbs, garlic, ½ cup olive oil, 2 tablespoons sherry vinegar, ½ teaspoon red chile flakes if you're using them, and a sprinkle of salt and pepper in a food processor. Process until smooth, scraping down the sides as necessary. Taste and adjust the seasoning.

5. When the vegetables are done, remove the baking sheet from the broiler and slip the steak(s) under the heat. Cook, turning once, until the steak(s) are charred but still a bit pinker inside than you like, 3 to 8 minutes total.

6. Transfer the steak(s) to a cutting board. Transfer the vegetables to a platter. Pour the chimichurri into a serving bowl. Slice the steak(s) and serve with the vegetables and chimichurri to pass at the table.

● recipe continues →

Variations

Pork Chops and Vegetables with Chimichurri. Chops are untraditional—but excellent—with this sauce. Instead of the beef, use 4 center-cut bone-in pork chops, each about 1 inch thick. They will take a little longer to cook in Step 5; if you have room in your broiler, you can cook them at the same time as the vegetables. You want them firm but still a little pink inside, 10 to 15 minutes total, depending on their thickness. Everything else stays the same.

Chicken and Vegetables with Chimichurri. Substitute 1 pound boneless, skinless chicken thighs for the beef. They'll take 10 to 15 minutes total cooking time in Step 5; you want them browned in places and no longer pink inside. If you have room in your broiler, you can cook them at the same time as the vegetables.

Big Beans and Vegetables with Chimichurri. By "big" beans I mean large lima beans—sometimes known as "gigantes." Canned, they're commonly called "butter beans"; sometimes you see them frozen. There are more choices if you buy them dried and cook up a batch yourself (see page 505). All varieties are a wonderful alternative to meat in this recipe. Use 2 (15-ounce) cans or about 3½ cups cooked; rinse and drain them well. Before broiling in Step 5, toss with 1 tablespoon olive oil, sprinkle with salt, and spread them out in a single layer on a rimmed baking sheet. Broil, shaking the pan a couple times, until they're blistered and browned in spots, about 5 minutes.

Broiling and Maybe Some Grilling

Whether your fuel is gas, electric, or charcoal, the two cooking methods that put food in the most direct contact with a heat source are broiling or grilling. People tend to underutilize their broilers, so I encourage you to think of them as a grill flipped upside down. Here are some tips to make the most of these cooking methods.

Maximizing Your Broiler

With most ovens, you can control the speed at which food cooks by moving the rack closer to or farther away from the heat. Some broilers boast intense and powerful heat, while others are weak. One way to see what kind of firepower you're dealing with is to broil a slice of bread about 4 inches away from the heat. If the top turns crusty and dark brown in about a minute, your broiler is pretty powerful; if it takes 3 minutes or longer, you've got a wimpy one. I try to give time ranges to account for all kinds of broilers. If yours is strong, lean toward shorter cooking times; if it's weak, broil for longer or move the food closer to the heat.

The Broiler Pan

If your broiler is a drawer that pulls out from under your oven, it likely comes with a deep pan fitted with a top piece that drains fat into the bottom. Some people love them, but I prefer the larger surface area of shallower rimmed baking sheets.

Heating Broilers

No matter what kind of broiler you have, it's important to let it run for 5 minutes before you start cooking; this time allows the roof of the broiler and the inside air temperature to heat up, which enables faster and more even cooking. Generally, you should turn on the broiler when you start a recipe; that way by the time the food is ready to broil, the heat will be raring to go.

Controlling the Heat

Some broilers have heat settings "high" and "low" that you can control with the turn of a knob, but most don't. Even those that claim to often don't have any difference between them. The one fail-safe way to adjust the heat during broiling is to change the position of the rack. Say you're cooking vegetables that are getting singed on the outside but are still crunchy in the middle: Move them farther away from the heat. Or if a steak isn't getting the kind of char you want, move it closer.

If a food is charring too quickly, another option is to cover the pan loosely with foil, which will slow the browning while continuing to cook the food. Unlike an oven, a broiler doesn't lose most of its effectiveness when you open the door, so don't be shy about checking on the progress of your food often and turning food or adjusting the rack position as needed.

Long-Distance Versus Regular Broiling

Most foods that you're going to broil—tender vegetables and seafood, or steaks, chops, or chicken pieces an inch or less thick—benefit from being positioned close to the heat, about 4 inches away.

Then there's something I call "long-distance broiling," which means putting the rack farther away from the heat—about 6 inches—so that food cooks more slowly. This is best for thicker pieces of meat or vegetables that take longer to cook. If you put them too close to the heat, they'll burn on the outside before cooking through in the middle. While it's obviously not as fast as regular broiling, it is a wonderful and quicker alternative to roasting.

Moving the Kitchen Outside

The obvious difference between broiling and grilling is that the broiler is in your kitchen, and—for most home cooks at least—the grill is outside. The flow of prepping and cooking these recipes is much smoother when you don't have to run back and forth from the kitchen to the backyard. But there are times you want to cook outside. So let's talk logistics.

Gas Grilling

Broilers and gas grills are virtually interchangeable when it comes to heating and cooking times, which is why a handful of recipes here give you the option of either. If you're lucky enough to have a gas grill positioned right outside of your kitchen—or if you're cooking with a friend and can share tasks—then use it in place of the broiler whenever you like, even if it's not specified as an option. Since I'm not counting on that, any recipe here that calls for grilling takes those outside trips into account.

Charcoal Grilling

Grilling over charcoal provides deeper flavor and better char than grilling over gas, and the cooking itself is quick. But charcoal grilling, overall, is too slow to call "fast," simply because it takes so much time to get the coals going. However, if you're willing to add a little extra time to fire up a charcoal grill, you can use one for any of the grilling—or broiling—recipes in this book.

Multitasking

If you're into cooking outdoors big-time, then you'll want to start using the grill as a stove. Nothing is stopping you from bringing out your pots and pans to make sauces and sides. (Just be aware that they can sometimes blacken, so cast iron or carbon steel is generally the best bet.) In fact, you can use these recipes to give it a try. Move the cutting board outside too if you have some extra workspace.

WHAT ABOUT A GRILL PAN?

Yes, you can get grill marks and excellent searing with a good grill pan. Some cover two burners, and you'll be able to use them exactly the same way as described in the recipes for grilling directly over a flame. If your pan only covers one burner, then you might need to cook something in the grill pan and something under the broiler.

To use a grill pan instead of a broiler, just remember the heat will be coming from the bottom, so shift the directions in the recipes accordingly. Same deal as in the previous paragraph applies in terms of whether you'll be able to fit everything into a single grill pan.

Flank Steak and Cherry Tomatoes with Soy Drizzle

Soy sauce is a classic marinade for steak, and its savoriness—or umami—also pairs wonderfully with sweet cherry tomatoes. In our time frame, however, a soy marinade before cooking won't have much impact. Instead, let's "marinate" the meat and vegetables after cooking with a quick drizzle sauce. Warm bread or spaghetti tossed with olive oil and red chile flakes will easily round out the meal. **Serves 4**

Ingredients

2 pints ripe cherry tomatoes

2 tablespoons good-quality vegetable oil

Salt and pepper

1 pound flank steak

3 cloves garlic

1 inch fresh ginger

⅓ cup soy sauce

1 tablespoon sesame oil

2 scallions

▢ Prep · Cook

1. Turn the broiler to high; put the rack 4 inches from the heat. Put a large skillet over high heat. (Beware: There's going to be some smoking.)

   ▢ Trim any stems from the cherry tomatoes if necessary. Put them on a rimmed baking sheet, toss with 1 tablespoon vegetable oil, and sprinkle with a little salt and pepper.

   ▢ Cut the steak in half if necessary to fit it in the skillet.

2. Sprinkle the bottom of the skillet with some salt and add the steak. Cook undisturbed until it browns and releases easily from the pan, 3 to 5 minutes. Pick it up with tongs or a fork over the pan, swirl in 1 tablespoon vegetable oil, and put the uncooked side of the steak into the hot oil. Cook until it's one stage pinker inside than you ultimately want it; this could be as little as 1 minute or up to 4. Transfer the steak to a cutting board. Remove the skillet from the heat.

3. Put the baking sheet with the tomatoes under the broiler and cook, shaking the pan occasionally, until they're charred in spots and starting to burst, 4 to 6 minutes.

   ▢ Peel 3 cloves garlic and 1 inch ginger; chop them together.

4. To make the drizzle sauce, put the garlic and ginger in the skillet used for cooking the steak over medium heat. Add a couple tablespoons water and scrape up any browned bits until the water evaporates. Add ⅓ cup soy sauce, another ½ cup water, and 1 tablespoon sesame oil. Warm the sauce, stirring occasionally, until it just starts bubbling; turn off the heat.

   ▢ Trim and chop the scallions.

5. When the tomatoes are ready, transfer them to a platter with a slotted spoon. Carefully pour any pan drippings into the drizzle sauce. Taste the sauce and add salt and pepper if you like.

6. Slice the steak against the grain as thickly as you'd like and nestle the slices next to the tomatoes. Pour any accumulated drippings over the steak. Garnish with scallions and serve with drizzle sauce.

Variations

Flank Steak and Cherry Tomatoes with Mustard Drizzle. Omit the ginger. Instead of the soy sauce and sesame oil, make the drizzle sauce with 2 tablespoons red wine vinegar, 2 tablespoons Dijon mustard, ½ cup water, and 1 tablespoon olive oil.

Flank Steak and Green Beans with Soy Drizzle. Instead of the tomatoes, trim 1 pound green beans but leave them whole. Toss, season, and broil as described in Step 3.

Flank Steak and Asparagus with Lemon Drizzle. Omit the ginger. Instead of the tomatoes, trim 1 pound asparagus. Toss, season, and broil as described in Step 3. Instead of the soy sauce and sesame oil, whisk together the zest and juice from 1 lemon with 2 tablespoons mayonnaise, ½ cup water, and 1 tablespoon olive oil.

Beef and Mushroom Kebabs with Spicy Pepita Sauce

Chipotle–pumpkin seed sauce adds kick to these skewers and helps the beef char beautifully in the broiler. To speed things up even more, you can always skip the skewers and just spread the mushrooms—then the beef—on a baking sheet. Tuck into warm corn tortillas for tacos; serve with rice or beans, tortilla chips, and salsa; or with a big salad. **Serves 4**

Ingredients

½ pound button or cremini mushrooms

1 pound boneless beef sirloin

4 tablespoons good-quality vegetable oil

Salt and pepper

1 clove garlic

1 cup pepitas (hulled green pumpkin seeds)

1 large or 2 small bunches fresh cilantro

2 limes

1 or 2 canned chipotle chiles with some of their adobo, or more to taste

2 teaspoons sesame oil

□ Prep · Cook

☐ If you're using wooden skewers, soak 8 in water.

1. Turn the broiler to high; put the rack 4 inches from the heat.

   ☐ Trim the mushrooms, leaving them whole.

   ☐ Cut the beef into 1½-inch chunks.

2. Thread the mushrooms on 3 or 4 skewers and the beef on 3 or 4 separate skewers; the goal is to leave enough space around the pieces to brown them well. Coat with 2 tablespoons vegetable oil and sprinkle with salt and pepper.

3. Put just the mushroom kebabs on a rimmed baking sheet under the broiler and cook, turning as necessary, until they are tender and browned in places, 10 to 15 minutes.

   ☐ Peel 1 clove garlic and put it in a food processor or blender.

4. Put the pepitas in a large skillet over medium heat. Cook, shaking the skillet frequently, until they brown in spots and you hear them start to pop, 3 to 5 minutes. Remove the skillet from the heat.

5. Put the beef kebabs on the baking sheet next to the mushrooms and broil, turning the kebabs once or twice, until the mushrooms are browned on all sides and the beef is cooked to your liking; cut into a piece of beef to peek inside after about 5 minutes. When you check, you can remove any mushroom kebabs that are ready and let the others keep cooking until all are done, 2 or 3 minutes more.

   ☐ Pull about 2 cups sprigs from the cilantro bunch.

   ☐ Halve 1 lime; cut the other lime into wedges.

• recipe continues →

6. Add the pepitas and the cilantro sprigs to the garlic in the blender or food processor along with 1 or 2 (or more) chipotle chiles and some adobo, 2 tablespoons vegetable oil, 2 teaspoons sesame oil, ½ cup water, and a sprinkle of salt and pepper. Squeeze in the juice from the lime. Purée, stopping to scrape down the sides once or twice, until a sauce forms; add more water a tablespoon at a time until the sauce is spoonable. Taste and adjust the seasoning.

7. When all the kebabs are ready, remove the meat and vegetables if you'd like and serve with the sauce and lime wedges on the side.

Variations

Beef and Jícama Kebabs with Spicy Pepita Sauce. Instead of the mushrooms, peel 1 pound jícama and cut into 1-inch chunks. Working with the tip of the skewer pointing down into each piece (as opposed to holding them in your hand), carefully thread the jícama onto skewers. Thread the beef onto others and proceed with the recipe. The jícama will cook a couple minutes faster than the mushrooms.

Pork and Mushroom Kebabs with Spicy Pepita Sauce. Instead of beef, use 1 pound boneless pork loin or sirloin chops. Figure they will take about 5 minutes longer to cook than the beef. Everything else stays the same.

Hearty Bread and Mushroom Kebabs with Spicy Pepita Sauce. You'd be amazed how satisfying this vegan meal is. Instead of the beef, cut about 1 pound whole grain bread into 1-inch chunks (crust and all). Thread them on separate skewers from the mushrooms and drizzle with 2 to 3 tablespoons olive oil. Broil them as described in Step 5, only watch them closely to make sure the bread doesn't burn.

The Better Burger

To me, a burger is a real treat, so when I have one, it's got to be good. If there's one dish that rewards spending the time to grind your own beef, this is it. The no-frills recipe here benefits from a side or two, like a green salad or steamed vegetable. You can of course use store-bought ground meat to save several minutes and extra cleanup. Just be sure to get a kind that has at least 10 percent fat in it to keep the burgers juicy. The packages are usually labeled now in reference to what percent "lean" the meat is, so it's easy to know. **Serves 4**

Ingredients

Good-quality vegetable oil as needed

1½ pounds boneless beef sirloin (not too lean) or chuck

Salt and pepper

Lettuce, tomato, onion, and pickles (optional)

Condiments of your choice

4 hamburger buns

☐ Prep · **Cook**

1. Prepare a charcoal or gas grill for direct cooking over medium heat or put a large skillet or grill pan on the stove over low heat. Make sure the grill grates are clean and oiled or if you're using a pan, that it's well seasoned. If not, add a thin film of good-quality vegetable oil.

   ☐ Cut the beef into chunks; put them in the food processor.

   ☐ Pulse until the beef is coarsely ground; transfer to a bowl and sprinkle with salt and pepper.

2. With gentle and light handling, shape the beef into 4 patties about 1 inch thick.

3. If you're cooking in a skillet or grill pan, raise the heat to medium-high. Grill or pan-cook the burgers, turning once, until they're cooked as you like—3 minutes per side for very rare and another minute per side for each increasing stage of doneness. Nick the thickest part with a small knife to check inside.

   ☐ Get the toppings and condiments ready.

4. Split the buns and toast them if you'd like. Remove the burgers from the grill or pan as they're ready. Serve on the buns with whatever toppings and condiments you like.

● recipe continues →

• **The Better Burger,** continued

Variations

The Better Pork and Scallion Burger. Substitute boneless pork shoulder for the beef and add ¼ cup chopped scallions along with the salt and pepper before shaping into patties. Cook until the pork is just cooked through and no longer pink inside, about 5 minutes per side.

The Better Lamb and Red Onion Burger. Most people like their lamb less rare than beef so figure another 2 to 3 minutes on the cooking times in the main recipe. Substitute boneless lamb shoulder for the beef and add ¼ cup chopped red onion along with the meat to the food processor. Thick full-fat Greek yogurt is a delicious smear for the buns, or tuck these into pita wraps.

The Better Cheeseburger. Grated or thinly sliced aged cheddar, thick slabs of fresh mozzarella, coarsely crumbled blue cheese—all are fair game. Top each burger with about 1 ounce cheese (more or less to taste) after you flip them. The surface that you put the cheese on needs to be quite hot so the cheese melts before the burgers overcook. So cover the grill; or if you're using a skillet, make them diner style: Top with cheese, put a small splash of water in the skillet, then quickly put a lid on top. The steam melts the cheese in a flash.

Sloppy Joes

An excellent sloppy joe is a game changer: homemade meat sauce, open-face on a bun—or as the variations show, spooned over other components—with way more vegetables than you're probably used to. And the fast cooking time keeps the flavors fresh and bright. If you want to speed things up or brown the beef darker, cook it in a separate skillet with the spices and garlic while the vegetables soften; then combine them and proceed from Step 4. Either way it's a knife-and-fork adventure. Green Salad (page 487) is a natural side dish. There are two vegan options among the variations, which also give you some ideas about serving the joes other ways besides on buns. **Serves 4**

Ingredients

2 tablespoons olive oil

1 onion

2 celery stalks

8 ounces zucchini (1 medium)

2 bell peppers (any color)

3 cloves garlic

8 ounces ground beef

1 teaspoon chili powder

1 teaspoon ground cumin

Salt and pepper

1 (15-ounce) can crushed tomatoes

¼ cup ketchup

1 teaspoon Worcestershire sauce, or more to taste

1 teaspoon soy sauce

4 hamburger buns

▫ Prep · Cook

1. Put 2 tablespoons olive oil in a large skillet or large pot over medium-high heat.

   ▫ Trim, peel, and chop the onion; add it to the skillet.

   ▫ Trim and chop 2 celery stalks and the zucchini; add them to the skillet.

   ▫ Trim, core, seed, and chop the bell peppers; add them to the skillet.

2. Cook, stirring occasionally, until the vegetables soften, 5 to 10 minutes.

   ▫ Peel and mince 3 cloves garlic.

3. When the vegetables are soft, add the garlic, beef, 1 teaspoon chili powder, 1 teaspoon ground cumin, and a sprinkle of salt and pepper. Cook, stirring occasionally, until the meat loses its pink color, 5 to 10 minutes.

4. Stir in the tomatoes, ¼ cup ketchup, 1 teaspoon Worcestershire, and 1 teaspoon soy sauce. Bring the mixture to a steady bubble, and cook, stirring occasionally, until it is thick and the flavors come together, 5 to 10 minutes.

   ▫ Split the buns; toast them if you like.

5. Taste and adjust the seasoning. Serve open-face on the split buns.

• recipe continues →

● Sloppy Joes, continued

Variations

Sloppy Rice Bowl. Start by getting a pot of rice going. Substitute ground pork for the beef; 1 bunch scallions for the onion; 1 inch fresh ginger, chopped, for the chili powder; 1 jalapeño chile, trimmed and chopped, for the ground cumin; ¼ cup hoisin sauce for the ketchup; and an extra 1 or 2 teaspoons soy sauce for the Worcestershire. Serve a scoop of the meat and vegetable mixture over a bowl of rice. Garnish with chopped cilantro if you like.

Sloppy Pita. Substitute white or whole wheat pita breads for the buns. Use red onion, ½ cup chopped dried apricots instead of the celery, ground lamb instead of the beef, 1 teaspoon ground coriander and ½ teaspoon ground cinnamon instead of the chili powder, and 2 teaspoons chopped fresh oregano or 1 teaspoon dried instead of the Worcestershire and soy sauce. If you have harissa, replace 2 tablespoons of the ketchup with it. Spoon the saucy meat and vegetables over the pita and garnish with chopped parsley if you like.

Sloppy Spaghetti. Start by boiling spaghetti until just tender, and reserve about 1 cup cooking water. When the vegetables and meat are ready in Step 4, toss them with the spaghetti and enough of the reserved cooking water to keep everything saucy. Wouldn't hurt to toss ½ cup or so grated Parmesan cheese in there too.

Sloppy Beans. Easy to turn this vegan. Instead of the meat, drain 3½ cups cooked or canned kidney or pinto beans (two 15-ounce cans). Mash them with a fork or potato masher before beginning the recipe until they're broken up, and continue. If the pan starts to look dry while cooking them with the vegetables in Step 3, add a little more olive oil.

Sloppy Tempeh. Another vegan approach. Substitute 8 ounces tempeh for the ground beef. Crumble it into the skillet with the vegetables in Step 3, adding more olive oil to prevent sticking.

Skillet Meat Loaf

Flattening out meat loaf to cook it in a skillet reduces cooking time and also dramatically increases the surface area to maximize crunch. I'll go ahead and say it: faster, better, revolutionary. Serve with Dressed Cooked Vegetables (page 487) or Steamed Vegetables (page 498) and warm bread or rolls. Or make a batch of Skin-On Mashed Potatoes (page 503). And the leftovers make a couple terrific sandwiches. **Serves 4, with leftovers**

Ingredients

1 tablespoon olive oil

1 cup bread crumbs

½ cup milk

1 pound ground beef

1 pound ground pork

Salt and pepper

2 ounces Parmesan cheese (½ cup grated)

1 clove garlic

1 egg

¼ cup ketchup

▫ Prep · **Cook**

1. Heat the oven to 425°F. Pour 1 tablespoon olive oil into a large skillet (preferably cast iron) and put it in the oven to heat while you prepare the meat loaf.

2. Combine 1 cup bread crumbs, ½ cup milk, the ground beef, ground pork, and a sprinkle of salt and pepper in a large bowl.

    ▫ Grate ½ cup Parmesan and add to the bowl. Peel and chop 1 clove garlic and add to the bowl.

    ▫ Crack the egg into the bowl.

    ▫ Gently mix the ingredients together with your hands; avoid over-handling.

3. When the skillet is hot, carefully transfer the mixture into the pan with a spoon or spatula, gently pressing down so the meat loaf has an even thickness. Spread ¼ cup ketchup on top.

4. Bake until the loaf is firm, 15 to 20 minutes; a quick-read thermometer inserted into the center should read 160°F.

5. Turn the broiler to high and put the rack 4 inches from the heat. Move up the meat loaf and broil until the top is brown and crisp, 2 to 5 minutes.

6. Cut into wedges and serve hot, warm, or at room temperature.

● recipe continues →

Variations

Skillet BBQ Meat Loaf. Omit the Parmesan cheese or replace it with grated Jack cheese. Drizzle the top with barbecue sauce instead of ketchup.

Skillet Miso Meat Loaf. Omit the ketchup. Substitute ½ cup any miso for the Parmesan (remembering that lighter is milder than red and brown) and 1 inch fresh ginger, peeled and chopped, for the garlic.

Skillet Chicken Meat Loaf with Salsa. Any kind of cooked or jarred salsa is good, but I especially like a green tomatillo-chile salsa here. Substitute ground chicken for the beef and pork and crumbled queso fresco for the Parmesan. Spread ½ cup salsa over the top of the meat loaf.

Stir-Fried Beef and Broccoli

I never get tired of this combination, especially when I skew the balance toward the broccoli and cook it a tad beyond crisp-tender. You'll be amazed how the meat flavors the broccoli and vice versa, while they both retain every bit of their uniqueness. Serve over rice or quinoa, or toss with egg noodles or linguine. **Serves 4**

Ingredients

1 pound boneless beef sirloin, flank, or rib-eye steak

4 tablespoons good-quality vegetable oil

Salt and pepper

1 inch fresh ginger

2 cloves garlic

1 medium head broccoli (1 to 1½ pounds)

4 scallions

1 tablespoon sesame oil

2 tablespoons hoisin sauce

□ Prep · Cook

1. Put a large skillet over high heat.

   □ Slice the beef against the grain as thinly as you can; better to have it shred a little than be too thick.

2. Put 2 tablespoons vegetable oil into the skillet and immediately add the beef; sprinkle with salt and pepper. Cook undisturbed until it browns and releases from the pan, about 3 minutes. Then stir occasionally until it's more browned but still a little rare in places, just another minute or two. Transfer the meat to a plate with a slotted spoon. Reduce the heat under the skillet to medium-high.

3. Add ¼ cup water to the skillet and scrape up any browned bits as it bubbles; pour the pan juices into a small bowl. Return the skillet to medium-high heat.

   □ Peel 1 inch ginger and 2 cloves garlic; mince them together.

   □ Trim the broccoli and break or chop it into small florets; cut the stems into thin coins or sticks.

4. Add 2 tablespoons vegetable oil to the skillet. Add the broccoli and cook, stirring occasionally, until it browns slightly, 3 to 5 minutes. Add the ginger and garlic. Cook, stirring, until fragrant, about a minute. Add ¼ cup water and the reserved beef juices, cover the skillet, and cook until the broccoli is as tender as you like it, another 3 to 5 minutes.

   □ Trim and chop the scallions.

5. Return the beef to the skillet along with the scallions, 1 tablespoon sesame oil, and 2 tablespoons hoisin sauce.

6. Toss to coat everything with the sauce and heat the beef through. Taste and adjust the seasoning, and serve.

● recipe continues →

Variations

Stir-Fried Beef and Carrots with Chiles. Substitute carrots for the broccoli. After trimming and peeling, slice them into coins about ¼ inch thick. Add 1 or 2 jalapeño chiles, trimmed and chopped, along with the ginger and garlic.

Stir-Fried Beef and Eggplant. Substitute eggplant (large globes or the small varieties) for the broccoli. After trimming, cut into 1-inch chunks. In Step 3, increase the water to ½ cup and cook until fully tender, an extra 3 minutes or so.

Stir-Fried Chicken and Celery. Substitute 1 pound boneless, skinless chicken thighs for the beef and 1 celery heart (several stalks with leaves) for the broccoli. Trim the celery, reserving the leaves and tender stalks at the center; slice the remaining stalks into 1-inch pieces at an angle. Chop the reserved leaves and stalks for garnish. The chicken will take a little longer to cook in Step 2.

WOK OR SKILLET?

Since most home cooks stir-fry in a pan rather than a wok, I recommend a heavy-bottomed 12-inch skillet for the recipes in this book. In other words, avoid aluminum and enameled metal alloys in favor of carbon steel, stainless steel with a bonded core bottom, or even cast iron. All will hold and distribute heat pretty well and, since you're usually working in batches anyway and stirring almost constantly, searing shouldn't be an issue. If you've got a professional-style wok setup or a flat-bottom wok you love, then of course go ahead and use it.

Stir-Fried Pork with Edamame and Scallions

Edamame add vibrant color and heft to stir-fries. Add them right out of the freezer bag toward the end of cooking with a little water, and suddenly you have a flavorful pan sauce. Serve over salad greens or steamed or microwaved bok choy, or wrap into warm flour tortillas or other flatbread. **Serves 4**

Ingredients

3 tablespoons good-quality vegetable oil

1 pound boneless pork loin or sirloin chops

Salt and pepper

1 inch fresh ginger

2 cloves garlic

4 scallions

2 cups frozen shelled edamame

1 lemon

1 tablespoon soy sauce, or more to taste

Prep · Cook

1. Put 2 tablespoons vegetable oil in a large skillet over medium-high heat.

   ☐ Slice the pork against the grain as thinly as you can; better to have it shred a little than be too thick.

2. Add the pork to the skillet, sprinkle with salt and pepper, and cook undisturbed until it browns and releases easily, about 3 minutes. Then cook, stirring occasionally, until it's only a little pink in places, another couple minutes.

   ☐ Peel 1 inch ginger and 2 cloves garlic; chop them together.

   ☐ Trim and chop the scallions, keeping the white and light green bottoms separate from the dark green tops.

3. Add the ginger, garlic, and scallion bottoms to the pork. Cook, stirring, until fragrant, about a minute. Transfer the pork mixture to a plate with a slotted spoon.

4. Add 1 tablespoon vegetable oil to the skillet along with 2 cups edamame, ¼ cup water, and a sprinkle of salt and pepper. Increase the heat to high and cook, stirring occasionally, until the beans are tender and heated through, about 3 minutes.

   ☐ Halve the lemon.

5. Squeeze in the juice from the lemon through a strainer or your fingers to catch the seeds and add 1 tablespoon soy sauce; toss to coat. Return the pork to the skillet along with any juices and stir in the scallion tops. Taste and adjust the seasoning, and serve.

• recipe continues →

Variations

Stir-Fried Pork and Black Beans. Instead of scallions, trim and chop 1 medium red onion; add it all in Step 3. Use 1½ cups drained cooked or canned black beans (one 15-ounce can) instead of the edamame and cider vinegar instead of the lemon and soy sauce. Garnish with cilantro sprigs.

Stir-Fried Pork and Corn. Awesome finished with avocado cubes and chopped cilantro. Omit the soy sauce. Substitute 1 chopped poblano chile for the ginger, frozen or fresh corn kernels for the edamame, and lime for the lemon.

Stir-Fried Pork with Peas and Shallots. Substitute olive oil for the vegetable oil and frozen peas for the edamame. Instead of the garlic, ginger, and scallions, peel and thinly slice 3 shallots; add them to the skillet with the pork in Step 2. Keep the lemon and season the sauce with 1 tablespoon Dijon mustard instead of the soy sauce.

Seared Pork Chops with Apples and Onions

Pork chops, apples, and onions rank way up there among my favorite flavor combinations, especially for fall or winter. So why not extend the idea into other seasons by using different fruit? This is a good time for a relatively thin bone-in cut so the meat doesn't dry out. All you need on the side is warm bread, though a salad is always welcome. **Serves 4**

Ingredients

2 tablespoons olive oil

4 bone-in pork chops
(about 1 inch thick, 1½ to
2 pounds total)

Salt and pepper

1 pound tart apples
(like Honeycrisp or Jonagold)

1 large yellow onion

½ cup chicken stock or water,
plus more as needed

1 tablespoon butter

Prep · Cook

1. Put 2 tablespoons olive oil in a large skillet over medium-high heat.

   ☐ Pat the pork chops dry with a towel and sprinkle with salt and pepper.

2. When the oil is hot, add the chops. Cook undisturbed until the chops brown and release from the pan, 3 to 5 minutes. Turn and cook on the other side. You want them to be still pink inside; nick with a small knife so you can peek.

   ☐ Core and slice the apples. (No need to peel them unless you really want to.)

   ☐ Trim, peel, halve, and slice the onion.

3. When the chops are browned but still pink inside, transfer them to a plate. Add the apples and onion to the skillet along with ½ cup stock or water. Sprinkle with salt and pepper and cook, scraping up any browned bits from the bottom of the pan. Adjust the heat so the mixture bubbles steadily but gently.

4. Nestle the chops into the apples and onions and pour in any accumulated juices from the plate. Cover the skillet and cook until the chops are tender and cooked through, 5 to 10 minutes.

5. When the chops are ready, transfer them to a platter. If the apples and onions are dry, add a splash of stock or water to make them slightly more saucy, then stir in 1 tablespoon butter. Taste and adjust the seasoning. Spoon the apples and onions on top of the pork and serve.

● recipe continues →

Variations

Seared Pork Chops with Apricots and Sweet Onion. Substitute fresh apricots for the apples and sweet onion (like Vidalia or Walla Walla) for the yellow. Pit the apricots and slice them thinly. Everything else stays the same.

Seared Pork Chops with Plums and Red Onion. Substitute any kind of plum for the apples and red onion for the yellow. Pit the plums and slice them thinly. Everything else stays the same.

Seared Pork Chops with Oranges and Leeks. Substitute oranges or any kind of winter citrus (like satsumas, tangerines, or mandarins) for the apples. Peel and chop them into bite-sized chunks, removing any seeds as you go. Instead of the onion, use 1 large or 2 medium leeks. Trim the root ends and the darkest green tops, then slice them crosswise about 1 inch thick, put them in a colander, and rinse them well under cold water. Everything else stays the same.

BBQ Baby Back Ribs

Baby back ribs are the meaty, small, curved bones from one side of the pork loin. They cook much faster than spareribs, which run along the other side and often have an extra flap of meat still attached. Sometimes you might only find baby back ribs untrimmed; the directions will help you if that's the case or just ask the butcher at the meat counter to help. A long-distance run under the broiler yields crusty, saucy, finger-licking barbecue in a hurry. Warm soft rolls, assorted pickles, and Chopped Salad or Dressed Cooked Vegetables (page 487) turn this main dish into a feast. **Serves 4**

Ingredients

2 to 3 pounds baby back ribs (1 large slab)

Salt

1 tablespoon sugar

2 teaspoons ground cumin

Pepper

5 teaspoons chili powder

1 tablespoon smoked paprika

2 cloves garlic

1 cup ketchup

¼ cup red wine or water

2 tablespoons red wine vinegar

1 teaspoon soy sauce

☐ Prep · **Cook**

1. Turn the broiler to high; put the rack 6 inches from the heat.

   ☐ If the ribs still have an extra flap of meat on one side, carefully run a small sharp knife between it and the bones, working away from you. As you cut, pull away the flap to separate it; freeze or refrigerate the meat for a stir-fry.

   ☐ Combine 1½ teaspoons salt, 1 tablespoon sugar, 2 teaspoons ground cumin, 1 teaspoon pepper, 2 teaspoons chili powder, and 1 tablespoon smoked paprika in a small bowl.

2. Rub the spice mixture all over the ribs; place them on a rimmed baking sheet. Broil, turning once, until both sides are browned, 10 to 15 minutes.

   ☐ Chop 2 cloves garlic; put them in a medium saucepan.

3. Add 1 cup ketchup to the saucepan along with ¼ cup red wine or water, 2 tablespoons vinegar, 1 teaspoon soy sauce, 1 tablespoon chili powder, and a sprinkle of salt and pepper. Bring to a simmer and cook, stirring occasionally, while the ribs broil.

4. Set aside half the barbecue sauce in a small bowl for serving. When the ribs are browned on both sides, start basting with the sauce in the saucepan. Broil, turning a couple times, until the exterior is caramelized and the inside is no longer pink at the bone, 5 to 10 minutes.

5. Cut the slabs into portions or individual ribs if you prefer and serve with the remaining sauce on the side.

● recipe continues →

Variations

BBQ Ginger-Hoisin Baby Back Ribs. Substitute five-spice powder for the paprika, ½ cup hoisin sauce for ½ cup of the ketchup, rice vinegar for the wine vinegar, and 2 tablespoons chopped fresh ginger for the garlic. Everything else stays the same.

BBQ Maple-Dijon Baby Back Ribs. Replace ½ cup of the ketchup with ¼ cup each Dijon mustard and maple syrup.

BBQ Tofu. Use the seasonings and sauce in the main recipe or either of the first two variations to make this go-to plant-based barbecue main dish or snack. Instead of the ribs, use 2 bricks firm tofu (14 to 16 ounces each). Turn a brick onto one side so that the widest sides are perpendicular to the cutting board and cut the brick in half. Cut each half crosswise into planks about ½ inch thick. Repeat with the other brick. Grease the baking sheet with 2 tablespoons good-quality vegetable oil, arrange the tofu in a single layer, then rub the tops with a little more oil before rubbing in the spice mixture. Cook and sauce as directed.

Cumin-Rubbed Pork with Mangoes

Pork tenderloin is a perfect cut for this kind of broiling because the outside browns in the same time it takes to cook through; a generous rub of cumin creates a little crust. And while all that is going on, you have time to prepare a mango salsa you'll warm in the same skillet.
Serves 4

Ingredients

1 tablespoon ground cumin

Salt and pepper

3 tablespoons good-quality vegetable oil

1 pork tenderloin (1 to 1½ pounds)

2 mangoes

1 small red onion

1 small bunch fresh cilantro

2 limes

☐ Prep · **Cook**

1. Turn the broiler to high; put the rack 6 inches from the heat.

   ☐ Combine 1 tablespoon ground cumin with a sprinkle of salt and pepper in a small bowl.

2. Drizzle 2 tablespoons vegetable oil all over the tenderloin and sprinkle with the spice mixture; rub to coat the meat all over. Put the tenderloin in a large broiler-proof skillet and broil, rolling it once in a while, until browned all over and slightly pink inside, 10 to 15 minutes. Nick with a small knife at the thickest part to check.

   ☐ Peel, pit, and chop the mangoes into ½-inch chunks.

   ☐ Trim, peel, and chop the onion.

   ☐ Chop ½ cup cilantro tender stems and leaves.

   ☐ Halve the limes.

3. When the pork is done, transfer it to a cutting board and tent with foil.

4. Carefully move the hot skillet to the stove, add 1 tablespoon vegetable oil, and turn the heat to medium-high. Add the mango and onion and sprinkle with salt and pepper. Cook, stirring once or twice, until they begin to soften, 3 to 5 minutes.

5. Squeeze in the lime juice and add the accumulated meat juices from the cutting board to the salsa. Remove from the heat. Stir in the cilantro. Taste and adjust the seasoning.

6. Slice the pork crosswise as thick as you'd like and serve with the salsa on the side.

Pork and Zucchini with Fresh Mint

An assertive yogurt marinade gives chunks of pork and zucchini plenty of punch before broiling—no skewers necessary, though you certainly can thread the pieces to make kebabs if you like. There's minimal checking and turning, so use the downtime to make a quick side, toasted pita, or start rice or orzo before beginning the recipe. **Serves 4**

Ingredients

2 lemons

1 small bunch fresh mint

3 cloves garlic

½ cup Greek yogurt

¼ cup olive oil, plus more for drizzling

¼ cup red wine

1 tablespoon dried oregano

Salt and pepper

1 pound zucchini

1 pork tenderloin (1 to 1½ pounds)

Several sprigs fresh parsley

▢ Prep · Cook

1. Turn the broiler to high; put the rack 4 inches from the heat.

   ▢ Halve one of the lemons; squeeze the juice into a medium bowl through a strainer or your fingers to catch the seeds.

   ▢ Chop ½ cup mint leaves and add them to the bowl.

   ▢ Peel and mince 3 cloves garlic; add them to the bowl.

2. Add ½ cup Greek yogurt, ¼ cup olive oil, ¼ cup red wine, 1 tablespoon dried oregano, and a sprinkle of salt and pepper to the bowl. Whisk to combine, then put half the marinade in another medium bowl.

   ▢ Trim the zucchini, cut it crosswise into slices about 1 inch thick, and add it to one bowl.

   ▢ Slice the pork tenderloin crosswise into 12 pieces (about ½ inch thick) and add it to the other bowl.

3. Toss the zucchini in the marinade, then transfer to one half of a rimmed baking sheet, leaving the excess marinade in the bowl. Broil until sizzling, about 2 minutes.

4. Carefully remove the baking sheet and add the pork to the other half. Discard any remaining marinade. Cook, turning everything once, until the zucchini is tender and the pork is browned in places and just cooked through, 5 to 10 minutes. Cut into a piece to check; it should be slightly pink at the thickest part.

   ▢ Strip the leaves from several parsley sprigs and chop.

   ▢ Cut the other lemon into 8 wedges.

5. Transfer the pork and zucchini to a platter. Drizzle with a little more oil if you like, garnish with parsley and lemon wedges, and serve.

Five-Spice Pork Meatballs with Bok Choy

Grinding your own meat doesn't seem like a shortcut, but once the food processor is in use, you can use it for everything—no mincing by hand—and you only have to clean it once. Most important: Be sure your chops have a little fat on 'em or the meatballs will be dry. **Serves 4**

Ingredients

4 tablespoons good-quality vegetable oil

1 large head bok choy (1½ pounds)

2 scallions

1 inch fresh ginger

Several sprigs fresh cilantro

Salt and pepper

1 pound boneless pork loin or sirloin chops

1 teaspoon five-spice powder

½ cup bread crumbs

1 egg

Soy sauce for serving

◻ Prep · **Cook**

1. Put 2 tablespoons vegetable oil in a large skillet over medium-high heat.

   ◻ Trim the bok choy; cut the leaves into wide ribbons and thinly slice the stems, keeping them separate.

2. Add the bok choy stems to the skillet and cook, stirring occasionally, until they start to soften, 3 to 5 minutes.

   ◻ Trim and chop the scallions.

   ◻ Peel and chop 1 inch ginger.

   ◻ Chop the tender stems and leaves from several cilantro sprigs.

3. When the bok choy stems soften, add the leaves to the skillet and sprinkle with salt and pepper. Cook, stirring occasionally, until they also soften and the stems are nearly tender but still have some crunch, about 3 minutes.

   ◻ Cut the pork into 2-inch chunks.

4. When the bok choy is done, transfer it to a platter and cover to keep warm. Remove the skillet from the heat and wipe it out.

5. Put the scallions, ginger, and cilantro in a food processor and pulse until finely chopped. Add the pork, 1 teaspoon five-spice powder, and ½ cup bread crumbs, and crack in the egg. Sprinkle with salt and pepper. Pulse, scraping down the sides of the bowl as necessary, until the pork is ground and the mixture is combined but not puréed.

6. Add 2 tablespoons vegetable oil to the skillet and return it to medium-high heat.

7. Use 2 spoons to shape meatballs; drop them into the skillet as you go. Cook, turning occasionally and adjusting the heat so they sizzle without burning, until they are browned all over and no longer pink inside, 8 to 10 minutes. Serve with the bok choy, passing soy sauce at the table.

Seared Ham Steak with Maple-Glazed Beets

Ham steaks are better and easier to find than they were when I wrote the first edition, and they're a great addition to your fast-cooking pantry. Since they're smoked and precooked, the time in the pan is minimal, and you can focus on cooking the gorgeous beets, which soak up caramelized bits of maple-mustard glaze. If you can't find smoked ham steaks, have the deli slice some extra-thick pieces of their best sandwich ham. **Serves 4**

Ingredients

2 tablespoons good-quality vegetable oil

¼ cup maple syrup

1 tablespoon cider vinegar

1 tablespoon Dijon mustard

Salt and pepper

1 pound ham steak (½ to 1 inch thick)

1½ pounds beets

½ cup beer, chicken stock, or water

▢ Prep · **Cook**

1. Put 2 tablespoons vegetable oil in a large skillet over medium-high heat.

2. Combine ¼ cup maple syrup, 1 tablespoon cider vinegar, and 1 tablespoon Dijon mustard in a small bowl with a little salt and pepper.

3. Put the ham steak in the skillet and cook until the bottom browns, 3 to 5 minutes. Turn and cook until the other side browns, another 3 to 5 minutes. Lower the heat to medium-low and cook, turning once more, until the ham is heated through.

   ▢ Trim, peel, and halve the beets stem to tip. Lay them flat side down on a cutting board, and slice into half-moons about ¼ inch thick.

4. When the ham is ready, transfer it to a cutting board and lightly tent with foil to keep warm. Add ½ cup beer, stock, or water to the skillet, stirring to scrape up any browned bits from the bottom.

5. Add the beets and the glaze. Cover and cook, stirring occasionally, until they're tender, 5 to 10 minutes.

   ▢ Cut the ham into thick strips.

6. When the beets are tender, raise the heat to medium-high and cook, turning, until the sauce thickens and becomes a glaze, a minute or two. Taste and adjust the seasoning and serve with the sliced ham.

Variations

Seared Ham Steak with BBQ-Glazed Kohlrabi. Use kohlrabi instead of the beets. Substitute ½ cup barbecue sauce for the maple syrup, vinegar, and mustard.

Seared Ham Steak with Maple-, BBQ-, or Honey-Glazed Brussels Sprouts. Follow either the main recipe or the first variation. Instead of the beets, use 1 pound Brussels sprouts. Trim the ends and either slice them thinly crosswise into ribbons or run them through the slicing disk of a food processor.

Braised Pork with Cabbage and Beer

How can you go wrong with pork and cabbage? Here the meat is thinly sliced and the cabbage shredded to get them as tender as possible during their quick simmer. Buttered egg noodles (page 493) are the obvious side dish. **Serves 4**

Ingredients

2 tablespoons good-quality vegetable oil

1 pound boneless pork loin or sirloin chops

Salt and pepper

1 yellow onion

1 small head savoy or green cabbage (about 1 pound)

1 teaspoon caraway seeds

1 teaspoon mustard seeds

1 cup beer

2 tablespoons cider vinegar

☐ Prep · Cook

1. Put 2 tablespoons vegetable oil in a large skillet or large pot over medium-high heat.

   ☐ Thinly slice the pork against the grain.

2. Add the pork to the skillet, sprinkle with salt and pepper, and cook undisturbed until it browns on the bottom and releases easily from the skillet, 3 to 5 minutes. Then cook, stirring occasionally, until the pieces brown on both sides but are still a little pink in places, another couple minutes.

   ☐ Trim, peel, halve, and slice the onion.

3. Add the onion to the skillet and cook, stirring occasionally, until it softens, 3 to 5 minutes.

   ☐ Trim, quarter, core, and cut the cabbage into thin ribbons.

4. Add the cabbage to the skillet along with 1 teaspoon caraway seeds, 1 teaspoon mustard seeds, 1 cup beer, 2 tablespoons cider vinegar, and a sprinkle of salt and pepper. Bring the mixture to a boil, then adjust the heat so that it bubbles steadily.

5. Cook, stirring occasionally and adding more liquid if the pan starts to get dry, until the cabbage is tender and the liquid becomes a sauce, 5 to 10 minutes. Taste and adjust the seasoning, and serve.

Variations

Braised Chicken with Cabbage and Beer. Substitute 1 pound boneless, skinless chicken thighs for the pork, cutting them into strips or chunks. Everything else stays the same.

Braised Pork with Red Cabbage and Red Wine. Instead of the savoy or green cabbage, use red cabbage and red onion for the yellow. Substitute a fruity red wine for the beer.

Homemade Chorizo with Pinto Beans

Unlike Spanish chorizo, which is cured until dried, Mexican-style chorizo is a fresh sausage: essentially finely ground spiced pork you cook in a skillet. That means you can whip up a batch any time you'd like to cook loose meat for tacos or burritos. I like to add beans to cut the richness. This dish is also great with poached or fried eggs on top and warm tortillas on the side. If you don't feel like dragging out the food processor, just use store-bought ground pork.
Serves 4

Ingredients

2 cloves garlic

1 pound boneless pork loin or sirloin, or shoulder if you can find that small a piece

1 teaspoon ground cumin

1 tablespoon chili powder

¼ teaspoon cayenne

Pinch of ground cinnamon

Pinch of ground cloves

1 teaspoon cider vinegar

Salt and pepper

2 tablespoons vegetable oil

1 large onion

1¾ cups cooked or canned pinto beans (one 15-ounce can)

1 lime

1 small bunch fresh cilantro

Prep · Cook

- Peel 2 cloves garlic. Pulse in the food processor until minced.

- Cut the pork into 2-inch chunks.

1. Add the pork to the food processor along with 1 teaspoon ground cumin, 1 teaspoon chili powder, ¼ teaspoon cayenne, a pinch each of ground cinnamon and ground cloves, 1 teaspoon cider vinegar, and a sprinkle of salt and pepper. Pulse until the pork is coarsely ground but not puréed.

2. Put 2 tablespoons vegetable oil in a large skillet over medium-high heat.

   - Trim, peel, and chop the onion.

3. When the oil is hot, add the chorizo mixture and the onion. Cook, stirring occasionally, until the chorizo is cooked through and crisp in places, 5 to 10 minutes.

   - If you're using canned beans, rinse and drain them.

   - Cut the lime into wedges; chop ½ cup cilantro tender stems and leaves.

4. Stir in the beans and cook, stirring occasionally, until they heat through. Taste and adjust the seasoning. Garnish with cilantro and serve with lime wedges.

• recipe continues →

Variations

Homemade Chorizo with Chickpeas. The flavor of cured Spanish chorizo, made fresh: Substitute 1 tablespoon smoked paprika for the chili powder, cayenne, ground cinnamon, and ground cloves. Use sherry vinegar instead of cider vinegar and olive oil in place of vegetable oil. Substitute chickpeas for the pinto beans, lemon for the lime, and fresh parsley for the cilantro.

Homemade Italian Sausage with Cannellini Beans. Replace the ground cumin, chili powder, cayenne, ground cinnamon, and ground cloves with 1 tablespoon fennel seeds and ¼ teaspoon red chile flakes. Substitute red wine vinegar for the cider vinegar and olive oil for the vegetable oil. Replace the pinto beans with cannellini beans, the lime with lemon, and the cilantro with fresh basil.

Homemade Tempeh Chorizo or Sausage. A vegan option that works with the main recipe and either of the previous variations. Substitute 1 pound tempeh for the pork.

Braised Sausage and Escarole

The near-perfect combination of rich sausage and pleasantly bitter escarole needs very little embellishment. They benefit each other by cooking together, even if the braising time is short. Let the variations get you rolling with more vegetable ideas beyond greens, like cubes of butternut squash or eggplant, sliced mushrooms, fresh or canned tomatoes. Serve with toasted bread or toss with pasta, and you'll be set. **Serves 4**

Ingredients

2 tablespoons olive oil

4 hot or sweet Italian sausage links (about 1 pound)

1 pound escarole

1 lemon

2 ounces Parmesan cheese (½ cup grated)

Salt and pepper

½ cup chicken stock, white wine, or water

Prep · Cook

1. Put 2 tablespoons olive oil in a large skillet over medium heat. When it's hot, add the sausages and cook, turning a few times, until they are browned all over but still underdone at the center, 5 to 10 minutes.

   - Trim and chop the escarole.

   - Grate the zest from the lemon; refrigerate the fruit for another use.

   - Grate ½ cup Parmesan.

2. Transfer the sausages to a plate. Spoon off all but 2 tablespoons of the fat. Turn the heat to high and add the escarole to the skillet. Sprinkle with salt and pepper and cook, stirring constantly, until it softens, just a minute or two.

3. Return the sausages to the skillet along with ½ cup stock, wine, or water; stir to scrape up any browned bits. Adjust the heat so the mixture bubbles steadily but not vigorously; cover and cook, stirring once or twice, until the sausages are firm and fully cooked at the center and the escarole is quite tender, 5 to 10 minutes. Remove from the heat.

4. Taste and adjust the seasoning. Spread everything in a single layer and scatter the lemon zest and Parmesan over the top. Serve straight from the skillet if you like.

● recipe continues →

Variations

Braised Sausage and Radicchio. Replace all or some of the escarole with radicchio. Instead of using the lemon zest, finish the dish with a drizzle of balsamic vinegar and lots of black pepper before adding the cheese.

Braised Sausage and Peppers. Substitute at least 1 pound any peppers for the escarole; trim, core, seed, and slice. Sweet or hot long Italian-style varieties are terrific here if you can find them. If not, then use any mix of green, red, yellow, or orange bell peppers, or try stemmed whole shishitos or sliced poblano chiles.

Braised Sausage and Broccoli Rabe. Instead of the escarole, chop about 1 pound broccoli rabe into bite-sized chunks.

SPEEDIER SAUSAGE

You can slice the sausages or crumble them out of the casings into the pan before cooking. When they're lightly browned, add the escarole and proceed as directed.

Bangers and Mash

The British meat-and-potatoes staple often uses the rendered sausage fat as the base of a gravy. Instead you can mash the potatoes right in the skillet that you used to cook the sausage. A nifty trick for steaming the potatoes ensures they're tender well before the 30-minute mark. Peas or peas and carrots are perfect on the side, as is a bottle of Worcestershire or HP Sauce on the table. **Serves 4**

Ingredients

Salt

2 pounds russet or Yukon Gold potatoes

2 tablespoons olive oil

4 mild sausage links
(or 8 to 12 breakfast links;
about 1 pound total)

Several sprigs fresh sage or
2 teaspoons dried

½ cup milk, plus more as
needed

4 tablespoons (½ stick)
butter

1 teaspoon cider vinegar

1 teaspoon dry mustard

Pepper

◻ Prep · **Cook**

1. Fill a large pot with 1 to 2 inches water; add a big pinch of salt and turn the heat to high.

   ◻ I don't bother to peel the potatoes, but if you want to, do that first. Halve the potatoes lengthwise and cut them into thin half-moons, dropping them into the pot as you go.

2. When all the potatoes are in the pot, they should be swimming but not fully submerged; add a little more water if necessary. When the water comes to a boil, adjust the heat so it bubbles vigorously and cook, stirring occasionally, until the potatoes are tender and just breaking apart, 10 to 15 minutes.

3. While the potatoes cook, put 2 tablespoons olive oil in a large skillet over medium heat. Add the sausages and cook, turning occasionally, until they're browned all over and no longer pink inside, 10 to 15 minutes. Transfer them to a plate.

   ◻ If you're using fresh sage, strip the leaves from several sprigs and chop.

4. Add the fresh or 2 teaspoons dried sage to the skillet. Cook, stirring constantly, until sizzling and fragrant, just a minute or so. Add ½ cup milk to the skillet and stir to scrape up any browned bits.

5. When the potatoes are tender, drain them in a colander, reserving about 1 cup cooking liquid. Add them to the skillet. Add 4 tablespoons butter, 1 teaspoon cider vinegar, 1 teaspoon dry mustard, and a sprinkle of pepper.

6. Mash the potatoes with a potato masher or fork, adding more milk or reserved cooking liquid to get the consistency you like. Taste and adjust the seasoning. Serve with the sausages.

● recipe continues →

Variations

Fish and Mash. Cod is the obvious choice, but any thick fish fillet or steak is fine. Instead of the sausage, cut 1 to 1½ pounds fish fillet into 4 portions, or use 4 steaks. Cook them as described in Step 3, turning once, just long enough to form a crust on the outside and become opaque at the center, 5 to 10 minutes total, depending on the type and thickness of the fish. Instead of the dry mustard and vinegar, season the potatoes with the grated zest and juice of 1 lemon.

Burgers and Mash. Instead of the sausage, season 1 pound any ground meat or poultry with salt and pepper, and gently form into 4 or 8 patties, each a little less than 1 inch thick. Cook as described in Step 3, turning just once and checking the inside for your desired doneness.

Mushrooms and Mash. A vegetarian option. Instead of the sausage, trim the stems from 4 portobello mushrooms. Increase the olive oil to 3 tablespoons. In Step 3, put them into the skillet gill side up, sprinkle with salt, and cover the pan for the first 3 minutes of cooking. Then proceed as directed.

8 Other Vegetables to Mash

Peel before boiling:

1. Turnips
2. Rutabagas
3. Parsnips
4. Celery root
5. Sweet potatoes
6. Beets
7. Winter squash
8. Kohlrabi

Lamb Chops with Balsamic Couscous

Lots of ways to go here in terms of cuts. For a big splurge, choose double-thick lamb rib chops. They take longer to cook than the thinner ones, but since you can fit all four chops in the skillet at once, you end up saving time. Plus, those meaty chops are easier to keep rare or medium-rare so they burst with juice. For a more economical option, choose lamb shoulder chops (which will have a bone) or leg chops—either one cut about 1 inch thick. The cooking cues will help you adjust the time to achieve your desired doneness. With the minty tomato couscous, you don't need much else unless you want one of the cooked vegetable recipes (page 498) on the side. **Serves 4**

Ingredients

2 tablespoons balsamic vinegar, plus more for serving

2 tablespoons olive oil

4 double-thick lamb rib chops or other chops
(1 to 1½ pounds total)

Salt and pepper

2 cups chicken stock, vegetable stock, or water

1 cup couscous

2 large ripe tomatoes

1 bunch fresh mint

□ Prep · **Cook**

1. Put a large skillet over medium-high heat.

   □ Combine 2 tablespoons balsamic vinegar and 2 tablespoons olive oil in a large bowl. Add the lamb chops and toss to coat.

2. When the skillet is hot, sprinkle the bottom with salt and pepper and add the lamb chops. (Reserve the marinade.) Sprinkle with salt and pepper and cook undisturbed until the chops brown on the bottom and release easily from the skillet, 3 to 5 minutes. Turn and cook until the chops are one stage rarer at the center than you ultimately want them, 2 to 5 minutes more (nick with a small knife to peek inside).

3. When the lamb is ready, transfer the chops to a plate and tent with foil to keep warm. Carefully pour in 2 cups stock or water to the skillet (it will bubble furiously at first), along with the reserved marinade and a sprinkle of salt. Boil for about 3 minutes, scraping up any browned bits from the bottom of the pan.

4. Stir in 1 cup couscous, then cover the skillet and turn off the heat. Let the couscous steep until it's tender and the liquid is absorbed, about 5 minutes.

   □ Core and chop the tomatoes.

   □ Strip ¼ cup leaves from the mint sprigs and chop.

5. When the couscous is ready, add the tomatoes and mint and fluff with a fork. Taste and adjust the seasoning. Serve the couscous alongside or underneath the lamb, drizzled with any accumulated juices from the plate and a few drops more vinegar.

Stir-Fried Lamb and Green Peppers with Cumin

Lamb seasoned with cumin is a beloved combination in many food cultures. Add green bell peppers and red chile flakes, and the flavors are eye opening. If you can't find a small quantity of the cuts listed below, substitute ground lamb or beef sirloin. Brown rice is good on the side, or tuck this into a pliable, chewy flatbread like lavash. **Serves 4**

Ingredients

4 tablespoons good-quality vegetable oil

1 pound boneless lamb leg, shoulder, or chops

2 teaspoons ground cumin

1 teaspoon red chile flakes, or to taste

Salt and pepper

1 inch fresh ginger

2 cloves garlic

2 large or 3 medium green bell peppers (1 pound)

3 scallions

1 tablespoon soy sauce, or to taste

▢ Prep · Cook

1. Put 2 tablespoons vegetable oil in a large skillet over medium-high heat.

   ▢ Slice the lamb against the grain into bite-sized pieces.

2. Add the lamb to the skillet, sprinkle with 2 teaspoons ground cumin, 1 teaspoon red chile flakes (or to taste), and some salt and pepper. Cook, stirring frequently, until the spices are toasted without burning and the lamb is browned and cooked through, 3 to 5 minutes.

   ▢ Peel 1 inch ginger and 2 cloves garlic; chop them together.

   ▢ Core, seed, and thinly slice the bell peppers.

3. Add the ginger and garlic to the skillet with the lamb. Cook, stirring, until fragrant, about a minute. Transfer the lamb mixture to a bowl.

4. Add 2 tablespoons vegetable oil to the skillet and reduce the heat to medium. Add the peppers and cook, stirring frequently to scrape up bits of lamb and spice, until they're lightly browned and just tender but still have a little crunch, 3 to 5 minutes.

   ▢ Trim and chop the scallions.

5. When the peppers are done, return the lamb to the skillet and add 1 tablespoon soy sauce and the scallions. Toss everything to combine. Taste and adjust the seasoning, and serve.

Variations

Stir-Fried Lamb and Green Peppers with Sichuan Peppercorns. This tingly, slightly hot spice isn't a true pepper—it's actually related to roses. You'll need to grind it with a mortar and pestle or on a cutting board with the flat side of a knife, but it's worth the little bit of work. Substitute 1 tablespoon ground Sichuan peppercorns for the ground cumin.

Miso Lamb Chops with Carrots

I stand by this assertion from the first edition: The sweet-saltiness of lamb, carrots, and miso is both unfamiliar and wonderful. Serve small bowls of plain rice or cooked grains on the side. **Serves 4**

Ingredients

4 double-thick lamb rib chops or other chops (1 to 1½ pounds total)

2 tablespoons good-quality vegetable oil

Salt and pepper

1 pound carrots

3 scallions

½ cup chicken stock, white wine, or water

3 tablespoons any miso

1 teaspoon soy sauce

▢ Prep · **Cook**

1. Put a large skillet over medium-high heat.

   ▢ Rub the lamb chops with 1 tablespoon vegetable oil and sprinkle all over with salt and pepper.

2. When the skillet is hot, add the chops. Cook undisturbed until they're browned on the bottom and release easily from the pan, 3 to 5 minutes. Turn and cook until the chops are one stage rarer at the center than you ultimately want them, 2 to 5 minutes more (nick with a small knife to peek inside).

   ▢ Trim, peel, and slice the carrots at an angle into ovals about ¼ inch thick.

3. When the chops are done, transfer them to a platter and tent with foil to keep them warm. Add 1 tablespoon vegetable oil to the skillet.

4. Add the carrots and cook, stirring occasionally, until they are lightly browned and just tender, 3 to 5 minutes.

   ▢ Trim and chop the scallions.

   ▢ Whisk together ½ cup stock, wine, or water; 3 tablespoons miso; and 1 teaspoon soy sauce in a small bowl until smooth.

5. Add the miso mixture to the carrots. Stir, scraping up any browned bits from the bottom of the skillet and coating the carrots with the sauce.

6. Taste and adjust the seasoning. Serve the carrots over the lamb chops, garnished with scallions.

Desserts

'm happy to say you don't have to be a baker to enjoy homemade desserts after dinner, even on weeknights. Instead you'll assemble store-bought and fresh ingredients into something that says, "Hey, can you believe I made this?"

There are a lot of ways to satisfy a sweet tooth, and they needn't be elaborate. With that mindset, all sorts of dishes qualify. Many of these recipes can be prepared ahead, sometimes even a day or two before serving. Others are so fast you can pull them together while someone else clears the table and brews the coffee.

The simplest things can hit the spot. A surprising uncooked pudding. Homemade bonbons. A seasonal fruit crisp you make on the stove. All of them are desserts that are welcome, impressive, and, yes, delicious.

If you're really short on time, offer whole pieces of gorgeous seasonal fruit, or whip up one of the sauces on page 465 or 469 to serve over ice cream or a simple cake from a nearby bakery. You'll be glad you made the effort. Dessert is always festive; it keeps everyone at the table lingering and chatting after the meal—even the kids. And isn't that why you wanted to get out of the kitchen so fast?

Caramelized Bananas

Decadence—with so little work. All you need is a spoon. For an even more indulgent treat, serve caramelized bananas over vanilla, chocolate, or, for a wild card, coffee ice cream. They're also good over yogurt, angel food or pound cake, and thick slices of toasted challah or brioche. **Serves 4**

Ingredients

4 tablespoons (½ stick) butter

½ cup packed brown sugar

2 tablespoons honey

Pinch of salt

4 ripe bananas

Prep · Cook

1. Put 4 tablespoons butter, ½ cup brown sugar, 2 tablespoons honey, a pinch of salt, and ¼ cup water in a medium skillet over medium heat. Cook, stirring frequently, until the sugar dissolves and the mixture thickens and darkens, about 10 minutes.

   □ Peel and slice the bananas at an angle into ovals about ½ inch thick.

2. Add the bananas to the skillet and cook until warm and coated with caramel sauce. Serve warm or at room temperature.

Variations

Caramelized Maple-Rum Bananas. Instead of the honey, use 3 tablespoons maple syrup. Instead of water, use ¼ cup light or dark rum.

Caramelized Chile-Lime Bananas. Use ¼ cup lime juice instead of the water and add 1 teaspoon chili powder or ground chile (like ancho or chipotle), to taste.

Chocolatized Bananas. Substitute ½ cup cream for the butter and water and 4 ounces chopped dark chocolate for the sugar and honey. You can also use white chocolate if you like.

ALL-PURPOSE CHOCOLATE SAUCE

A jar of spoonable chocolate gives you the power to turn anything into dessert: the usual cookies or ice cream or yogurt, but also cut fruit, fresh or frozen berries, nuts, graham crackers or saltines (yes!)—even lightly toasted bread. It's super-easy: In a small saucepan, combine 4 ounces chopped dark chocolate (defined by at least 70% cocoa solids), 4 tablespoons (½ stick) butter, ¼ cup sugar, ¼ cup water, and a pinch of salt. Cook, whisking, over very low heat until the chocolate melts and the mixture is smooth. Whisk in 1 teaspoon vanilla extract. Serve hot, or cool and refrigerate for up to several days. Warm before using. Or eat it with a spoon.

Fruit Slush

Imagine a cross between a snow cone and granita made with frozen fruit in less than 10 minutes. All it takes is a food processor with a grating disk and a bag of frozen fruit. To expand your options, you can cut fresh fruit into chunks and freeze it for several hours before grating. Ditto for other flavorful liquids; see the first variation to get you thinking in that direction. Serve in bowls or, for a state fair or urban street corner experience, in little paper cups. **Serves 4**

Ingredients

½ lemon

¼ cup sugar, plus more as needed

1 pound frozen fruit (any combination)

☐ Prep · Cook

☐ Squeeze the juice from the lemon half into a medium bowl through a strainer or your fingers to remove the seeds. Add ¼ cup sugar. Stir to dissolve.

1. Fit the food processor with the grating disk and turn it on. Push the frozen fruit through the feed tube a few pieces at a time. When it's all grated, transfer to the bowl with the sweetened lemon juice.

2. Stir gently with a fork to combine. Taste and add more sugar if necessary. Serve right away.

Variations

Coconut Slush. Combine the lemon juice and sugar with 2 (14-ounce) cans coconut milk (reduced fat is fine but will be less luxurious than the full-fat kind). Add more sugar to taste if needed. Freeze the mixture in 2 or 3 ice cube trays. Use the coconut ice cubes instead of the fruit in Step 1. No need to add anything else in Step 2. Serve.

Fruit Sorbet. Instead of using the grating disk, fit the food processor with the metal blade. In Step 1, put the fruit, lemon juice, and sugar in the work bowl and process, stopping to scrape down the sides of the bowl if necessary, until the fruit is just puréed. (It only takes a minute.)

Fruit Sherbet, Dairy or Nondairy. Instead of using the grating disk, fit the food processor with the metal blade. In Step 1, put the fruit and sugar (no lemon juice) in the work bowl with ½ cup milk or a nondairy alternative like coconut, oat, or nut milk.

8 Frozen Fruits to Try for Ice, Sorbet, or Sherbet

1. Strawberries
2. Raspberries
3. Blackberries
4. Pineapple
5. Mangoes
6. Peaches
7. Sweet or sour cherries
8. Any kind of melon

Orange Cream Sundaes

A simple orange syrup poured over vanilla ice cream re-creates the tangy-on-creamy flavor of the retro Creamsicle ice cream and sherbet pop. The fast trick is to reduce the juice in a broad skillet, not a saucepan; but if you don't have one coated in enamel or ceramic or made of stainless steel, use a big pot. (Cast iron, aluminum, or carbon steel will react with the juice.) Fresh orange juice is the key, so either squeeze your own or buy the good stuff. The advantages to doing it yourself are that you can use other orange-ish citrus like satsumas or tangerines and cut off some lovely strips of zest for garnish. To speed things up even more—and if a soupy sundae sounds appealing—don't bother to chill the syrup. And lots of other combinations work too (see the variations). **Serves 4**

Ingredients

2 cups orange juice

½ cup sugar

1 quart vanilla ice cream

Strips of zest from 1 orange (optional)

▫ Prep · **Cook**

1. Put 2 cups orange juice and ½ cup sugar in a large skillet over high heat (see the headnote). Cook, stirring occasionally, until the mixture is reduced by half and thickens into a syrup, 10 to 15 minutes.

2. Transfer the syrup to a shallow dish and put it in the freezer to cool, about 10 minutes.

   ▫ Take the ice cream out of the freezer to soften.

3. Scoop 1 cup vanilla ice cream into each of 4 bowls and drizzle the orange syrup over the top. Garnish with zest if you like.

Variations

Cider Sundaes. Replace the orange juice (and optional zest) with apple cider and reduce the sugar to ¼ cup. Serve over cinnamon or caramel ice cream.

Blueberry-Lemon Sundaes. Omit the orange juice and optional zest. Add 2 cups blueberries, ½ cup water, and the zest of a lemon to the skillet along with the sugar.

Bring to a boil, then let bubble gently but steadily until the blueberries break apart and thicken into sauce, 15 to 20 minutes. Taste and add more sugar if necessary. Serve the sauce warm over lemon frozen custard, sherbet, or sorbet instead of the vanilla ice cream.

Cranberry Sundaes. Great for fall over pumpkin ice cream. Omit the orange juice

and optional zest. Add 2 cups cranberries, ½ cup port wine or water, and the zest of a lemon to the skillet along with the sugar. Bring to a boil, then let bubble gently but steadily until the cranberries break apart and thicken into sauce, 15 to 20 minutes. Taste and add more sugar if necessary. Serve warm over ice cream.

Salted Chocolate Peanut Butter Bonbons

Based on one of the most popular recipes from the first edition, now with more variations. Imagine what would happen if you rolled a peanut butter cup into a ball—one that you don't care much about being perfectly round. If you have a few extra minutes, before freezing, roll them in finely chopped peanuts or unsweetened shredded coconut (the finest stuff you can find). **Makes 36 balls**

Ingredients

2 tablespoons butter

4 ounces dark chocolate

1 cup peanut butter

1 cup powdered sugar, plus more as needed

Salt (the flaky kind is best here)

☐ Prep · Cook

1. Put 2 tablespoons butter in a medium microwave-safe bowl.

    ☐ Chop 4 ounces chocolate; add it to the bowl.

2. Microwave the mixture on high heat, checking and stirring occasionally, until the butter and chocolate melt, a minute or two.

3. Add 1 cup peanut butter and stir until it's evenly incorporated. Add 1 cup powdered sugar and stir until the mixture is smooth.

4. Put a piece of wax or parchment paper on a rimmed baking sheet. Use 2 teaspoons to drop 1-inch balls of dough onto the sheet. Sprinkle with a little salt.

5. Put the baking sheet in the freezer and freeze just until the balls firm up a bit, 10 to 15 minutes. Serve right away or store in an airtight container for up to a couple days in the refrigerator or several weeks in the freezer.

Variations

Salted Chocolate Almond Butter Bonbons. One logical spin on the original. Use almond butter instead of peanut butter.

Chocolate Coconut Bonbons. Omit the salt. One quick extra step gets you a giant leap closer to a Mounds bar. Replace the peanut butter with unsweetened shredded coconut. Put it in a food processor with 1 tablespoon water and let the machine run for 30 seconds or so. Stop and scrape down the sides. You're looking for the texture of nut butter, so if you're not there yet, repeat, adding water 1 teaspoon at a time until you are. Then proceed with the recipe from Step 3, substituting the coconut paste for the peanut butter.

Chocolate Cherry Bonbons. Works with any dried fruit really. Omit the salt and peanut butter. Bring 1 cup water to a boil in a small saucepan and add 1 cup dried sweet or tart cherries. Remove from the heat, cover, and steep until the fruit is fully tender, 10 to 15 minutes. Drain well, reserving the liquid. Purée the cherries into a paste following the directions in the preceding variation, using the reserved soaking liquid to reach the desired consistency. Proceed from Step 3.

Chocolate Orange Pudding

Using silken tofu is the easiest and fastest way to make, well, silken pudding. Orange and chocolate are a winning combination. For more flavor ideas, be sure to check out the variations. **Serves 4 to 6**

Ingredients

¾ cup sugar

8 ounces dark chocolate, plus 1 ounce for garnish

1 orange

1 brick silken tofu (14 to 16 ounces)

1 teaspoon vanilla extract

▢ Prep · Cook

1. Put ¾ cup water and ¾ cup sugar in a small saucepan and bring to a boil. After it boils, stir to dissolve the sugar crystals, then remove the syrup from the heat.

   ▢ Chop 8 ounces chocolate.

2. If you have a double boiler, put the chocolate in the top. To make a double boiler if you don't have one, put the chocolate in a heatproof bowl you can set securely over a small or medium saucepan. Put about 1 inch water in the double boiler bottom of the saucepan. Adjust the heat so the water simmers. Fit in the double boiler top or rest the bowl on top. Stir the chocolate frequently until it's melted and completely smooth.

   ▢ Grate 1 tablespoon orange zest; refrigerate the fruit for another use.

3. In a blender, combine the melted chocolate, sugar syrup, silken tofu, orange zest, and 1 teaspoon vanilla. Blend, stopping as necessary to scrape down the sides, until the mixture is completely smooth.

4. Divide the mixture among four to six 6-ounce ramekins or serving bowls; freeze them until the pudding firms up a bit, 15 to 20 minutes. To serve, shave 1 ounce chocolate over the tops using a vegetable peeler or fine grater.

Variations

Banana Pudding. Serve this with vanilla wafers and it's pretty close to the retro classic. Replace the chocolate and orange zest with 2 ripe bananas. Skip Step 2.

White Chocolate–Orange Pudding. Use white chocolate instead of dark.

Coconut Pudding. Omit the chocolate and orange. Instead of water, use coconut milk to make the syrup; add ½ cup unsweetened shredded coconut to the saucepan in Step 1. Skip Step 2. Garnish with toasted shredded coconut or pistachios.

Pumpkin Mousse

Pie in the sky that eats like air. You can dig into these right away if you want, but a quick
chill in the freezer firms them up perfectly. Like all classic mousses, this contains raw eggs; if
you're at all worried about that, see the egg-free variation. **Serves 6 to 8**

Ingredients

½ cup cream

4 tablespoons sugar

3 eggs

1 (15-ounce) can pumpkin
(not pumpkin pie mix)

½ teaspoon ground cinnamon

¼ teaspoon ground nutmeg

¼ teaspoon ground cloves

¼ teaspoon ground cardamom

□ Prep · Cook

1. Put ½ cup cream and 2 tablespoons sugar in a medium bowl. Using an
   electric mixer, beat the cream until it holds soft peaks.

2. Separate the eggs and add the whites and 2 tablespoons sugar to a clean
   medium bowl. Discard the yolks, or refrigerate them to save for another
   use. Wash and dry the beaters and beat the egg whites until they hold
   soft peaks.

3. Add the pumpkin, ½ teaspoon ground cinnamon, ¼ teaspoon ground
   nutmeg, ¼ teaspoon ground cloves, and ¼ teaspoon ground cardamom
   to the egg whites. Gently fold them in with a rubber spatula. Fold in the
   whipped cream just until no streaks of white remain.

4. Spoon the mousse into 6-ounce ramekins or small bowls and put in the
   freezer for 15 minutes to chill before serving.

Variations

Chocolate Mousse. Instead of
the pumpkin and spices, heat
4 ounces chocolate, chopped,
and 2 tablespoons butter in
a bowl or the top of a double
boiler set over simmering
water until almost completely
melted; remove from the heat
and stir until smooth. Fold
the whipped egg whites into
the chocolate, then fold in the
whipped cream.

Jam Mousse. Really any jam,
preserves, or marmalade you
like is excellent here, but let's
start with a personal favorite.
Omit the sugar (the jam will
make the mousse pleasantly
sweet). Instead of the
pumpkin and spices, use 1 cup
apricot jam or preserves and
increase the cream to ¾ cup.
Everything else stays the same.

**Whipped Cream Pumpkin,
Chocolate, or Jam Mousse.**
For an egg-free version that
works for the main recipe
or either of the variations,
try this. Omit the eggs.
Combine the pumpkin, melted
chocolate, or jam with any
of the accompanying spices
in a small bowl. Increase the
cream to 1½ cups and, if using
pumpkin or chocolate, beat in
all 4 tablespoons sugar. With
the beaters on low, incorporate
the pumpkin, chocolate, or
jam mixture into the whipped
cream ¼ cup at a time.

Individual Tiramisus

Assembled right in the serving bowls, with minimal shortcuts, this is a lightning-fast, crowd-pleasing dessert. For a boozy version, see the variations. **Serves 4**

Ingredients

Instant coffee or espresso powder

12 ladyfingers

1 cup cream

½ cup mascarpone cheese

1 cup powdered sugar

Cocoa powder for dusting

☐ Prep · Cook

1. Brew 1 cup instant coffee or espresso, using enough powder so it's a little bit stronger than you'd drink it.

2. Dip 12 ladyfingers in the coffee and divide them among the bottoms of 4 shallow bowls.

3. Using an electric mixer, beat 1 cup cream in a medium bowl until it holds soft peaks.

4. Combine ½ cup mascarpone and 1 cup powdered sugar in a separate bowl. Starting slowly so the sugar doesn't fly everywhere, beat with the electric mixer until it's fully incorporated. Gently fold the mascarpone mixture into the whipped cream. Spread it on top of the ladyfingers. Dust some cocoa powder over the top and serve.

Variations

Boozy Tiramisus. Add 2 tablespoons crème de cacao, crème de menthe, Marsala, or grappa to the coffee. Everything else is the same.

Strawberry Tiramisus. Omit the cocoa. Hull and slice 1 pint strawberries, put them in a small bowl, drizzle them with 1 tablespoon balsamic vinegar, and stir; let them sit while you make the puddings. Instead of the coffee, mix ½ cup strawberry preserves with 1 cup water; use this for dipping the ladyfingers. Top each tiramisu with a spoonful of the balsamic strawberries.

Green Tea Tiramisus. Instead of the coffee, brew 1 cup double-strong green tea and use that to dip the ladyfingers. Garnish with chopped hazelnuts instead of cocoa.

Skillet Apple Crisp

When you deconstruct the fruit and topping components of a crisp, you get a beloved dessert in a fraction of the time. And you don't even have to turn on the oven. The variations provide two of many alternatives and a whole different topping that works on any fruit. Use whatever is in season: peaches, plums, pears, berries—even bananas, mangoes, or pineapple. Cooking time is variable, just a few extra minutes one way or the other; you check for tenderness frequently. **Serves 4 to 6**

Ingredients

8 tablespoons (1 stick) butter

2 pounds apples

½ cup walnuts or pecans

½ cup rolled oats

¼ cup unsweetened shredded coconut

½ cup packed brown sugar

½ teaspoon ground cinnamon

Salt

Prep · Cook

1. Put 1 tablespoon butter in a large skillet over medium heat.

   □ Core and chop the apples, leaving the skin on.

2. Add the apples to the butter and cook, stirring frequently and adding water 1 tablespoon at a time if the pan starts to look dry, until the apples are tender, 5 to 10 minutes.

3. Put 7 tablespoons butter in another large skillet over medium heat.

   □ Chop ½ cup nuts.

4. When the butter is melted, add the nuts, ½ cup rolled oats, ¼ cup shredded coconut, ½ cup brown sugar, ½ teaspoon ground cinnamon, and a pinch of salt; toss to coat. Cook, stirring frequently, until the topping is golden and crisp, 6 to 8 minutes.

5. When the fruit is soft, divide it among serving bowls. Scatter the topping over the fruit and serve.

• recipe continues →

Variations

Skillet Blueberry Crisp.
Instead of the apples, use 3 pints fresh blueberries or 6 cups frozen. Omit the ground cinnamon in the topping, or substitute 2 teaspoons lemon zest if you like. In Step 2, don't add any water to the skillet; cook the berries until they just start to burst, 3 to 5 minutes.

Skillet Peach Crisp. Instead of the apples, use 2 pounds peaches. Pit them; peel them if you like. Slice them into thin wedges. The ground cinnamon

in the topping is optional—I like ¼ teaspoon ground cardamom instead.

Skillet Fruit Crisp with Crunchy Phyllo Topping.
Omit the oats and coconut. Heat the oven to 375°F. In Steps 3 and 4, combine 7 tablespoons butter, ½ cup brown sugar, ½ teaspoon ground cinnamon, and a pinch of salt in a small saucepan over medium-low heat. Cook, swirling the pan until the butter melts and the sugar dissolves. Stack 12 frozen

phyllo sheets on top of one another; cut them into shreds. Spread them out on a rimmed baking sheet; scatter the chopped nuts on top. Drizzle with the butter mixture and toss with 2 forks to coat. Transfer the baking sheet to the oven (it's okay if the oven's not fully heated) and bake, tossing once or twice, until the phyllo is golden and crisp, 20 to 25 minutes. Use this to top the cooked fruit in Step 5.

Components and Sides

We Americans are now a long way past expecting our dinner plates to have a hunk of meat in the center with spoonfuls of something starchy and something green or orange on the side. So think of these "sides" as companions to mix and match with the recipes elsewhere. I usually give you a suggestion or two in the headnotes, but I encourage you to do whatever makes you and the people you're cooking for happy.

Timing is also up to you. There's always something else on the stove or in the oven, so these recipes dovetail with your kitchen choreography. You attend to them periodically, but they need not dominate your activity. And almost none needs to be served piping hot, which means you can start them before the main dish and let them sit around for a little bit.

The "components" are master recipes—basic dishes like simply cooked beans, grains, and sauces you can make ahead and keep on hand so you can minimize the amount of take-out and processed foods in your diet. Though many take longer than 30 minutes, having them handy is undeniably convenient.

Fresh Tomato Salsa

The main recipe is a pico de gallo–style chopped salsa. The variation demonstrates how to take the same ingredients and do something totally different with them. The list covers ingredients to try both ways. **Serves 4** (**about 2 cups**)

Ingredients

1 small white onion, or less than half of 1 large

1 or 2 limes

2 or 3 large ripe tomatoes (1 pound)

1 fresh hot green chile (like serrano or jalapeño), or more to taste

1 clove garlic

1 bunch fresh cilantro

Salt and pepper

▢ Prep · Cook

▢ Trim, peel, and chop the onion and put it in a medium bowl.

▢ Halve the lime. Set aside the other half and reserve the second lime to cut later if you need it.

▢ Core and chop the tomatoes and add them to the bowl.

▢ Trim the chile and remove the seeds if you like; chop as finely as you can manage and add it to the bowl.

▢ Peel and chop the garlic; add it to the bowl.

▢ Chop ½ cup cilantro tender stems and leaves; add it to the bowl.

1. Sprinkle with salt and pepper and stir to combine the ingredients. If possible, let the salsa sit for about 15 minutes to develop flavor and juiciness.

2. Before serving, taste and adjust the seasoning, adding juice from the reserved lime, more chile, and/or cilantro. Stir again and serve right away, or store in the refrigerator for a day or two.

Variation

Cooked Salsa. For a smooth or slightly chunky sauce that keeps in the fridge for a week, all you have to do is put the ingredients in a blender instead of a bowl. Purée until the mixture is the texture you want, then transfer the salsa to a medium saucepan. Bring to a boil, then reduce the heat so the salsa bubbles steadily but gently. Cover and cook, stirring occasionally, until it thickens a little and looks saucy, 15 to 20 minutes. To make it thicker, uncover and boil off some of the extra liquid for a few minutes more.

10 Ingredients to Use in Salsa Instead of Some or All of the Tomatoes

1. Peaches
2. Nectarines
3. Plums
4. Mangoes
5. Any melon
6. Cherries
7. Strawberries
8. Pineapple
9. Green (unripe) tomatoes
10. Black beans

Eggs, Cooked Four Ways

The fastest way I know to turn something light into a satisfying meal is to put an egg—or two—on it. Scrambled eggs are the most forgiving since the yolk is already broken, so let's start there with a foolproof way to make sure the texture is exactly how you like it. The variations cover how to cook eggs hard-boiled, fried, and poached. **Makes 2 to 4 servings**

Ingredients

2 tablespoons butter or olive oil

4 eggs

Salt and pepper

☐ Prep · Cook

1. Put 2 tablespoons butter or olive oil in a medium skillet over medium-high heat.

   ☐ Crack the eggs one at a time on a flat, hard surface and open them over a bowl. Sprinkle with some salt and pepper and whisk until the yolks and whites are just combined.

2. When the butter has melted or the oil is hot, pour the eggs into the skillet. Let the eggs cook for just a few seconds to heat up, then begin stirring frequently and scraping the sides of the pan. A wooden or silicone spatula is a good tool for this job, but any big spoon can work too.

3. As the eggs begin to solidify, some parts may look like they're drying out; whenever you see that, remove the pan from the heat and continue stirring until the cooking slows down a bit. Then return the pan to the heat and continue cooking. The eggs are done when they're creamy and soft but still a bit runny. Even after you take them off the heat, they can quickly become overcooked, dry, and tough. (If you like them that way, that's fine too.) Serve right away.

Variations

Hard-Boiled Eggs. No butter or oil needed. The method I like is this: Fill a medium saucepan halfway full with water and bring to a boil. Gently lower 4 eggs straight from the fridge (or not) into the water with a spoon so they don't crack. Or use as many as will fit without bumping around. Cover and turn off the heat. For standard large eggs, figure 8 minutes for a jammy yolk, 1 minute longer up to 12 for each degree of doneness; by 12 they'll probably turn chalky and get that green ring between the yolk and the white. Drain the eggs and rinse them under cold water until cool. Peel and serve right away, or refrigerate in the shell for up to a week.

Fried Eggs. When the butter has melted or the oil is hot in Step 2, swirl it around to coat the bottom of the skillet. Crack the eggs into the skillet

• recipe continues →

and cook, spooning some of the pooling butter or oil on top if you like, until the whites are no longer translucent, 2 to 3 minutes. Turn the heat to low and sprinkle the eggs with salt and pepper. Cook undisturbed until the whites are firm and the yolks are as runny as you like, just a couple minutes more. Gently lift the eggs out of the pan with a spatula. Serve right away.

Poached Eggs. Put 1 to 2 inches water in a medium saucepan and bring to a boil.

Lower the heat so the water barely bubbles. Crack 1 egg on a flat, hard surface and open it into a shallow bowl, being careful not to break the yolk. Gently slip the egg into the water. Repeat with the remaining 3 eggs, slipping each into different spots in the saucepan. Cook the eggs undisturbed for 2 to 5 minutes, depending on how hot the water is and your desired doneness. My ideal is just until the white is set and the yolk has filmed over. The longer you cook them, the thicker the

yolks become. Lift the eggs out of the water with a slotted spoon, letting as much water drain off as possible. If you want to make them look fancy, trim off any raggedy edges with kitchen scissors while the egg is in the spoon. Transfer them to a paper towel–lined plate to drain. Serve right away, sprinkled with salt and pepper.

11 THINGS TO ADD TO SCRAMBLED EGGS

Add sauces and cheeses directly to the eggs as you scramble them. With the other ingredients, decide if you want to cook them in the butter or oil to soften before pouring the eggs into the skillet. For the last two on the list, I always do that to cook away any liquid so the eggs don't become watery.

1. 1 teaspoon chopped fresh strong herbs like oregano, tarragon, or thyme
2. 1 tablespoon chopped fresh mild herbs like parsley, chives, chervil, basil, or mint
3. Tabasco, Worcestershire, or other prepared sauce, to taste
4. Up to ½ cup grated or crumbled cheddar, goat, or other melting cheese
5. Up to ¼ cup grated Parmesan cheese
6. 1 or 2 chopped scallions
7. 1 cup chopped cooked mushrooms, onion, spinach, or other vegetables
8. Up to 1 cup chopped smoked salmon or other smoked fish
9. Up to 1 cup chopped cooked shrimp, crab, or lobster; or oysters, any way you like them
10. 1 or 2 chopped ripe tomatoes
11. Up to ½ cup any cooked salsa

Vinaigrette

Even though the salads in this book all have dressings built into the recipe, I'm including a master recipe to spin many different ways to use whenever you'd like. Because if you have a jar in the fridge, you will use it on a lot more than salads. And what you have in the jar will beat the stuff in a bottle every time.

The main recipe lists many options for the vinegar. All have different flavor nuances and colors; the idea is to use what you have and what you like, adjusting to taste and customizing the flavor. See the variations that follow, and you'll immediately get a sense of the possibilities. **Makes about 1⅓ cups**

Ingredients

1 cup olive oil

6 tablespoons vinegar
(sherry, red wine, white wine, or balsamic)

2 teaspoons Dijon mustard

Salt and pepper

Honey or sugar to taste
(optional)

□ Prep · Cook

1. Put 1 cup olive oil, 6 tablespoons vinegar, 2 teaspoons Dijon mustard, and a sprinkle of salt and pepper in a jar or other airtight container with a tight-fitting lid. Shake vigorously until the oil and vinegar blend together (emulsify). They will likely separate again, but all you have to do is shake to recombine them.

2. Taste the vinaigrette and see what it needs. You may want to add more vinegar, a teaspoon at a time, until the balance tastes right to you. Or perhaps add a bit of honey or sugar to balance out the sharpness of the mustard until it is the way you like it.

3. Serve the vinaigrette right away. It will keep for several days to a week or more, depending on the extra ingredients.

Variations

Creamy Vinaigrette. Replace half the olive oil with mayonnaise, yogurt, silken tofu, or cream. If using yogurt or tofu, whisk until the vinaigrette is smooth.

Soy Vinaigrette. Substitute 5 tablespoons good-quality vegetable oil and 1 tablespoon sesame oil for the olive oil; use rice vinegar for the vinegar. Before adding salt, add 1 teaspoon soy sauce, then taste and see if you want another 1 or 2 teaspoons.

Lemony Vinaigrette. Instead of the vinegar, use the juice and zest from 1 lemon and the juice from another. (Be sure to strain out the seeds first.)

Green Salad

The side that goes with more dishes than any other. Fortunately, you never have to make it quite the same way twice, especially if you skip the dressing here and make a batch of homemade vinaigrette from the previous recipe. The benefit of having the dressing in the bottom of the bowl is that you can make the salad up to an hour ahead without risking wilted leaves: Don't toss it right after adding the greens; instead drape the bowl with a damp kitchen towel and refrigerate until you're ready to serve it; then toss. **Serves 4**

Ingredients

⅓ cup olive oil

2 tablespoons any vinegar or lemon juice

Salt and pepper

1 pound romaine lettuce or any other salad greens (see page 11)

☐ Prep · Cook

1. Put ⅓ cup olive oil and 2 tablespoons vinegar in a large bowl and sprinkle with salt and pepper. Whisk with a fork to combine.

   ☐ Trim the lettuce and tear the leaves into bite-sized pieces (you should have about 6 cups). Add the greens to the bowl.

2. Toss gently, lifting from the bottom to coat with dressing. Taste and adjust the seasoning; toss again. Serve right away.

Variations

Chopped Salad. More like a slaw than salad really, and a great way to use up odds and ends in the produce drawers. Anything you like to eat raw is fair game: cabbage, radishes or jícama, bell peppers, cucumbers, scallions or red onions, zucchini or summer squash, cauliflower, broccoli, kohlrabi, fresh herb leaves— you get the point. Before you make the dressing in Step 1, trim and peel what you've got as necessary and chop enough to fill 6 cups. Add them to the bowl with the dressing, toss, and serve.

Dressed Cooked Vegetables. Eat them hot, at room temperature, or chilled—as you like. If you don't have any leftover plain cooked vegetables, make a batch of Steamed Vegetables (page 498). Drain well. The formula here dresses 6 cups, so do the math accordingly. Or make Vinaigrette (page 485) and drizzle or toss the vegetables with some of that.

Pick-a-Fruit (or Tomato) Salad. So you remember this is always a side dish or dessert option. Omit the olive oil. Instead of the vinegar, put 6 tablespoons fresh lime, lemon, or orange juice in the bowl. Or use balsamic vinegar alone or with some of the citrus juice. Instead of the romaine, add 6 cups cut fruit, halved strawberries, or whole berries. And remember, tomatoes are technically a fruit. The seasoning is up to you: Use salt and pepper, or salt and chili powder or ground chile, or a tablespoon or so of sugar. If you want to experiment, try adding curry powder, ground cumin, or ground cardamom and go as sweet and savory as you like.

Croutons

The quickest—and crunchiest and tastiest—way to croutons is in a skillet. Never a big deal, since you can do them on the stove while you're making dinner, even with something else going in the oven or broiler. Use whatever oil you're using for the salad dressing—or soup, or wherever the croutons will ultimately land. **Makes 2 to 3 cups**

Ingredients

¼ cup olive oil or good-quality vegetable oil, plus more as needed

8 ounces any bread (sliced or from a whole loaf, including corn bread; figure 3 to 4 cups once cubed)

Salt and pepper

▢ Prep · Cook

1. Put ¼ cup olive or vegetable oil in a large skillet over medium heat.

   ▢ Cut the bread into cubes any size you like; usually ½ to 1 inch is about right. Just leave the crust on, I always say.

2. When the oil is hot, add the bread to the skillet and sprinkle with salt and pepper. Toss to coat with the oil and cook, tossing occasionally and adjusting the heat so the croutons sizzle and toast. Add a little more oil if the pan dries out (it likely will).

3. Cook until the bread is lightly browned all over. Use right away or cool and store in an airtight container for a few days.

Variations

Bread Crumbs. These are best when bread is no longer spongy but not so dry you can't tear it. With the same amount of bread, this will make about 1 cup. Omit the oil and salt and pepper; skip Steps 1, 2, and 3. Cut or tear the bread into 2-inch pieces and put them in a food processor. Pulse a few times to break up the bread, then continue pulsing until it reaches the consistency you want: coarse (pea-sized), fine (like coarse grain), or somewhere in between. Use right away, or if the bread is quite dry, you can store it in an airtight container in the pantry for up to 1 month or in the freezer for up to 3 months.

Fried Bread Crumbs. Follow the directions for grinding the bread crumbs as described in the previous variation. Then switch back to the main recipe and season and fry them as described for the croutons, only toss them more frequently with a spatula and assume they'll brown a little faster.

Fastest Vegetable Stock

Sure, there's nothing like a stock that simmers on the stove all afternoon, but this is the next best thing and still way better than store-bought boxes and cans. **Makes about 2 quarts**

Ingredients

4 large carrots

2 large onions

1 large russet potato

4 celery stalks

5 or 6 cloves garlic

8 ounces button or cremini mushrooms

3 or 4 ripe or canned whole roma (plum) tomatoes

1 small bunch fresh parsley or at least 5 parsley stems

Salt

☐ Prep · **Cook**

1. Put 10 cups water in your largest pot and bring to a boil.

   ☐ After rinsing or scrubbing and trimming the vegetables as necessary, cut them like this and drop them into the pot as you work:

   ☐ Peel 4 carrots if you like; cut them into thick coins.

   ☐ Leave the skin on the 2 onions, but quarter them.

   ☐ Cut 1 potato (with the skin) into big chunks.

   ☐ Halve or quarter 4 celery stalks.

   ☐ Toss in 5 or 6 trimmed (but not peeled) cloves garlic.

   ☐ Halve 8 ounces mushrooms if they're big.

   ☐ Halve 3 or 4 fresh tomatoes; leave the canned tomatoes whole but reserve their juice for another use.

   ☐ Toss 1 bunch parsley right in.

2. Bring the water back to a boil, then adjust the heat so the water bubbles steadily without splattering everywhere. Cook until the vegetables are tender, 30 to 60 minutes, depending on how much time you have and your taste. The longer it goes, the deeper the flavor.

   ☐ Set a colander or large strainer over a heatproof bowl or another pot big enough to hold at least 2 quarts.

3. When you've decided the stock is ready, carefully pour or ladle it into the colander or strainer, including the vegetables. Lift the colander out of the liquid if necessary and press on the vegetables to extract as much liquid as possible. Taste and add salt to taste. Use right away or put in airtight containers (different sizes are handy, as is filling an ice cube tray with stock). Refrigerate for up to a week or freeze for up to 6 months.

• recipe continues →

Variations

Fastest Chicken Stock. Follow the prep and cooking steps in the main recipe, using the following ingredients: 3 to 4 pounds bone-in, skin-on chicken parts (this is the perfect place for whole wings, thighs, backbones, and/or necks), 2 large carrots (cut into chunks), 2 celery stalks (cut into chunks), 1 large onion (quartered), and 2 bay leaves. Cook for a full hour. After straining and cooling, pick through the chicken to pull out all the meat; use that for chicken salad or a quick stir-fry. And skim as much fat as you can off the top with a large spoon. (This becomes easier after the stock cools.)

Fastest Beef Stock. Follow the prep and cooking steps in the main recipe, using the following ingredients: Rinse 3 to 4 pounds meaty beef bones like shin or oxtail under cold water. Add 2 large carrots (cut into chunks), 2 celery stalks (cut into chunks), 1 large onion (quartered), 2 bay leaves, and a handful of black peppercorns. You'll need to simmer the full hour to make the most of the beef bones; 90 minutes would be even better. Strain and skim the fat off the top.

Fastest Seaweed Stock. Essentially Japanese dashi, a ubiquitous everyday base for all sorts of soups, stir-fries, braises, and sauces. You can make it vegan or with seafood.

Since this stock doesn't freeze very well, I've adjusted this variation to make about 6 cups, or enough for 4 servings with maybe a little left over. Omit all the vegetables, aromatics, and herbs. Instead, combine one 4- to 6-inch piece dried kelp (kombu) and 8 cups water in a large pot over medium heat. Don't let the mixture come to a boil; as soon as it's about to, turn off the heat and remove the kelp; you can slice it up for salads or stir-fries if you like. The stock is ready to use. Or to make more traditional dashi, add ½ to 1 cup dried bonito flakes to the pot after removing the kelp and stir; cover and let sit for a few minutes, then strain.

Tomato Sauce

Okay, so here's the third most useful sauce there is (after salsa, page 480, and vinaigrette, page 485) and hopefully incentive to forget about ever buying sauce in a jar. Plus you can spin the basic recipe in any number of directions, some of which follow. You can also add chopped fresh garlic with the onion, or olives, herbs, or fresh chiles toward the end of cooking. The recipe is easily doubled, and once cooled it will keep in an airtight container in the fridge for several days or in the freezer for up to 6 months. Pack the sauce in small quantities (say ½- or 1-cup containers) to avoid ever having to thaw more sauce than you want. **Serves 4 (about 2 cups)**

Ingredients

2 tablespoons olive oil or butter

1 small onion

1 large (28-ounce) can whole peeled tomatoes

Salt and pepper

□ Prep · Cook

1. Put 2 tablespoons olive oil or butter in a large skillet over medium heat.

   □ Trim and peel the onion; chop it.

2. When the oil is hot or the butter is melted, add the onion and cook, stirring occasionally, until soft, 2 to 3 minutes.

   □ Carefully pass a knife through the tomatoes in the can (or grab and crush them in your hands) to break them up a little.

3. Add the tomatoes and their juice and a sprinkle of salt and pepper to the skillet. Cook, stirring occasionally, until the tomatoes break down and thicken the sauce, 10 to 15 minutes. Taste and adjust the seasoning. Serve warm, or cool and store as described in the headnote.

Variations

Mushroom Tomato Sauce. Depending on how mushroomy you want the sauce, add 1 to 2 cups chopped or sliced mushrooms along with the onion in Step 2. Cook until the vegetables are soft, the water from the mushrooms has evaporated, and the pan is dry again. Then add the tomatoes and proceed.

Meat Sauce. Start by heating the olive oil or butter and browning 8 to 12 ounces ground beef or pork (1 to 1½ cups) or sweet or hot Italian sausages (4 to 6 links), chopped or meat squeezed from the casings. Cook, stirring frequently, until the meat is no longer pink and is browned in places, 5 to 10 minutes. Spoon off all but 2 tablespoons fat, add the onions, and proceed with Step 2.

Fresh Tomato Sauce. Works with the first two variations too. Substitute 2 pounds ripe tomatoes, cored and chopped or puréed, for the canned, adding them in Step 3. The cooking time will be about the same.

Pasta or Noodles, Plain (or Tossed with Butter or Oil)

You probably don't need a recipe for cooking pasta, but here it is the fastest way I know—the trick being to use the bare minimum amount of water—with a few variations for my favorite Asian noodles. Boiling the water takes longer than the actual cooking, so be sure to get that going before you start anything else. **Serves 4 to 8, depending on the rest of the meal**

Ingredients

Salt

1 pound any pasta or egg noodles

2 tablespoons butter or olive oil (optional)

Pepper (optional)

Additional flavorings from the list on page 495 (optional)

☐ Prep · Cook

1. Fill a large pot halfway full of water and bring to a boil; salt it.

2. When the water boils, add the pasta. If you have long strands, hold them in a bundle above the pot and gently swirl them in the water until the bottom of the strands soften and you can fit the rest in the pot.

3. Stir frequently with a fork or tongs to keep the pasta or noodles from sticking together. Start tasting after 5 minutes.

4. When the pasta is tender but not mushy, drain it, reserving about 1 cup cooking liquid (even if you don't think you'll need it). Return the pasta to the pot along with any seasonings you like: 2 tablespoons butter or olive oil, more salt, or some pepper; add a spoonful or 2 of the reserved cooking liquid and any of the possible flavorings from the list that follows and stir. Otherwise toss the pasta with the sauce you've prepared or use it in another dish. Serve hot or warm.

• recipe continues →

Variations

Rice Noodles, Plain or Tossed with Oil. Flat or round, thin or wide, they all cook the same; only the time changes, and the window of doneness is shorter than with wheat noodles. Usually 12 ounces is enough for 4 servings. After adding the noodles to the boiling water in Step 2, stir constantly until they're soft. Start checking the thinnest vermicelli after 30 seconds; the thickest noodles might take more than 5 minutes to become tender. Drain the noodles when they're slightly less tender than you want them. Return them to the pot and toss with good-quality vegetable oil instead of the butter or olive oil. A little sesame oil is good too; no need to add cooking liquid. If you don't need them right away, when the noodles are in the colander, rinse them with cold water to stop the cooking and remove some starch. Then transfer the noodles directly from the colander to a big bowl of cold water for up to an hour. Drain them again before tossing with oil and using.

Soba Noodles, Plain or Tossed with Oil. Soba are made from buckwheat, usually combined with wheat for a slightly nutty, earthy flavor. Like rice noodles, 12 ounces should be enough for 4 servings. Cook as directed in the main recipe, only start checking after 3 minutes. Then drain, rinse with cold water, and handle as described in the rice noodle variation.

Sweet Potato Noodles (Japchae) or Bean Threads, Plain or Tossed with Oil. Thankfully, this terrific, slightly gelatinous, and pleasantly chewy Korean staple—and all sorts of clear or "glass" noodles made from different bean and vegetable starches—has become easier to find. Usually 8 ounces is enough for 4 servings. Cook as directed in the main recipe, only start checking after 3 minutes. (The widest, thickest strands can take up to 10 minutes.) Drain and handle as described in the rice noodle variation.

5 Ways to Flavor Plain Pasta or Noodles

Stir in any of the following along with the butter or olive oil:

1. 1 to 2 tablespoons chopped fresh rosemary, thyme, oregano, or sage
2. ½ cup chopped fresh parsley or basil
3. 1 teaspoon grated lemon zest
4. Up to 1 cup grated Parmesan cheese
5. 1 cup cored and chopped ripe tomatoes

White Rice

The happy truth about rice and grains is that you can cook almost every kind perfectly using the simple minimal-measuring method here. The most notable exception is couscous (see the variation that follows). The only significant variable is the timing. With the cues in this recipe, the eyeballing method here is easy, especially the more batches you make. See the list that follows for a few ideas for flavoring rice or grains once they are cooked.

The other happy truth is that rice and grains are easy to reheat. The microwave works best—just pop them in there in a covered dish—but a small pot on the stove works well too. Scatter some drops of water from your hands on top, set the heat to medium-low, cover, and cook. Start checking after 5 minutes, then fluff with a fork. Cold rice and grains are perfect for stir-frying. Fried rice anyone? (See page 207). Though for salads, I prefer the texture when rice or grains are slightly warm or at room temperature. **Serves 4**

Ingredients

1 cup white rice (any long-, medium-, or short-grain; basmati is always a safe bet)

Salt

▫ Prep · Cook

▫ Put 1 cup rice in a large saucepan, fill the pan with water, and swirl. Let the rice settle to the bottom of the pot and carefully pour off the water. Repeat a couple more times until the water is noticeably clearer.

1. Add enough water to the saucepan to cover the rice by about an inch. Toss in a big pinch of salt. Bring to a boil, then adjust the heat so the mixture bubbles gently.

2. Cover and cook undisturbed until little holes appear on top of the rice and most of the water is gone; start peeking after 10 minutes. Test a few grains. Like pasta, the rice should retain a little bite when it's done; you want it cooked without being mushy.

3. If the rice isn't ready, tip the pan to see if any water remains. If not, add a splash before re-covering and returning the rice to the heat to cook for another 5 minutes before you check again.

4. When the rice is ready, remove it from the heat and let it sit for at least 5 minutes or up to 20. Fluff with a fork; taste and add more salt if necessary. Serve right away or season further first; the list that follows has lots of ideas.

Variations

Brown Rice. This works for long-, medium-, or short-grain brown rices but not wild rice, which can take as much as twice as long to cook. Follow the main recipe, only in Step 1, cover the rice with about 1½ inches water. The methods for cooking, testing, and adjusting remain the same, but the cooking time can range from 30 to 45 minutes, depending on the size and variety of the rice.

Plain Whole Grains. Works for anything but couscous. Follow the main recipe, only in Step 1, cover the grains with about 1½ inches water. (If you're using quinoa, rinse the grains in a strainer under running water, stirring them with your hands to thoroughly rinse them.) The methods for cooking, testing, and adjusting remain the same, but the cooking time can range from 10 to 30 minutes, depending on the grain, so be sure to check frequently for doneness.

Couscous, White and Whole Wheat. Your choice; same unique method. Since couscous is tiny bits of pasta, even the whole wheat type is quite fluffy. If you're cooking the larger pearl couscous (also called "Israeli couscous"), follow the directions for pasta and noodles on page 493, only start checking after it's been boiling for 3 minutes. For 4 to 6 servings: Put 2 cups couscous in a medium saucepan; add 3 cups water and a big pinch of salt. Bring to a boil. As soon as the water boils, cover the pan and remove from the heat. Let it sit until the couscous is tender and has absorbed all the water, 5 minutes for white, 10 to 15 minutes for whole wheat. Fluff with a fork and serve, or season first using the list that follows.

11 Ways to Flavor Cooked Rice and Grains

Start by adding 2 tablespoons butter, olive oil, or good-quality vegetable oil. Add any of the following (alone or in combination), then fluff the cooked grains with a fork to combine.

1. 1 to 2 tablespoons chopped fresh herbs
2. A drizzle of Vinaigrette (page 485)
3. Black pepper
4. Up to 1 cup grated or crumbled cheese
5. 1 to 2 cups cooked beans, peas, or lentils
6. Up to 1 cup chopped dried fruit
7. 2 chopped scallions
8. Up to 1 cup tomato sauce or salsa
9. Ground spices (like curry powder or garam masala, five-spice powder, or chiles or chili powder), to taste
10. Up to ½ cup chopped pitted olives
11. Up to ½ cup chopped nuts

Steamed Vegetables

By thinking of vegetables in three wildly general categories—greens, tender, and hard—all you need is this recipe and the variations that follow to prepare and cook virtually everything. The "greens" category includes the most delicate, like watercress, spinach, and arugula, as well as those that require longer cooking, like collards and escarole. What I call "tender" vegetables are those that are firm but pliable when raw: celery, green beans, asparagus, snow peas, sugar snap peas, broccoli, cauliflower, and mushrooms, and those that fit the description when you chop or slice them, like eggplant, zucchini, cabbage, onions, leeks, shallots, and fennel. Everything else is "hard": root vegetables, tubers (like potatoes), and winter squashes.

For each vegetable in a category, you control how long it takes by choosing how to cut or slice it. Even hard vegetables like beets and sweet potatoes will cook relatively quickly when they're cut in pieces less than 1 inch thick; they'll cook fastest if you grate them. Making peace with the peels—which are nutritious and can actually be delicious—saves you several minutes, prep time. Let's get right to it. **Serves 4**

Ingredients

1½ pounds any vegetable

Salt

2 tablespoons butter, olive oil, or good-quality vegetable oil (optional)

Juice of 1 lemon (optional)

Pepper (optional)

▢ Prep · Cook

▢ If you have a pot with a steaming insert, lucky you—use that and add enough water to almost reach the insert. Or set up a steamer by choosing a large pot with a tight-fitting lid. If you've got a collapsible steamer basket, put it in the pot and open it up. If you don't have a basket or liner, rig a steamer with two heatproof plates: Put one upside down in the water, the other right side up on top of the first. Add enough water to the pot so that it almost reaches the basket or submerges the upside-down plate.

▢ Trim the vegetables and peel them if necessary.

▢ For greens, chop them if you like, especially any sturdy stems. For vegetables, cut them into chunks or slices no more than 1 inch thick.

1. Bring the water in the pot to a boil. Put the vegetables in the insert or basket or on the plate, and adjust the heat so the water bubbles vigorously without splashing onto the food. Cover the pot.

2. Start checking for doneness after 2 minutes by piercing with the tip of a knife. Since the vegetables will continue to cook even when they're out of the steamer, take them out when they're slightly firmer than you

• recipe continues →

ultimately want them. The tenderest greens and smallest chunks will be ready in as little as 2 minutes; root vegetables might take up to 15. So just check until you get the hang of estimating.

3. Sprinkle the vegetables with salt and transfer them to a serving bowl with tongs. Dot with 2 tablespoons butter or drizzle with 2 tablespoons oil if you like. Or to reserve the vegetables for another use, stop the cooking by shocking them (see page 501); let the vegetables cool, drain them, then store in airtight containers in the refrigerator for up to a week.

Variations

Boiled Vegetables. I don't recommend this cooking method for peppers, chiles, eggplant, or mushrooms— or anything else you don't want to absorb water. Before preparing the vegetables, fill a large pot halfway with water, add a big pinch of salt, and bring to a boil. To boil sturdy greens, first add only the stems to the boiling water; when the stems are almost tender, 3 to 4 minutes, add the leaves. For everything else, drop all the pieces in the pot at once. Cooking times and finishing directions are the same as in the main recipe.

Microwaved Vegetables. Put the vegetables on a microwave-safe plate or in a shallow bowl along with a splash of water; don't drown them. Cover loosely with a paper towel, a vented microwave cooking lid, or another microwave-safe plate. Since timing will depend on your oven's power, cook in 2-minute bursts on high until you're comfortable. Every minute or two, stop the machine and—being careful of wafting steam—check for doneness. Finish the vegetables as described in the main recipe.

Roasted Vegetables. Heat the oven to 425°F. Instead of using a pot, put the prepared vegetables on a rimmed baking sheet. Drizzle with 2 tablespoons olive oil or good-quality vegetable oil, sprinkle with salt, and toss. Put the baking sheet in the oven. Roast, occasionally turning the vegetables with a spatula and checking for doneness, until the vegetables are browned in places and as tender as you like. If they are browning too quickly, lower the temperature to 400°F and stir more frequently. Doneness is a continuum: Delicate greens will be ready in 5 minutes; start checking hard vegetables, cut in chunks or sliced as described in the Prep, after 20 minutes. Everything else falls somewhere in between, so checking after 10 minutes is a good rule of thumb. Taste and adjust the seasoning. Serve hot or at room temperature.

5 Ways to Flavor Cooked Vegetables

Toss any of the following with the vegetables after cooking and dressing with butter or oil:

1. Chopped fresh herbs
2. Citrus juice or grated zest
3. Fried Bread Crumbs or Croutons (page 488)
4. Chopped nuts
5. Vinaigrette (page 485)

SHOCKING VEGETABLES

Quickly chilling vegetables to stop cooking leaves them brightly colored and puts you in control of when and how you serve them. It's easy really: Fill a clean sink or large bowl with ice water. As soon as the vegetables are crisp-tender and vibrantly colored, grab them with tongs or drain them and plunge them into the ice water for a minute or so until they're cool to the touch; drain again. Then use them for salads, reheat in a pan with butter or oil, or put into airtight containers and refrigerate for another time.

ROASTED PEPPERS

Though you can easily buy good ones in jars, this is something I still prefer to make myself. Here's how: Heat the oven to 450°F; turn the broiler to high and put the rack 4 inches from the heat; heat a charcoal or gas grill to moderately high heat and put the rack 4 inches from the heat; or turn on a few gas burners on your stove. Roast or broil on a rimmed baking sheet, grill, or cook the peppers right in the gas flame, turning as necessary until they're dark brown or black all over and they collapse in on themselves. Roasting can take up to an hour total, broiling and grilling about 15 minutes, and cooking in the gas flame about 10 minutes. Wrap the cooked peppers in foil or put them in a bowl and cover it with a plate or foil; the steam will help the skins peel off easily. When they are cool enough to handle, remove the skins, seeds, and stems—doing this under cold water is easiest. It's okay if they fall apart a bit. Now they're ready to serve or transfer to airtight containers and store in the fridge for a week or freezer for a few months.

Skin-On Mashed Potatoes

You only realize how long it takes to peel potatoes when you stop doing it. The other tricks that put mashed potatoes in your grasp are slicing thinly and not having a ton of water in the pot. Russet potatoes make a fluffier mash, while all-purpose Yukon Golds tend to be a little creamier in texture. **Serves 4**

Ingredients

Salt

1½ pounds russet or Yukon Gold potatoes

½ cup milk, plus more as needed

4 tablespoons (½ stick) butter or ¼ cup olive oil

Pepper

☐ Prep · **Cook**

1. Fill a large pot with about 2 inches water; add a big pinch of salt and put over high heat.

   ☐ Scrub the potatoes, halve them lengthwise, and working with the flat sides down on the cutting board, cut into slices no more than ½ inch thick. Drop them into the pot as you go.

2. Once you've added the potatoes to the pot, cover it and wait for the water to boil. Adjust the heat so the action is vigorous without bubbling over. Cook, letting the water boil the whole time, until the potatoes are tender and just breaking apart, 15 to 20 minutes.

3. Drain the potatoes well and return them to the pot; set it over medium-low heat.

4. Add ½ cup milk, 4 tablespoons butter or ¼ cup olive oil, and a sprinkle of salt and pepper. Mash with a potato masher or fork, adding more milk if needed to reach the consistency you prefer. Taste and adjust the seasoning, and serve.

• recipe continues →

Variations

Stir-Fried Potatoes. Please try these if you never have. Omit the milk. Choose whether you want to cook the potatoes in butter, olive oil, or good-quality vegetable oil. After scrubbing the potatoes, shred them in a food processor fitted with the grating disk or on a box grater; put them in a kitchen towel–lined colander, bundle them up, and squeeze out as much liquid as you can. To cook, melt the butter or heat the oil in a large skillet, scatter in the potatoes, and sprinkle with salt. Cook undisturbed until they sizzle, brown a little, and release easily from the bottom of the skillet, 3 to 5 minutes. Then cook, stirring occasionally and scraping any bits from the pan with a spatula, until they're browned in places and tender but not mushy, about another 5 minutes. Taste and adjust the seasoning, adding pepper if you like. Serve hot, at room temperature, or chilled and dressed like salad.

Mashed or Stir-Fried Sweet Potatoes. Substitute sweet potatoes (any kind or color) for the potatoes. These you've got to peel, but it's relatively fast since the peels are thick. Wash and peel them before preparing as described in the main recipe or the first variation. When you stir-fry them, they won't get quite as crisp as regular potatoes but will bring their other appealing characteristics to the dish.

Roasted Potatoes or Sweet Potatoes. Worth the extra 5 to 10 minutes when you really want 'em. Heat the oven to 425°F. Use 1½ pounds any potato or sweet potato you like. Choose whether you want to cook the potatoes in butter, olive oil, or good-quality vegetable oil; if using butter, melt it. If you're using sweet potatoes, peel them. Then cut the potatoes into ½-inch chunks. Put them on a rimmed baking sheet; sprinkle with salt. Drizzle with oil or melted butter and toss to coat. Spread the pieces into a single layer and roast undisturbed until they release easily from the baking sheet when you turn them with a spatula, about 15 minutes. Cook, stirring once or twice more, until they're browned in places and fork-tender, another 15 minutes.

5 More Ways to Flavor Mashed Potatoes

Stir in any of the following in Step 4 of the main recipe:

1. 1 or more tablespoons Dijon or whole grain mustard
2. ½ cup chopped fresh parsley, basil, or dill
3. 1 tablespoon chopped fresh oregano, rosemary, thyme, or a mix
4. 1 cup grated Parmesan cheese or another melting cheese like cheddar or Gruyère
5. ½ cup or more cream or buttermilk instead of the milk

Cooked Beans

There's nothing hard about cooking beans. And if you've got some in the fridge or freezer at all times, they're as convenient as opening a can. So the choice between canned and those you cook yourself from dried boils down to whether you plan ahead a little. This flexible method gives you beans done the way you like them, with skins mostly intact, along with some flavorful cooking liquid. **Serves 6 to 8** (**about 8 cups**)

Ingredients

1 pound dried beans, any kind (except lentils and split peas; for them see the variation)

Several bay leaves (optional)

Salt and pepper

▫ Prep · Cook

▫ Rinse the beans in a colander under cold water and discard any that are broken or discolored. Look for small bits of foreign matter and get rid of those too.

1. Put the beans in a large pot and cover with cold water by 2 to 3 inches. Add the bay leaves if you're using them. Bring to a boil, then reduce the heat so the liquid bubbles gently.

2. Cover the pot and cook 30 minutes before checking the first time. After that, stir once in a while and add a little water if the beans are no longer submerged, checking for doneness every 10 minutes.

3. When the beans start to get tender, add a generous pinch of salt and some pepper and continue cooking until the beans are slightly less tender than the way you ultimately want them, about 45 minutes for mung and other small beans and up to an hour or more for other varieties, depending on their size, shape, and age.

4. When the beans are done, remove them from the heat, but keep them covered for up to another 30 minutes to finish cooking in the hot water. Remove the lid and stir to cool a bit. Taste and adjust the seasoning. Transfer the beans and cooking liquid to airtight containers in the portions most useful to you. (If you go with a scant 2 cups and include some liquid, you've essentially got a can ready to go.) Refrigerate for up to a week or freeze for up to 6 months.

● recipe continues →

Variations

Cooked Lentils, Split Peas, or Split Beans. In addition to working for all kinds of lentils and yellow and green split peas, these directions work for many of the small legumes used for Indian dals. Follow the main recipe, but start by covering the beans or peas with no more than 2 inches water, and start checking them after about 15 minutes. If they look dry, add water ¼ cup at a time. Split peas and split beans will break down quickly and become soupy. For intact lentils, check more frequently and transfer them to a colander set over a bowl the moment they get tender, but before their skins crack. Reserve the cooking liquid if you like, and rinse the lentils under cold water to stop their cooking.

Cooked Fresh Shell Beans. More work. More time. More incredible. So grab 'em when you see 'em, usually in midsummer. Chickpeas, edamame, black-eyed peas, favas, and cranberry beans are the most common beans sold fresh. Shell the beans if they're still in the pods and follow the directions in the main recipe, but cover the beans with only about 1 inch water. Start checking them after 20 minutes and every 5 minutes thereafter. The cooking time will vary wildly from bean to bean and batch to batch but rarely takes more than an hour.

Cooked Frozen Shell Beans. Lima, edamame, and fava beans are the most common types sold frozen. You don't have to make a whole pound at a time; I usually just cook the whole bag, however much that happens to be. Follow the directions in the main recipe, but cover the beans with only about 1 inch water. Start checking them after 5 minutes and every minute or so thereafter. Or cook them, covered by ½ inch water, in a covered dish in the microwave set on high. Start checking after 1 minute, and thereafter in 30-second intervals.

15 Ways to Flavor Cooked Beans

I prefer to cook beans plain and spruce them up to my tastes and whims of the moment as I use them. That's why you made a big batch, isn't it? Some ideas:

1. Chopped, cored ripe tomatoes
2. Leftover cooked vegetables, like greens or peppers
3. Chopped fresh herbs or crumbled dried herbs
4. Any vinaigrette
5. Soy sauce
6. Olive oil, good-quality vegetable oil, or butter
7. Sesame oil
8. Spice blends, like curry or chili powder
9. Chopped fresh chiles, fresh ginger, or garlic
10. Balsamic or any wine vinegar
11. Chopped toasted nuts or seeds
12. Crumbled cooked bacon or sausage
13. Mashed anchovies
14. Grated sharp cheese like Parmesan, pecorino Romano, ricotta salata, or Manchego
15. Crumbled feta, blue cheese, or queso fresco

Cook-Ahead Roasts, Starting with Chicken

If you've got an hour, you can roast some kind of simple protein for no good reason other than to have it handy. And that saves a ton of time in the long run. Plus, since you made it at home, you end up with a super-high-quality, economical component for soups, salads, sandwiches, stir-fries, and pastas, to combine with fresh vegetables and season on a whim.

If you're wondering what happened to the beef, it cooks so quickly anyway—unless you're doing a slow braise—I say it's best to stick to steaks and ground beef for fast meals. Whatever protein you choose, divide it into portions if you like and refrigerate in airtight containers for several days or freeze for a couple months. **Makes 4 to 8 servings, plus bones for stock**

Ingredients

1 whole chicken or cut-up bone-in, skin-on chicken parts (3 to 4 pounds total)

2 tablespoons olive oil or good-quality vegetable oil

Salt and pepper

□ Prep · Cook

1. Heat the oven to 450°F and put a rack near the bottom. Put a heavy ovenproof skillet (preferably cast iron, or carbon or stainless steel) on the oven rack to heat.

   □ Trim any excess fat from the chicken. Rub the whole chicken or parts with 2 tablespoons olive oil or vegetable oil, and sprinkle all over and inside with salt and pepper.

2. When the oven is hot, carefully (since the pan will be very hot) put the whole chicken, breast side up, or the chicken parts skin side up, in the heated skillet. Roast undisturbed for 40 to 50 minutes for a whole bird and 30 to 40 minutes for parts. The chicken is done when a quick-read thermometer inserted into the thickest part of a thigh registers 155° to 165°F; when you cut into a thigh close to the bone, the juices should run clear and there should be no traces of pink in the meat.

3. Transfer the chicken or parts to a platter or cutting board to collect the juices and let it rest for at least 5 minutes. Quarter the whole bird with a sharp knife or cut it into parts with kitchen scissors. Return any accumulated juices to the skillet and warm gently. Serve with some of the pan juices spooned over the top and the rest passed at the table.

4. To store the chicken for another meal, let it cool to room temperature, then cut it into parts or pull the meat from the bones in as big pieces as you can; save the skin and bones for stock. (I keep containers in the freezer and add chicken and vegetable trim to them until I have enough to fill a stockpot.) Put the meat in airtight containers along with the pan juices, and store as described in the headnote.

• recipe continues →

Variations

Roast Pork Loin. For this purpose a boneless pork loin—not the extra-lean tenderloin or a bone-in cut—is best. Look for one that weighs about 2 pounds and has a visible but thin fat cap on one side. Heat a large skillet, rub the pork with the oil, and season as described in the main recipe. Roast for 20 minutes before checking for doneness. A quick-read thermometer is handy here, but you can always nick it with a sharp knife and peek at the thickest part to see how pink it is inside. Turn the roast once if you like, but you don't need to. You want to remove it from the oven when it's one stage less than your desired doneness. If it's close, keep checking every 5 minutes; still quite rare, check every 10 minutes. The total cooking time will range from 20 to 40 minutes depending on the thickness of the roast. When it's done, cut the pork into portions, drizzle with the pan juices, and serve immediately. Or refrigerate or freeze as described in the headnote. Eat cold or let sit out for a few minutes to come to room temperature, or gently reheat in stir-fries or pasta sauces just before serving.

Roast Salmon (or Other Fish Fillets). Instead of the chicken, roast about 2 pounds any thick fish fillets or steaks. Salmon, cod, bass, and rockfish are particularly good, but bluefish, tuna, and mackerel are also delicious. Use a rimmed baking sheet, but don't put it in the oven to heat. Instead, rub the baking sheet with 2 tablespoons vegetable oil. Put the fish fillets on the pan skin side down (if there's no skin, you can tell because it's the smoother of the two sides). Steaks go in one side or the other. Sprinkle with salt and pepper and rub all over with another 2 tablespoons vegetable oil. Transfer the pan to the hot oven. Turn thick steaks or fillets once they release easily from the baking sheet; no need with fillets less than an inch thick. Roast until the fish is firm and barely opaque inside; a thin-bladed knife will pass through it fairly easily. Thin fillets will take 5 to 10 minutes total; start checking after 5 minutes. Thick pieces might take up to 20 to 30 minutes; start checking after 15 minutes. I love eating cooked fish chilled. If you'd rather warm it first, use the microwave on low or put it on a baking sheet, tent it with foil, and reheat it at 325°F until it's just steaming; the timing will depend on its thickness and how cold it was going in the oven.

Roasted Tofu. Use roasted tofu anywhere you'd use meat—sliced, cubed, or cut into thick planks. The texture of tofu transforms in the oven; when you do whole bricks, the outside gets crunchy while the inside becomes custardy but stays firm enough to slice thinly. Instead of the chicken, roast 2 or 3 (or more) bricks firm tofu (14 to 16 ounces each). You don't need the oil. Heat the oven to 400°F. Line a rimmed baking sheet or large skillet with parchment paper; don't heat it in the oven before roasting. No need to pat the tofu dry, just drain the water away. Rub the tofu all over with salt and put on the parchment paper. Roast, turning a couple times to brown evenly, until it's golden brown all over and springy when you press on it, about an hour. Cool on a wire rack, then portion if you like and refrigerate or freeze as described in the headnote.

Roasted Tofu,
page 509

Index

A NEW KIND OF RECIPE

Hummus and Vegetable Pita Pockets

Pita is the ideal vehicle for hummus: Spread it thickly inside slightly crisp pockets, then fill with fresh vegetables and briny feta. The recipe here gives you about 2 cups hummus, enough for a generous ½ cup for each sandwich. For a lighter approach, halve the portion of hummus, refrigerate the rest for up to a few days, and finish with lettuce, olives, or more cucumbers. The variations and list that follow will inspire your own creations and include directions for handling pocketless pitas. And you can always use cannellini or fava beans to make the hummus. **Serves 4**

Almost every recipe in this book is a main dish.

Ingredients

A list for shopping—or putting out on the counter. You don't prep the food here; you'll do that later.

Four 8-inch pitas with pockets

¼ cup olive oil, plus more for drizzling

Salt and pepper

1 lemon

2 cloves garlic

1¾ cups cooked or canned chickpeas (one 15-ounce can)

½ cup tahini

1 teaspoon ground cumin or paprika

2 or 3 medium ripe tomatoes

1 large cucumber

4 ounces feta cheese (1 cup crumbled)

▢ Prep · Cook

1. Turn the broiler to high; put the rack 4 inches from the heat.

   ▢ Drizzle the pitas with olive oil (about ½ teaspoon per side) and rub it over all with your fingers. Sprinkle salt and pepper on both sides and spread the pitas out on a large rimmed baking sheet.

   ▢ Halve the lemon; squeeze the juice into a food processor or blender through a strainer or your fingers to catch the seeds.

   ▢ Peel and chop 2 cloves garlic.

   ▢ If you're using canned chickpeas, rinse and drain them.

2. Add the garlic and chickpeas to the machine along with ½ cup tahini, ¼ cup olive oil, 1 teaspoon ground cumin or paprika, and a sprinkle of salt and pepper. Let the machine run, adding water, chickpea-cooking liquid, or more olive oil a tablespoon at a time until the purée is smooth but not watery. Taste and adjust the seasoning.

   ▢ Core the tomatoes and cut them into chunks; put them in a medium bowl.

   ▢ Peel the cucumber if necessary, cut it in half lengthwise, and scoop out the seeds with a spoon if you like. Chop the flesh and add it to the bowl.

3. Put the pitas on a rimmed baking sheet and grill, turning once, until browned—even slightly charred—on both sides, 2 to 5 minutes total.

   ▢ Crumble 1 cup feta cheese and add to the tomatoes and cucumber. Sprinkle with salt and pepper, drizzle with a little olive oil, and toss.

A Prep step often takes place *while* other cooking is happening to take advantage of downtime. Here, you prep the feta while the pitas brown.